QA
135.5
.M3676

The Mathematical Education of Exceptional Children and Youth

An Interdisciplinary Approach

Edited by
Vincent J. Glennon
University of Connecticut

Editorial Panel
Frances Connor, Teachers College, Columbia University
William M. Cruickshank, University of Michigan
Daniel P. Hallahan, University of Virginia
J. Fred Weaver, University of Wisconsin—Madison
Stephen S. Willoughby, New York University

National Council of
Teachers of Mathematics

Tennessee Tech. Library
Cookeville, Tenn.

315601

Copyright © 1981 by
THE NATIONAL COUNCIL OF TEACHERS OF MATHEMATICS, INC.
1906 Association Drive, Reston, Virginia 22091
All rights reserved

Library of Congress Cataloging in Publication Data:
Main entry under title:

The Mathematical education of exceptional children and
  youth.

  Bibliography: p.
  1. Mathemathics—Study and teaching (Elementary)—
Addresses, essays, lectures. 2. Exceptional children—
Education—Mathematics—Addresses, essays, lectures.
I. Glennon, Vincent Joseph, 1915–   II. Connor,
Frances.
QA135.5.M3676   371.95   80-29518
ISBN O-87353-171-X   AACR1

Printed in the United States of America

Table of Contents

iii

Preface

It is propitious that the manuscripts for this professional reference book were written during the International Year of the Child, 1979. It is my hope that the book will contribute to ameliorating the many problems that presently exist in the mathematical education of exceptional children and youth in the United States and other nations. Many of their unique problems in learning mathematics begin in the quality of the teaching of mathematics. And much of this inadequate teaching is due to the teacher's and the special educator's lack of a sound knowledge of the characteristics of the learner, of the mathematics itself, or of the variables in an instructional psychology.

Properly conceptualized, the mathematical education of all children and youth should draw on several basic disciplines—developmental psychology, neurology, cognitive psychology, physiology, biochemistry. And the mathematical education of exceptional children, because of the unique problems involved with each single condition and with multiple-handicapping conditions, requires even more attention to the basic disciplines. Mathematics education, then, is an interdiscipline that, like medical education, is built on, and eventuates out of, the substrate sciences in varying amounts. And the disciplines between and among the disciplines are the most socially important disciplines.

The interdisciplinary editorial panel reflects in equal numbers the community of mathematics educators and the community of special educators. The panel decided that the first two chapters should be written first and used to provide a general structure for chapters 3 through 9.

Chapters 3 through 9 each discuss a specific kind of exceptionality. In each instance the planning and writing of these chapters was a cooperative effort between a mathematics educator (the first author named) and a special educator. The purpose in having both disciplines represented was to ensure that the content would represent sound scholarship both in the characteristics of each kind of exceptionality and in the instructional psychology of mathematics applied to that condition. In other words, each writing team sought to provide the principles and practices for establishing a good psychoeducational match between the learner's characteristics and cognition.

Chapter 10 fittingly concludes the volume with a discussion of the improvement of preservice and in-service programs of mathematics education for exceptional children and youth. It is of critical significance for teachers and special educators to keep uppermost in mind the very useful statement that "the fine tuning of the individual child's or youth's curriculum is the teacher's role and responsibility." By attending to that wise insight, teachers and special educators will know that a sound psychoeducational match cannot be a ready-made published textbook or workbook program even though it may be advertised or otherwise represented as a program for learning disabled or other exceptional children or youth.

This book is intended for several professional groups, each of which impacts uniquely on the mathematics education program of exceptional children and youth. First is the very large number of general classroom teachers who are increasingly being held responsible for teaching mathematics to these children and youth. The general classroom is very often perceived, wisely or not, as the least restrictive environment. For most general classroom teachers, having a blind child or a mentally retarded youth in the classroom is a new and anxiety-inducing situation. This book should serve this very large readership in many useful ways.

Second among the professional groups for whom this book is intended is the special educator. The special educator is often asked by the classroom teacher to prescribe mathematics programs for exceptional children. However, the lack of adequate preparation both in the mathematics and the instructional psychology of mathematics in the teacher education program raises serious doubts about the quality of such prescriptions. Therefore, special educators can profit by a thorough reading of, and reflection on, the ideas in this unique interdisciplinary approach to the mathematical education of our exceptional people.

Third, the school psychologist, school counselor, and related support personnel—the pediatric neurologist, the pediatrician, the school administrator, and the curriculum coordinator—all will acquire new professional insights for the improvement of instruction in mathematics by a study of this book.

Finally, and very important, are those who are responsible for the quality of the professional preparation of the people who will staff the nation's classrooms. College and university faculties who teach the preservice courses and conduct in-service development programs for the general classroom teachers, the special educators, and the supportive personnel have the ever-present responsibility of keeping up to date on the mathematical education of exceptional children and youth. This reference is recommended to them by the editor, who has had a long association with college and university teacher education programs.

I am deeply grateful to the editorial panel and the many authors for

their generous donation of precious professional time and wisdom, for prompt attention to correspondence, for devotion to the tasks of meeting a demanding writing schedule that required the setting aside of other tasks, for excellence in professional collaboration and professional writing, and for highly professional and exhaustive critiques of manuscripts.

I am indebted to Deanna M. Korner, secretary to the faculty in mathematics education at the University of Connecticut, for going beyond her duties in typing and retyping manuscripts and attending to the many details involved in correspondence and record keeping, and to Daphne E. Johnson for her assistance with editing the manuscripts.

VINCENT J. GLENNON, *Editor*

Exceptional Children in Changing Times

Howard H. Spicker
Indiana University

James McLeskey
Indiana University

Howard H. Spicker, Ph.D., is professor of education and chairman, Department of Special Education, Indiana University. He is a member of the Indiana State Advisory Committee for Gifted and Talented; chairman, State Advisory Committee, Mentally Retarded and Developmental Disabilities; consultant, U.S. Office of Education, Bureau of Education for the Handicapped; and recipient, Paul Witty Fellowship for Gifted and Talented Leadership Conference and Indiana Governor's Special Service Citation. He has been listed in Who's Who in American Education.

James McLeskey, Ph.D., is director of undergraduate programs in the Department of Special Education at Indiana University. His teaching interests are in the areas of assessment and methods for mildly handicapped children and procedures for educating the mildly handicapped child in the regular classroom. McLeskey's present research interests center on attentional, problem-solving, and concept-formation deficits that impede the learning of mildly handicapped children.

U NTIL the advent of Public Law 94-142, the Education for All Handicapped Children Act of 1975, the formal education of exceptional children and youth was the sole responsibility of special educators. With little warning (and even less in-service education to facilitate it) the new law mandated a shotgun marriage in the fall of 1978 between regular and special educators. Reluctant, if not wary, attempts are still being made today to consummate that marriage.

EXCEPTIONAL CHILDREN AND THE LAW

We believe, perhaps idealistically, that most regular educators as well

as special educators agree that exceptional children are entitled to an education. However, we suspect that many regular educators are confused if not downright hostile toward some of the specific provisions mandated by PL 94-142. By discussing the law's major provisions as well as the underlying rationale for their inclusion, we hope to clear up the major confusions and, in so doing, perhaps reduce some of the hostilities.

The Right to a Free Appropriate Public Education

Until recently, most states provided free educational programs for exceptional children on a voluntary basis only. If money, classrooms, and teachers were available and the child's handicapping condition was not too severe, a special education program was provided by the local education agency. If the school was unwilling or unable to provide an educational program for handicapped children, parents had little recourse other than keeping such children at home, institutionalizing them, or placing them in a costly private school. Prior to the passage of PL 94-142 in 1975, it was estimated that approximately 1 million handicapped children had been "excused" from state-mandated public school attendance. The school exclusion practices specific to mentally retarded children were legally challenged in 1971 in the case of the *Pennsylvania Association for Retarded Children (PARC)* v. *Pennsylvania*. The association contended that regardless of the severity of their handicap, all retarded children are capable of benefiting from an educational program. An appropriate education for some might result in learning to use the toilet or partially learning to feed themselves; for others it might mean learning those self-care, language, and social skills needed for working in a sheltered workshop or living in a group home. Applying the equal protection and due process guarantees of the Fifth and Fourteenth amendments, PARC successfully argued that whereas the state of Pennsylvania had undertaken to provide a free public education for its children, including some of its mentally retarded children, it could not deny a free program of education and training for any of its retarded children.

Once the court recognized the educational rights of one group of handicapped children, it was not long before similar rights were demanded for all handicapped children. Washington, D.C., had a long history of excluding from public school not only those children who were moderately, severely, or profoundly retarded but also children with behavior disorders, severe vision or hearing impairments, and those with multiple handicapping conditions. *Mills* v. *Board of Education of the District of Columbia* ended those exclusion practices when the court ruled that the D.C. policy violated the children's constitutional rights of due process and equal protection.

The final major right-to-education case was the *Maryland Association for Retarded Children (MARC)* v. *Maryland*. It had been the practice of public school corporations in Maryland to transfer certain handicapped

children (particularly the severely retarded) to private day or residential schools. Very often these private schools had long waiting lists, and during the interim the schools placed the children on homebound instruction. Even when a private school had an opening, the school corporation covered only 20% to 50% of the actual cost of the program. Baltimore County's circuit court not only reiterated the right of handicapped children to a free appropriate public education regardless of the severity of their handicap but, in addition, mandated that private school placements by public schools and also transportation to and from such schools must be fully paid for by the public system. The court also ruled that homebound instruction could be justified for mentally retarded children only when their physical condition prevented them from attending school (Turnbull & Turnbull, 1978).

It is quite apparent that the provision of PL 94-142 ensuring the right to a free appropriate public education was an attempt to assure that handicapped children were given the rights of due process and equal protection, granted by the Fifth and Fourteenth amendments, that had been denied to them these many years.

Nondiscriminatory Assessment

Of all the traditional categories of exceptional children, none carries a greater stigma than mental retardation. Although research findings have for some time now discredited the many negative stereotypical ideas that tend to be associated with mental retardation (e.g., that all mentally retarded individuals possess a strange physical appearance, have a tendency toward criminality, are socially incompetent, are incurable, and that their condition is genetically caused), such ideas continue to be accepted as truth by much of the general population. This, coupled with our inability to demonstrate that special education programs are more effective than regular programs in increasing the academic and social skills of most educable mentally retarded children, makes it understandable that many parents become upset when their children are labeled mentally retarded by the schools.

Parents of children from Mexican, black, Puerto Rican, native American, and other ethnic and racial minority groups have become particularly upset by the discovery that their children are disproportionately represented—overwhelmingly so—in special education programs for the mildly retarded. Several lawsuits by parents from minority groups were necessary to convince the schools that these children were being improperly tested and therefore improperly labeled and improperly placed in programs for the mildly retarded.

In Southern California a group of Mexican-American parents filed a class action suit against the state of California, charging that their children had been improperly placed in special classes for the mentally retarded because the instruments used to make the placement decision had been ad-

ministered in English rather than in the children's primary language (*Diana* v. *California State Board of Education*). The court decided for the plaintiffs and directed the schools to retest in their native language all "mildly retarded" children whose native language was not English. As a result of the court's decision, approximately 50% of the Mexican-American children in special classes for the mildly retarded were removed from that classification and placed back into a regular classroom appropriate to their age. After a shaky beginning, many of these children have been successfully reintegrated, particularly when the schools have adopted a transition program that includes a multicultural curriculum presented by bilingual teachers (MacMillan, 1977).

In San Francisco, a similar class action suit (*Larry P*. v. *Riles*) was filed by a group of black parents. They argued that the reason for the disproportionate representation of black children in special classes for the mentally retarded was the direct result of using intelligence tests that were appropriate to the experiences of middle-class white children but not necessarily appropriate to the experiences of culturally different black children. After a long, bitter struggle, the court ruled in favor of the parents. No longer can such intelligence tests as the Stanford-Binet or the Wechsler Scales be used as the sole basis for labeling and classifying minority children as mentally retarded.

PL 94-142 incorporates the *Diana* and *Larry P*. decisions by mandating that children be tested with racially and culturally nondiscriminatory assessment instruments in their native language. As these nondiscriminatory testing procedures are implemented around the country, large numbers of educationally deprived (predominately lower-class minority) children will be removed from such classifications as mentally retarded or emotionally disturbed and placed back in regular classrooms. Unfortunately, the reading and mathematics difficulties, as well as the behavior problems, that were the cause of the children's referral to special education will come with them. It is quite possible that such children can be motivated toward higher achievement if materials are used (i.e., readers and mathematics texts) that include current sports and music heroes as well as the positive historical contributions that their own racial and ethnic groups have made to American life.

An Appropriate Education

Prior to the passage of PL 94-142, it was estimated that approximately half of the 8 million handicapped children enrolled in public schools were not receiving an education appropriate to their needs. Specialized instruction for most exceptionalities was either nonexistent or tended to consist of watered-down academics in an atmosphere of supervised baby-sitting. For example, children diagnosed as educable mentally retarded were thought to

possess common learning characteristics for which a homogeneous curriculum would be appropriate. Similar assumptions of group homogeneity were entertained for most categories of exceptional children despite mounting evidence accumulated over several decades that the behavioral characteristics of exceptional children were extremely heterogeneous. PL 94-142 finally recognized the unique differences among handicapped children within categorical groups and, therefore, required an individualized education program (IEP) for each child.

The Individualized Education Program

Although producing IEPs for each individual as required by law is extremely time-consuming, the educational benefits to the 4 million previously neglected or mistaught children are enormous. The time may well come when establishing annual goals and short-term objectives will be recognized as a sound educational practice not only for the handicapped but for all children.

The Least Restrictive Environment

To the maximum extent appropriate, handicapped children are to be educated with nonhandicapped children. This, the least restrictive environment (LRE) provision of PL 94-142, is without question the most misunderstood portion of the law. Prior to the law it was common practice to bar handicapped children from regular classrooms and place them with children of like handicaps in special classes, schools, or institutions. Studies investigating the efficacy of such placement for the mildly handicapped have offered little evidence to justify it. Despite smaller classes, special curricula, and specially trained teachers, the academic and social gains of retarded children in special settings tended to be no better than those made by retarded children receiving their education in regular classrooms (Dunn, 1968, 1973; Kaufman & Alberto, 1976; Mosley & Spicker, 1975). Similarly discouraging reports were coming from state residential schools for the hearing and visually impaired. However, none of these studies was as devastating to segregated treatment for handicapped children as the court cases involving the public residential schools and hospitals for the mentally retarded at Partlow in Alabama (*Wyatt* v. *Stickney*, 1971, 1972), Willowbrook in New York (*NYARC* v. *Rockefeller*, 1973, 1975), and Pennhurst in Pennsylvania (*Halderman* v. *Pennhurst*, 1977). The courts held that the physical deprivation, the lack of basic sanitation, the overcrowding, the lack of physical exercise, the inadequate diet, the unchecked violence of residents against each other and of employees against residents, the lack of adequate medical and psychiatric care, and the abuse of solitary confine-

ment and restraint practiced in these institutions constituted cruel and unusual punishment in violation of the rights of mentally retarded citizens as guaranteed by the Eighth and Fourteenth amendments. Furthermore, since retarded or disturbed individuals give up such fundamental rights as the right to travel, freedom of association, and the right to privacy, the district court in Alabama stated: "Adequate and effective treatment is constitutionally required because without treatment, the hospital is transformed into a penitentiary where one could be held indefinitely for no convicted offense" (*Wyatt* v. *Stickney*, 1971).

The combination of inadequate treatment and restrictions on personal freedoms requires that alternatives to institutions be found. Many of our federal courts now adhere to the guidelines suggested by Chambers (1976):

> Courts should not permit involuntary commitment if home care or a community group home can provide the needed protection and better equip the individual for independence. Courts and agencies should not permit placement in separate schools for mentally retarded children when extra assistance in regular public schools can properly educate the child and avoid the social stigma attendant upon segregation. Guardianship that denies a retarded citizen the right to make important life decisions should be avoided when the individual merely is incapable of handling one or two separable and specific kinds of responsibilities. (p. 489)

Under PL 94-142, these guidelines apply to all handicapped children. As further stated by Chambers (1976), when government has a "legitimate communal interest to serve by regulating human conduct it should use methods that curtail individual freedom to no greater extent than is essential for securing that interest. When you swat a mosquito on a friend's back, you should not use a baseball bat" (p. 486). Similarly, a blind child needing only instruction in braille should not be placed in a distant state residential school for blind children for 24 hours a day, 7 days a week.

To ensure that educators will use "fly swatters" rather than "baseball bats" to provide appropriate individualized programs in appropriate settings for handicapped children, PL 94-142 includes the LRE guidelines. It is important to understand that the placement of handicapped children with nonhandicapped children is mandated only when the IEP case conference participants agree that a regular class setting is likely to provide handicapped individuals the highest probability of attaining the IEP short- and long-term objectives established for them. However, as stated in the final rules and regulations governing the act (*Federal Register*, August 23, 1977), "Where a handicapped child is so disruptive in a regular classroom that the education of other students is significantly impaired, the needs of the handicapped child cannot be met in that environment. Therefore, regular placement would not be appropriate to his or her needs" (Sec. 121a.552, p. 42513).

Due Process for Parents and Children

Before PL 94-142 was passed, the labeling, placement, and school exclusion practices applied to handicapped children throughout the United States seldom involved parental consent. More likely than not, parents were informed by school officials that their child had been tested, found to be handicapped, and should therefore be placed in a special education program designed for his or her specific handicap. Even in those communities where parental consent was required for placement in special education, it was unusual for a school district to request parental consent to conduct the individual assessment leading to the decision, and even more unusual to involve parents in determining the child's educational program or appropriate placement. Decision making for handicapped children without parental involvement resulted in the inappropriate labeling of minority children (as mentally retarded, emotionally disturbed, etc.), the homogeneous, rather than individualized, programming for children with similar labels, the segregated placement of handicapped children in self-contained programs, and the exclusion of children whom the schools arbitrarily declared incapable of benefiting from the regular educational program.

Under PL 94-142 the schools must obtain parental consent before conducting an individualized assessment. Parents have a right to expect a reasonable rationale for the evaluation. It is therefore imperative that specific objective observations of a given child's deviant behaviors be recorded by teachers and other school personnel and shared with the parents. In most instances, such observational data will be sufficient to obtain the necessary parental consent for an individual preplacement assessment. If the evaluation data indicate a possible need for special education services, the parents must be given an opportunity to participate in the case conference that might lead to the development of an IEP for their child. Parents have the right to examine and question all information that is being used by the school to determine the nature of their child's problem. They must be allowed to participate in the determination of long- and short-term educational goals for their child and, in addition, must approve the educational placement that appears to be the most appropriate for implementing the instructional program designed for the child.

Should the parents refuse to give consent for a preplacement evaluation or disagree with the school's diagnosis, educational program, or placement recommendations, either the parents or the public agency (the school) has the right to ask for an impartial due process hearing. The hearing officer assigned to the case has an obligation to render a decision that is in the best interest of the handicapped child.

Once the schools accept parents as partners in educational decision making for handicapped children, recognize the children's right to a free appropriate education, and expand the range of options for delivering ser-

vices to them, the number of due process hearings conducted in behalf of handicapped children should greatly diminish. It is unfortunate that it took court action to provide handicapped citizens their educational rights. Legal mandates, especially those that are poorly understood, tend to be resented by those given the responsibility for implementing them. It is our fervent hope that this background has convinced you that PL 94-142's provisions are necessary to guarantee appropriate educational opportunities to children who have been denied those opportunities much too long.

The Gifted and Talented Children's Education Act of 1978

As educational opportunities became available to handicapped children under PL 94-142, the lack of similar educational services for gifted and talented children became increasingly apparent. Not only was our country losing many of its future problem solvers but, even worse, a high percentage of gifted children failed to graduate even from high school, not to mention college. This waste of our nation's greatest resource was brought to the attention of numerous congressional leaders. The result was the passage of the Gifted and Talented Children's Education Act of 1978 on October 15, 1978. The act authorized an expenditure of $25 million for fiscal year 1979 with an increase of $5 million each year to a maximum of $50 million by 1983.

The purpose of the law is to provide financial assistance to state and local educational agencies, institutions of higher education, and other public and private agencies and organizations so that they are able to plan, develop, operate, and improve programs designed to meet the special educational needs of gifted and talented children.

Not since the National Science Foundation push following the launching of Russian satellites in the late 1950s has the federal government become so actively involved in the talents of gifted children. The impetus of the new law has been remarkable. States that have yet to invest one cent of their own money for gifted and talented educational programs are suddenly finding themselves with a federally funded state supervisor in that area. Statewide in-service education programs for teachers of the gifted are being held in most states. Pilot programs for gifted and talented children, including those from economically disadvantaged families, are springing up everywhere. This momentum should certainly be maintained so that, at last, appropriate educational programs will exist to help gifted and talented children reach their full potential.

TOWARD AN UNDERSTANDING OF EXCEPTIONAL CHILDREN

Although a positive attitude toward exceptional children and a recognition of their educational rights are important ingredients for teaching them,

the teacher must also understand the positive and negative behaviors that are likely to be associated with a given exceptionality. Only then can appropriate instructional modifications be made if needed.

Although great variability exists among the characteristics of persons who have been labeled exceptional at one time or another, categories of exceptionality have proved useful in indicating gross characteristics of exceptional children. According to Kirk (1972),

> An exceptional child is a child who deviates from the average or normal child (1) in mental characteristics, (2) in sensory abilities, (3) in neuromuscular or physical characteristics, (4) in social or emotional behavior, (5) in communication abilities, or (6) in multiple handicaps to such an extent that he requires a modification of school practices, or special education services in order to develop to his maximum capacity. (p. 4)

Special education is thus designed to—

> ensure adequate attention to those whose school learning is either hindered by handicapping conditions, or sufficiently above or below school standards to require programs in addition to or instead of regular classroom instruction so as to maximize student growth and development. (Lilly, 1979, p. 1)

Exceptional children who are most frequently taught in regular class settings are categorized under the following headings:

1. Mild learning and behavior problems
   A. Specific learning disabilities
   B. Socially maladjusted and emotionally disturbed
   C. Slow learner and mentally retarded
2. Sensory handicaps
   A. Visually impaired
   B. Hearing impaired
3. Physical and health impairments
4. Gifted and talented

Each of these categories is reviewed in the sections that follow. Included is information detailing how exceptional children are identified. Also included is an overview of behaviors and characteristics that are symptomatic of specific exceptionalities.

Mild Learning and Behavior Problems

Children with mild learning and behavior problems are estimated to constitute approximately 7% of the school-aged population. These children are characterized by an inability to progress academically and adjust socially as rapidly as their peers. This inability to adjust to the demands of a

school setting frequently leads to frustration when they are faced with school-related tasks. A child who is having such difficulty is likely to be labeled lazy, unmotivated, or a troublemaker. Unless the child's specific needs are identified and met in the early school years, a vicious cycle of frustration and acting-out behavior on the part of the child may result in increasing academic failure and social maladjustment.

Children experiencing mild learning and behavior problems have been traditionally categorized under the labels *specific learning disability, socially maladjusted and emotionally disturbed,* or *slow learner and mentally retarded.* Criteria for each of these categorical labels and characteristic behaviors exhibited by many of the children so labeled are outlined below.

Specific Learning Disability

Children exhibiting specific learning disabilities are defined in PL 94-142 as follows:

> Those children who have a disorder in one or more of the basic psychological processes involved in understanding or in using language, spoken or written, which disorder may manifest itself in imperfect ability to listen, think, speak, read, write, spell, or do mathematical calculations. The term includes such conditions as perceptual handicaps, brain injury, minimal brain dysfunction, dyslexia, and developmental aphasia. The term does not include children who have learning problems which are primarily the result of visual, hearing, or motor handicaps, of mental retardation, of emotional disturbance, or environmental, cultural, or economic disadvantage. (Sec. 5(b) (4))

Three criteria are frequently used for classifying a child as learning disabled. First, the child must not be emotionally disturbed, mentally retarded, sensorially impaired, or environmentally disadvantaged. Thus the child must appear to be normal, except for the specific learning disability. Second, the child must be an underachiever in one or more academic areas. This determination is frequently made by comparing actual achievement level to an anticipated achievement level gauged from the child's chronological age, mental age, and years in school. Finally, children are labeled *learning disabled* only after attempts are made to improve or compensate for weak academic areas in the regular class setting. This final criterion is crucial in that whereas many children have difficulty with academic subjects, only those with the most severe problems should be labeled learning disabled.

The only behavioral characteristic shared by all specific learning disabled children is underachievement. Some children labeled learning disabled are characterized as introverts and others as extroverts; some are hyperactive and others hypoactive. Nonetheless, certain characteristics are frequently observed among learning disabled children. These merit mention, especially those that influence classroom instruction.

Hyperactivity. A small number of children considered to have a specific learning disability are also extremely active. These children must be involved in a structured task throughout the school day; otherwise, they walk around the classroom, fidget, and are in constant motion.

Inattention. A significant number of children with learning disabilities have difficulty attending; when attention is attracted to a general task, these children frequently have difficulty determining the relevant aspects of the task. Instructions for academic tasks must be explicit so as to direct attention to the relevant dimensions of the task.

Memory disorders. A frequently noted behavior of learning disabled children is a tendency to remember something one day and forget it the next. Frequent repetition in a variety of contexts is often required before basic information is retained.

Lack of motivation. A frequently noted characteristic of learning disabled children relates to a lack of motivation. After repeated failure in attempts to learn academic skills, many children respond by doing nothing, with an attitude based on the idea "If I don't try, I can't fail." Obviously, such a circumstance leaves children extremely frustrated, since they cannot succeed no matter what the response. This frustration may precipitate many characteristics frequently exhibited by learning disabled children, namely, inattention, acting-out behavior, and impulsive response patterns.

Motor incoordination. A difficulty that frequently characterizes learning disabled children but only infrequently interferes with academic success is motor incoordination. If a high premium is attached to handwriting and other motor skills in a given classroom, some learning disabled children may experience difficulty; otherwise, this characteristic is of little consequence.

Block to learning. A problem that eludes characterization is frequently referred to by teachers as a "block to learning." Much controversy surrounds the nature of this blockage. Some have suggested that brain dysfunction is the primary culprit, and others have referred to modality weaknesses (i.e., visual or auditory learners) and language deficits. Although the cause of this blockage is unclear, the resulting behavioral manifestations are obvious. Some children do not seem to be able to learn reading or mathematics content no matter how good the teacher, how elaborate the methods, and how persistent the effort. These children are frequently labeled *dyscalculic*, *dyslexic*, *aphasic*, or *specific learning disabled*.

Socially Maladjusted and Emotionally Disturbed

Graubard (1973) has defined behavioral disabilities of children who are classified socially maladjusted or emotionally disturbed as

a variety of excessive, chronic deviant behaviors ranging from impulsive and aggressive to depressive and withdrawal acts (1) which violate the perceiver's expectations of appropriateness, and (2) which the perceiver wishes to see stopped. (p. 246)

Two primary criteria are frequently used to identify children who exhibit behavioral disabilities. First, these children must chronically exhibit deviant behavior that violates the expectations of a teacher, school psychologist, or other authority figure. It is obvious that any decision regarding behavior disabilities is subjective, based on the specific perspective of the person doing the labeling. Nonetheless, most teachers have fairly specific criteria regarding the types of behaviors that they perceive as deviant and the extent to which these behaviors will be tolerated in their classrooms. The subjective nature of behavior disabilities makes it difficult (and perhaps undesirable) to determine specific criteria for how much and what types of deviant behavior a classroom teacher should tolerate before referring a child as a candidate for the label *socially maladjusted* or *emotionally disturbed*. The second criterion frequently noted when classifying a child exhibiting behavior disabilities is underachievement. When a child is involved in chronic off-task behavior in the classroom, it is obvious that little time is devoted to academic achievement. Underachievement is thus a concomitant behavior frequently noted as characteristic of children labeled socially maladjusted or emotionally disturbed.

All children labeled socially maladjusted or emotionally disturbed have been viewed by an authority figure as persons who cannot or will not "fit in" to a given setting. The characteristic behaviors resulting in this lack of fit vary greatly. Quay (1969) has attempted to bring some clarity to the process of labeling and teaching socially maladjusted and emotionally disturbed children by categorizing the types of children exhibiting behavioral disabilities:

1. Conduct disorder: These children act out in class and are often aggressive and attention seeking.

2. Anxious-withdrawn: These children tend to be overlooked, since they are shy, lack self-confidence, and infrequently interact with teachers or peers.

3. Inadequate-immature: This type of child is characterized by apathy, daydreaming, and failure to complete work. They also cause problems in a classroom by playing with toys, making noise with pencils or sticks and so forth, and writing on walls or desks.

4. Socialized delinquent: These children are characterized by social maladjustment, since they are capable of following the rules of school, but decide to participate in gang activities or abide by the ethics determined by peers or members of their subculture.

Bower (1969, pp. 22–23) has noted other behaviors, including the following, that have been frequently noted as characteristic of children in Quay's four categories:

1. An inability to build or maintain satisfactory interpersonal relationships with peers and teachers
2. Inappropriate types of behavior or feelings under normal conditions
3. A general, pervasive mood of unhappiness or depression
4. A tendency to develop physical symptoms, pains, or fears associated with personal or school problems

Other behaviors considered characteristic of specific learning disabled children are frequently exhibited by socially maladjusted and emotionally disturbed children. These behaviors include hyperactivity, inattention, and lack of motivation.

Slow Learner and Mentally Retarded

Mental retardation is formally defined as "significantly subaverage general intellectual functioning existing concurrently with deficits in adaptive behavior, and manifested during the developmental period" (Grossman, 1973, p. 11). Intellectual functioning is typically measured with an individual intelligence test; a score below a cutoff (usually two standard deviations below the mean or approximately 70) is used as evidence of possible retardation. Slow-learning children generally score between 70 and 90 on measures of intelligence. Stimulated by the prevalent view in education and psychology that intelligence test scores are culturally biased and may be poor indicators of academic potential, psychologists have included adaptive behavior as an integral part of the definition of mental retardation. Adaptive behavior is viewed from a broad perspective as a person's ability to adapt to new and ever-changing social and cultural situations in a manner appropriate to a given social/cultural milieu. More succinctly stated, measures of adaptive behavior are used to determine if a person has an aptitude for nonacademic endeavors, whereas intelligence tests are used to measure academic potential. For example, a child may have difficulty learning basic mathematics facts in a classroom setting yet demonstrate great facility in counting and estimating probabilities when playing games of chance with dice—shooting craps, for instance. Mentally retarded children, or those who are characterized as slow learners, thus have difficulty with both social and academic development, consistently lagging behind peers in both areas.

The most relevent characteristic of slow learners and mentally retarded children with respect to classroom instruction is that they develop in school

at only 50% to 80% of the rate of the normal child. This rate of development is reflected in the need for frequent repetition of material in a variety of contexts and at differing conceptual levels before mastery can be achieved, and in the need to expect that somewhat less than a year's material can be covered in a year's time (Kirk, 1972).

Slow learners and mentally retarded children also frequently exhibit behaviors described earlier as being characteristic of specific learning disability, social maladjustment, and emotional disturbance. These behaviors include hyperactivity, inattention, lack of motivation, a lag in social-emotional development, and conduct disorders. Other frequently noted characteristics that influence classroom instruction include the following:

Language and speech problems. Many mentally retarded and slow-learning children have problems acquiring language and frequently require assistance in learning to articulate clearly the words they learn. These limited language skills may lead to difficulty when these children are faced with acquiring reading or conceptual skills that require the use of language. For example, children may progress through basic arithmetic facts with few problems, but when they are faced with word problems and conceptual skills on a higher level, deficient language will surely impede learning.

Learning from the concrete. Mentally retarded children find it much easier to learn from concrete materials and concrete experiences than from abstract experiences. They tend to have difficulty transferring information from one context to a similar, related context. These characteristics necessitate that instruction begin on a low (concrete) conceptual level, gradually proceeding to abstractions. It is also necessary to teach retarded and slow-learning children every aspect of a task to be learned, never depending on transfer or "common sense."

Low maximum achievement level. Mentally retarded children usually reach a second- to sixth-grade level of achievement at the end of their formal schooling (Kirk, 1972). This and other previously noted characteristics of the mentally retarded and slow learners result in the need to carefully select curriculum to meet the individual academic and vocational needs of the child.

Sensory Handicaps

Children with sensory handicaps—that is, visual or auditory impairment—are estimated to compose approximately 1% of the school-aged population. These children vary greatly in their ability to adapt to the regular classroom setting, since there is little correlation between sensory impairment and the ability to achieve academically. The key to successful achievement for sensorially impaired children is presenting information to

them in a form that they can understand and process. The limitations that visual or auditory impairment place on the child make this task more difficult, but it is by no means impossible.

Visually Impaired or Blind

Children with visual impairments are traditionally categorized according to the degree of visual acuity and defects in the field of vision. This approach to the definition of visual impairments has not proved to be educationally relevant; therefore, terminology used by educational practitioners deals with the functional nature of the impairment. Partially seeing children who can read large print or regular print under special conditions are categorized as visually impaired, whereas children who must use braille are categorized as educationally blind (Dunn, 1973).

Most children experiencing visual difficulty are identified before entering school; however, some children compensate for their visual impairment to the extent that their handicap is not noticed until extensive visual activities are required in school. Teachers should be aware of the warning signals for visual problems: red eyelids; watery eyes or discharge; eyes that do not appear to be straight; excessive rubbing of the eyes; shutting or covering one eye or tilting the head; difficulty with close work, perhaps resulting in facial distortions; a tendency to reverse or confuse letters or numbers; poor spacing in writing; and difficulty in "staying on the line" (Gearheart & Weishahn, 1976).

One of the greatest hurdles to be overcome in accepting and integrating visually impaired children into the mainstream of public schools is the attitude of peers, teachers, and others who come in contact with these children. Specific attitudes vary widely but are often strongly felt. Attitudes range from pity and the view that the blind are helpless to awe that a person with so devastating a handicap could achieve so much. The blind are often expected to play a role characterized by dependence, melancholy, helplessness, and docility (Scott, 1969). Most visually impaired children wish to be treated like everyone else and will frequently respond favorably to such treatment. If the teacher and the visually impaired child are willing to discuss the impairment with classmates, it may help alleviate anxiety. This process will also impart to peers a more realistic perspective of the strengths as well as the limitations of a visually impaired child.

Visually impaired children have little problem adjusting to a regular classroom setting. They have as much ability to learn as children with normal eyesight, but they often lag behind academically because of limited visual experiences. Their greatest academic difficulty is with concept development. Visual input seems to be the great unifier in concept development; we can feel, smell, and hear an airplane, for example, but the visual image of an airplane pulls all these pieces together. Concept development

should be emphasized and attempts made to let the child experience an airplane on a concrete level through as many senses as possible. It is also important that such children use any remaining useful vision; often, the more their vision is used, the more efficient it will become (Turnbull & Schulz, 1979).

Another consideration that influences classroom instruction is reading rate. Blind children who depend on braille, and partially sighted children who require large-print material, read at only 25% to 50% of the rate of sighted children. This slow rate necessitates adjusting assignments for visually impaired children to allow for completion in a reasonable amount of time.

A blind child will need some initial assistance in becoming oriented to the classroom—learning the location of desks, exits, and so on. Most of them, however, will have already received training in orientation and mobility skills and will adapt quickly to new settings. Few classroom adaptations are required other than those instructional materials and procedures that help circumvent the child's visual deficit.

Hard of Hearing or Deaf

Children are classified hard of hearing or deaf on the basis of auditory acuity measures obtained using a pure-tone audiometer. The audiometer measures the loss of both frequency (pitch) and intensity (loudness). Although specific cutoffs for frequency and intensity hearing losses may be used to categorize children as hard of hearing or deaf, McConnell (1973) offers definitions with more educational relevance. He defines the hard of hearing or partially hearing as

> those whose hearing loss in the prelingual period or later is not of sufficient severity to preclude the development of some spoken language, and those who have normal hearing in the prelingual period but acquire hearing loss later. (p. 352)

The deaf are defined as

> those whose hearing loss is so severe at birth and in the prelingual period (before two or three years of age) that it precludes the normal, spontaneous development of spoken language. (p. 352)

Thus, factors included in determing the severity of a hearing loss include the child's age at the onset of the impairment, the severity of the frequency and intensity losses, and the influence the loss has on language development.

Most children with moderate to severe hearing loss are identified before entering school; however, some children, especially those with mild loss, are not identified until afterward. Warning signs include a lack of attention, turning or cocking the head, difficulty following directions, reluc-

tance to participate in oral activities, and dependence on classmates for instructions (Gearheart & Weishahn, 1976).

The greatest problem faced by hard of hearing or deaf children is their difficulty in acquiring language. Limited language skill is the primary reason for the lack of educational achievement often experienced by these children, since a language deficit often leads to difficulty in acquiring higher level language skills, such as reading and writing. The ability to adapt to this problem depends on a number of factors, including the degree of impairment, intellectual development, and personal-social development (Kirk, 1972; McConnell, 1973).

Degree of impairment. Children with some residue of hearing may be able to develop some language and speech and thus interact and function more effectively in a regular class. Deaf or extremely hard of hearing children who do not develop some language and speech progress much more slowly and require extensive special educational services.

Intelligence. The intellectual abilities of deaf and hard of hearing children are apparently equivalent to those of normal children, although hearing impaired children tend to score lower on intelligence tests that require extensive language skills. Their educational progress is greatly influenced by their rate of learning and ability to generalize, draw conclusions, and make use of subtle cues (Kirk, 1972).

Personal-social development. The lack of language skills that is frequently characteristic of children with hearing deficits produces major problems in developing personal and social skills. Extremely limited language reduces personal-social contacts and thus limits the child's chances for social development (McConnell, 1973).

Thus, many factors influence the educational development of hard of hearing and deaf children. Many of these children will adjust quickly and easily to the regular classroom setting, although some adaptations are needed to ensure that the individual needs of each child are met.

Physical and Health Impairments

The most obvious result of recent federal legislation for the handicapped has been the increased accessibility of public buildings to the wheelchair bound and physically handicapped. This exposure of the physically handicapped to the general public has led to an increasing acceptance as the handicapped have gained the opportunity to demonstrate that they can become productive, contributing members of society when they have equal access to resources. Access to resources is the key by which the physically handicapped, cerebral palsied, and others experiencing health impairments can realize their full potential.

The physical and health problems that, to a greater or lesser degree, interfere with educational progress are as varied as the children who have them. No single term can apply to them all (Wilson, 1973). These impairments include disorders of the nervous system, such as cerebral palsy and epilepsy; orthopedic handicaps resulting from crippling injuries or diseases, such as rheumatoid arthritis or osteomyelitis; and general health impairments, such as asthma, diabetes, and tuberculosis. The impact of these impairments varies greatly depending on the severity of the condition and the coping ability of the impaired person. The academic achievement level of persons having these conditions varies from the very high, gifted range to the severely retarded. One should not conclude that a child who is, for example, cerebral palsied cannot achieve academically. A substantial number of cerebral palsied people do well in school, finish college, and have productive careers.

Many other physical and health impairments—multiple sclerosis, muscular dystrophy, and cystic fibrosis, for instance—are occasionally encountered in public schools. For a detailed review of these conditions, see Bigge and O'Donnell (1976), Bleck and Nagel (1975), Dunn (1973), or Gearheart and Weishahn (1976).

The ability of physically handicapped and health-impaired children to adjust to a public school setting varies in relation to the severity of the condition, the age of the child at its onset, and the child's psychological and intellectual development. These factors should be considered when planning educational programs for them.

Most of these children will require few, if any, classroom adjustments. Adaptations of curriculum, methods, and materials are needed only when (a) the severity of the disability greatly influences future vocational and social competency; (b) special circumstances, such as extended absences from school or working at reduced speed, extend the time required to complete coursework; and (c) intellectual deficits require the use of special methods and materials (Wilson, 1973).

Specific problem areas that could interfere with academic progress follow.

Communication Problems

Children with health and physical impairments may have difficulty formulating and uttering speech. Writing can be a problem for many cerebral palsied children and others who have difficulty controlling or moving the hands and arms. These difficulties may interfere with language development and educational achievement. For example, a cerebral palsied child whose speech is slow and slurred may well be hesitant to interact in class discussion or individually with teachers or peers. These impediments must be compensated for before such children can reach their full potential.

Mobility Problems

Most schools and classrooms can be readily adapted for children who need a wheelchair or crutches through the use of ramps, wide aisles and doorways, special rest-room facilities, and the removal of any barriers. Most physically handicapped children in public schools will be fully independent and will require little classroom adaptation.

Social-Psychological Development

Children with health and physical impairments are often labeled "different" or "odd" by peers. Children who experience epileptic seizures, although perfectly normal otherwise, may be viewed by classmates as anything from mysterious to possessed. Open discussion of health and physical impairments can help alleviate fears experienced by exceptional children as well as their classmates. A second, perhaps more acute problem relates to the manner in which impaired children view themselves. Although many readily accept a handicapping condition, some do not adjust well and become dependent on family and friends. It is important that impaired children be given all the responsibility they can handle so that they might develop functional skills and a positive self-concept.

The Gifted and Talented

Gifted and talented children are defined as those who possess demonstrated or potential intellectual ability, creative or productive thinking, specific academic aptitude, leadership ability, or talent in the performing or visual arts. Such children require differentiated education or services beyond those normally offered by the regular school system in order to realize their potentials (Title IX-a: Gifted and Talented Children's Act of 1978). This definition includes not only children who score in the upper range on intelligence tests but also those who demonstrate talents and creative ability in areas other than those addressed by the standard curriculum of public schools.

Identifying gifted children has traditionally involved tests of intelligence, academic achievement, special aptitudes, or creative abilities. Coupled with these tests should be observation and interaction on the part of the teacher to determine if the child has potential for high performance. The specific criteria for categorizing a child as gifted or talented vary according to the nature and objectives of the program for which children are being selected. For example, the criteria used to select children for a special mathematics class should be different from those used to select children for a special music class.

Terman's classic longitudinal study has shown that intellectually gifted children tend to have better health, fewer social and emotional problems, and better athletic ability than children with average intelligence. They also

adapt quickly to change and require few cues before understanding concepts and generalizations. Whereas Terman's subjects were from predominantly white, middle- and professional-class families, these characteristics should be used with caution when planning for lower class children in general and nonwhite minority children in particular. Most traditional public school programs group children according to chronological age and, in high school, by potential for success in college. Few school corporations provide such needed alternatives as acceleration, special homogeneous groupings, or intellectual enrichment. Each of these classic approaches to the education of the gifted has a specific advantage.

Acceleration. Children who have learned to read or have learned basic mathematics prior to kindergarten have little to gain academically by being kept in class with children of their chronological age. Not one study has yet shown that entering kindergarten or school early, skipping grades, or entering college early has had a detrimental effect on the academic or social-emotional growth of gifted children as a whole. The few exceptions can easily be avoided by basing decisions to accelerate on individual rather than on group criteria. Since gifted children do not always excell in all subjects, it is likely that specific content acceleration in such subjects as mathematics will be more beneficial to children with specific academic talents than an overall grade acceleration.

Special groupings. It is difficult to meet the needs of highly gifted children in a regular classroom. If at all possible some portion of time should be arranged whereby gifted children can share their creative and critical thinking skills with children like themselves. This is beneficial not only for their intellectual growth but even more so for their social-emotional development. Gifted children must be given the opportunity to discover that there are other children like themselves and that they are not freaks.

Intellectual enrichment. Regardless of educational placement, it is necessary to adapt both the curriculum and teaching methods to meet the needs of gifted and talented students. These children quickly learn grade-level material and thus require an enriched curriculum that allows for continued learning and insight through an in-depth study of specific topics and special projects. Gifted and talented children also are capable of grasping concepts and generalizations more rapidly and with fewer cues than their classmates; thus teaching methods should be directed toward the discovery method rather than drill and the dissemination of information.

Other characteristics of gifted and talented students influence classroom instruction. As noted earlier, many gifted and talented children and youth quickly grasp regular school material and concepts and become bored with school. This leads to a high drop-out rate, even at the college

level. This difficulty is further aggravated when one considers the mismatch between the convergent thinking often required in the standard school curriculum and the divergent thinking frequently exhibited by gifted and talented children. As an example, a child who was learning the concept of regrouping in subtraction produced the following solution:

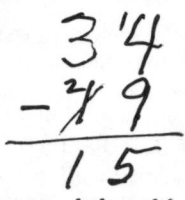

Fortunately, the teacher understood that this child was applying the principle of compensation. Once this principle was grasped, other methods for solving similar problems were quickly learned. Divergent or nontypical approaches to school tasks are not viewed as appropriate by all teachers; thus they may lead to problems for gifted and talented children as a mismatch occurs between the child's skills and aptitudes and the teacher's expectations. This can precipitate frequent conflict in the classroom if the curriculum and methods are not matched to the individual needs of the child.

SUMMARY

This chapter was written to give the regular educator an overview of the legislation and litigation that has led to the placement of many exceptional children in regular classes. Descriptive information was included regarding how children are placed in various categories of exceptionality. Behaviors that characterize different categories and influence classroom instruction were also reviewed. An understanding of the plights—past and present—of the handicapped is but a beginning in meeting the needs of all children in our public schools. We hope this information, coupled with the specific methods that will be reviewed in subsequent chapters, will result in the effective mathematics instruction to which exceptional children are entitled.

REFERENCES

Bigge, J. L., with O'Donnell, P. A. (Eds.). *Teaching individuals with physical and multiple disabilities.* Columbus, Ohio: Merrill, 1976.

Bleck, E. E., & Nagel, D. A. (Eds.). *Physically handicapped children: A medical atlas for teachers.* New York: Grune & Stratton, 1975.

Bower, E. M. *Early identification of emotionally handicapped children in school* (2nd ed.). Springfield, Ill.: C. C. Thomas, 1969.

Braga, J. L. Early admission: Opinion versus evidence. *Elementary School Journal,* 1972, 72, 35–46.

Chambers, D. Right to the least restrictive alternative. In M. Kindred et al. (Eds.), *The mentally retarded citizen and the law.* New York: Free Press, 1976.

Diana v. *State Board of Education*, C-70-37 F.R.P. (N.D. Cal. 1970, 1973).

Dunn, L. M. *Exceptional children in the schools*. New York: Holt, Rinehart & Winston, 1973.

Dunn, I.. M. Special education for the mildly retarded—Is much of it justifiable? *Exceptional Children*, 1968, *34*, 5–22.

Federal Register, Vol. 42, No. 163, August 23, 1977.

Gearheart, B. R., & Weishahn, M. W. *The handicapped child in the regular classroom*. St. Louis: C. V. Mosby, 1976.

Graubard, P. S. Children with behavioral disabilities. In L. M. Dunn (Ed.), *Exceptional children in the schools*. New York: Holt, Rinehart & Winston, 1973.

Grossman, H. (Ed.). *Manual on terminology and classification of mental retardation*. Washington, D.C.: American Association of Mental Deficiency, 1973.

Halderman v. *Pennhurst*, No. 74-1345 (E.D. Pa. 1977).

Kaufman, M. E., & Alberto, P. A. Research on efficacy of special education for the mentally retarded. In N. R. Ellis (Ed.), *International review of research in mental retardation, volume 8*. New York: Academic Press, 1976.

Kirk, S. A. *Educating exceptional children* (2nd ed.). Boston: Houghton Mifflin, 1972.

Lilly, M. S. *Children with exceptional needs*. New York: Holt, Rinehart & Winston, 1979.

MacMillan, D. L. *Mental retardation in school and society*. Boston: Little, Brown, 1977.

Maryland Association for Retarded Citizens v. *Maryland*, Equity No. 100/182/77676 (Cir. Ct. Baltimore Cty., filed May 3, 1974).

McConnell, F. Children with hearing disabilities. In L. M. Dunn (Ed.), *Exceptional children in the schools*. New York: Holt, Rinehart & Winston, 1973.

Mills v. *Board of Education of District of Columbia*, 348 F. Supp. 866 (D.D.C. 1972).

Mosley, W. J., & Spicker, H. H. Mainstreaming for the educationally deprived. *Theory into Practice*, 1975, *14*, 73–81.

New York Association for Retarded Children v. *Rockefeller*, 357 F. Supp. 752 (E.D. N.Y. 1973), final consent judgment entered, Civil Nos. 72 C 356, 72 C 357 (E.D. N.Y. entered, May 5, 1975).

Pennsylvania Association for Retarded Children v. *Pennsylvania*, 334 F. Supp. 1257 (E.D. Pa. 1971) and 343 F. Supp. 279 (E.D. Pa. 1972).

Quay, H. C. Dimensions of problem behavior and educational programming. In P. S. Graubard (Ed.), *Children against schools*. Chicago: Follett, 1969.

Scott, R. A. *The making of blind men: A study of adult socialization*. New York: Russell Sage Foundation, 1969.

Turnbull, A. P., & Schulz, J. B. *Mainstreaming handicapped students: A guide for the classroom teacher*. Boston: Allyn & Bacon, 1979.

Turnbull, H. R., III, & Turnbull, A. P. *Free appropriate public education: Law and implementation*. Denver: Love, 1978.

Wilson, M. I. Children with crippling and health disabilities. In L. M. Dunn (Ed.), *Exceptional children in the schools*. New York: Holt, Rinehart & Winston, 1973.

Wyatt v. *Stickney*, 344 F. Supp. 387 F. Supp. 373 (M. D. Ala. 1972), 334 F. Supp. 1341, 325 F. Supp. 781 (M. D. Ala. 1971), aff'd sub nom *Wyatt* v. *Aderhold*, 503 F. 2d 1305 (5th Cir. 1974).

2

Variables in a Theory of Mathematics Instruction for Exceptional Children and Youth

Vincent J. Glennon

University of Connecticut

Vincent J. Glennon, Ph.D., is a fellow of the American Association for the Advancement of Science. He was a teaching fellow at Harvard University and a teaching assistant to John R. Clark, Teachers College, Columbia University. He was professor and director of the Arithmetic Studies Center and Clinic, Syracuse University, and professor and director of the Mathematics Education Center, University of Connecticut. He is a former teacher and supervisor in the Massachusetts public schools.

A THEORY of instruction in general and of mathematics instruction in particular can be perceived as a set of interrelated variables to be drawn on in varying amounts for the purpose of selecting, organizing, and transmitting the culture in a maximally efficient manner. The history of education over the past 3000 years is a litany of varied attempts by scholars to achieve this end. Each educator focused on the variable or variables he or she perceived as most significant to the instructional process for facilitating learning by children and adults.

Prior to the rise of scientific psychology in the mid-19th century, the long saga of the improvement of instruction reflected the educational wisdom of the rational psychologists and their close intellectual allies—those philosopers who concerned themselves in some significant way with the educational process. Excellence in teaching was achieved intuitively. Exemplars of teaching can be found in all eras. In the 5th century B.C. Plato wrote of Socrates' teaching style. Plato showed how Socrates, using the dialogue method, was able to teach precise thinking to someone whose thoughts were expressed inaccurately or ambiguously. The central variables in the Socratic style of teaching were a one-to-one, or face-to-face, dyad

and a method of investigative conversation aimed at developing rigor in thinking.

Other teachers, also acclaimed for their excellence, capitalized on these variables, namely, the size of the groups and the method, in very different ways. Over the centuries many teachers have been remembered for their ability to teach large groups, rather than one person, and to do so using a method that is generally referred to as the "lecture" method (from the Latin verb *legere*, to read). Ralph Waldo Emerson (1803–1882) and George Lyman Kittredge (1860–1940), among others, were superbly endowed with the ability to organize and deliver lectures.

The long history of instructional psychology, both rational and scientific, could be drawn on in the same way for countless instances to illustrate how renowned teachers have used one or more of the several variables that should constitute a theory of instruction in an unusually skillful manner to facilitate learning.

THE NEED FOR A THEORY OF INSTRUCTION

A properly formed theory of instruction permits the teacher to make wise decisions concerning such very different questions as the following:

1. What mathematics is of most worth for teaching to an educable mentally retarded young adult? To a gifted but dyscalculic 12-year-old? To an emotionally disturbed child in the middle grades?

2. What source of motivation is likely to yield the greatest response from a talented but underachieving child? From a mildly emotionally disturbed child? From a highly motivated gifted child?

3. What teaching method is most appropriate for a teenager who is unable to tolerate frustration? Unable to focus attention? Unable to store and retrieve the basic facts?

These and an infinite number of other questions concerned with maximizing the teaching-learning process relate to what Cruickshank (1975) calls "the psychoeducational match" (pp. 71–112). In a very real sense, the task of making a good psychoeducational match, or cognitive "fit," is to select from among the several variables that constitute a theory of instruction those that are appropriate to the particular teaching-learning situation at hand.

A well-formed theory of instruction will make it possible for the teacher to ask appropriate professional questions and make reasonable decisions. Decision making is a never-ending part of the teaching process. According to Shavelson (1950),

> Decision-making is pervasive in teaching. Descriptive studies have even suggested that the list of instructional decisions made by classroom teachers is

infinite. Regardless of the actual number, decisions—sometimes conscious but more often not—are involved in almost every aspect of a teacher's professional life, especially in planning, implementing and evaluating instruction. (p. 372)

Today the cognitive fit, or psychoeducational match, is commonly referred to as "matching teaching and learning styles." This terminology is useful but incomplete. It suggests that the quality of an instructional situation is largely determined by two, and only two, variables—differences in how the teacher teaches and differences in how the learner learns. It fails to address several other, equally important variables. One such variable encompasses the different sources of the curriculum (i.e., *what* the teacher will seek to teach and, it is hoped, what the child will learn). Other variables include the different sources of motivation for learning and the different theories about the developmental nature of the learner.

Teaching-learning styles, in the fullest sense of the term, would then include curriculum, teaching, learning, motivational, and developmental styles and their interactions. These five variables (and perhaps others) and their interrelationships would form the basis for a theory of instruction by which appropriate decisions and sound psychoeducational matches would be determined.

In recent years and after a century of scientific psychology, several significant attempts have been made to create a theory of instruction. Most notable, perhaps, is Bruner's (1966) short essay, "Notes on a theory of Instruction," in which he identifies and briefly describes four major features of such a theory:

> First, a theory of instruction should specify the experiences which most effectively implant in the individual a predisposition toward learning. . . .
> Second, a theory of instruction must specify the ways in which a body of knowledge should be structured so that it can be most readily grasped by the learner. . . .
> Third, a theory of instruction should specify the most effective sequences in which to present the materials to be learned. . . .
> Finally, a theory of instruction should specify the nature and pacing of rewards and punishments in the process of learning and teaching. (pp. 40–41)

Hosford (1973), after a long and careful study of the complex problem of developing a theory of instruction, suggests that Bruner "did more than has anyone else. He dared to propose an outlined sketch of a theory of instruction" (p. 8). Hosford goes on to suggest that it is regrettable that Bruner did not pursue a *general* theory of instruction (italics added)—and, one might add, a more *complete* theory of instruction. To be complete a theory of instruction would have to provide answers to questions other than those concerned with *implementing* a curriculum. It would also have to provide a source for answers to all the questions related to the instructional process, including the *curriculum itself*.

More specifically, Bruner's partial theory of instruction could not be found useful for answering, say, even the first question above—What mathematics is of most worth for teaching to an educable mentally retarded young adult? Nor would it serve well the teacher who used it to seek answers to any of a myriad of questions that need to be answered in any school day.

To be of educational significance to the more than one million classroom teachers, a theory of instruction must be complete, general, readily comprehended, and easily applied. Creating a theory that fulfills these requisites is not a simple task, and perhaps that is the reason none has been developed.

SOME ESSENTIAL VARIABLES

Clearly, there are variables in a theory of instruction that must be well known to all teachers of exceptional children and youth, whether regular classroom teachers or special educators. Although perhaps not all variables are of equal importance when deciding about the mathematics program for a particular child at a particular time, all are essential to a complete repertoire, and all need to be drawn on in appropriate ways to make a good psychoeducational match for each learner. Unfortunately, space does not permit a discussion of all the variables applicable to a theory of instruction; the essential variables discussed in this essay are (a) the mathematics itself, (b) sources of the mathematics curriculum, (c) sources of the teacher's methodology, (d) sources of motivation for learning, and (e) consolidating learning.

The Mathematics Itself

It is unreasonable to expect that one who knows little or nothing about the discipline of chemistry can be an effective teacher of chemistry or that one who knows little or nothing about Mandarin Chinese can be an effective teacher of that subject. In the same way, it is unreasonable to expect the teacher or special educator who is deficient in a knowledge of the structure of the mathematics used in the middle school program to be a competent teacher of that subject to those children, or a competent writer of textbook material, or a competent constructor of tests for those children.

First among the equally essential variables that constitute a theory of instruction of mathematics, then, is a thorough knowledge of the mathematics itself that is *appropriate* to the child, youth, or group being taught. This is the sine qua non of instruction—whether the instruction is in an initial teaching situation or a diagnostic–remedial situation and whether it is with learners who are retarded or talented, physically disabled or learning disabled. The necessity of a knowledge of one's subject rests on the very simple principle that one cannot teach well something that one does not

understand well. If a teacher is responsible for teaching in a mathematically meaningful way the rationale of the algorithm for dividing a decimal by a decimal (e.g., $4.2 \overline{)6.0}$), one can do so only if one understands well the mathematical processing of the numerals. If one's understanding is limited to the mechanical procedure for manipulating the decimal points (the caret method), which was learned in childhood and usually without mathematical understanding (i.e., learned associationally but not conceptually), then all that one can teach to others is the same low-level nonmathematics.

Many research studies, perhaps beginning with the study by Glennon (1948), have consistently shown that general mathematics teachers or regular classroom teachers understand only about one-half the mathematics commonly taught to children in Grades K–6. Furthermore, special education teachers usually have even less preparation in both the mathematics and the instructional psychology of mathematics than regular classroom teachers. Hence, there is still much to be done regarding this first variable of a well-formed theory of instruction—a sound knowledge of the mathematics itself—if those who work with exceptional children and youth are to be competent.

Sources of the Mathematics Curriculum

A second variable in an instructional psychology is a thorough knowledge of the three *main* sources of the mathematics curriculum (Glennon, 1965). All mathematics is not of equal worth to exceptional children and youth. The ability to read a clock, digital watch, or calendar is surely of greater educational or practical significance to youth of limited mental ability than the ability to divide a fraction by a mixed number. An inquiry into the properties of modular number systems may be highly stimulating and appropriate for a child who is gifted in the ability to learn mathematics. But the same topic would be wholly inappropriate for the gifted child who is both dyscalculic and unable to focus attention on cognitive tasks for substantial periods of time.

The psychoeducational match or mismatch is a direct function of the teacher's knowledge of the sources of the curriculum and the ability to apply that knowledge to the subject of school mathematics. It is not uncommon to observe a teacher of educable mentally retarded children trying to teach a topic that is inappropriate to their present stage of cognitive development and future needs. Similarly, it is also not unusual to witness a classroom situation of some 20 heterogeneously grouped children in which the 2 or 3 who are talented or gifted are required to learn at the same comparatively slow rate as the children of average ability.

How, then, can the teacher make wise decisions on the daily question—What mathematics is of most worth for each exceptional child and youth? Over the years we have seen the rather clear delineation of three

theories (or subtheories) of curriculum that can be drawn on to answer this question. These are generally known as the logical theory, the sociological theory, and the psychological theory. Each rests on certain assumptions; each has certain advantages and certain limitations. A brief discussion of each will help the reader firmly establish these three theories as cognitive anchors and thus have them solidly in mind for future use as one variable in an instructional psychology.

The Logical Theory

The logical theory dates back to the years of the Roman Empire and was known in mathematics as *numerorum scientia*, the science of numbers. It was the curriculum of the patricians. Simply stated, the logical theory today suggests that the structure essential to the facilitation of teaching, learning, retention, transfer, and problem solving resides in the discipline itself. No discipline is as well or elegantly structured as mathematics. For example, only 11 properties or basic generalizations form the structure of the real number system.

From the point of view of the logical theory of curriculum, the making of a good psychoeducational match is essentially that of determining if the child or youth has already firmly in mind all the necessary prior cognititve learnings that are prerequisites for facile learning of the new. If so, the new learning will take place quickly. That is, the amount of time on task, or engaged time, is reduced to a minimum. Conversely, a poor psychoeducational match eventuates in increased time on task, increased difficulty in learning, decreased retention, greater retroactive inhibition and inability to transfer learning to new, related situations, and difficulty in problem solving.

Of the several assumptions basic to the logical theory, five are listed here:

1. Mathematics content can be arranged in a logical order.

2. Mathematics is learned best when it is arranged in logical order.

3. Readiness to learn a new topic is a function of the sequencing of prior learnings.

4. The content selected and its sequencing can best be determined by specialists in mathematics education.

5. The best way to ensure that the mathematics program is arranged in a sequentially sound manner is to arrange it according to its logical structure.

There are several advantages to teaching the mathematics program in a way that gives primary emphasis to its logical structure:

1. This approach can help students appreciate mathematics as an en-

joyable experience in itself; they then may well have a better awareness of its applicability to other situations.

2. Textbooks, which are the major source of instructional material in U.S. schools, are organized sequentially and with concern for the logical structure of the subject.

3. When the curriculum is organized with due regard to the structure, there is greater assurance that there will be fewer gaps or omissions in the teaching.

4. A structured and sequential curriculum provides a greater guarantee that the cognitive readiness needed for learning new, related topics will be adequate.

Limitations to the structured teaching of mathematics include these:

1. The subject matter seems to take first place; the child or youth comes second.

2. The teaching can become too formal, dull, and unrelated to the needs and interests of the learners.

3. Logical readiness for new learning does not also ensure psychological readiness or sociological readiness.

4. Stress on teaching mathematics as mathematics may interfere with integrating the program into the whole school day.

The Sociological Theory

The sociological theory, too, was a basis for curriculum decision making in the Roman Empire and was called *logistica*. It was the source of the curriculum for the plebeians. Today we would refer to it as applied, or socially useful, mathematics—the mathematics that is needed for proficiency or competence in real-life situations, the mathematics that is "basic." Clearly, numbers and operations used in everyday money situations, such as counting change in a grocery store, would be socially *useful* mathematics. Also clearly, learning to perform the basic operations using the numeration system of base four would be socially *useless* mathematics. Establishing a good psychoeducational match, then, becomes the task of finding and capitalizing on socially significant and sensible problem situations faced by children and adults.

What mathematics do adults commonly use in everyday-life situations? If we can determine the answer to this question, we can then teach these same competencies for mastery to children and youth and thereby prepare them for effective adulthood, at least in all nonspecialized mathematical situations. Unique uses of mathematics, such as in measuring and computing three-place decimals in a particular business or industry, would be

left to on-the-job training. Such is the rationale of those who advocate the primacy of the sociological theory.

Much investigation of the adult needs for arithmetic was carried out from 1911 to the early 1950s by Wilson (1951) and his students. This theory of curriculum was all but forgotten in the late 1950s and the 1960s, when the pendulum shifted abruptly to the point of view espoused by the mathematicians—the logical-structure theory (discussed above). However, the newfound concern for proficiency or competence as evidenced in the back-to-the-basics movement and in the concern for an *appropriate* educational program for the handicapped as required by the federal Public Law 94-142 (The Education of All Handicapped Children Act) suggests a renewed interest in the sociological theory of curriculum. Surely one criterion for a sound psychoeducational match would be social relevance.

Four assumptions that are basic to the sociological theory of curriculum are these:

1. Certain persistent, recurring personal and social situations require mathematics that can be identified and built into the school curriculum. Such a curriculum is the best preparation for competent adulthood.

2. Learning is best when it involves solving problems that are real and important to the individual.

3. A satisfactory level of competence or proficiency in arithmetic can be achieved through a curriculum that is centered in everyday personal and social problems.

4. Since children are social beings, their curriculum should be developed from the problems of social beings.

There are advantages to a sociologically based curriculum theory:

1. Only mathematical topics and problems of high social significance are included in the curriculum. All others are omitted.

2. A reduced curriculum permits more teaching time per topic. Presumably, greater mastery results from this increased time on task.

3. Increased motivation will result from a curriculum that is based on real-life situations.

4. A socially significant mathematics program can be more readily integrated into the whole school day.

And there are limitations:

1. The social situation that may be real to an adult may not be perceived as real by the child when that same situation is contrived for classroom purposes.

2. Basing a school mathematics program exclusively on social situa-

tions may fail to develop adequate knowledge of basic mathematical relationships and structure.

3. A curriculum that is based solely on socially useful mathematics represents a low level of competence.

4. Mathematics that is seen only as socially significant may not be learned well, may not be transferred well to new, related situations, and may not be used intelligently in problem-solving situations.

The Psychological Theory

With the rise of progressive education in this century, the psychological theory of curriculum received a great impetus. The idea that the curriculum should result from the immediate needs or expressed needs of the learners was not a new one. It had been inherent in the thoughts and writings of earlier rational psychologists and educational philosophers with interests in human development and the educational process.

However, the psychological theory of curriculum of the 20th century was new in the sense that it was a natural extension of the three successive thrusts of progressive education—the child-development thrust, the concern for social reform, and the flowering of scientific psychology. The Progressive Education Association, later called the American Education Fellowship, formally disbanded in 1951, claiming that it had accomplished what it set out to do. The three thrusts are still significant concerns of American education.

In its most radical form, the psychological theory of curriculum is referred to as the expressed-needs-of-the-child point of view. This holds that only the children themselves are truly capable of knowing and expressing their immediate needs. These immediate needs cannot be known by studying what they may need as adults and then benignly imposing these needs on the learners while in school. Rather, children must be provided with an environment in which they are free to set their own learning goals, plan their own learning experiences, and evaluate their own learning. Truly there are few schools in which "freedom to learn" is interpreted so liberally. Perhaps the best known of these is the Summerhill School in England. In a fairly recent discussion of the school the late headmaster presents succinctly the place of curriculum development in mathematics (Neill, 1960):

> Whether a school has or has not a special method for teaching long division is of no significance, for long division is of no importance except to those who *want* to learn it. And the child who *wants* to learn long division *will* learn it no matter how it was taught. (p.5)

Here, establishing a sound psychoeducational match is a fairly simple matter for the teacher. It consists of waiting until the child expresses a need

for learning long division, or whatever. Is such a theory of curriculum appropriate as a source of mathematical topics for emotionally disturbed and socially disordered children? For talented and gifted children? For learning disabled or dyscalculic youth?

Some basic assumptions of the psychological theory are these:

1. The child learns best when the content is directly related to an immediate need.

2. The learning situation in which there is the greatest freedom to learn is the one in which the greatest learning will take place.

3. The learning that takes place in a free environment is not only adequate to meet the problems that arise in school but also adequate to meet the problems that arise in life outside the school. Solving real personal problems today is the best preparation for adult life.

Some claimed advantages include the following:

1. The child and her or his expressed needs take first place; the subject matter is of secondary importance.

2. A child-centered curriculum facilitates and increases learning, retention, transfer of learning, and ability to solve real-life problems.

3. A child-centered curriculum contributes to the integrated, well-rounded development of the child—physically, mentally, socially, and emotionally.

4. The child learns the importance of freedom and how to use it wisely.

Some limitations are these:

1. Attempts to teach concepts or skills for which the child has an immediate need but not the prerequisite learnings (cognitive readiness) will be unnecessarily difficult, even unsuccessful.

2. Incidental learning is likely to be accidental learning.

3. The centrality of immediacy of the individual's mathematical needs does not give adequate attention to either the needs of society or the role of the logical structure of mathematics.

Glennon (1965) and Glennon and Wilson (1972) have developed a number of simplified models that assist in understanding the more important variables of an instructional psychology. One is used to show the major sources of the curriculum.

A Model for Sources of the Curriculum

Since there are three, and only three, major sources of the curriculum, or subtheories, a region bounded by an equilateral triangle is used as a model for this variable (see Figure 2.1). The region identified by the 0

represents the ideal curriculum for the child of average ability. The curriculum draws equally, or at least equitably, on all three constituent theories. It can be represented as being held in place by the equal "pulls," or tensions, on the three springs. If a learner's mathematical learning rate is somewhat slower than normal, the source of that child's curriculum would be more "in balance" near region A.

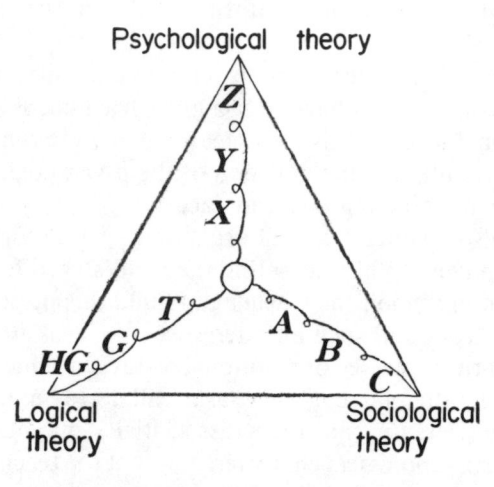

Figure 2.1. Major sources of the curriculum.

For children who are still slower in their rates of learning, appropriate adjustments in the source of the curriculum have to be made in order to attain a good psychoeducational match in this important variable of a theory of instruction. If the learner is mentally retarded but educable (EMR), the source of the curriculum approaches, say, the region identified by B. Basic literacy and "numeracy" for present needs and minimum adult consumer needs become the behavioral goals. At the same time, the pull from the other two sources is lessened. For example, counting change is a more socially significant goal for this type of learner than the unique factorization theorem.

If the learner is trainable mentally retarded (TMR), the curriculum's center of balance shifts to the region of C, and a very rigorous interpretation of needs is employed to select the curriculum. The TMR learner needs to be able to receive and express ideas using only the very basic quantitative language of "how many" and "how much."

Gallagher (1960, pp. 4–6) has distinguished among the talented, gifted, and highly gifted. The *talented* learner has the ability to accomplish learning of the school type that is between 1 and 2 standard deviations above the population mean. This includes about 14% of all children and youth.

Gifted learners are those whose ability is between 2 and 3 standard deviations above the mean—about 2% of the population. And the *highly gifted* are those whose academic ability is 3 or more standard deviations above the mean, or about 0.1% (1 out of 1000).

Although Gallagher's classification of the talented and gifted may be arbitrary, it does help us to see the need for increasingly rigorous interpretation of the logical structure of mathematics as the primary source of their curricula. His groupings would conform roughly to the regions *T, G,* and *HG* on the model.

For the child or youth who is emotionally disturbed or socially disordered, the teacher will have to use great teaching skill to find a good psychoeducational match. This may mean moving the center of balance of the learner's curriculum in the direction of the psychological theory of curriculum. While maintaining a warm, accepting, and objective role, the teacher must also maintain a well-organized, psychologically structured learning environment. While accepting the child's need to work on, say, a stamp collection in school, the teacher can build this person's mathematics program, in part, around such an interest.

As these learners' degree of emotional disturbance increases (*X, Y,* and *Z*), their ability to attend to cognitive tasks will decrease, their tolerance for frustration may decrease, and their dissociativity may increase—to name just a few of the psychological characteristics that the teacher must be aware of and compensate for with curriculum adjustments.

In the same way, the model above can be used as the theoretical basis to develop a sound psychoeducational match of the mathematics curriculum for other kinds of exceptional children—the blind and visually impaired, the deaf and hearing impaired, and the physically disabled.

Summary and Implications

This second variable in a theory of instruction of mathematics—the sources of the curriculum for children and youth—seeks to provide the basis for finding reasonable and wise answers to the question, "Of all the mathematical knowledge available, what is of most worth, is most appropriate, for a particular exceptional learner?"

As mentioned above, the quality of any psychoeducational match is a result, in part, of the teacher's knowledge of the theories of curriculum and of the appropriateness of each one for children of varying conditions of exceptionality. Keeping in mind that a typical classroom instructional time for mathematics might be 45 minutes, which totals about 135 clock hours a year (0.75 × 180 days), we see that each hour must be used wisely if maximum learning is to take place. Only part of the 135 clock hours are devoted to the developmental lessons of new concepts and skills. And still further, since a particular child is attending only part of the time to the task to be learned

("engaged time"), the originally available 135 clock hours a year are greatly eroded. How very important it is, then, for the teacher of exceptional children and youth to have clearly in mind a model of curriculum theory. Such is needed to assist in the tasks of deciding what mathematics is of most worth and of making a good psychoeducational match.

Sources of the Teacher's Methodology

If the curriculum variable—what mathematics is of most worth to justify the use of school teaching time—is a difficult area for decision making, the variable of the teacher's methodology is even more complex. The three basic sources of methodology are herein considered to be the fundamental *strategies* of teaching. These strategies describe the essence of each major role of the teacher in the classroom. A good psychoeducational match, or fit, requires that the basic methodology of the teacher be the one that facilitates learning, retention, transfer of learning, and problem solving better than some other method for a given child or youth.

The three basic methodologies are teaching as telling, teaching as guiding discovery, and teaching as psychotherapy (Glennon, 1965). Each will be presented briefly, followed by a model that relates all three and also brings into perspective the very important hybrid method, teaching through discussion.

Teaching as Telling

This method has the longest and perhaps most distinguished recorded history. Plato illustrated how Socrates used telling in the form of questions to convey information to a person whom he had engaged in a dialogue. Telling is the major source of most instructional tactics used today. Research in interaction analysis shows that when telling is being used in a typical classroom, most of the talking is done by the teacher, not by the students.

But the textbook also "tells" the reader; the tape recorder tells the listener; the TV set tells the viewer; the visiting resource person tells the group; the math-laboratory card tells the participant; the annual play of the dramatics club tells the audience; the computer-assisted program and other programmed instructional materials tell the users; and, of course, the visiting lecturer tells the listeners. These tactics are all variations of one basic method—telling—the direct presentation of subject matter, or didactic exposition.

Worthy of mention here is a recent yearbook of the National Society for the Study of Education, *The Psychology of Teaching Methods* (1976), which discusses one of the three basic methods of teaching—the lecture method. Most of the book is concerned with the several *tactics* by which the basic strategy of teaching through telling is carried out. These include chapters on programmed instruction and computer-assisted instruction

(CAI), both of which are tactics for telling. Also discussed is tutoring, in which the basic method could be telling or perhaps discussion. Other chapters on the use of simulations and games and on television and films are also illustrations of teaching through telling. Notably missing are treatments of the psychologies of the other two basic methodologies—teaching as guiding discovery and teaching as psychotherapy.

In recent years, and despite the best efforts of competent instructional psychologists to counteract them, attempts have been made to denigrate the telling method. At the same time, putative advantages have been assigned to teaching through discovery, and a small group would vigorously claim that the only real way to teach is through the method of psychotherapy.

One pejorative adjective for characterizing the method of telling is that it is "authoritarian." Ausubel (1961) discussed this criticism, arguing that

> there is nothing inherently authoritarian in presenting or explaining ideas to others as long as they are not obliged . . . to accept them on faith. Didactic exposition has always constituted the core of any pedagogic system, and I suspect, always will, because it is the only feasible and efficient method of transmitting large bodies of knowledge. (p. 23)

The proper use of the method of teaching through telling is related to many personal, social, and cognitive variables. One of these is the kind of cognitive material in mathematics (or any other subject) being learned. A simple and useful way of classifying cognitive content is that of Brownell and Hendrickson (1950, pp. 92–128): the mathematics to be learned can be (a) arbitrary associational material, (b) concepts, (c) generalizations, and (d) problem solving.

Associational material can be defined as informational material for which there is no meaning or understanding to be learned at the time the child or youth is ready to learn. By way of an illustration, there is no reason that can or need be given to a child on why the symbol 7 is formed or written in the conventional manner when he or she is ready to learn the orthography. The child learns the visual-motor skill through being told, "This is a seven," and through an appropriate amount of practice. In the same way, the youth is told the word (not the concept) *pi* for the ratio between a circumference and diameter and its orthography, π.

A concept can be defined as a common response to different stimuli. A child has acquired a concept for "fourness" when, no matter what the physical appearances may be, he or she is able to say "four" as a correct response to the question, "How many are there?" A concept is an abstraction. A child does not have a concept of "four" when he or she can use the word correctly *only* as the answer to the single question (stimulus), "How old are you?" or *only* in response to the single question, "How many wheels are there on your cart?"

Concepts cannot usually be taught as well through telling as the arbitrary associational type of material discussed above can. Rather, concepts must be developed out of the schemata of prior experiences and the readiness that those experiences generate. The learner's concept of "four" matures slowly. At a later date, 4 is understood as the length of a side of a square that has exactly 16 square units of area. Still later, it is understood as the product of $^-2 \times {^-2}$.

A generalization can be defined as the relationships that exist between two or more concepts. A child has acquired the generalization that the order of the factors does not affect the product when he or she knows that this holds for every instance. As with concept learning, telling a generalization for which adequate experiential readiness has not been acquired is neither effective nor efficient.

The ultimate goal of the mathematics program is the use of arbitrary associations, concepts, and generalizations to solve problems—whether of the contrived, verbal, in-school type or the real problems that arise in daily living or the puzzles and games of recreation. As with the teaching of concepts and generalizations, problem-solving ability cannot be acquired well through telling unless the learner already has stored and has available the necessary schemata (readiness) for receiving the message.

We have all taught and learned much through telling and will continue to do so in the future, particularly if we know well the conditions under which it is most effective. Carroll (1968), in his presidential address to the Division of Educational Psychology of the American Psychological Association, summed up his beliefs about the method of telling:

> Despite its relative neglect in educational psychology, learning from being told has a glorious past. Its future may be even more glorious if we will take the trouble to examine it with the attention we have paid to other—less interesting—ways of learning. (p. 10)

In summary, our first general method of teaching, telling, has a solid place in the teacher's repertoire when the material being taught is arbitrary associational material. Its usefulness with the other three kinds of cognitive learning is directly related to the child's previously developed cognitive readiness to acquire the new learning. Making a good psychoeducational match on when to use the method of telling for the exceptional learner requires sound judgment of a high order on the part of the teacher.

Teaching as Guiding Discovery

It has become fashionable in the past decade or two to advocate the method of teaching through discovery as a panacea for the ills of mathematical instruction. Discovery was to be the basic method by which the logical structure of the new math of the 1960s was to be taught. As with

most reform movements in education, a few extremists within it formed a cultlike group that nearly lost sight of the values inherent in teaching through telling and teaching as psychotherapy.

When defined in its most rigorous manner, "pure" discovery would center on the learning rather than the teaching process. The role of the teacher would become that of providing a learning atmosphere in which children are free to (a) determine their own learning purposes, (b) determine their own learning experiences and materials, (c) learn some subject matter that is new to them, and (d) even contribute new knowledge to society. All four of these conditions for pure discovery would rarely, if ever, exist in school situations.

Hence, discovery as a method of teaching and a style of learning subject matter needs to be modified by some adjective such as *guided* to identify and characterize accurately the role of the teacher. On a continuum like that as shown in Figure 2.2, the method of pure telling (such as an uninterrupted lecture) would be at the far left. As the method increasingly takes on more of the aspects of teacher-guided discovery of subject matter and cognitive styles, the shift on the scale is increasingly to the right. The question mark at the far right suggests the rare, perhaps impossible situation in which all four conditions for a method of pure discovery would exist in a school environment.

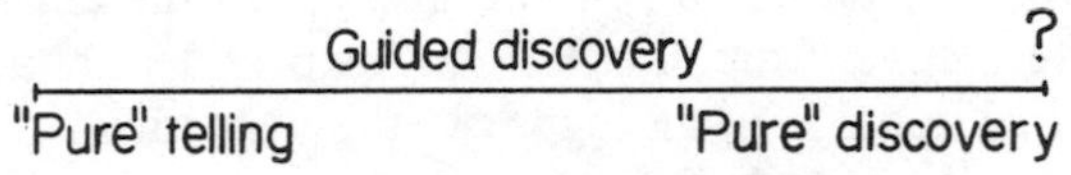

Figure 2.2. The telling–discovery methods continuum.

We have discussed the method of telling in regard to each of the four kinds of subject matter—arbitrary associations, concepts, generalizations, and problem solving. In the same way, it is important to consider briefly the appropriateness of guided—discovery in the learning of each.

Would it be wise to withhold telling children the name and orthography of the Greek letter π, used to denote the ratio of a circumference to a diameter, on the grounds that it would be better methodology to guide them in the discovery of that arbitrary association? Or is telling more efficient and therefore more appropriate for such learnings of the associational type?

In some preceding developmental lessons out of which the generalization for the ratio was developed (and out of which the need for the symbol π arose), should the teacher's basic method have been that of telling? Or should it have been some form of guided discovery? Would the additional time required to teach through guided discovery be well spent? That is, would it yield increased facility in learning, increased long-term memory, increased transfer of learning, or increased problem-solving ability?

Bruner (1961), without regard to the several kinds of subject-matter learning and the very likely different relationships that exist between the method of teaching and the kind of learning, viewed discovery as a whole piece of cloth and suggested four benefits that result from discovering for oneself: (a) an increase in intellectual potency, (b) a shift from extrinsic to intrinsic rewards, (c) learning the heuristics of discovering, and (d) an aid to memory processing.

Cronbach (1962) saw discovery and telling as a function of the stage of development of the learner:

> We need experiments that carefully control the time allocated to discovery, to know how much slower it is. I think we will find that a rich mixture of "discovery-to-presentation" (telling) is best to get the learner started, but that after he is well on the road, a leaner mixture will make for faster progress and greater economy. (p. 13)

In general, it can be said that the method of teaching through telling is most appropriate for arbitrary associations and the simpler types of conceptual learning. As the kind of learning increases in complexity through the higher concepts, generalizations, and problem solving, the method should shift increasingly to the right of center on the continuum (see Figure 2.2).

Although a modest body of firm knowledge is available regarding the relationship between each of the four kinds of subject matter named above and the appropriateness of the two methods shown on the continuum, considerably less is known about the many varying characteristics of exceptional children and their interactions with the methods of telling and guided discovery. One characteristic that has received attention in recent years is the pupil's anxiety toward mathematics. How does a teacher establish a good psychoeducational match when "personological" variables are included in the task of selecting a basic method of teaching? This leads us into our discussion of the third major method of teaching, teaching as psychotherapy.

Teaching as Psychotherapy

School personnel have generally agreed that the instructional psychology of classroom teaching includes more than a concern for the learning of subject matter. The competent teacher is also interested in the learner's attitudes and aptitudes, anxieties and hopes, personal and social values, habits and appreciations. In a word, the good teacher is concerned with the total development (cognitive, affective, and psychomotor) of the learner—not an easy task to carry out!

What method of teaching seems particularly appropriate for the affective outcomes of instruction? Here we must keep in mind, of course, that these goals are not taught independently of the cognitive goals. There is no

time in the school day when one teaches a certain appreciation of mathematics—say, the efficiency of the base-ten numeration system over the system of Roman numeration—without also teaching both these systems.

The third major method of teaching, psychotherapy, is primarily concerned with the affective domain of objectives. The other two major methods, described above, are concerned with both the cognitive and psychomotor domains. That the good teacher has always been concerned with the development of the whole person is not a new idea. In a sense, it is as old as rational psychology itself. However, in this century, and contemporaneously with the origins and development of the mental health movement (which began with the publication of Beers's (1910) book, *A Mind That Found Itself*), teaching as psychotherapy became a significant component in the competent teacher's repertoire. It is a necessary professional complement to the other two basic methods. It is needed if one is to make a good psychoeducational match for many children.

There are several similarities and several differences between the process of education and the process of psychotherapy. Symonds (1949) listed these similarities:

1. Both teachers and therapists should treat children as individuals with potentialities for progressively taking over direction of themselves.
2. Both teachers and therapists are counseled to accept the child as he is—no matter how stupid, lazy, dirty, resistive, or disorderly.
3. Both teachers and therapists have a responsibility to understand the child.

And he listed these differences, among others:

1. A teacher is primarily concerned with the world of reality and his task is to help children to become effective in the real world. A therapist, on the other hand, according to Carl Rogers, gives his attention primarily to the feelings expressed by a child.
2. A teacher feels and expresses love, but avoids hate; a therapist does not express either love or hate.
3. The teacher stimulates, encourages, guides, directs. The therapist, on the other hand, consistently avoids using any influence in the form of suggestion, advice, or encouragement (pp. 7–10).

Rogers (1969) is the preeminent leader in advancing the cause of psychotherapeutic methods in the teaching situation. The title of his recent book, *Freedom to Learn*, identifies the primacy of the property of freedom for the learner. The aim of education is the facilitation of learning. And the facilitation of learning requires freedom—freedom on the part of the learner to decide what to learn, when to learn, if to learn, how to learn, where to learn, how to evaluate the worthwhileness of the learning, and so

on. In all these aspects of the learning situation, the role of the "teacher" must be that of a *facilitator*.

Rogers suggests 10 guidelines for the person who would be a facilitator of learning, including these 4:

1.   The facilitator has much to do with setting the initial mood or climate of the group or class experience.
2.   The facilitator helps to elicit and clarify the purposes of the individuals in the class as well as the more general purposes of the group.
3.   He regards himself as a flexible resource to be utilized by the group.
4.   Throughout the classroom experience, he remains alert to the expressions indicative of deep or strong feelings. (pp. 164–166)

As noted above, under the discussion of theories of curriculum, there are few schools in which the teacher is perceived and behaves as a facilitator of learning. Summerhill is notably one of the few schools in which the centrality of the concept of freedom is undiluted.

A Model for Sources of the Teacher's Methodology

In our discussion we have identified the three major sources of the teacher's methodology—the basic *strategies* of telling, guiding discovery, and psychotherapy. Other so-called methods, such as computer-assisted instruction, the use of textbooks, films, audiotapes and videotapes, and so on, are *tactics* for teaching and should not be thought of as basic sources of methodology.

As with the three theories or sources of the curriculum, we can represent the three disparate sources of the teacher's methodology by using a triangular shape (see Figure 2.3). The question mark near the extremist position of "teaching as discovery" suggests the rare, almost impossible school situation in which all four criteria for true discovery (listed above) would be found. The region in the center is labeled "discussion method" to suggest that this method, although neither pure nor basic in itself, draws on all three basic methods.

Establishing a good psychoeducational match between the characteristics of an exceptional child or youth and the method to be used in teaching is a sure way to maximize learning. If the child is fully ready to learn and if the subject matter to be learned is either associational or of the simple conceptual sort, it is quite likely that the method should be in the region of "telling." As the conceptual load gets more complex and the heuristics of learning become more important outcomes, the method should shift increasingly toward teacher-guided discovery. As affect increases in significance as the goal or objective, the method should shift toward the region indicated as psychotherapy.

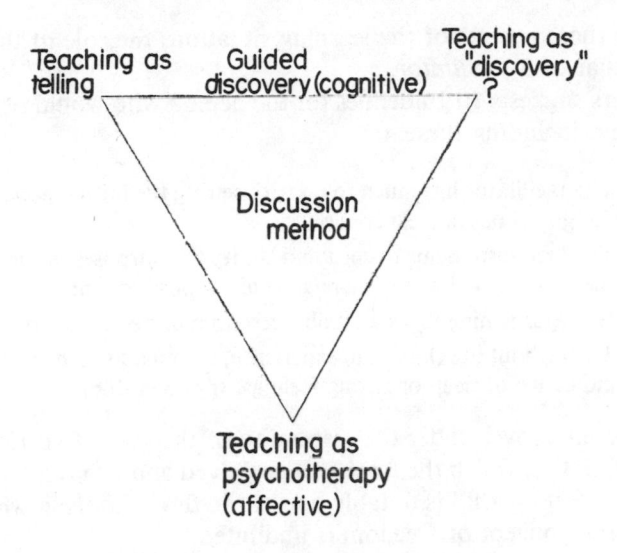

Figure 2.3. Major sources of the teacher's methodology.

Sources of Motivation for Learning

Up to this point we have discussed three basic components of an instructional psychology that are essential if one seeks to establish a good psychoeducational match for exceptional children and youth. These three components are (a) the mathematics itself; (b) the sources of the mathematics curriculum (i.e., what mathematics is of most worth for a particular exceptional person?); and (c) the sources of the teacher's methodology (i.e., what method is best or most appropriate for a particular exceptional person?).

The complexity of human learning suggested by the interactions, both positive and negative, among these three variables almost boggles the mind. Yet, an instructional psychology that is limited to these three components is incomplete. As a fourth variable, we must also include a discussion of the theories of motivation. Motivation is the energizer of learning, and a good psychoeducational match is not possible without due consideration of it.

The concept of motivation addresses the question of "why" people behave the way they do. This question is more complex than either that of the teacher's methods or that of the appropriateness of the curriculum.

Maslow (1943) developed a theory of motivation in which he suggested a hierarchy of five needs: (a) the "physiological" needs of food and homeostasis, or chemical balance in the body; (b) the safety needs; (c) the love needs; (d) the esteem needs; and (e) the need for self-actualization. This structure assumes that basic human needs are organized into a hierarchy of relative prepotency. A lower need dominates the behavior of the person un-

til it is satisfied. Then higher needs emerge as controllers of behavior. Maslow points out that the order is not as rigid and immutable as the framework implies. The usefulness of this hierarchy as a basis for the classroom teacher's source of motivation has been questioned by others. They cite instances such as the youth who will opt for a difficult course and the knowledge it will yield even at the risk of failing in lieu of a less difficult course in which the student will succeed, gain self-esteem, and ensure her or his "safety." Countless other school situations that seem to contradict the hierarchical order of needs can be cited.

Three Major Types of Motives

Sears and Hilgard (1964) provided the teacher with a more functional exposition of the motivation variable. They identified three major sources of motivation for learning—the social motives, the ego-integrative motives, and the cognitive motives.

Social motives. Social motives are those that arise out of one person's interactions with others. The social environment is the source of a variety of forces that are received by the individual, are integrated into her or his present schemata, and determine how her or his behavior will be expressed. The learner's behavior is shaped by modeling that of a peer, a significant adult, a television personality, and so forth.

Ego-integrative motives. The ego-integrative motives refer to the arousal of the learner's feelings, needs and drives, habits and instincts, and attitudes and appreciations. It includes those qualities that make one uniquely human and caring and that cause a person to seek to maintain and enhance one's concept of oneself.

Cognitive motives. Cognitive motives are those ways of arousing interest in the subject matter that is to be learned. If the source of the cognitive motivation resides outside the learner, it is referred to as *extrinsic* motivation. This has been described as the teacher's finding ways and means to get the learner to do willingly what must be done anyway. The ways and means can range from positive rewards, such as gold stars on papers, good grades, special recognition and membership in honors programs, to punishment, such as failing grades and even physical abuse.

If the source of the motivation resides, as we hope it does, in the learner's desire to learn mathematics as a good in itself, it is referred to as *intrinsic* motivation. The source of arousal of motivation in the short run is some sort of real or contrived problem solving. Putatively, the stimulation to want to engage in the cognitive behavior is the response to the learner's recognition of a novel situation. This perceived problem may be a task of pure mathematics or a puzzle or game that is pursued simply because it is good and satisfying in itself, or it may be an applied, socially significant

situation that is studied because of its usefulness in real-life, out-of-school situations.

In the long run, the source of cognitive motivation resides in the learner's awareness and acceptance of the need for success at a given grade level or in a given course as a necessary prerequisite to subsequent courses, which in turn ensures success in the vocational preparation needed for the desired future occupation.

As with the variables of curriculum sources and teacher's methodology (discussed above), the three types of motives suggested by Sears and Hilgard can be shown in the form of a triangle (see Figure 2.4). This model suggests that within the region any one point, A, represents a source of motivation that is a mixture of all three basic sources.

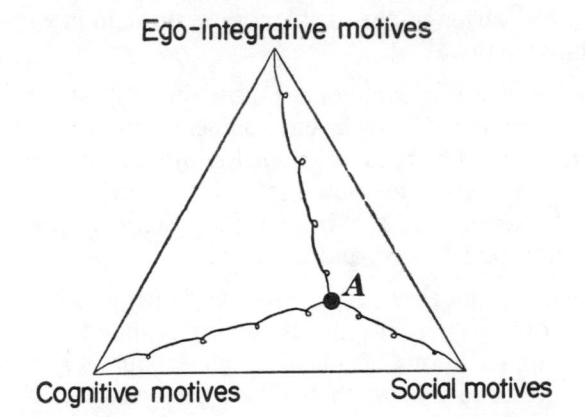

Figure 2.4. Three major sources of motivation.

Social Class and Three Levels of Reinforcement

When studied from a developmental point of view, investigations of the relative effectiveness of the three sources of motivation have been concerned with (a) tangible or material things (candies, toys, etc.), (b) social reinforcers in the form of social approval, and (c) knowledge of results (90%, "correct," etc.). Each type represents a level or stage in development. The material rewards supposedly correspond with the lower socioeconomic level and the social reinforcers and knowledge of results with the middle class. The developmental theory also assumes a shift in locus of control from external to internal, which occurs more rapidly among middle-class children and youth.

Schultz and Sherman (1976) made a critical study and evaluation of the research and concluded that "social class differences in reinforcer preferences *cannot* be assumed. Claims that the findings of social class dif-

ferences in reinforcer effectiveness are consistent . . . are simply unfounded and misleading" (p. 39).

The teacher of the exceptional child or youth who wishes to establish a good psychoeducational match between the type of learning reinforcement used and the child's social class would do better to treat each learner as a unique person. The type of reinforcer that is best for a particular learner is idiosyncratic and independent of social class.

Applied Behavior Analysis

The use of intrinsic motivation is not effective with all exceptional children and youth. Further, there are times when learners will be aroused neither by expected peer or adult approval nor by a knowledge of results and weekly progress charts. When these sources of motivation are insufficient, inappropriate, or inadequate, the teacher should have ready access to, and command of, the basic strategy of conditioning and some easily and immediately usable tactics for modifying behavior. One behavior-modification or behavior-shaping technique that is commonly used is the "time-out room" to which the deviant child is sent for a "cooling off" period. Being removed from the peer group for an extended period of time causes some children to reflect on their behavior and change it to a more socially acceptable and conforming kind. Here, the locus of control shifts immediately and completely to the teacher (external). The children will perhaps realize that if they wish the locus of control to return to them (internal), they must "shape up."

Another tactic for modifying undesirable behavior is that of ignoring the behavior. When the behavior is ignored, it is unrewarded. Unrewarded behavior is often extinguished. Rewarding desirable behaviors and punishing undesirable behaviors by drawing on the principles of conditioning as well as using other tactics may make it possible to establish a good psychoeducational match and thereby bring about educational progress when other, more desirable kinds of motivation momentarily fail.

Consolidating Learning

No set of variables that purports to suggest a theory of instruction would be complete if it did not provide the teacher with an awareness of the need for consolidating learning. A functional knowledge of the principles of teaching that are concerned with receiving, storing, recalling, and expressing learning *with facility* is essential to a useful instructional psychology.

The consolidation of learning has been referred to in the past as *drill* or *practice*. There are two types of consolidation experiences—*integrative* and *repetitive*. Integrative experiences have as their goal the development of meaningful concepts, generalizations, and problem-solving abilities. The learning activities are many in number and varied in kind.

The goal of repetitive practice is to facilitate, fix, maintain, increase, or restore a skill or ability that has already been acquired. The learning experiences, which may be many in number but few in kind, are essentially concerned with attempting to repeat a level of performance that has already been attained.

By way of an illustration, in initially learning to rename in the addition of whole-number examples of the form 16 + 9, the child might engage in a variety of learning experiences with things, with pictures, and with different algorithms or symbols—all for the purpose of *integrating* this new learning into her or his present schemata. This new learning will then be mathematically meaningful but not necessarily facile.

However, to raise this learning to the reasonably high level of facility and efficiency required by society for numerical competency, the learner will need to resort to *repetitive* practice. Here the teacher must be aware of the child's thought processes. If this child is finding the sum of 16 and 9 by "counting on by ones" from the digit of greater value in the ones place, then engaging in repetitive practice will increase proficiency in doing just that. The child will not necessarily develop to a more mature cognitive style. The drill, in this situation, will fix or arrest the child's development at a level that is less mature than society believes is desirable.

Burton (1962) has summarized the principles underlying the use of *repetitive* practice. Nine out of 14 (slightly reworded) are listed:

1. Practice should be only on the kinds of learnings that require repetitive practice. These are mental skills, motor skills, and arbitrary associations.

2. Repetitive practice should be held to a minimum until the learner has attained the level of meaningfulness desired.

3. Practice periods at the beginning should have a large diagnostic emphasis.

4. Practice for speed should be subordinated to practice for accuracy at first, and then the two should be progressively balanced.

5. Practice periods should be relatively short and distributed over a period of time (scheduled reinforcement or spaced reviews).

6. Practice periods should be lively, interesting, and pleasant.

7. Practice should proceed under a reasonable amount of tension, anxiety, or pressure. According to the Yerkes-Dodson law, anxiety increases learning when the level is between the extremes of apathy at one end of a continuum and wild excitement or uncontrolled emotion at the other end.

8. Progress should be apparent to the pupil.

9. Practice should eventually be individualized. (pp. 458–459)

CONCLUSION: SOME INTERACTIONS AMONG VARIABLES IN AN INSTRUCTIONAL PSYCHOLOGY

We have thus far considered five variables that are essential to an instructional psychology—a knowledge of the mathematics itself, sources of the curriculum, sources of the teacher's methodology, sources of motivation, and the consolidation of learning. For lack of space, other variables have not been discussed. However, in the following hypothetical case study, enough information is presented to be able to indicate the complexity of the interactions, positive and negative, that can and do arise in the classroom as teacher and child attempt to work together.

Mary is in Grade 3. She is 8 years old, lives in an inner-city neighborhood, and attends a school near her home. She is below average in measured mental ability and is stronger in visual-spatial ability (right hemisphere) than in verbal ability (left hemisphere). She is better at associational learning than conceptual learning. She has a low tolerance for frustration. She prefers the security and structure of a teacher-centered classroom, and she learns better when motivated by extrinsic rewards than by intrinsic rewards. Her conceptual tempo is impulsive rather than reflective. Her attitude toward mathematics is neutral, and her expressed self-concept is negative. (Other cognitive and affective characteristics could be listed.)

To appreciate fully the possible interactions, we must also consider the characteristics of Mary's teacher. Betty Smith has several years' experience in teaching Grade 3 in that school. She has a high tolerance for frustration, and she prefers to teach mathematics through guided discovery. She believes that conceptual learning is important and that intrinsic motivation is preferable to other types of motivation. She professes to have an "open" classroom atmosphere but does not think that hands-on materials are necessary or useful. She believes that drill or practice is unnecessary, even harmful.

Other needs of both child and teacher could be listed and would need to be considered if a good psychoeducational match were to be attained. But what are some of the interactions among the few noted traits and characteristics of the child and the teacher?

First, recall that Mary is below average in measured ability to achieve learning of the school type. Her rate of learning is slower than that of an average child. In mental age, Mary is more like a first-grade child. Does she really "need" to learn to rename in the subtraction of whole numbers (e.g., $52 - 17 = n$) simply because this topic is in the third-grade textbook and all third graders are using that book? Or should this topic be delayed until Mary is in Grade 4 or Grade 5? The interaction between mental ability and cognitive success is obvious. The educational implications are clear.

Second, since Mary is stronger in visual-spatial ability than in verbal ability, the teacher must base her initial instruction more on the concrete (enactive) and pictorial (iconic) modes than on the written symbolic mode only. But Miss Smith is opposed to using hands-on materials such as bundles of tongue depressors and pictures of number lines. There is a substantial conflict here that may result in a poor psychoeducational match, or cognitive fit, for Mary.

Third, Mary has a low tolerance for frustration—a low boiling point, a short fuse. Miss Smith likes to teach mathematics by guided discovery, which means the withholding of information and reluctance in telling. But Mary cannot easily accommodate her own preferred learning style to Miss Smith's preferred teaching style. A strong negative interaction exists, perhaps unknown to the teacher, that may be the cause of Mary's outbursts during math lessons.

Fourth, Mary is more strongly motivated by material rewards than by intrinsic rewards. Miss Smith, however, does not believe in "coddling" with candies, trinkets, and so on. Knowledge is its own reward. Again, a negative interaction exists between the pupil's learning style and the teacher's preferred teaching style.

Even though we have only scratched the surface of the many possible interactions, cognitive and affective, on the data of this abbreviated "case study," we have shown that the variables in a teaching-learning situation interact in many and complex ways.

Admittedly, much has yet to be learned and used in the classroom to maximize the psychoeducational match for all children and youth who have the kinds of exceptional learning needs discussed in the subsequent chapters of this professional reference. In each chapter the authors first discuss the characteristics of the children and youth possessing a specific kind of exceptionality. Then they discuss how to draw on instructional psychology to establish a good psychoeducational match for these youth in the teaching and learning of mathematics.

REFERENCES

Ausubel, D. P. Learning by discovery: Rationale and mystique. *Bulletin of the National Association of Secondary School Principals*, 1961, *45*(269), 18–58.

Beers, C. *A mind that found itself*. Garden City, N.Y.: Doubleday, 1910.

Brownell, W. A., & Hendrickson, G. How children learn information, concepts, and generalizations. In *Learning and instruction*, Forty-ninth Yearbook of the National Society for the Study of Education (Pt. 1). Chicago: University of Chicago Press, 1950.

Bruner, J. S. The art of discovery. *Harvard Educational Review*, 1961, *31*, 21–32.

Bruner, J. S. *Toward a theory of instruction*. Cambridge, Mass.: Harvard University Press, Belknap Press, 1966.

Burton, W. H. *The guidance of learning activities*. New York: Appleton-Century-Crofts, 1962.

Carroll, J. B. On learning from being told. *Educational Psychologist*, 1968, *5*(2), 10.

Cronbach, L. J. *Issues current in educational psychology*. Paper read at the Social Science Research Council Conference on Mathematical Learning, New York, May 4–6, 1962.

Cruickshank, W. M. The psychoeducatonal match. In W. M. Cruickshank & D. P. Hallahan (Eds.), *Perceptual and learning disabilities in children: Psychoeducational practices.* Syracuse, N.Y.: Syracuse University Press, 1975.

Gallagher, J. J. *Analysis of research on the education of gifted children.* Urbana, Ill.: Office of the Superintendent of Public Instruction, 1960.

Glennon, V. J. *A study of the growth and mastery of certain basic mathematical understandings on seven educational levels.* Unpublished doctoral dissertation, Harvard University, 1948.

Glennon, V. J. And now synthesis: A theoretical model for mathematics education. *Arithmetic Teacher*, 1965, *12*(2), 134–141.

Glennon, V. J., & Wilson, J. W. Diagnostic-prescriptive teaching. In *The slow learner in mathematics*, Thirty-fifth Yearbook of the National Council of Teachers of Mathematics. Washington, D.C.: The Council, 1972.

Hosford, P. L. *An instructional theory: A beginning.* Englewood Cliffs, N.J.: Prentice-Hall, 1973.

Maslow, A. H. A theory of motivation. *Psychological Review*, 1943, *50*, 370–396.

National Society for the Study of Education. *The psychology of teaching methods*, Seventy-fifth Yearbook. Chicago: University of Chicago Press, 1976.

Neill, A. S. *Summerhill: A radical approach to child rearing.* New York: Hart, 1960.

Rogers, C. *Freedom to learn.* Columbus, Ohio: Merrill, 1969.

Schultz, C. B., & Sherman, R. H. Social class, development, and differences in reinforcer effectiveness. *Review of Educational Research*, 1976, *46*(1), 25–29.

Sears, P., & Hilgard, E. (Eds.). *Theories of learning and instruction*, Sixty-third Yearbook of the National Society for the Study of Education (Pt. 1). Chicago: University of Chicago Press, 1964.

Shavelson, R. J. Teachers' decision making. In *The psychology of teaching methods*, Seventy-fifth Yearbook of the National Society for the Study of Education (Pt. 1). Chicago: University of Chicago Press, 1950.

Symonds, P. M. Educational psychotherapy. *Journal of Educational Psychology*, 1949, *40*, 5–20.

Wilson, G. M. *Teaching the new arithmetic.* New York: McGraw-Hill, 1951.

3

Teaching Mathematics to Children and Youth with Perceptual and Cognitive Processing Deficits

Vincent J. Glennon
University of Connecticut

William M. Cruickshank
University of Michigan

Vincent J. Glennon, Ph.D., is a fellow of the American Association for the Advancement of Science. He was a teaching fellow at Harvard University and a teaching assistant to John R. Clark, Teachers College, Columbia University. He was professor and director of the Arithmetic Studies Center and Clinic, Syracuse University, and professor and director of the Mathematics Education Center, University of Connecticut. He is a former teacher and supervisor in the Massachusetts public schools.

William M. Cruickshank, Ph.D., is professor of child and family health, psychology and education, Program of Child and Family Health, School of Public Health; and director emeritus, Institute for the Study of Mental Retardation and Related Disabilities, University of Michigan. He is president of the International Academy for Research in Learning Disabilities. Formerly he was Margaret O. Slocum Distinguished Professor of Psychology and Education and director, Division of Special Education and Rehabilitation, Syracuse University.

LEARNING DISABILITIES, a confusing and all-too-inclusive term, has been perplexing some professional educators and psychologists since 1963, when the term was, with some degree of accident, first thrust upon unwary professionals. The term, insofar as concepts and study are concerned, actually goes back far earlier than 1963 (Wiederholt, 1974), and other terms have both preceded and followed it as one professional after another has attempted to define it and make order out of the misunderstandings that surround it (Cruickshank, 1979; Cruickshank & Paul, 1980).

To orient the reader, it will be necessary to examine briefly the inclusive nature of the term *learning disabilities* and to define it insofar as teaching

and developmental mathematics are concerned. Two figures may help. It is impossible for a single illustration to encompass all the dimensions of this complicated problem, but Figure 3.1 does contain a paradigm that may clarify some elements of the issue. Learning disabilities do not form a single entity, nor are they a single syndrome. They are, as the figure illustrates, a complicated set of factors that singly or in combination can adversely affect learning and adjustment. These factors group themselves into two major constellations, namely, (a) the psychosocial, emotional, and genetic determinants that are noted in the top flaps of the paradigm and (b) the determinants in the nature of various neurophysiological dysfunctions noted on the front face of the construct.

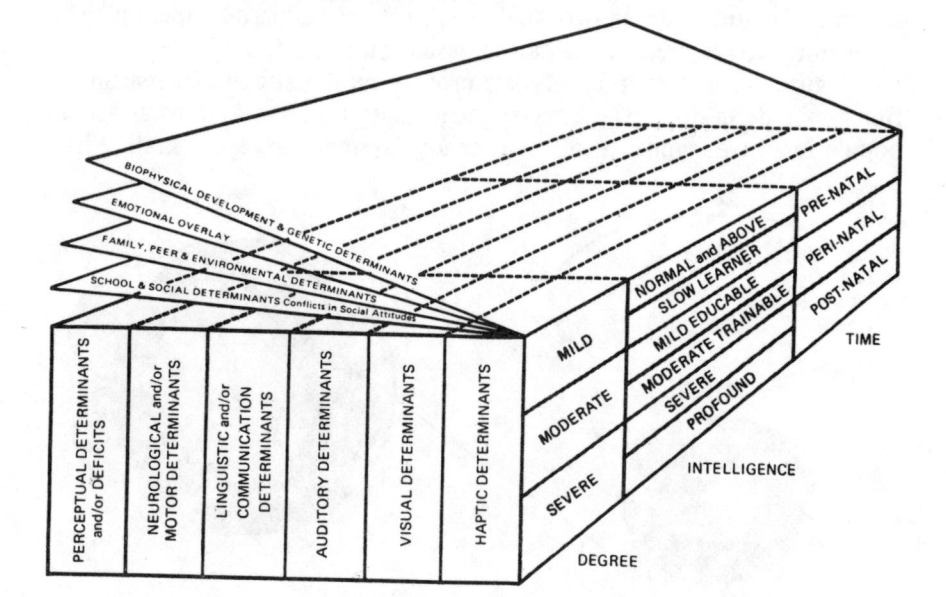

Figure 3.1. The complexity of learning disability. (Reproduced with permission from W. M. Cruickshank, W. C. Morse, & J. S. Johns, *Learning Disabilities: The Struggle from Adolescence to Adulthood:* Syracuse: Syracuse University Press, 1980.)

Overall, learning disabilities can be manifested at different levels of severity: mild, moderate, or severe. Learning disabilities affect all levels of intelligence, from the lowest to the highest. (This statement, while absolutely true, is disputed by organizations of parents, which almost universally have defined learning disabilities as a set of psychological conditions in children at or above a so-called normal IQ. This situation is being modified through a more thoughtful consideration of Public Law 94-142, and state cut-off levels are rapidly disappearing.)

Learning disabilities have their etiology in prenatal, perinatal, and, to a lesser extent, postnatal developmental periods and generally within the neurological system of the organism. There may be biophysical and genetic determinants to the problem, and almost always emotional overlays exist in the child that complicate and confuse the underlying issues of learning disability. There may be family and environmental determinants as well as school, social, and economic determinants.

Likewise, on a different plane, learning disabilities may have a definite or presumed neurophysiological basis and may be associated with perceptual processing determinants (involving one or all of the sensory modalities), perceptual determinants or deficits (which are of neurological origin), or linguistic and communication dysfunctions (which may be the secondary manifestations of visual, auditory, or haptic dysfunctions of a perceptual nature, i.e., audio-motor, visual-motor, etc.).

Figure 3.2 may help clarify the problem and assist one in reaching a functional definition. The cone-shaped illustration shows a total school population in a hypothetical local school system, large or small. First,

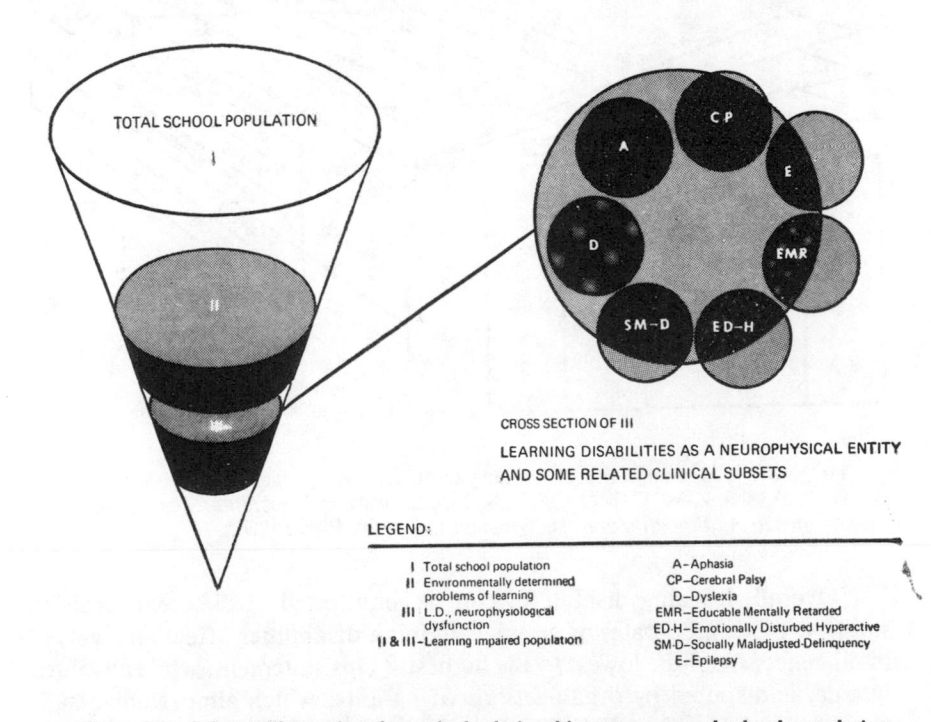

TOTAL SCHOOL POPULATION

CROSS SECTION OF III

LEARNING DISABILITIES AS A NEUROPHYSICAL ENTITY
AND SOME RELATED CLINICAL SUBSETS

LEGEND:

I   Total school population
II Environmentally determined
    problems of learning
III L.D., neurophysiological
    dysfunction
II & III–Learning impaired population

A–Aphasia
CP–Cerebral Palsy
D–Dyslexia
EMR–Educable Mentally Retarded
ED-H–Emotionally Disturbed Hyperactive
SM-D–Socially Maladjusted-Delinquency
E–Epilepsy

Figure 3.2. Schema illustrating theoretical relationship among a total school population, learning impaired populations, and selected subsets of the specific learning disability group. (Reproduced with permission from W. M. Cruickshank, W. C. Morse, & J. S. Johns, *Learning Disabilities: The Struggle from Adolescence to Adulthood*. Syracuse: Syracuse University Press, 1980.)

toward the middle of the cone is a group of children defined as those whose learning problems are the result of environmental pressures or impairments. In Figure 3.1 it was suggested that the problem of these children originated in psychosocial determinants. Currently these are included in the generally accepted group of children and youth with learning disabilities and are encompassed within the general definition of the issue as it is popularly conceived. This group of children was not originally included in the thinking of those who were concerned with the problem prior to 1963. However, the learning disabilities and characteristics of the children and youth in this group are often very similar to a second group to be discussed momentarily, and thus they can be included in the definition, providing practitioners know what they are doing, understand the nature of an accurate definition, and have good etiological and diagnostic information on which to base differential programs of teaching and learning.

Contrary to popular thinking and to that of some professionals, the size of the two groups is not accurately known. No definitive epidemiological or demographic studies exist, and this fact in and of itself makes planning for instruction difficult within a state or local school system.

The second group of pupils in Figure 3.2 consists of those included in the original concept of the term, prior to 1963, and are pupils whose learning disabilities are the result of some dysfunction of the central nervous system of a prenatal, perinatal, or postnatal origin. It is these children who present the most serious instructional problems to teachers, not discounting the seriousness and importance of the problems in the previously discussed group that retard learning and that are related to environmental deprivation and social disorganization. Children whose learning and adjustment problems are related to central nervous system dysfunction and to perceptual processing deficits will be the primary focus of this chapter, for their needs are significant and are those which educators are least prepared to handle. Their problems frequently preclude their inclusion in a successful program of mainstreaming (Cruickshank & Paul, 1980). A definition of this group of children has been carefully developed by Wepman and his associates (1975, p. 300) and gives form to the discussion that follows.

The reader will note in Figure 3.2 several small circular inserts in the cross section of Level III. In the legend below these are identified as aphasia, cerebral palsy, and so on. Their position in the paradigm is not accidental; that is, all children with aphasia (A) and accurately defined dyslexia (D) have perceptual processing deficits similar to learning disabilities as we have defined them here. About 90% of cerebral palsied children (CP) under 16 years of age show similar perceptual processing deficits. As a matter of record, much of what is known about these problems in learning disabilities came from research completed with cerebral palsied subjects.

No definitive data exist regarding the other clinical subtypes noted in the paradigm. The percents of the various populations are estimates only, albeit estimates based on extensive clinical observations and some clinical research data. Many children with a variety of clinical problems have the added problem of one or more perceptual processing deficits.

BASIC ARITHMETICAL CONCEPTS AND FACTS

Two fundamental concepts must be kept in mind as one moves to provide mathematical experiences for children with learning disabilities. First, as with all children, their acquisition of arithmetical and mathematical understandings is developmental and must be approached from a developmental point of view. Second, it cannot be forgotten that in the normal course of developing physically, children with perceptual and cognitive processing deficits have not, by reason of their disabilities, progressed normally from the point of view of concepts, ideational experiences, abstract or concrete ideas, values, or other essential elements basic to movement from one growth level to another. The teacher who expects to meet these children's needs does not begin instruction—remediation is not the appropriate concept—at the chronological level of the child but begins developmentally at the lowest functional level at which a genuine success experience can be obtained. In working with a 23-year-old man of good intelligence and capacity, Cruickshank found in early exploratory activities that the first genuine success experience that could be obtained was in terms of eye-head coordination, a skill normally acquired by a child before 18 months of age (Cruickshank, Morse, & Johns, 1980, chap. 13).

It goes without saying that we believe mathematical skills are socially useful and that they have market value for the learner. Specifically, with respect to learning disabilities, we know that "mathematics has structural qualities which, when grasped, not only enhance its social utility, but lend mathematics a beauty which children should be led to see and enjoy for its own sake" (Cruickshank, Marshall, & Hurley, 1971, Vol. 1, p. 5).

We emphasize structure throughout the approach to the education of children with learning disabilities—structured environment and space, structured teaching materials, structured programs, and a structured teacher-pupil relationship.

> To help the child sense mathematical structure, none of the specific mathematical learnings [can be developed] as separate unrelated entities. For example, as concepts for *set, subset* and the relations of *equivalence, inclusion, greater than,* and *less than* are developed, their relevance to and uses in developing geometric and number concepts [must be] presented immediately in a spiral manner. (ibid.)

Of particular concern is the manner in which the teacher must translate the

long-term goal of helping the child move toward self-esteem. This will come only through bona fide success experiences.

> The activities for each of the major mathematical concepts and skills [must be] analyzed into a detailed and graduated series of steps [steps more finite and elemental than for the normal child]. Each step [must aim] at an immediately attainable, limited aspect of the concept. More importantly, the criteria by which achievement of the objective of each step is determined must readily be seen by the child himself. The lessening of the learner's reliance on outside authority, and resultant increasing self-evaluation, bring benefits to self-esteem which cannot be overemphasized. (ibid.)

These desirable ends can be achieved only by the substitution of trial-and-error behavior on the part of the learner with genuine success experiences, and this can be securely achieved only by understanding a developmental sequence that begins so low in the child's learning level that success is a guaranteed outcome. As the teacher becomes acquainted with the characteristics of children and youth with learning disabilities, it will become apparent rather quickly that concepts of *lowest level, development, structure,* and *success experience* are interwoven and constitute the fabric out of which positive growth and achievement for these children will take place. Although these concepts are generally recognized by all good teachers, teachers of the learning disabled must recognize that they must consciously plan for them and integrate them into every aspect of their teaching.

CHARACTERISTICS OF THE LEARNING DISABLED

We shall now characterize the child or youth with learning disabilities. Although the implications of these characteristics for teaching and learning mathematics will compose the latter half of this chapter, we shall illustrate each characteristic with a practical implication for some specific aspect of developmental mathematics. We have indicated that learning disabilities for this group of children and youth involve perceptual and cognitive processing deficits, which are the result of a diagnosed or presumed neurological dysfunction. Probably *perceptual and cognitive processing deficit* would be a more accurate term than *learning disabilities* (Cruickshank, 1977b), although admittedly this is cumbersome and does not carry the popular appeal of the other term. However, irrespective of terminology, if the educator has an accurate understanding of the problem, the label is not too important. Perception and cognition fall within the purview of educators and psychologists in the teaching situation and can be dealt with without a technical background in neurology, although it is always helpful if good pediatric neurology is represented on the professional diagnostic team. There is, on the one hand, little a teacher can do with the neurological prob-

lem per se. It is essential, however, to understand that neurophysiological data should serve as a background to the educator's operational plan. There are, on the other hand, a tremendous number of things an insightful teacher can do to alleviate processing deficits in a child—deficits that are inherent in neurological dysfunction and that may involve all sensory modalities. Just what the details are regarding the actual bridge between neurological dysfunction and perceptual and cognitive processing deficits is not fully known in all their complicated aspects, but enough is known to permit conclusive educational planning and instruction to take place.

Attention Disturbances and Attention Span

A pervading characteristic of the great majority of learning disabled children is their inability to refrain from reacting to extraneous stimuli—extraneous to the task immediately at hand. For example, on psychological tests, such as the Rorschach, these children give a preponderance of small-detail responses rather than organize the inkblot into a single meaningful concept. In practical situations these children are distracted by any auditory, tactual, visual, or olfactory stimuli—by colors, by street sounds, by movement in the classroom, by both external and internal stimuli, indeed by any stimulus to which a response can be made. Tight clothing, lack of a bowel movement, hunger, the stimulus of clothing against the skin—each or all of these may in certain children serve as distracters from the task at hand. As a result of the inability to refrain from reacting to both sensory and motor stimuli, these children often have almost unusable attention spans in terms of the tasks to be accomplished in the classroom. A child with a measured attention span of 120 seconds may experience nearly total failure in an arithmetic drill that ordinarily requires about 20 minutes of attending time. Not all children with learning disabilities have such short attention spans, but many do. It is very common to encounter learning disabled children with usable attention spans of under 5 minutes, and herein lies an immediate cause of conflict and misunderstanding between child and teacher. The pupil violates the planned classroom time schedule.

This lack of attending ability often leads to students' being characterized as hyperactive, and hyperactive they are. But the hyperactivity we describe is the result of both the inability to attend to appropriate stimuli and the inability to refrain from reacting to extraneous stimuli. Alfred A. Strauss used to speak of these children as being "stimulus bound," that is, tied to stimuli. The end result, however, is pupils who are distracted meaninglessly to things around them, who react purposelessly to specific stimuli that are suddenly introduced into the classroom (a stranger coming into the room, a book dropping, an adolescent pinching or tickling a classmate sitting nearby). A fire alarm may actually cause such children to swing around in their chair and fall from it. Falling out of chairs is common among wig-

gling learning disabled children in elementary school. One helpful antidote for this behavior is to reduce extraneous stimuli in the immediate learning area of the classroom for these children (Cruickshank, Bentzen, Ratzeberg, & Tannhauser, 1961; Cruickshank, 1977b). The impact of forced responsiveness to extraneous stimuli, however, is seen in dramatic ways that have more specific influences on learning.

Figure-Ground Pathology

The influence of figure-ground reversal has been understood in psychology for a long while, although its impact on instruction has not been so widely recognized. Figure and ground reversal means exactly what it says—the background assumes greater attraction than the figure itself in a given situation. This phenomenon is a good example of the learning disabled child's inability to attend to central stimuli for a period of time appropriate for accurate discrimination. In most background situations the stimuli outnumber those in the figure; hence, they take precedence over the figure. Consider what this means in an arithmetic drill involving 12 two-digit addition problems (with their plus signs and lines), all placed on a single standard-sized piece of white paper. Each problem, for the normal child, stands alone. But on that piece of paper, considering four distinct elements for each problem (two numerals, a plus sign and a line), are 28 individual stimuli. This number is compounded by angles, the different shapes of numerals, spaces between and around numerals and sets of numerals, likes and differences among numerals, and myriad other factors, each and every one a stimulus extraneous to the task at hand: correctly perceiving and solving a given problem. Each problem is surrounded by dozens of other stimuli. For the child who is so driven, the potential for attending to these extraneous stimuli and thus reversing field, so to speak, is great indeed. The child may know the number fact, but before an appropriate intellectual decision can be reached and recorded, visual or motor distraction has taken place and the child may not be able to redirect himself or herself to the actual figure (problem) and then to solve it correctly. Placing one problem alone on a single and otherwise blank piece of paper may obviate much of this problem.

It is quite obvious that whereas standard textbooks and workbooks have their places in the instructional program, they are very often inappropriate for the pupil with learning disabilities. From the point of view of figure-ground discrimination, the usual basal texts and workbooks contain entirely too many stimuli on a given page.

Dissociation

Dissociation, from our point of view in this discussion, is the inability of the individual to conceptualize parts into wholes visually and often

auditorily. For example, individual numerals may not be integrated into a whole concept of an addition or subtraction problem. The individual parts assume greater significance than the whole. In large measure this may be due to the inability of the child to attend and to the issue of forced responsiveness to extraneous stimuli. Dissociation, or the inability to conceptualize elements as a unity—as a gestalt—constitutes a fundamental disability for the individual with learning disabilities insofar as the conceptualization of form is concerned. This issue is observed in numerous children in their inability to conceptualize letters, numerals, and combinations of letters in words, sentences, or paragraphs leading to ideas; to complete puzzles or form boards; to lace up shoes or button clothing; and in other related practical aspects of daily living.

Memory Dysfunction

Another characteristic of those with learning disabilities related to neurophysiological dysfunction is poor performance on tasks requiring either short- or long-term memory function. Even though this can also be related to intellectual level and to emotional tension, it is, in the learning disabled child, primarily related to the issues of attention span and sensory and motor hyperactivity. Both *retroactive inhibition,* where new learning interferes with earlier learning, and *proactive inhibition,* where earlier learning interferes with later learning, are indeed factors to be seriously considered by educators who work with learning disabled youth.

A child may indeed have responded appropriately to a given aspect of learning and may have apparently learned something for the moment. The same child, however, whose attention span is interrupted successively by numerous, perhaps hundreds of stimuli, will not retain that learning, and repetitive teaching may be required day after day for long periods of time. Thus, multiplication tables or concepts of renaming ("borrowing" and "carrying") in addition and subtraction can be seemingly insurmountable hurdles for both child and teacher. If there is one characteristic of the learning disabled child or adolescent that tests the teacher, this is it. Patience is required from the adult, sometimes almost beyond any expected limits. It is not that the child is behaving negatively or consciously attempting to misbehave. The child is seriously distracted and cannot attend properly. As a result, the memory of recently learned facts or concepts is often exceedingly limited. For this reason, if the concept of multiplication, for example, is learned, the availability of a hand calculator is so important in providing repeated successful experiences for the child.

Sequencing

A most interesting characteristic of many children and youth with learning disabilities is the inability to sequence in a proper order. This may

be observed in some children as a very minor aspect of the disability, but in others it may be very significant. "John, please come to my desk," asks a fourth-grade teacher. John is learning disabled. "Take this note to the principal's office; have his secretary sign it. Then take the note to Miss Jones in Room 208, give it to her, and she will give you a package to bring to me. Please hurry." The package is likely never to be delivered. There are too many memories involved; ordering these memories may be limited or impossible, and a success experience is most unlikely.

Within the process of solving arithmetic problems, sequencing is also very important. Assume that the three two-digit numbers shown here are to be added. Renaming is involved. First the problem must be correctly copied

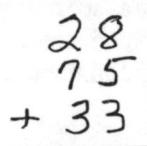

from the chalkboard (visuo-motor activity); then three digits must be added and a ten carried to the left-hand column; then four digits must be added and an appropriate answer written under the line. Task analysis helps delineate the sequence of functions necessary to solve the problem. Substraction, division, and multiplication usually involve even greater sequencing skills. The reader should keep in mind that failure to function in this realm is often found in pupils of high intellectual ability. It is not just associated with restricted mental ability. Learning disabilities are respecters of no single intellectual level.

In terms of both classroom activities and instructional procedures, these children will respond more satisfactorily within good concepts of structure than under essentially permissive programs. Structure is used as a tool of learning. Thus, the program is repetitive from day to day and week to week. New activities are inserted with much advance warning, and the teacher expects confusion for a while on the part of a given child or group of children. The child always sits in the same place; the appearance of the room does not vary significantly from day to day. The school day starts with a given activity. This is followed by an order of learning activities that does not vary much from day to day. As a result of this structure, a secure framework is developed from which children can predict events and operate more efficiently. Structure also aids children with sequencing problems and lends support to those with maladaptive learning characteristics (i.e., impulsivity, distractibility, disorganization, etc.).

Discrimination

One of the unique characteristics of pupils with learning disabilities is

their inability to recognize "fine differences between auditory and visual discriminating features underlying the sounds used in speech and the orthographic forms used in reading," writing, and spelling (Wepman et al., 1975, p. 306). Obviously, attending problems are inherent here as with many of the other characteristics. However, the lack of the ability to discriminate is fundamental to the problems of learning these children often demonstrate. The inability, for example, to discriminate the numeral 8 from the capital letter *O* or a zero (0) can be fundamental to success or failure in copying arithmetic problems or reading them from a chalkboard or text. The letters *m* and *n* are often confusing, as are *v* and *w*. The letters *d, b, p,* and sometimes *g* or *j* can likewise cause serious confusion. The lower-case letter *l* and the numeral 1 are so nearly identical that children with discriminatory dysfunctions experience failure. The arithmetic and the reading teachers must work hand in hand on many of these characteristics.

Directionality and Body Parts

It is essential to a child's success in mathematical processes to have a command over issues of directionality. It is interesting, but often very sad, to observe elementary school children (and quite often youths in junior and senior high school) unable to discriminate between *left* and *right, above* and *below, over* and *under.* "Walk to the end of the room and turn left just before you reach the wall," says a teacher to a learning disabled child in a practice situation. The child walks to the end of the room as commanded, but then hesitates, not knowing exactly which way to go, needing to glance at the teacher or others for assurance, and then turning on the basis of trial and error rather than with real orientation. Obviously in this situation there is a 50% chance for failure when a 100% insurance of success is desired. Directional skills are essential in most mathematical skills. Pupils carry to the left-hand column in addition; they borrow from left to right in subtraction. Perplexity marks the faces of a group of learning disabled children when directionality is required.

The lack of directional skills is closely related to a lack of knowledge regarding body parts, and this deficiency in turn is closely related to poor self-concepts. Accurate and spontaneous recognition of *left hand, right hand, left foot, right foot, left eye, right ear, top of the head, under the chin*—all this directional nomenclature, expected to be fully understood by the time the child reaches first grade—is all too often wholly lacking in children and youths with learning disabilities. These vocabulary concepts have mathematical implications that are normally achieved early in the child's life, but when they aren't, they may become the responsibility not only of the mathematics teacher but of the English and physical education teachers as well. One of the authors employed a 16-year-old youth with learning disabilities as a dockboy during the summer. The youth was told,

"When the wind blows from the south or east, tie the boats on the left side of the dock. When the wind comes from the north or west, moor the boats on the right side of the dock." The expression of near horror on his face quickly reminded the adult that practice regarding the relationships between right and left and west and east was required, if not also some system of color coding for wind direction and the placement of valuable boats to prevent wind damage. When this was done, failure was completely precluded, and the youth expressed genuine pride that he "never made a mistake all summer." Perceptual and cognitive processing deficits can be and are translatable into the daily activities of living as well as into the concrete and abstract aspects of instruction and learning. "Place your name in the upper right-hand corner of your paper," requests the teacher. "Where's that?" mumbles the 12-year-old boy recently assigned to sixth grade, who then quickly looks over at his neighbor for modeling and for help. Confusion can turn into terror when the neighboring child mistakes the need for help as an attempt to copy and so informs the whole class that "the new kid is copying from me, Miss Smith!" In contrast, the teacher can discuss with the class the new child's problems as an aspect of individual differences characteristic in varying forms of all the members of the class, and she can ask neighboring children to assist the learning disabled children when misunderstandings or confusions take place.

Spatial and Temporal Disorientation

The example involving the docking of boats illustrates also the trouble some learning disabled children have with spatial orientation. These children are often confused by concepts of time, not only in terms of the exact time as seen on the face of a clock but also time in broader generalities, such as morning, afternoon, day versus weeks, weeks and months, years, holidays, and weekends. Such abbreviations as A.M., P.M., eve., wk., mo., or yr. add still another dimension to the child's general confusion. Estimating time is developmental. A child whose development has been interrupted by perceptual and cognitive processing deficits may not have the capacity to estimate or predict time. "We shall go next week," says the mother of a 10-year-old learning disabled girl. "How long is that?" "When is next week?" "What is a week?" To respond to such questions once might not be so difficult, but when the same questions are asked repeatedly, patience wears thin even when the behavioral dynamics are fully understood by the adult. A birthday party is held in a school for a schoolmate. "When is my birthday?" the learning disabled child asks. "Not until February," responds the teacher. It is now only the month of May, but for the learning disabled child, February should be today or at least no later than tomorrow! These are not the responses of severely mentally retarded children; these inconsistencies with what are supposedly developmental skills and learnings

are those of children with good intelligence but with significant processing deficits.

Obtaining Closure

A visuo-motor problem known as failure to achieve closure (the inability to make cognitive and perceptual responses in a complete and comprehensible manner) is often apparent in children and youth with learning disabilities and has an impact on their success rate in reading and arithmetic. This condition may take the form of finding it difficult to reach closure verbally—while talking, for example—or conceptually, while attempting to think through a process. This condition, as illustrated in the following example, may be related to distractibility or possibly to something more fundamental. However, its appearance is frequently observed in writing. For example, the numerals *6, 9,* and *4* and the letters *a, d, o, p,* and so on may look as illustrated in Figure 3.3 when the child's paper is submitted (see also Cruickshank, Morse, & Johns, 1980, chap. 12–14). Dissociation can also be observed in these examples. Obviously there is great possibility for misunderstanding the child who exhibits these errors—errors that he or she may see as a perfectly good performance. Errors of closure can be misinterpreted for sloppiness. They are really deep-seated eye-hand coordination problems. Psychologists observe this phenomenon frequently when the child is asked to reproduce figures of the Bender-Gestalt test, for example, or from the child's responses on the Rorschach test. Teachers, however, have in the daily written assignments of children a continuous built-in method of observing this problem, one that can have serious negative influences on performance and success.

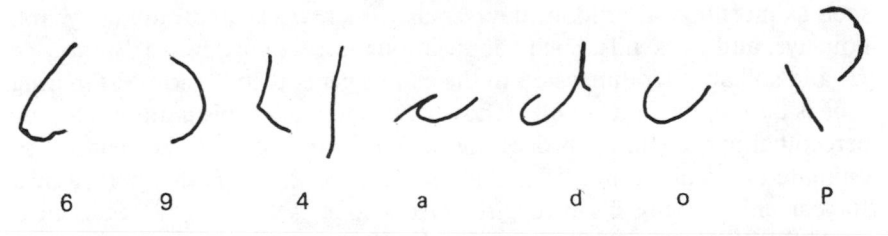

| 6 | 9 | 4 | a | d | o | P |

Figure 3.3. Samples from a 15-year-old youth's writing illustrating dissociation and failure of closure.

Perseveration

Perseveration can be variously defined and is often observed in the response behavior of the mentally retarded and in psychotic or neurotic patients. On a somewhat different level perseveration can also be observed in those with learning disabilities, particularly if an emotional overlay is also present. Perseveration, from our point of view, is the inability of the in-

dividual to move easily from one concept to another or, in another view, the inability of the individual to switch with ease from one stimulus situation to another. It has also been defined as the prolonged aftereffect of a stimulus. It is not the opposite of hyperactivity or of compulsive responses to many stimuli. It is the overattention of the individual to a single stimulus and the inability to negate that stimulus in order to attend to another. Stories or jokes might be repeated endlessly to anyone who will listen. A certain physical movement might be repeated until external efforts by others are necessary to stop it. During an arithmetic practice situation a child might be asked to write the numeral 4 followed by an 8, followed by a 4, and so on. The teacher later observes that the paper contains a line of 4s. The child cannot make the change from 4 to 8. The response noted in Figure 3.4 was produced by one 10-year-old child.

Figure 3.4.

Perseveration is a difficult psychological characteristic to modify, and teachers must be prepared for this. Psychological therapy is usually needed, and when this happens, the psychologist or psychiatrist and the educator must work hand in hand for the benefit of the learning disabled child.

Intersensory Disorganization

Much has been written about the problems of children and youth with learning disabilities, particularly those behaviors involving visual and motor activity, auditory and motor behavior, and, to a lesser extent, the other sensory modalities. Consider, however, this situation. The teacher speaks to her class. "Listen, boys and girls; listen to me" (auditory input). "Look at the blackboard" (auditory and visual input). "See what I have written there?" (visual input). "Now copy what you see on your paper, and solve the arithmetic problems. Write your name in the upper right-hand corner of the paper. Be neat, and place five addition problems on each line. There are 15 problems for you to complete, and we will have about a half hour" (auditory and visual input; motor output). Other factors are involved in this situation also—sequencing, directionality, and the ability to separate 15 problems into three sets of 5. More important for the immediate discussion is that more than one sensory modality is involved. The children must integrate auditory and visual input with motor output. They may hear accurately; they may see accurately; but when the learning disabled are re-

quired to integrate these functions into a motor act requiring accuracy, they may be unable to do so. Eating skills, shoe lacing, bicycle riding, accuracy on a trampoline, and an endless list of other skills requiring the integration of two or more sensory-motor systems—all require specific, and often excessive, training before success is experienced. Worksheets in arithmetic, for example, cut down the requirements of *looking at* a blackboard and *copying* (visuo-motor). Listening to an assignment read by someone else may reduce the *visual* input while increasing the *auditory* input, and if a motor skill is subsequently involved, it, too, can be approached in a unitary rather than a coordinated manner. Coordinating sensory activities is difficult for these children, who can often function quite satisfactorily along a single sensory or motor avenue.

In respect to sensory-motor integration, a final characteristic might also be mentioned. This has to do with those activities that require the child to *cross the midline*. The midline refers to the spinal cord, and such activities involve the simultaneous integration of the two hemispheres of the brain or two sides of the body—right side with left side. Writing activities that require the child to hold the paper with one hand while writing with the other (see Figure 3.5) may result in failure from both the teacher's and the child's point of view. A child considered *clumsy* may be observed to be clumsy only when she or he must coordinate one side of the body with the other. Teachers can often develop ways to reduce this problem within the normal activities of the classroom. Figure 3.5 illustrates the traditional writing position for a right-handed child. Figure 3.6 suggests a position for

Figure 3.5 (left). Traditional position for handwriting, involving interhemispheric coordination and midline crossing.

Figure 3.6 (right). Setup for handwriting (for a right-handed pupil) involving fixing the top and bottom of the paper with masking tape and no interhemispheric coordination or midline crossing. The left hand can be held in place on the knee if necessary with a sandbag, or tied loosely to the upper leg.

a desk and a piece of paper in relation to a child who has trouble with hemispheric incoordination. Here the paper is held down by masking tape, and it is placed to the right (or left if the child is left-handed) of the center of the child's body. The unused hand can be placed on the lap, or if necessary (if motor hyperactivity is a problem) the unused hand can be covered with a sandbag or tied down to help the child relax. Writing or computing arithmetic problems can often be done quite successfully with this procedure.

Summary of Characteristics

We have stressed a series of the most significant characteristics of children and youth with learning disabilities. These are the ones most likely to have an immediate negative influence on the child's learning in the home and school situation. We need to stress that these characteristics, although most common in elementary school children, will often be observed in learning disabled students in both junior high school and senior high school classes. All levels of public and private education must be prepared to meet this challenge.

TEACHING THE LEARNING DISABLED

We have listed 11 general characteristics of the symptomatology of children and youth (and adults, too) who are handicapped in their ability to receive, store, process, and express perceptual and cognitive experiences. These deficits can make it very difficult for them to achieve up to their native ability. When their learning disability is in the specific area of mathematics, it is usually referred to as *developmental dyscalculia*. (Acalculia, which is different from dyscalculia, is the condition evidenced by a total or partial loss of mathematical ability. This loss may be due to cerebral insult from an injury, a cerebral stroke, a tumor or lesion, the effects of surgery, and the like.)

Developmental dyscalculia, or simply dyscalculia, then, is a dysfunction in the neurophysiological system that limits one's ability to achieve or mature in mathematics up to his or her estimated capability. The number of variables that may be implicated in this impairment and the complexity of their many possible interrelationships was indicated by Figure 3.1. The relevance of these variables for an instructional psychology of mathematics is the main concern of this part of the chapter.

Accepting the estimation of competent researchers and practitioners that about 15% of the school population is dyscalculic, ranging from mild to serious and with a ratio of four males to one female, what are some of the problems that must be addressed in order to help these exceptional people? We have identified for discussion the following questions:

1. How do we distinguish between those who are dyscalculic and those who have received inadequate teaching (dyspedagogia)?

2. How do we identify the dyscalculic?

3. What is the need for an educational evaluation of the dyscalculic?

4. What are the major considerations (components, variables) in a well-formed instructional psychology of mathematics applied to the dyscalculic?

DYSCALCULIA OR DYSPEDAGOGIA—WHICH?

It is fashionable among some school and university personnel to cite poor teaching as the cause of one's failure to learn mathematics up to estimated ability and at the same time to deny or at least denigrate the existence of the abnormal neurophysiological conditions that may cause dyscalculia. Although there is little question that the existence of dyspedagogia—inadequate teaching—is real, it is also true that dyscalculia is equally real. How then, does the teacher or school psychologist distinguish between the two conditions as the cause of the learning problem?

The presence of one or more of the 11 general characteristics of the learning disabled may be suggestive of dyscalculia but not necessarily conclusive evidence for a particular child or youth. That is, it is possible for a person to have mild deficits in, say, attention and memory and yet be able to cope with mathematics well enough to be unrecognized as dyscalculic by the special educator, the classroom teacher, or the school psychologist. Furthermore, since people can be dyscalculic regardless of whether they are talented, above average, average, slow, or retarded in their rate of learning, it makes the task of distinguishing between dyscalculia and dyspedagogia even more difficult.

In order to be able to identify children or youth who have no clearly recognizable handicapping condition and are therefore seemingly capable of learning mathematics at a rate consistent with their ability, teachers or other school personnel should have a thorough professional knowledge of the school mathematics program. They should know what is normal mathematical achievement and what is anomalous. By way of a simple illustration, they should know that whereas making tally marks and counting them in order to find the sum of $6 + 9$ is normal developmental behavior for many 7-year-olds (second graders), the same behavior is immature, anomalous, even possibly abnormal behavior for 11-year-olds (sixth graders) of average ability. In normal 11-year-olds, that behavior could be either a symptom of developmental dyscalculia or the failure that resulted from several years of inappropriate teaching.

If the behavior in question (counting marks, for instance) is merely the

consequence of poor teaching, that is, of failure to diagnose, teach, or reteach and consolidate mature learning of the addition factions, it will usually respond quickly to skillful telescoped reteaching. If the immature behavior does not respond to such high quality teaching, the teacher can be reasonably confident that this behavior suggests developmental dyscalculia. If so, the instructional psychology for the remediation of the behavior is considerably more complex than that required for the normal child who has experienced years of inappropriate or dysfunctional teaching. That is, making a good psychoeducational match (see chap. 2) is a considerably more difficult professional task for the teacher of the dyscalculic than it is for the teacher of children and youth who have no impairment of the neurophysiological system.

In the same way, if a student in Grade 6, after a teaching-learning unit on, say, dividing a whole number by a fraction ($3 \div \frac{3}{4} = ?$), cannot respond appropriately to a question that asks her to draw a picture of the sentence using, say, pie shapes, the diagnostician cannot automatically assume she has an intersensory dysfunction (visuo-spatial motor integration deficit). It may well be (and in all likelihood is) that this ability was never developed in the initial teaching of the lesson(s). More seriously, since it is well known that the average elementary or middle school teacher understands only about half of the mathematics in the K−8 program, it may be that in this case the concretizing of the number ideas and the picturizing of them was not taught in the unit because the *teacher* did not have the mathematical knowledge and the teaching ability to do so.

However, if indeed the visuo-spatial understanding and representation of $3 \div \frac{3}{4} = ?$ was well taught (including the model ⊕⊕⊕, which shows four sets of ⊖ ⊖ ⊖ ⊖) and yet the student of average or above-average ability was unable thereafter to represent the sentence in picture form, then this disability may suggest a neurophysiological impairment of the right (visuo-spatial) hemisphere. And if so, the remediation will be complex. If good standard teaching procedures do not remediate the problem in a reasonable amount of time, an intensive diagnosis of the student's learning styles will be needed in order to establish an optimum psychoeducational match, or fit, between goal and method.

The ability to assess accurately the readiness to learn and the limits of educability of the dyscalculic child, youth, or adult is the *primus inter pares,* first among equals, of the professional competencies of those teachers who are responsible for these perceptually and cognitively handicapped people.

IDENTIFYING THE DYSCALCULIC

We have given two instances of post hoc *clinical* procedures for identifying children and youth with learning disabilities in mathematics. We have

suggested that the unusually skillful teacher is one who knows well the developmental patterns of children of different mental abilities and knows equally well the content and instructional psychology of mathematics. By drawing on these domains of professional knowledge, the teacher can find many of the children and youth who have been unable to learn mathematics even when it was well taught. But what other "child-find" means are available? There are two general categories: psychometric testing and scientific procedures.

Psychometric Testing Procedures

The Education for All Handicapped Children Act of 1975, Public Law 94-142 (see chap. 1) defines children and youth aged 3–21 with specific learning disabilities as

> those children who have a disorder in one or more of the basic psychological processes involved in understanding or in using language, spoken or written, which disorder may manifest itself in imperfect ability to listen, think, speak, read, write, spell or do mathematical calculations. (p. 89, Stat. 794)

This law suggests the use of a discrepancy score between children's capacity for academic learning and their level of achievement. We mentioned in the first part of this chapter 11 behavioral characteristics that can be used to help find those children and youth whose perceptual and cognitive processing abilities are impaired. In addition to these observable behaviors, what kinds of psychometric testing programs are usually used?

According to Coles (1978) the 10 most frequently recommended tests and related procedures for a learning-disabilities battery in the past 10 years are these:

Illinois Test of Psycholinguistic Abilities

Bender Visual-Motor Gestalt Test

Frostig Developmental Test of Visual Perception

Wepman Auditory Discrimination Test

Lincoln-Oseretsky Motor Development Scale

Graham-Kendall Memory for Designs Test

Purdue Perceptual-Motor Survey

Wechsler Intelligence Scale for Children

A neurological evaluation by a neurologist

An electroencephalogram

In order to determine a discrepancy score between aptitude for school-type learning (a specific kind of intelligence) and achievement, one or more of the commonly used standardized achievement tests should be added to the list.

The administration of a selected group of these tests, together with their scoring (and evaluation, preferably by a mature school or cognitive psychologist), may take from 3 to 8 hours. On the basis of the results, the examiner assesses the person's psychological and educational developmental levels as they affect his or her ability to learn and present level of achievement. The measure (size) of the discrepancy between the two variables (capacity and achievement) suggests the magnitude of the learning disability.

In general, if a fifth grader of average mental ability is achieving in mathematics at fourth-grade level, the learning disability is educationally significant but not severe. If, however, that same child is achieving at a second-grade level, there is much justifiable cause for believing him or her to be dyscalculic. An individualized educational plan is indicated.

If Tim, a slow learner in Grade 10, is achieving in mathematics at a Grade 7 level, there is little cause for concern because there is probably no educationally significant discrepancy between his capacity and his achievement. He may well be at grade level. However, a third-grade level of achievement by the same person would indicate a substantial hiatus between capacity and achievement. A well-planned intervention program is required in this latter situation.

And if Marian, a very bright 8th grader who has the capacity to achieve at the 10th- to 11th-grade level, is performing at the 8th-grade level, her "at grade level" is cause for great concern. Again, the criterion for psychometric evaluation is not how well students are doing in relation to peers or to the grade-level curriculum but how well they are doing in relation to their own ability to learn mathematics.

Using psychometric formulas. In implementing Public Law 94-142, which requires school personnel to find handicapped children and youth and provide an appropriate education for them, educators commonly use some psychometric formula. Several are available. Each purports to provide a measure (score) of expected achievement (aptitude) of the child or youth. This measure is then used as the sum. From it the measure of the child's actual achievement level in mathematics is subtracted. The difference suggests the magnitude of the discrepancy between expected level of achievement and actual achievement and, hence, suggests the educational significance of the learning disability. Obviously, the greater the difference between the scores, the greater the degree of dyscalculia.

Here are three commonly used formulas (CA = calendar or chronological age; MA = mental age; GA = grade age):

1. The Michigan State Education Department (1977) formula:
   Expected grade equivalent $= \dfrac{IQ \times CA}{100} - 5$

2. The Harris (1970) formula:

Expected grade equivalent $= \dfrac{2MA + CA}{3} - 5.2$

3. The Myklebust (1968) formula:

Expected educational age $= \dfrac{MA + CA + GA}{3}$

A word of caution is needed here on the use of simple discrepancy scores as a basis for finding those who are learning disabled in mathematics. Although it is customary to find the learning disabled by subtracting the actual achievement score from the expected achievement, it is in fact not all that simple, particularly if one is concerned with a *scientific study* of how factors other than aptitude are related to achievement. In studies of this kind, Thorndike (1963) suggests more rigorous procedures using the prediction equation or regression equation (pp. 44–45).

However, here we are primarily concerned with identifying *individual* children and youth, not with carrying out a scientific study. We need to use both *nomothetic data* (scores on norm-referenced tests) and *idiographic data* (personal documents, such as case studies, observations, anecdotal materials, individual interviews, etc.). Many of the data needed to identify and verify the 11 general characteristics in a particular child or youth are gathered through idiographic procedures, not nomothetic tests. Hence school personnel can feel highly confident that a professional use of idiographic methods is most appropriate, even necessary, when the purpose is to identify those who are learning disabled.

Using the WISC to help identify the dyscalculic. One of the most widely used psychometric tests of intelligence is the Wechsler Intelligence Scale for Children—Revised (WISC-R). When it is cautiously used, it can also be helpful as a simple test to suggest those who may be dyscalculic. The WISC-R provides the examiner with measures (scores) on two aspects of intelligence—verbal and performance. Both sections have six subtests. The subtests of the verbal section are Information, Comprehension, Arithmetic, Similarities, Vocabulary, and Digit Span (optional). The performance subtests are Picture Completion, Picture Arrangement, Block Design, Object Assembly, Coding, and Mazes (optional).

Of these subtests, four seem to be more useful than others in helping to find children and youth who may be dyscalculic. These four are the Arithmetic and Digit Span verbal tests and the Block Design and Coding performance tests. When children score generally well in other areas but remarkably lower in these four tests, there is a good possibility that they are experiencing unusual difficulty in learning mathematics commensurate with their general aptitude.

The WISC-R Profile in Figure 3.7 shows that this 10-year-old boy (A. B.) had *educationally* significantly lower scores in the cluster of the four tests discussed above, which suggested the possibility of dyscalculia. And A. B. was indeed experiencing much cognitive difficulty and anxiety in his school mathematics program.

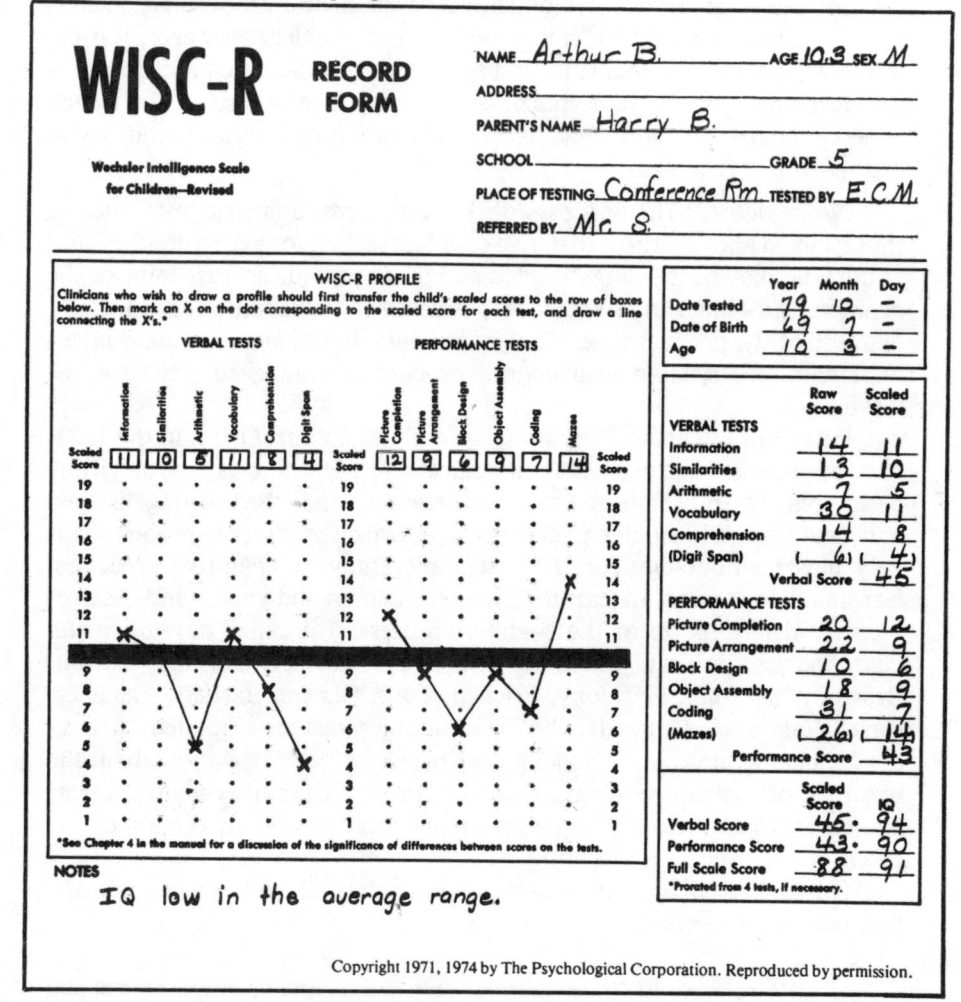

Copyright 1971, 1974 by The Psychological Corporation. Reproduced by permission.

Figure 3.7. WISC-R Test Profile.

Even single WISC-R scores can be educationally significant to the classroom teacher, the diagnostician, and the school psychologist if properly interpreted. By way of an illustration, if a child's score on the Digit Span test is remarkably lower than that of children of comparable age and learning aptitude, this might suggest a short-term memory deficit that will very likely interfere with learning. Other single WISC-R tests can be used to

identify disabilities or deficits that might limit one's learning of mathematics.

Scientific Procedures for Identifying the Learning Disabled

By and large, school personnel use psychometric procedures, such as those discussed above, to identify the learning disabled. However, it is extremely important for them also to be aware of the scientific procedures being developed for the same purpose. We shall briefly discuss three such areas of inquiry: neurometrics, the clinical analysis of hair, and brain asymmetry.

Neurometrics. The purposes of the several psychometric tests, such as those named above, are (a) to derive data (soft signs) to suggest children and youth who may be learning disabled and (b) to provide at least some of the characteristics that can be specifically isolated for remediation. Both sets of data are of the product type. That is, the data do not yield any hard information on the specific neurological *process* or etiological basis for the disability.

Although researchers beginning as early as Samuel Orton in the 1920s have approached the problem of impairment of learning as neurologically based, only recently have attempts been made to study the learning disabled and neurologically similar people from a brain functions approach. This very new methodology for the systematic study of cognitive processes, learning, and memory in learning disabled children and youth (and old people with deterioration of the cognitive processes) is called *developmental neurometrics,* or simply neurometrics (John, Karmel, Corning, Easton, Brown, Ahn, John, Harmony, Prichep, Toro, Gerson, Bartlett, Thatcher, Kaye, Valdes, & Schwartz, 1977). Computer methods applied to electroencephalograms (EEG) make it possible to derive information about the brain's processes for receiving, encoding, processing, and evaluating information that is not readily apparent simply from a visual inspection of the EEG.

How effective are neurometrics? John and his colleagues made the following statement:

> Neurometric EEG measures not only discriminated between normal and LD children better and were more concordant with preclassification than the psychometric measures, but reflected processes more intimately related to brain function. Not only do psychometric measures in this study account for little of the independent variance related to the distinction between normal and LD children, but their relation to brain function is far more inferential. These findings cast doubts on whether these psychometric measures, which included many tests commonly used to assess for organicity in learning disability, possess any significant specific sensitivity to brain dysfunction. (p. 1405)

The most striking feature of these results is the high percentage of LD children who displayed multiple types of dysfunction in multiple regions [of the brain]. The high incidence of pervasive dysfunction suggests widespread occurrence of some severe, generalized insult, such as pre- or perinatal trauma, malnutrition, or stimulus deprivation. (p. 1408)

In view of the fact that neurometric procedures can yield better results in a shorter time than psychometric procedures, which now require up to a full day of testing (6 to 8 hours), we can look forward to mass screening on a large scale for the early identification of children who might be high-risk dyscalculics. Early detection and remediation of perceptual and cognitive disabilities caused by neurophysiological disease would lessen the present costs, human and economic, of our inability to identify those children at an early age.

Clinical analysis of human hair. A second method for identifying learning disabled children and youth that, like neurometrics, does not require invading the brain through surgical, anaesthetic, or psychopharmacological procedures (hence, is noninvasive) is through the analysis of hair samples for heavy and trace chemical elements. The influence of these elements on human physical behavior has been well studied and reported. Much less has been done on the relationship between amounts of these elements and human learning disabilities.

In the study reported by Pihl and Parkes (1977), the laboratory procedure of atomic absorption spectroscopy was used. It is a quick, inexpensive, and unobtrusive method for measuring the level of heavy chemical elements. Hair samples from groups of learning disabled and normal children were compared for their content of 14 chemical elements. Appropriate statistical procedures "revealed that by using cadmium, cobalt, manganese, chromium, and lithium, all subjects could be classified as LD or normal with ninety-eight percent accuracy, a result that was quite unexpected" (p. 205).

The researchers concluded that "the high levels of [statistical] significance reported here . . . and the general failure of educative techniques with many LD children suggests that [chemical] element patterns may prove not only a fruitful diagnostic procedure, but may also provide answers pertaining to etiology and treatment" (p. 206).

Brain asymmetry: architectural and functional. The architecture of the brain and the cognitive (as well as affective and psychomotor) functions it performs have been a long-standing area of inquiry. It has been known for a long time that the left hemisphere, for most right-handed people, performs verbal functions and that the right hemisphere performs visuo-spatial functions. Knowledge of the specific region of each hemisphere that controls specialized tasks in arithmetic or algebra or geometry has been of more re-

cent concern to neuropsychologists, cognitive psychologists, and psychoneurologists.

Very recently effort has been directed to finding the precise ways in which one hemisphere differs from the other and how such differences suggest the etiology or basic cause of learning disabilities. Although most of the attention is being directed toward dyslexia, we can logically infer that similar findings will implicate dyscalculia.

Galaburda and Kemper (1979) examined "in excruciating detail" the cortex of a deceased 20-year-old dyslexic male. They found in the left hemisphere misshapen clumps of convoluted tissue in the ridges (gyria). And whereas in a normal brain that area (where the abnormalities occurred) is usually larger in the left hemisphere than in the right, in this instance the areas were of equal size. The neurologists stated that the abnormality of tissue suggested that dyslexia (dyscalculia is numerical dyslexia) is not solely—or perhaps even primarily—a psychological problem.

Areas for scientific research studies such as the three above (neurometrics, hair analysis, and brain asymmetry) may shortly provide school personnel with highly accurate and almost immediate identification of dyscalculic children and youth. Findings from research to date provide firm support for Cruickshank's (1977c) statement on the etiology of learning disabilities, that "LD is the result of a malfunction of the neurophysiological system of the organism which results in a *perceptual processing* deficit" (p. 1).

Specific Symptoms of Dyscalculia

In the first part of this chapter we discussed 11 *general* characteristics of learning disabled children and youth. These were attention disturbances, figure-ground pathology, dissociation, memory dysfunction, sequencing, discrimination—auditory and visual, directionality, spatial and temporal disorientation, closure, perseveration, and intersensory disorganization. A few specific illustrations of dyscalculic people were given. We reserved to this part of the chapter a fuller discussion of the *specific* symptoms of dyscalculia.

Kosc (1974) has identified, named, and given instances of six specific forms of dyscalculia. Although this categorization is helpful, some of the behavioral symptoms he uses to clarify the forms are naive and can be misleading. We shall discuss one of these following the presentation of his six categories (forms) of symptomatology:

> *Verbal dyscalculia* is manifested by the disturbed ability to designate verbally mathematical terms and relations, such as naming amounts and numbers of things, digits, numerals, operational symbols, and mathematical performances. There are cases of brain-damaged persons who are not able to identify the numbers dictated to them in the form of numerals (for example: to show

the dictated number of fingers) although they are able to read or write the respective number or to count the amount of things (sensory-verbal dyscalculia). Or, on the other hand, persons with verbal dyscalculia are not able to name the amount of presented things or the value of written numbers although they are able to read or write the dictated number (motor-verbal dyscalculia).

Practognostic dyscalculia. In these cases there is a disturbance of mathematical manipulation with real or pictured objects (fingers, balls, cubes, staffs, etc.). Mathematical manipulation includes the enumeration (single addition) of the things and comparison of estimates of quantity (without their addition). A patient with practognostic dyscalculia is not able to set out sticks or cubes according to the order of their magnitudes, not even to show which of two sticks or cubes is bigger or smaller, or whether they are the same size.

Lexical dyscalculia. This particular disorder is concerned with a disability in reading mathematical symbols (digits, numbers, operational signs, and written mathematical operations). By far the most serious form of lexical dyscalculia is when the child is not able to read the isolated digits and/or simple operational symbols ($+$, $-$, $\times$, $\div$, etc.). In the less serious forms, he cannot read multidigit numbers (especially with more than one zero in the middle), numbers written in a horizontal rather than a vertical line, fractions, squares and roots, decimal numbers, and so on. In some cases he interchanges similar looking digits (3 for 8, 6 for 9, and vice versa), or two digit numbers are read as reversed (12 as 21).

Graphical dyscalculia. This is a disability in manipulating mathematical symbols in writing, analogous to lexical dyscalculia. Graphical dyscalculia often occurs where there is dysgraphia and dyslexia with letters; eventually, in the most serious disabilities of this kind, the patient is not able to write numbers dictated to him, to write the words for written numerals, or even to copy them. Leischner (1957) presents a patient who wrote "6" and "9" in a combination of both symbols, like this 6. In less severe cases, where a person cannot write numbers with two or three digits, he writes them in the opposite direction or he isolates the separate elements (i.e., 1284 as 1000, 200, 80, 4 or 1000, 200, 84) or he ignores the zeros (i.e., 20073 as 273 or 20730); or he devises his own idiosyncratic manner. This person may not be able to write any mathematical symbol, even though he can write the word for the dictated number, e.g., to the dictated "8" he writes "eight."

Lexical and graphical dyscalculia are also called numerical dyslexia and numeral dysgraphia, and together both are labeled numerical dyssymbolia in the literature.

Ideognostical dyscalculia. This is a disability primarily in understanding mathematical ideas and relations and in doing mental calculation. Grewel (1952) calls this disability "asemantic aphasia," but it is more accurate to call it "ideognostic dyscalculia." In the most serious cases of this type of dyscalculia a person is not able to mentally calculate the easiest sums. Often, a person with brain dysfunction is able to read or write the written numbers but is unable to understand what he has read or written. For instance, he knows that 9 =

"nine" and that "nine" is to be written as 9, but he does not know that 9 or nine is one less than 10, or 3 × 3, or one-half of 18, etc. In these and similar cases, it is not possible to label this kind of dysfunction as numerical dyslexia or dysgraphia, or even as operational dyscalculia (see below). In this case the formation of ideas, agnostic function, is disturbed; it is appropriately called ideognostic dyscalculia.

Operational dyscalculia. In this case, the ability to carry out mathematical operations is directly disturbed. Hecaen et al. (1961) call this form of dysfunction "anarithmetia." A typical occurrence is the interchange of operations, e.g., doing addition instead of multiplication; subtraction instead of division; or substitution of more complicated operations by simpler ones (e.g., 12 + 12 = (10 + 10) + (2 + 2); 3 × 7 = 7 + 7 + 7 = 21; or in serious disturbances: 777). Typical also is a preference for written calculation of sums (tasks) which could be easily calculated silently, or calculation by counting on the fingers where the task could be easily solved silently or in writing and without counting fingers.

A disability like operational dyscalculia is most difficult to identify because of the necessity for carefully following the subject's procedure in completing the operations especially when the subject is a patient who cannot verbalize what (and how and why) he is doing according to his partial rules. In the cases of combined symptoms of different types of dyscalculia, especially the combination of ideognostic and operational dyscalculia, it is nearly impossible to discover when and how the wrong achievement was conditioned by one or by the other disability.

In every case it must be pointed out that incorrect results do not reveal what kind of disturbance is really involved in a particular task; it is quite possible to get correct results by means of incorrect procedures. Green and Buswell (1930) gave an example in which a student approached the task 86 − 4 as follows: "Six and four equals ten; ten and eight equal eighteen." Then he wrote his answer backwards: 81. His result differs from the correct answer by one, but the procedure was essentially wrong. This case clearly presents a symptom of operational dyscalculia.

It is obvious that various combinations of symptomatology of developmental dyscalculia occur mostly in combination with symptoms of other impaired symbolic functions of the brain (especially with dyslexia and dysgraphia with letters) or other disorders of the higher nervous system (within the frame of reference of minimal brain dysfunction), analogous to post-lesional dyscalculia or acalculia in adulthood resulting from brain damage. (*Note.* From pp. 49–50 of "Developmental Dyscalculia" by L. Kosc, *Journal of Learning Disabilities,* 1974, *7,* 46–59. Copyright 1974 by Professional Press, Inc. Reprinted by special permission of Professional Press, Inc.)

We mentioned earlier that some of the behaviors Kosc defined as symptoms of a specific form of dyscalculia are naively drawn and can be misleading. In general, any behavior is normal if it is congruent with the person's stage of cognitive development. Hence, counting on one's fingers to find "how many in all" in 3 + 4 is developmentally normal for a 6-year-

old of average ability but is abnormal, immature, for an 11-year-old of average ability. And the same behavior is normal for another 11-year-old who is mentally retarded but educable.

Whereas counting fingers or blocks or whatever represents a meaningful processing of the numbers for a 6-year-old child, the same behavior can be indicative of a school program that was inadequate over the years for an 11-year-old. An adequate program would have identified this child's immature behavior earlier, diagnosed the child's thought processes, and counteracted the situation through appropriate consolidation experiences designed to fix and facilitate the behavior on the most mature level of cognitive performance.

The same behavior—counting things or making tally marks to find the sum of 3 + 4—would suggest operational dyscalculia only if it continued to be used after an adequate, instructionally sound teaching of it had taken place. If the child failed to develop a mature thought processing of 3 + 4 = 7 as the outcome of an appropriate set and sequence of teaching-learning experiences, then the persisting immature behavior could suggest developmental dyscalculia.

Other behaviors that can suggest developmental dyscalculia are listed below. Whether in fact the child who exhibits these behaviors is indeed dyscalculic depends on whether or not the behavior, assuming the teaching was adequate, is consistent with normal developmental patterns for the child. By way of an illustration, if a given mathematical behavior is normal for an average child at age 7 or 8, that same behavior would also be normal for a slow learner at age 10 or 11. Hence, in order to use this list of suggested behaviors intelligently, the teacher or school psychologist must know what is normal behavior for children having different learning aptitudes. Typical of the questions to ask are the following:

Is the child having unusual difficulty in—

Ordering things by length, weight, size?

Ordering a set of pictures chronologically?

Ordering numbers and recognizing the betweenness of numbers?

Counting forward or backward?

Repeating a set of numbers forward or backward?

Writing numbers from dictation (for example, writing "one hundred four" as 1004)?

Writing a numeral without reversing the digits (such as "72" for "27")?

Writing numbers from dictation (rate, spacing, and quality of orthography)?

Copying exercises from the chalkboard (visuo-motor integration in far-point copying)?

Recalling the meaning and use of symbols (such as $+$, $-$, $\times$, $\div$, $=$)?

Recalling the basic facts?

Outgrowing immature, compensatory, or obviational behaviors?

Remembering the right-to-left direction for the addition, subtraction, and multiplication algorithms and left-to-right direction for the division algorithm?

Remembering the sequence of steps in the standard algorithms?

Perceiving visuo-spatial relationships (manifested in crowded written work, dysgraphia, and difficulty aligning digits in algorithms)?

Recognizing or describing an object that is seen from a different "angle" (angulation)?

Decoding verbal problems and encoding into number sentences?

Although these questions are mostly concerned with the mathematics program for Grades K–6, other questions appropriate to normal progress in the Grades 7–12 program can be asked to identify dyscalculic youth.

THE NEED FOR EDUCATIONAL EVALUATIONS

In many instances an elaborate, time-consuming, and costly psychometric workup may result in an evaluation of a child or youth that is too brief, superficial, trivial, or inaccurate to be of any educational significance to anyone. For example, a second-grade 8-year-old boy (who repeated Grade 2) was brought to a center for learning disabled children and youth. His combined neurological and psychometric assessment program required some 8 hours and cost about $200. The final report was 16 typewritten pages. Out of all this, the evaluative summary of his mathematical development was the following:

> Math computation skills are solidly within the normal range. He gives evidence of good understanding of addition and subtraction. He showed some difficulty with double integer [sic] subtraction and double integer [sic] addition. He is unfamiliar at this time with multiplication.

The psychometrist's basis for this trivial and quite useless evaluation was the administration and scoring of a standardized test. The evaluation was limited to cognitive products—that is, is the answer "right" or "wrong"? No attempt was made to probe the child's thought processes and to evaluate and report them. Seemingly, there was a lack of awareness of the developmental nature of human learning on the part of the psychometrist. For instance, the boy was asked to process $15 - 8$. He did this by writing on his paper ❘ ❘ ❘ ❘ ❘ ❘ ❘ ⨮ ⨮ ⨮ ⨮ ⨮ ⨮ ⨮.

He counted the remaining tally marks and wrote the addend, 7. In the evaluative summary above, no mention is made of this or other obvious evidences of the level of maturity or immaturity of the child's cognitive processes.

The test itself does not measure the "understanding" of the addition and subtraction operations; hence, the statement to that effect in this summary would be misleading to any reader of the report. Also, the reader is not provided with any of the specific difficulties the child had with addition and subtraction. Did his problem reside in a lack of knowledge of the addition and subtraction facts? Was there a visuo-spatial difficulty that hampered his efforts to align place values? Any difficulty with addition facts with bridging a ten? Renaming in subtraction? Exactly which constituent skills and understandings did he "show some difficulty with"? The report is of no help here.

And why wouldn't he be "unfamiliar" with multiplication in Grade 2? It is usually introduced for systematic instruction in Grade 3! By the same token, and facetiously, the child is also unfamiliar with the addition of fractions (Grade 5) and using the formula to find the area of a circular region (Grade 7 or 8)! Evidently the psychometrist was not sufficiently well informed on either the content or the instructional psychology of the mathematics program to be able to write a reasonable and useful evaluation of this child's learning ability or disability.

Cruickshank (1977b) brought to our attention the sorry state of affairs in the preparation of educational evaluations of learning disabled children and youth:

> It is always interesting, but a bit shocking, to this writer that in assessing the problems of a learning disabled child the educational diagnosis is always omitted. Even when school personnel themselves refer to a child, there is often no educational diagnostic data submitted or scheduled to be done later. Only rarely does an interdisciplinary team include an educator in the diagnostic phase. While the educator's contribution is not necessarily the most important factor, the information he is qualified to provide on learning disabled children is very important. It cannot be omitted. (p. 97)

It is very essential that the teacher, psychometrist, school psychologist, and special educator keep in mind that the term *evaluate* suggests *putting a value on* behavior. However, in order to be able to do so with professional competence, the evaluator must have a well-formulated value system for the essential variables in an instructional psychology of mathematics.

APPLYING AN INSTRUCTIONAL PSYCHOLOGY

In chapter 2, Glennon presented the need for an instructional psychology as the substrate for working in a professional way rather than a

mechanical way with exceptional children and youth. He identified and elaborated on five essential variables (components) that must be kept in mind when trying to effect an optimal psychoeducational match: (a) a sound knowledge of the appropriate mathematics itself; (b) the major theories (sources) of the curriculum; (c) the major teacher methodologies (not specific methods or techniques); (d) the basic theories of human motivation; and (e) the role of consolidation in human cognitive learning. The complexity of possible interactions, positive and negative, were then cited in a mini–case study form to illustrate the difficulty of making a good psychoeducational match. In the discussion that follows, we shall draw on these variables to suggest ways to develop the mathematics program for learning disabled children and youth.

We begin with the very obvious, but sometimes ignored, truism that it is not possible to publish a mathematics program that is *specifically targeted* for the dyscalculic. It is pedagogically ridiculous and professionally irresponsible to purport that a program can be so designed and written. Consider for a moment just a few of the 11 characteristics discussed at the beginning of this chapter: attention disturbances, figure-ground pathology, and memory dysfunction. How could a team of authors possibly write workbook lessons, units, page material, or textbooks to make a good psychoeducational match for the children and youth who have these characteristics?

If a lesson has several practice exercises on a page, the child who has an attentional disturbance will be unable to attend to a *single* exercise. That child will be distracted by the other exercises on the same page and, being unable to tolerate the frustration induced by a crowded page (figure-ground pathology), may well "explode." Yet, no publisher can afford to print a page with just a single computational exercise or a single word problem in the center of an otherwise blank page. Who would buy such a program?

In the same way, a busy page with, say, a picture to be used as a source for data for solving the word problems on that page would not make a good match for the child who has a figure-ground discrimination disability. Again, textbook programs are "expected" to have pictures, and yet pictures are contraindicated for the child who has this perceptual disability.

And the child or youth with a memory dysfunction may be unable to store and retrieve the multiplication facts as they are developed in a text or workbook program. This child may need the obviational advantages provided by a calculator, multiplication chart, or some similar device. Again, the usual textbook program, even if it purports to be published specifically for the learning disabled population is inadequate, even harmful, when used in its present format with learning disabled children and youth.

In the same way, the other characteristics of the learning disabled discussed at the beginning of the chapter cannot be readily incorporated in-

to textbook, workbook, or other conventional format of published mathematics programs.

And consider further that dyscalculic children and youth vary in aptitude for mathematics from the level of genius to trainable mentally retarded. How naive it would be, then, to suggest that a particular published program could be used in a professionally responsible way (that it could make a good psychoeducational match) with learning disabled children and youth who do vary so greatly in intelligence.

How, then, can the teacher adjust a standard mathematics program to the individual characteristics and learning rates of the learning disabled in mathematics?

A Sound Knowledge of the Mathematics Itself

First, the teacher, whether a general classroom teacher or special educator, must have a solid knowledge of the structure of the mathematics appropriate to the mental age and grade levels of the children and youth being taught. At first blush, this may seem obvious. After all, doesn't every teacher of elementary school mathematics understand how to add, subtract, multiply, and divide? Frankly, no! As was noted in chapter 2, research over the past 30 years shows that the typical K–8 teacher *understands* only about 50% of the mathematics in the K–6 program. Much of the difficulty that dyscalculic children and youth experience in learning mathematics begins with the teacher's and special educator's lack of knowledge of the structure of the mathematics itself. And this is often further compounded by the teacher's lack of interest and enthusiasm for the subject, or even anxiety and its negative effect.

Teachers whose knowledge of mathematics is limited to what they learned associatively, as a bag of mental tricks, are unable to teach the subject conceptually, that is, mathematically meaningfully. They are unable to psychologize the content and hence unable to teach it in such a way as to (a) facilitate meaningful learning, (b) increase retention, (c) increase transfer of learning, (d) decrease retroactive inhibition, and (e) increase problem-solving ability. The child or youth who is learning disabled in mathematics cannot be helped much by a teacher who is handicapped by his or her own lack of knowledge of the appropriate mathematics.

In particular, special education teachers may be more handicapped in their understanding of the logical structure of mathematics than general classroom teachers. This is due in large part to the few or even zero semester hours of appropriate work they often receive in mathematics education in the special education program. It is also due to some extent to the quality of that work. Too often that lack of quality of both the content and the instructional psychology is reflected in the methods books used in their course work.

Specifically, in one current methods book written by a special educator for use by students in special teacher education programs, we found such bizarre mathematics concepts, meaningless tricks, and even examples of *incorrect* mathematics, as these:

- Zero cannot be divided!
- Dividing by one is meaningless!
- In $10\overline{)2500}$ show the child the factoring method of striking tens, as $1\cancel{0}\overline{)250\cancel{0}}$.
- To multiply by 10, add [sic] a zero in one's place!

Needless to say, the student teacher or graduate student in special education who is so miseducated can hardly be expected to teach correct mathematics by correct methods. The learning disabled child who may be experiencing some difficulty when the mathematics is correctly structured will have even greater disability under these conditions.

What Mathematics Is of Most Worth?

A second component in an instructional psychology that is essential to establishing a good psychoeducational match is a functional knowledge of the three major sources of the curriculum and the logical implications of each for selecting specific topics for teaching. All mathematical topics are not of equal worth to all children and youth, dyscalculic or not. Wise choices have to be made in order to make optimum use of the relatively few clock hours that are available in one academic year for developmental lessons—that is, systematic, structured, sequential teaching of *new-to-the-child* mathematics.

The amount of time that appears in the daily schedule for mathematics instruction is referred to as *allocated time* (Berliner, 1978). The time that is available after the "starting up time," "putting away time," and so on, are subtracted leaves the *engaged time*. The amount of engaged time in which there is a good psychoeducational match between the new mathematics to be taught and the readiness of the child to learn is referred to as *academic learning time*. Berliner reported that in his study of second-grade mathematics programs the academic learning time was 30–58 hours in the school year. In fifth-grade classes the range was 18–53 hours. The dyscalculic child who is placed in a regular classroom as the least restrictive environment must share with many other children these few hours of academic learning time.

It is crucial, then, that the teacher of the learning disabled child select the mathematics topics according to some theory of curriculum. The three major theories of curriculum for determining what mathematics (or any other subject matter area) is of most worth are the logical-structure theory, the psychological (needs of the child) theory, and the sociological (needs of

adult society) theory. The reader may find it helpful to review these theories again in chapter 2.

The neurophysiological deficit referred to here as dyscalculia affects some children and youth in their rate of learning; it affects others in the quality of learning. Both of these perceptual and cognitive conditions have implications for deciding what mathematical topics are of most worth for a particular learner.

It is clear that dyscalculic children who have a slow rate of learning conceptual material will be unable to learn as many new topics in the given amount of academic learning time as those who have an average rate of learning, and even fewer than those children who learn rapidly. Hence the teacher will want to draw on the sociological theory of curriculum when selecting topics for the slow dyscalculic. Specifically, the topic $1/2 + 1/2 = \square$, for example, would meet the criterion of adult proficiency in numeracy, and the topic $1/5 + 1/13 = \square$ would *not* represent useful mathematics. Hence the former could be defended in the curriculum for the slow dyscalculic; the latter could not.

Quality of learning can be categorized as *associative* or as *conceptual*. Bright dyscalculic children who are able to conceptualize mathematical topics rapidly, which is often the case, but who have a serious deficit in the associational aspect of learning present a unique problem for the teacher. Whereas they may be able to learn the more complex understandings and solve both verbal and creative problems on the high school level consistent with their high rate of learning, they may also be strangely unable to learn, remember, and recall quickly some of the simpler conceptual facts on the Grade 2 and 3 levels, such as $6 + 9 = \square$, or $13 - 5 = \square$.

Al, a very bright fifth grader with whom one of the writers has worked for several years, is able to conceptualize mathematics well beyond his present grade level. At the same time, he still has considerable difficulty with the basic facts of the four operations with whole numbers, such as $5 + 7 = \square$, $6 \times 4 = \square$, and $15 - 7 = \square$. For him, the appropriate curriculum theory leans heavily toward the logical structure (see the model in chap. 2). But to prevent the deficit in remembering and expressing the basic facts from interfering with his progress in high-level conceptual work, Al uses a calculator as an obviational or coping technique.

Bill, a 15-year-old of above-average mental ability, was reasonably successful in the arithmetic program through Grade 8. Nothing in his school history suggested dyscalculia. In Grade 9 he failed algebra. A detailed diagnosis of Bill's thought processes in mathematics revealed that he had "succeeded" in Grades 1–8 by having a good capacity for associational (but not conceptual) learning and a good storage and retrieval system. Since most of his pencil-and-paper tests during the first 8 years were the memoriter type, Bill's conceptual disability did not show up. However, in

Grade 9 the more abstract, symbolic material to be learned required a higher quality of reasoning ability. Bill's reasoning ability was impaired, and his ability to associationalize learning was of little help when he needed to conceptualize, say, the distributive property and use it rationally in simple linear equations.

Al and Bill have different deficits and abilities. Al can conceptualize mathematics but has a storage and retrieval deficit. Bill can associationalize his learning, but his conceptualizing, or reasoning, is impaired. These different impairments have profound implications for deciding what mathematics is of most worth—considering what can be learned or mastered in the academic learning time available.

Thus, the teacher or team responsible for planning the curriculum for all learning disabled pupils in mathematics must understand well the sources of the curriculum and draw on them in some combination if they wish to make a good psychoeducational match in this particular component of an instructional psychology of mathematics.

The Sources of the Teacher's Methodologies (Styles)

The third major component in our instructional psychology relates to *how* one should teach. By this we do not mean the specific tactics and strategies, methods, and materials of classroom practice. Rather, we refer to the basic substrate of methodology. Over the past several thousand years, the study of the teaching act by philosophers, rational psychologists, and practitioners has yielded three *major* theories (sources) of methodology. These are commonly referred to as (a) teaching as telling, (b) teaching as guiding discovery, and more recently, (c) teaching as psychotherapy. Again, the reader is referred to Glennon's model in chapter 2 for relating all three theories to assist in the complex professional task of making a good fit between teaching styles and learning styles.

Among the characteristics of some dyscalculic children and youth, as discussed above, are motor disinhibition, figure-ground pathology, and short attention span. Adjusting teaching methodology to fit these characteristics requires a high degree of structure. The teacher needs to be aware of these disabilities and to adjust his or her teaching style accordingly. As Cruickshank (1977b) has stated:

> Teachers must teach to the disability of learning disabled children. The problems of educators and parents in dealing with learning disabled children, then, are quite different from those involved with children with only physical disabilities, and the distinction can be confusing. Instead of providing prosthetics which make it possible for the child to adjust to the normal world, it is necessary for adults to modify the environment to meet the needs of the learning disabled child. We must, therefore, teach to the disability; we must plan programs that take the disability into consideration. (p. 115)

One very important way of adjusting methodology to the learning disabled child or youth is to structure it to conform with the principles and techniques of teaching as telling, and "learning from being told," as John Carroll put it. This may mean using simple rather than compound or complex declarative sentences. It may mean making only limited use of teaching through guided-discovery methodology, since this requires a high tolerance for frustration—something the dyscalculic child or youth may be lacking.

Teaching as psychotherapy, in which the major role of the teacher is that of a facilitator and one who reflects the feelings of the learner, may be appropriate at times as a mental health methodology. But the kind of structure the learning disabled child usually needs is not the kind of structure found in this methodology. In general, the large amount of freedom to decide what I want to learn, when I want to learn it, how I want to learn it, and how I am going to evaluate what I learned—all essential ingredients of a psychotherapeutic methodology—may be highly inappropriate in making a good psychoeducational match between teaching style and learning style for the learning disabled.

Too, the teacher needs to ensure structure in methodology by maintaining consistency in the mathematical language, symbols, and algorithms used. Children and youth model their mathematical language after their teacher's language. If the teacher uses mathematically incorrect or meaningless language (such as "Zero cannot be divided"), the children may make those expressions a permanent part of their stored language. If the teacher still uses such terms as *borrowing, carrying, goes into,* and *cancelling* in developing the language of the algorithms, the children will think with these incorrect language forms the rest of their lives. Incorrect language patterns that are memorized and consolidated early are not easily replaced later with correct language.

The older child or youth who is still unable to store, integrate, and retrieve quickly the addition, subtraction, multiplication, and division facts (which are essential to processing all the algorithms), yet has no difficulty understanding the mathematical relationships, will require an obviational or coping technique or device. This may be in the form of a chart that contains the facts and is always at hand, or it may be the calculator. Other obviational techniques, coping methods, and compensatory procedures should be made available to dyscalculics in order to permit them to develop at their optimal rate.

Also, structure in the form of "telling" by the teacher is necessary to assist the child or youth in coping with the problem of dysgraphia and visuo-spatial difficulties. Figures 3.8 and 3.9 show the work of an eighth-grade boy who needs direct assistance in organizing and structuring his written work. This page of practice material, crowded with 33 exercises, was inappropriate for this boy. He needed to be shown (told) how to arrange his

work in order to avoid having a messy printed page and using additional practice paper. Learning to use his ruler to partition his page into blocks (unit regions) and doing one example in each block would be a simple technique for coping with his dysgraphia.

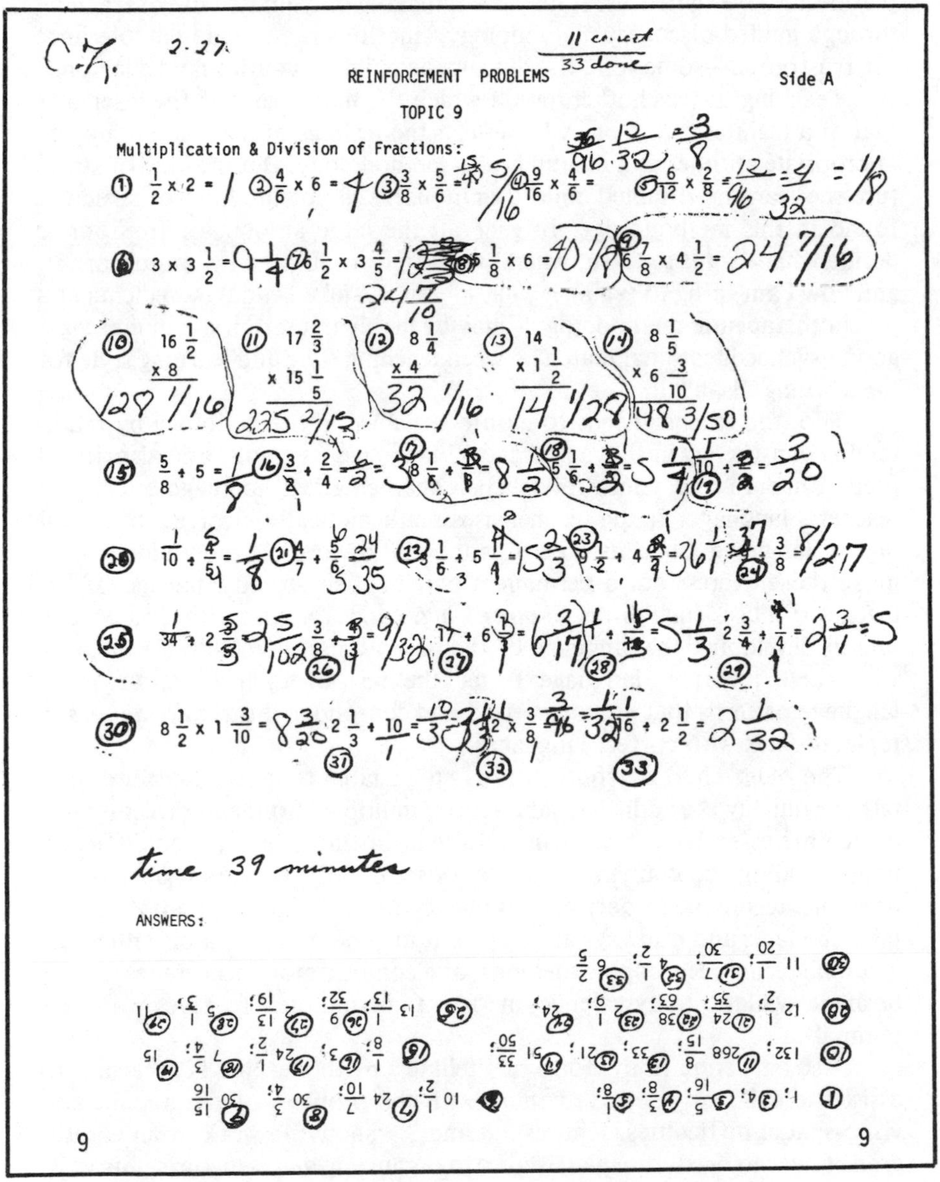

Figure 3.8. Dysgraphic work of an eighth-grade boy.

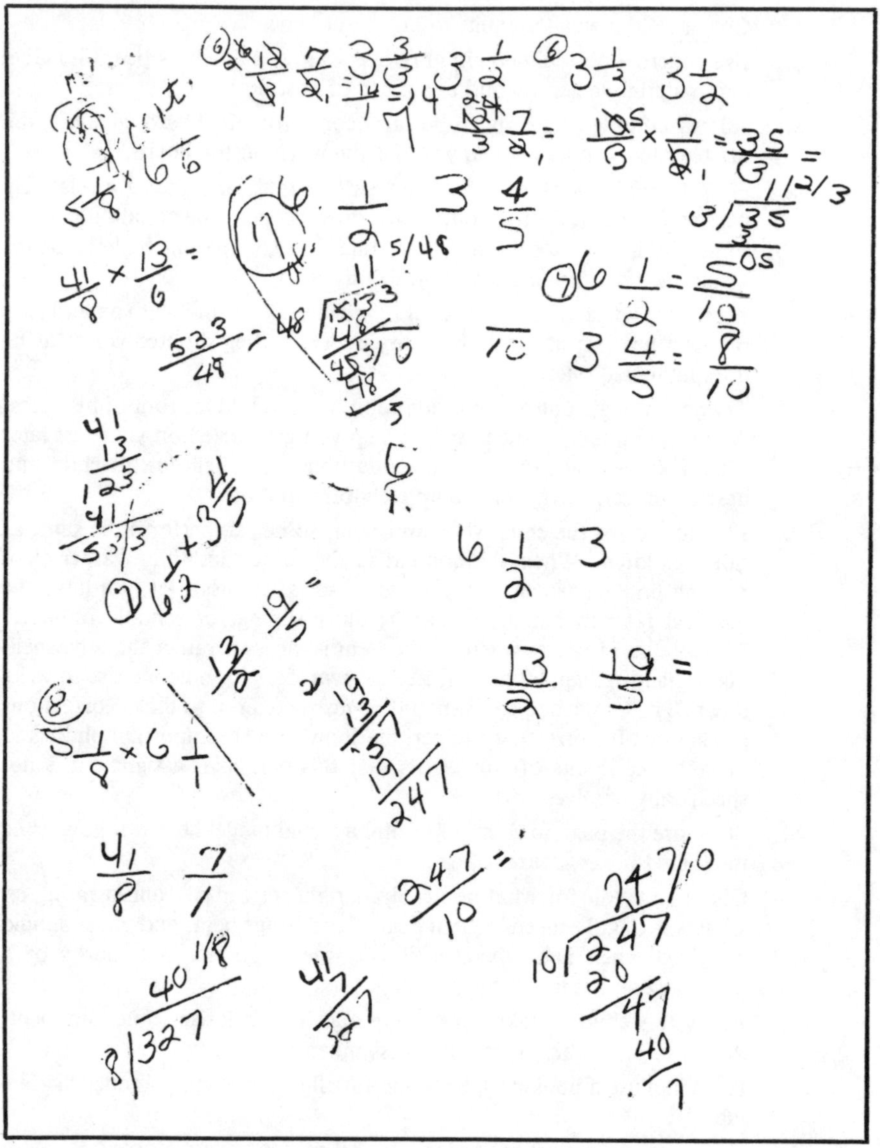

Figure 3.9. Dysgraphic work of an eighth-grade boy.

In addition to the three major *general* methodologies above, the teacher of learning disabled children and youth must have readily available a large reservoir of *specific* methods and techniques to be drawn upon as needed for particular situations. Cohen (1979) has prepared a list that is helpful:

1. Give a child a small amount to do at one time.

2. Use concrete objects and simplify everything as much as possible. Give him material he can do and avoid use of abstracts.

3. Allow him to work slowly. If he can't copy from the board, give him the master copy you used when you put the work on the board.

4. Have the child work at a "clean desk" or table and facing a relatively bare wall or area. Clutter confuses or distracts this type of child. What to some children would be an interesting and stimulating bulletin board would be a confusing distraction to this child.

5. Keep your voice at a moderate and even level. The child with an auditory problem has just as much difficulty understanding shouted words as he does mumbled ones.

6. Try not to single out or focus attention on this child in front of his peers. A careless statement such as "I'll help you get started on your test later since I know you can't read the questions" can belittle this child and destroy his self-image and completely turn him off.

7. Plan ahead for the child who can't read, so he can perform the same as other children. When the content is the important thing rather than reading practice (such as in a class of social studies), let him have the material read to him by a parent, older sibling, or school volunteer. Likewise, in instances where the content is the issue rather than the spelling or handwriting, let him dictate his own ideas to someone else to write down. The "someone else" should be instructed not to make corrections or changes. In correcting a paper, mark only for the important phase and do not take points off for errors that this particular assignment is not specifically involved with.

8. Structure the page for him. Give him a visual model he can follow using numbered boxes, columns, etc.

9. Give him credit for what he has done right instead of concentrating on what is wrong. He needs a great deal of encouragement, and praise should be given when and wherever it is earned. Do not put marks of a demoralizing nature on his paper.

10. Allow this child to take tests orally and have a longer time allotment. Avoid surprise quizzes or timed assignments.

11. Have him use a bookmark to block out all but one line to reduce distractability.

12. Have him use a marker to block out all but one math problem.

13. Present material orally and permit oral answers.

14. When he is given an assignment, show him how to arrange his paper in columns, rows, etc.

15. Ask short questions.

16. For the child with an auditory discrimination problem, seat him near the front at a point at which you can face him most of the time while you are speaking. Speak clearly and "mouth" your words. He can read your lips

to help him distinguish between similar sounds, i.e., bed from beg, cope from coke, pet from pat, etc.

17. For the child with an auditory memory problem, give directions in small single units. Instead of saying "take out your spelling book, turn to page 45, and using ink and white paper, copy the words in column one," say "Take out your spelling book—now turn to page 45—now take a sheet of white paper and your pen—find column one (demonstrate)—now copy the words in this column." This rule applies to older perceptually involved students as well as younger ones.

More hints for teachers. This child often:

1. Needs brief and specific directions with short term, easily attained goals.

2. Cannot make choices easily—should be directed often.

3. Finds it difficult to work with other children. He may want to participate but gets into difficulty easily. If he is joining a group, give him specific directions beforehand.

4. Is usually bright, may understand but not respond reasonable [sic] well, so let him sit with reading groups and follow along by listening. Give answers orally.

5. Is confused with too many symbols—suggest simplified work sheets, particularly in math.

6. Has difficulty shutting out noise and movement. Find him a quiet corner to work in for some periods of the day.

7. Is interested and willing to work with a tape recorder and head sets if the tape is clear in its directions and work.

8. Is physically immature in hand, eye, and body coordination. Emphasis on games and activities leading to better coordination should be encouraged.

9. Is subtly rejected by his peers. Make an effort for him to belong.

10. Prefers to work at some tasks alone. This should not be ignored but encouraged where he finds it difficult to work with others.

11. Has a very short attention span. Needs to be checked on constantly.

12. Needs directions repeated quietly to him again after they have been given to class. Have him repeat and explain directions to you.

13. Gets very upset. When this occurs it takes him a long time to "get in the groove." Give him freedom to move before he explodes.

14. Cannot read test questions or write the answers. Make arrangements to give him crucial tests orally. Does much better on multiple choice questions.

15. Cannot work under time pressure. Allow him time to work at his own pace. He will fall apart under pressure.

(*Note.* Copyright 1979 by *ACLD Newsbriefs*. Reprinted by permission.)

We have summarized and applied three of the essential components of an instructional psychology: the mathematics itself, theories of curriculum

for deciding what mathematics is of most worth for a dyscalculic person, and theories of teacher methodology for deciding how to match teaching style to learning style. We now summarize some thoughts on a fourth component: *What sources of motivation are the energizers of learning?*

The Sources of Motivation for Learning

We discussed in chapter 2 the three major sources for energy mobilization: the social motives, the ego-integrative motive, and the cognitive achievement motives. A functional awareness of these kinds of motivations is essential in the repertoire of the instructional psychology for general classroom teachers or other school personnel who are teaching dyscalculic children and youth.

For the student whose disability is evidenced only by unusual difficulty in learning mathematics and is not further complicated by unacceptable social behavior and emotional impairment, the teacher will find it a relatively easy task to draw on any one or all three theories of motivation to get the child to do willingly what society says is reasonable and what she or he must do anyway. Any number of specific techniques and methods are available to the creative teacher.

However, many dyscalculic children and youth with long histories of failure due to consistently inadequate psychoeducational matching of school tasks to readiness to learn have social-emotional impairments. These make the teacher's task of motivating them considerably more difficult. Several new sources for conceptualizing motivational strategies have gained acceptance in recent years. We shall discuss five of them briefly: *learned helplessness, field-dependence/independence, metacognition, locus of control,* and *behavior modification.* In some instances they relate closely to one another and to the three major theories of motivation.

Learned Helplessness

Learned helplessness (Thomas, 1979) is very often a characteristic of learning disabled children and youth (and adults, too!). It may be exemplified behaviorally in low self-concept, weak ego strength, lack of motivation, and chronic depression. The helplessness is learned by individuals who, after a period of continuous failure, acquire the belief that they have little or no control over a specific category of behavior, say, mathematics, or over life in general. Constant failure is enervating. The solution is often to give up, to avoid such ego-threatening situations. Dyscalculic children and youth in particular may perceive themselves as being unable to learn mathematics. Lacking confidence tends to interfere with acquiring competence. Lack of competence tends to reduce confidence still more. And so the cycle goes.

Not all dyscalculic children and youth perceive themselves as helpless.

Some are strongly motivated to achieve cognitively. However, for those who are not achievement motivated, the teacher has a difficult assignment. For one child a material reward may be a motivation; another child might be motivated by a symbolic reward such as a gold star or an "A." But for many children the most effective energizer will be the knowledge that they are overcoming the loss of control, the feeling of helplessness, in mathematical situations. Nothing suceeds like success. However, there is some reason to believe that a "success only" program, with never an experience of failure, may not always make as good a psychoeducational match as one in which there is a judicious mixture of occasional failure, but not devastating experiences (Thomas, 1979, p. 210).

Field-Dependence/Independence

We have referred to the importance of matching teaching style and learning style. A fairly new way of conceptualizing this need is that of field-dependence or field-independence (Witkin, Moore, Goodenough, & Cox, 1977). With the use of appropriate measurement items and techniques, people can be categorized as field-independent or field-dependent. Persons who are more analytic, more impersonal, better able to separate a figure from its background, less sensitive to social situations, and more interested in abstract content are considered to be field-independent. Those who look at things more globally, are more personable, warmer, more tactful and sociable, and work better with people than with abstract ideas are more field-dependent.

Evidence is now available that suggests that field-independent people respond better to intrinsic motivation than field-dependent people. When the motivating source is in the form of material rewards, field-dependent children do as well as field-independent ones. And when the theory of motivation is in the form of social reinforcers, such as praise, again the two groups do equally well.

Teachers of the dyscalculic will have to be flexible in their use of each of the three major sources of motivation when matching teaching and learning styles of field-independent and field-dependent children and youth.

Metacognition

Metacognition is a new area of cognitive-developmental study and research (Flavell, 1979). It is concerned with finding ways to develop the ability to learn about one's own learning processes. Specifically, it is concerned with acquiring the cognitive ability to evaluate one's learning processes, learning styles, learning products. For learning disabled children, this ability would mean an increased ability to ask, "Why is it that when I subtract from left to right example A is correct and example B is incorrect?"

$$\begin{array}{r} 47 \\ -15 \\ \hline 32 \end{array} \qquad\qquad \begin{array}{r} 62 \\ -18 \\ \hline 54 \end{array}$$

Example A   Example B

Development in metacognitive processes would suggest that children will grow in their ability to be less impulsive and more reflective in their behavior and, we hope, will increasingly be able to monitor their learning processes: attending, remembering, recalling, transferring learning, solving problems, and reconstructing prior learning temporarily forgotten.

Locus of Control

Among the general characteristics of the learning disabled mentioned at the beginning of this chapter are several that suggest that for many of these children and youth their behavior is motivated by stimuli in their environment. The adult who enters the classroom, the child who drops a book, the ambulance that passes by the school building—any such actions may cause an uncontrolled reaction by the learning disabled child. In a very real sense, their behavior is beyond their control. Learning to shift the locus of control from external events to within themselves is a very difficult and often a long-term task. Shifting the locus of control from impulsive-dominated behavior to reflective-oriented behavior is essential if the person is to behave in a manner that is acceptable in home, school, and community life.

Behavior Modification

The fifth source of newer strategies for motivating learning disabled children and youth is the best known. "Behavior mod" is a part of every teacher's professional vocabulary. It is also known as applied behavior analysis, contingency management, behavioral engineering, and stimulus control. Behavior modification techniques are particularly useful for the teacher of the dyscalculic child who is also emotionally or socially impaired. This is discussed at length in the chapter by Weaver and Morse. Here we shall simply list the commonly used techniques for modifying unacceptable behavior:

Setting rules	Contracting procedures
Stimulus change	Verbal feedback
Teacher praise	Reinforcement procedures
Shaping	Time-out

Modeling plus reinforcement of matching responses

Obviously, teachers of mathematics will not be successful if they do not have the ability to cause the child or youth to attend to the cognitive situation. It may require the combined efforts of both the teacher and the

school's counseling psychologist to find ways to modify the attentional dysfunction of the dyscalculic student in order for learning to progress at a rate consistent with aptitude.

SUMMARY

In this chapter we first identified and discussed the general characteristics of learning disabled children and youth. We then suggested some specific characteristics of those whose specific exceptionality is in the learning of mathematics—the dyscalculic students. Drawing on the essential variables in an instructional psychology, as presented in chapter 2, we offered specific suggestions for applying these variables to the teaching and learning of mathematics.

REFERENCES

Berliner, D. C. *Allocated time, engaged time and academic learning time in elementary school mathematics instruction.* Paper presented at the Annual Meeting of the National Council of Teachers of Mathematics, San Diego, April 12, 1978.

Cohen, L. Suggestions for teachers in helping children with learning disabilities. *ACLD Newsbriefs,* September/October 1979, p. 12.

Coles, G. S. The learning-disabilities test battery: Empirical and social issues. *Harvard Educational Review,* 1928, *48*(3), 313–340.

Cruickshank, W. M. Learning disabilities: A definitional statement. In E. Polak (Ed.), *Issues and initiatives in learning disabilities: Selected papers from the First National Conference on Learning Disabilities.* Ottawa: Canadian Association for Children with Learning Disabilities, 1979.

Cruickshank, W. M. *Learning disabilities in home, school, and community.* Syracuse, N.Y.: Syracuse University Press, 1977. (b)

Cruickshank, W. M. Perspectives on dyslexia. *Newsletter of the Orton Society* [Towson, Md.], May 1977, *2*(3), 1. (c)

Cruickshank, W. M., Bentzen, F. A., Ratzeberg, F., & Tannhauser, M. *A teaching method for brain-injured and hyperactive children.* Syracuse, N.Y.: Syracuse University Press, 1961.

Cruickshank, W. M., Marshall, E. D., & Hurley, M. A. *Foundations for mathematics.* Boston: Teaching Resources Corporation, 1971.

Cruickshank, W. M., Morse, W. C., & Johns, J. S. *Learning disabilities: The struggle from adolescence to young adulthood.* Syracuse, N.Y.: Syracuse University Press, 1980.

Cruickshank, W. M., & Paul, J. L. Psychological characteristics of children with learning disabilities. In W. M. Cruickshank (Ed.), *Psychology of exceptional children and youth* (4th rev. ed.). Englewood Cliffs, N.J.: Prentice-Hall, 1980.

Education for All Handicapped Children Act of 1975, Public Law 94-142, 94th Congress, S.6. November 29, 1975.

Flavell, J. H. Metacognition and cognitive monitoring: A new area of cognitive-developmental inquiry. *American Psychologist,* 1979, *34* (10), 906–911.

Galaburda, A. M., & Kemper, T. L. Cytoarchitectonic abnormalities in developmental dyslexia: A case study. *Annals of Neurology,* 1979, *6*, 94–100.

Harris, A. J. *How to increase your reading ability.* New York: David McKay, 1970.

John, E. R., Karmel, B. Z., Corning, W. C., Easton, P., Brown, D., Ahn, H., John, M., Harmony, T., Prichep, L., Toro, A., Gerson, I., Bartlett, F., Thatcher, R., Kaye, H., Valdes, P., & Schwartz, E. Neurometrics. *Science,* 1977, *196* (4297), 1393–1410.

Kosc, L. Developmental dyscalculia. *Journal of Learning Disabilities,* 1974, *7,* 46–59.

Myklebust, H. R. Learning disabilities: Definition and overview. In H. R. Myklebust (Ed.), *Progress in learning disabilities.* New York: Grune & Stratton, 1968.

Pihl, R. O., & Parkes, M. Hair element content in learning disabled children. *Science,* 1977, *198,* 204–206.

Strauss, A. A., & Lehtinen-Rogan, L. *Psychopathology and education of the brain-injured child.* New York: Grune & Stratton, 1947.

Thomas, A. Learned helplessness and expectancy factors: Implications for research in learning disabilities. *Review of Educational Research,* 1979, *49*(2), 208–221.

Thorndike, R. L. *The concepts of over- and under-achievement.* New York: Bureau of Publications, Teachers College, Columbia University, 1963.

Wepman, J., Cruickshank, W., Strother, C., Deutsch, C., & Morrissey, A. Learning disabilities. In N. Hobbs (Ed.), *Issues in classification of children* (Vol. 1). San Francisco: Jossey-Bass, 1975.

Wiederholt, L. Historical perspectives on the education of the learning disabled. In L. Mann & D. Sabatino (Eds.), *Second review of special education.* Philadelphia: J. S. E. Press, 1974.

Witkin, H. A., Moore, C. A., Goodenough, D. R., & Cox, P. W. Field-dependent and field-independent cognitive styles and their educational implications. *Review of Educational Research,* 1977, *47*(1), 1–64.

Teaching Mathematics to Socially and Emotionally Impaired Pupils

J. F. Weaver

The University of Wisconsin — Madison

William C. Morse

The University of Michigan

Dr. William C. Morse is professor of educational psychology and psychology and chairman of the Combined Program in Education and Psychology at the University of Michigan. He has spent his professional career working with socially and emotionally disturbed children and training special education teachers. He is a regular consultant to public school and institutional programs for disturbed children and youth. Morse has published articles and books dealing with the education of these youngsters.

TEACHING SOCIALLY AND EMOTIONALLY IMPAIRED PUPILS

(The material in this section is an abbreviated version of certain material by W. C. Morse in *The Education of Socially-Emotionally Impaired Children and Youth* [in preparation].)

The Problem

IT IS not difficult to define social-emotional disturbance in youngsters. In fact, there are almost as many definitions as state departments of education, and these variant descriptions are supplemented by a great number of

individual writers who develop their own. In common usage, each one of us has our own concept of *disturbance* that we apply to others when we use the term. Individual teachers differ widely when asked to identify disturbed pupils. Yet we are all quite confident that we know what the label means and whom it covers.

A group in Texas (Coulter, Morrow, and others at the Texas Learning Resource Center, Texas Education Agency, Department of Special Instruction, Austin, Texas) has embarked on an effort to codify the concept of emotional disturbance in special education. They have found a great variety of models, including the medical, educational, and sociological, each ascribing the problem to different sources: within the child, as an educational deficit, and as a consequence of environment. The most exhaustive treatment of the different meanings and theories concerning the nature of deviance (biological, psychodynamic, behavioral, and ecological being the primary ones) is to be found in the five volumes by Rhodes and Tracy (1972–1976).

The significance for the classroom teacher of the many ways of looking at disturbance is that those who are selecting the children who fit this special education category and who are indicating what the treatment should be do not share the same set of concepts. Defining this category is the most confusing in all of special education. Furthermore, and of utmost importance, social and emotional problems are found in combination with all other categories, regardless of label, even though the dual nature of many cases is ignored. It is the most pervasive special education component.

To repeat, it is not hard to define social-emotional disturbance. What is virtually impossible is to define the concept in a way that has anywhere near universal acceptance, interpretation, and implications. As an example, we shall examine the Bureau of the Education of the Handicapped definition as applied to Public Law 94-142. The emotionally disturbed category includes children who have had for a long period of time one or more of the following, and to such a marked degree that their educational performance is adversely affected: inability to build or maintain satisfactory interpersonal relationships with peers or teachers; inappropriate types of behavior or feelings under normal circumstances; pervasive mood of unhappiness or depression; and a tendency to develop physical symptoms or fears associated with personal or school problems. The definition further states that this term includes schizophrenic and autistic children. The socially maladjusted (a term that implies the delinquents) are not included unless they are also seriously emotionally disturbed. As any teacher knows, this last caveat is a cop-out. It is done to avoid responsibility for what is probably the largest group of school problems, and it probably represents a political and financial decision. Since the discrimination is both impossible to make and unwarranted in nature, as will be shown, this statement is not

germane to the present chapter. Furthermore, it is absurd to talk about children as if their total life were school. Are we to ignore those children not having irritating school responses? The definition is cast as if school were the cause and cure when the largest generator of child pathology is in the family and community life. Teachers know that this is a myopic view of the problem area, with a selective special clientele for special education, since they have as many problem pupils not certifiable in their classes as those who are certified. The term *social-emotional impairment* (SEI) used here is thus more inclusive and realistic than the typical definitions based on excluding certain children.

The overall approach to SEI special education is an ecological one. That is, behavior is a consequence of the interface of the person and the contemporary environment. To alter behavior, one approaches both the individual and the environment. This means we must study both the children and the classroom conditions as we plan interventions.

Although a figure of 1.5% of the child population is given as reasonable for this area of special education, the evidence is that at least 3% should be included in the very seriously socially-emotionally disturbed and that another 8–10% are in need of special help because of similar problems, to say nothing of the multihandicapped, of which one facet is disturbance. Since few schools have an active mental health program, those who do not fit special education are often left in limbo until they get "bad" enough to fit. All these come to the regular classroom where the teacher is supposed to provide a solution. How many and what type of special pupils, as defined above, are mainstreamed varies with school districts. In some districts mainstreaming has become a fetish; in others it is used moderately.

The Regular Teacher and the SEI Problem

Helping socially and emotionally impaired (SEI) pupils learn academic and social skills requires an intricate extension of the processes of accommodation to individual differences. The self-concept of these pupils differs from normal youngsters. Furthermore, the behavior of certain ones changes day by day and sometimes moment by moment. This puts a considerable burden on the sophistication and responsiveness of the teacher.

It should be recognized at the outset that in contrast to most categories of special education, the majority of SEI pupils have always been mainstreamed. Dedicated and effective teachers have always helped such children, often going to great lengths to find supportive methodology. So what is new? The opening chapter describes very well what is new. Pupils with these special problems must now be formally identified and taught in the least restrictive educational environment. Their education must be according to an individual educational plan (IEP). The IEP is to contain specific academic and behavioral goals. The teacher is accountable for

reaching the stated objectives—the elementary teacher for all academic goals and the secondary teacher for those in a given subject area—as well as assisting with the personal and social goals. There is no more hit or miss or dependence on the degree of responsibility felt by an individual teacher. Maximizing their pupils' skills is now the legal obligation of all teachers, and an obligation for which there is accountability. Often the goals are set by the diagnostic team and the special educators rather than the regular teacher who is to do the work. Help may be given to the mainstream teacher in terms of consultations, tutorials, a resource room, or a part-time special class. But for many SEI pupils, the program's success rests on the effort of mainstream teachers. When this new obligation was discussed with these regular secondary teachers, two important conditions became evident. One is that all teachers could remember disturbed pupils (whether formally identified by special education or not) for whom they had extended themselves far beyond the usual, sometimes with success and sometimes not. Secondary teachers who have been negatively stereotyped as oriented only to subject matter and little concerned with personal problems of children reported examples of special attention given to particularly disturbed adolescents. Teachers often go far beyond the call of duty for their pupils and keep trying against high odds, taking a great deal of emotional punishment in the process. Thus, again, the legal situation should not be thought of as bringing something entirely new to the regular teaching profession. There was an all-important second condition: these teachers listed the help they wanted in order to do an effective job. They wanted, not general advice about curriculum, but specific material and actual lessons that would be appropriate; not only theoretical discussions about the nature of the pupil's problem but what exactly to do when there was a refusal or management condition that could not be handled in class; finally, what would be reasonable expectations for pupil achievement and particularly how one should handle grading. What this indicates is that the regular teachers must become active in asking for what they need and not rest on what the consultants volunteer.

Options for Classroom Teachers

The miracle of effective classroom teaching, or more accurately stated, putting pupils with a wide array of individual differences in a position for effective learning in a group setting, rests on many professional skills. Including SEI pupils is expanding the perimeter of what a teacher already does. What are the dimensions on which these expansions take place?

Several options for accommodating one's teaching to SEI pupils are within the teacher's immediate control. One is the nature of the teacher-pupil relationship. Making this relationship useful or compatible rests on two aspects. One is greater self-knowledge. The other is greater knowledge of the self-concept of the pupil, on which rest acceptance, empathy, and

astute planning. Both of these are necessary if we are not to foul up the tenuous interpersonal dynamics that make the relationship useful and positive. A second dimension is modulating the input of the group dynamics of the classroom. On the one hand, we try to prevent acerbating conditions coming from the group. On the other hand, can we actually make the group supportive for this special pupil? The third dimension is the substantive area, the material we want the pupil to learn and the methods we employ. Here the regular teacher will find that what is taught and how it is taught are already known skills. The teacher must consider, however, the best fit for the particular pupil and perhaps the use of alternative methods. Although SEI pupils tend to be significantly retarded in academic achievement, this is not always true. The "behind" pupil is hardly a new phenomenon. Usually there are regular pupils who are as deficient as the disturbed ones.

The material on these dimensions will be incorporated in the two major sections to follow. One is teachers' self-understanding. The other is the pupils—their nature and classroom-relevant behavior. From these two, plus the regular teaching skills already part of the teacher's ability, are formed the adjustments that are in the teacher's domain. We do not imply, however, that these adaptations are easily made or easily maintained.

The Dimensions as Seen from SEI Pupil Self-Concepts

We recognize that the external behavior of the disturbed child is a consequence of what is going on inside him or her as well as the external confrontations. As we learn more of what is going on within, we find ourselves sympathetic with the pupil's feelings of confusion, frustration, dismay, pretense, disinterest, or anger, and we adjust our strategies therewith. As teachers, we are particularly attuned to the satisfactions of learning, the excitement normal children have of "getting it." We can recognize in them the self-enhancement that comes from conquering a piece of ignorance and the good feeling of putting skills to work for some personal goal. Unfortunately, the SEI youngsters live mostly in anxiety, defensive negativism, and failure and are continually grappling with a sense of inadequacy. The positive effect from learning is seldom theirs. They are behind their potential ability in actual achievement. School often connotes failure, and teachers are the taskmasters who "set you up to fail again." For most of them school is far from a happy place. What you learn there is not of the highest personal priority. All in all, a not pleasing picture for the teacher or pupil. When normal youngsters have temporary similar emotional states, a teacher can bring them around without too much difficulty. SEI pupils are programmed internally to follow their own deep-seated patterns. But once teachers understand the individual nature of SEI pupils, they are ready to get on with the business of teaching them. The fact is, the SEI pupil's covert first order of business is relationships—how to get along with authority,

peers, and even themselves. To consider yourself worthwhile, you have to have the concern of important people such as your teacher. The trouble is, you have considerable talent for provoking adults as well as peers. So much energy goes into the relationship area that there is little left over for academic enterprises. If teachers understood you better, they could offer more help.

We turn now to a brief overview of the patterns of SEI self-concept. In short, what we want is to know the overall generalizations of personality on which the imprint of the individual is still imposed. These patterns of deviation will be cast in terms of self-concept, since this is the typical way teachers generalize about youngsters. The explanation often used to account for "bad" behavior is a poor self-concept.

There are two aspects to the idea of self-concept: one is the nature of the self-structure and the other is self-esteem. Self-concept includes one's perceived talents and limitations and one's values, skills, and roles. The roles include family-member role, role as a student, peer role, and cross-sex role. One's identity (ethnic, religious, and sexual) is also embodied in the self-concept. Body image too is a part of it.

One's affective states are part of the self. Since some aspects of the real self are alien to what we can tolerate believing about ourselves, certain attributes may be denied or repressed. Then, too, we are not always consciously aware of all that we are. There is a layer of the self that is inferred from behavior and test data. The most important behavior and motivating conditions may stem from unrecognized features in our nature. The term *self-concept* is more functional than *personality*, since it is that which the person herself or himself defines or portrays. The pieces of the mosaic are idiosyncratic, though the areas mentioned above are common.

Self-esteem has to do with evaluation of the self. After the descriptors comes the judgment. Regardless of how academically proficient students may be objectively, the issue is, how do they feel about their status? Some children have high self-regard if they just pass; others, only if they are at the top of the class. Some could not care less, since the academic performance area holds little importance to them. Individuals have their own hierarchy of what counts most.

The self-concept–self-esteem cycle is the core knowledge we need in order to understand the pupil and plan for dealing with the symptomatic behavior. The same symptom—say, aggressive acting out toward the teacher—may stem from a self that expects to have its own way and wants no one to interfere. The teacher is the target but not in a personal sense. Or the behavior may stem from a displacement of anger really directed at parents, though the child is too afraid to direct the anger at them. One pupil resists mathematics because it makes no sense to the self he or she is; another is afraid of failure and has no personal risk capital. The symptom

of refusal is the same in each case to the teacher. The teacher's reactions that will help the pupil will be different.

How does one learn about the nature of the SEI self? Often children are very open and "tell all." Others may be reluctant even to think about it. If teachers are to base their plans on the nature of the pupil, they must accumulate an understanding of the pupil's self-concept. Some sources of information are listed below.

1. Theoretically, there should be material in the child's records that will aid in appreciating the pupil's self-concept and level of self-esteem. Past regular teachers and special workers may have clues. If the psychological testing has been adequate, there should be information on both the overt (acknowledged) and the covert self. The truth is, records often contain everything but the core of self and self-esteem.

2. But it is not always unfortunate that data are not in the file. Those things shared directly between teacher and pupil are more important than items in the record file. It is the sharing that makes the difference. Any SEI pupil should be interviewed by the teacher when she or he first comes to the classroom. As the teacher talks with the pupil, questions are raised that are central to their mutual experiences together. For example, "What has been your experience relative to arithmetic (or math)?" Is it easy, hard, useful, part of what you want to learn, and so on are touched on. Satisfactions related to achievement are noted. The defensive "pretend to know it all" cases are revealed through the conversation. One asks how one can best help the given pupil in this academic area, and the IEP goals are reviewed. Plans for getting needed help are discussed. Some children have no real knowledge about where they stand except that they are behind. There is nothing like this first-hand interchange to give the teacher a handle on the "arithmetic self," so to speak.

3. When there are ongoing social or academic difficulties, the teacher continues the talk. The term for these discussions is Life Space Interviewing, which is geared to an action setting and involves a nonpunitive, planning-oriented meeting of minds (see Long, Morse, & Newman, 1980).

The goal of Life Space Interviewing is to conclude with a mutually satisfactory procedure to meet the immediate problem. Classroom expectations are clarified. A teacher should not wait for a crisis to begin to get on speaking terms with the youngster. There is a tendency to let well enough alone until it gets intolerable. The suggestion is to establish a working rapport *before* there is a crisis.

We turn now to a brief look at four basic syndromes or styles of self-development in SEI children. We are dealing with the 3% of very seriously disturbed as defined in the first section. We recognize that these basic patterns will be overlaid with the special individualistic nature in a given pupil.

The unique nuances are what the teacher adds to make a specific strategy out of the general approach.

1. *Pupils in severe contemporary stress.* Whereas special education is supposed to include only long-term chronic SEI pupils, there are increasing numbers of youngsters who are suffering from situational stress too difficult for their coping capacity. Their behavior can be every bit as difficult as the classic syndromes.

To an increasing extent children are the victims of unfavorable social conditions. The number who have to deal with parental divorce is epidemic. Often these pupils are in families that have waited to divorce until the offspring are teenagers on the false assumption that it won't matter then. The reverse is true. At this age all of the fundamental life choices are impending—sexual behavior, marriage, careers, and independence—and then the bottom drops out of their established home life. Both older and younger children frequently show drastic drops in school achievement and worry about what is going to happen to them. Economic reverses or a new awareness of the limitations of poverty are other conditions of crisis. Moving from elementary to junior high school or the move to senior high school may demand resources a youngster does not have. Adolescence itself has been termed a time of crisis, and we know of the depression, frantic activity, and confusion that can result. Moving is often upsetting. The shock of confronting prejudice (which had somehow been escaped heretofore) can produce dismay and bitterness that flood the self. Child abuse, as we now realize, is much more prevalent as a cause of reactive disturbance. Sexual abuse is usually traumatic. The death of a parent, sibling, close friend, or relative may lead to a reactive crisis. Fears of a particular teacher can make one find ways to stay home. Youth who have been found delinquent and are awaiting their trial date are often consumed with anxiety. Getting involved in drugs or sexual activity beyond one's choice can make one feel helpless to meet and control the life forces.

Although a few naturally compensate by more school diligence, the opposite is the usual pattern. A previously adequate self with reasonable self-esteem is overwhelmed by life conditions. Energy for academic matters is nil. Often youngsters will say they can't concentrate or can't study, even though they used to be fair students. This change in itself adds a charge of anxiety and makes matters worse.

The teaching strategy with such pupils is to recognize their state and discuss what could be done to help them deal with their problem. In the meantime, back in the classroom, the teacher tries to find highly motivating work and makes the lessons brief and not overdemanding. The therapeutic value of keeping at the usual learning tasks as a balance is emphasized, even though it is recognized as difficult. We do not berate them with "You used to be . . ." or "What's the matter with you?" It is said to take a young

child a year to deal with a divorce (though the marks may well persist for life). Reactive children present many behavioral formats, but the essential thing is to provide any help and support possible. The need for professional assistance in coping with the central problem as well as the concomitant educational program can prevent a situational response from becoming the persistent nature of the self-concept.

2. *The neurotic selves.* Although all of us are neurotic to some extent, some children and youth are neurotic to the point of not being able to manage life over a long period of time. They have learned ways of responding that are self-defeating. The basic characteristics are low self-esteem and essential unhappiness. Theirs is a deep commitment to inadequacy learned by failure over and over. Although some have aspiration levels that are unusually high and unattainable (a reflection of adult expectations that they have incorporated), most of the neurotics would just like to get along with the normal quota of success. The etiology usually rests with how they were treated as they grew up. Family rejection, excruciating demands, school failure, peer rejection—almost any chronic misfit of capability and demand can set things awry. The main thing to remember is that these children have an internal struggle in the contrast between the values they have incorporated and their inability to behave reasonably. They *can* relate, and they *do* care.

The evolving neurotic self is an outcome of trying to deal with the conflict and the low self-esteem. Some of these children fight back in anger out of their frustration, often being sorry afterwards. They attack at the least stimulus to their inadequacy. To care even when the child is "bad" is the difficult remedial stance for the teacher.

Other neurotics simply quit trying. The "I can't" response is often a total behavior pattern. So we must find the level at which even they can easily perform, but this may even upset them because it is a "baby level." Some become loners, mistrusting relationships because they consider themselves useless. It takes a lot of persistent caring to overcome these fixated patterns. Some are so depressed that they feel hopeless and think of suicide. Laughter and enjoyment is foreign to their nature.

There are the "passive aggressives," who vacillate between acting out and acting in. Some neurotic children deny everything and pretend they are doing satisfactorily, or even very well indeed: First done, forget the errors. The false front must be penetrated so that they will try to work at the level on which they can do the tasks.

All these youngsters require specific curricular and method adjustments to remove their anxiety and fear of failure. Different methods not reminiscent of their failure should be used. Games for learning and short, small-step tasks are devised. Above all, one avoids failure.

They also need to be surrounded by caring from the teacher and, one

could hope, from peers. In one way or another they need to be protected from social derision and unfavorable group comparisons. Real progress, though it be small, should be recognized.

3. *Value-deficient SEI youngsters.* More and more teachers are confronted with pupils who are unmotivated to academic tasks either because they have never incorporated the usual age-related school values or because the values they have are alien to school activities. Some have not socialized in any area to speak of and thus take what they can from anyone. Certain delinquents are of this order.

Since most teachers have an articulate superego, it is difficult for them to identify with a pupil who does not care. Some of these youngsters love to argue "why should we study math" and always win, since they originate and act from an alien code of values. A number of these empty youngsters are expert con artists. Lying is often a simple solution to a problem they face. They are unabashed at being asked about undone homework. The point is, their self-concept does not contain the motivation we would like to use, and there is no damage to their self-esteem when they do not comply with expectations that are not a part of the self. Since they live in the moment, appeals to the value in the future make no sense. Many children learn to please the teacher regardless of their own views, and in this event the pupil-teacher relationship does the work: not so with the relationship-deficient ones.

It appears that we are producing more and more alien and relatively empty youngsters. At the worst, schools become a place of pandemonium where such pupils threaten the marginal and even the serious students and enjoy working them over and ridiculing teacher-accepted behavior. Losing one's cool, being dominated, giving in to authority, being laughed at by friends you hold high, being straight—these are the tender spots of self-esteem. Many, though not by any means all, delinquents have such a profile.

It is not their fault they have been so raised by society, and nothing is gained by being angry at them. We set the limits and make it clear what the limits are as well as the consequences. We expect the limits to be tested. To many, being excluded is the solution of choice. When we understand the makeup of the self, we don't argue; we are direct and frank. But we also decide with them when and under what conditions they can return.

The motivational problems are manifold. To some, games appeal if it's not like working and doesn't take too much effort. Others work only when watched. If the math can be made pragmatic to solve some life problem of personal worth, there may be a chance, but it is not always easy to convert numbers into cash. Money and excitement are the real goals of these youngsters. Sometimes, for the milder cases, a conference with parents or guidance counselors can supply a modicum of motivation, but it seldom

lasts too long at a stretch. The fact is that most schools are not designed to accommodate this type of self. The best promise is through cooperative study and job assignment. Applied math is a better bet than the usual algebra-geometry sequence.

4. *The psychotic.* There are two categories of SEI children who are the most profoundly disturbed—autistic and schizophrenic. Although their numbers are small, their impact is great. These deviations are believed to be organic in origin, although environmental stress may precipitate some of the behavior or add layers of disturbance to the organic base.

Autistic children have been well described by Paluszny (1979). These are children who exhibit very limited or even no language, a lack of typical relationships to people and things, and atypical affective responses. They may exhibit bizarre mannerisms and fixations on particular specifics. Except in rare instances, such children should not be mainstreamed for the significant part of their training.

The schizophrenic condition mainfests itself both in childhood and at puberty. These youngsters distort reality, have fixated notions, exhibit idiosyncratic thinking (often usefully penetrating in some areas), and tend to have inappropriate social behavior. Bizarre behavior may be present. Obsessive question asking is common.

Some of these pupils will find mathematics a preoccupation. Numbers may fascinate them.

It is important to foster any such combination of interest and ability that appears; in some instances it has led to careers using mathematics. More often, however, the rigidity of the schizophrenic youngster is upset by simple " + " and " − " operation signs—such a small way to them to indicate so much conceptual distinction. They usually are most secure with routines and defined tasks. They need to be able to trust the teacher. Clear directions are required. The teacher watches to see that their peers do not make fun of them. Adolescence is a particularly difficult time for this type of self. Expert consultation is essential for a teacher to appreciate psychotic pupils.

Dimensions of Adjustment as Seen from the Teacher's Viewpoint

Left to our own, most of us have a great deal more empathy for one type of a disturbed child than for others. The same teacher will have a long fuse for one pupil and a short one for another. What we must do is elevate our concern for all pupils to that level we already possess for some. Several psychological concepts can help accomplish this by enabling the teacher to plan, since there is no single set of techniques that will fit all SEI pupils. These concepts are in addition to the overall knowledge discussed in the previous section.

1. *Increasing our acceptance and empathy for SEI pupils.* It has been

indicated that most teachers already have in their repertoire adequate academic and personal responses to certain "different" children. The point is to make this capacity general for *all* SEI pupils. The goal is to break the cycle of pupil-teacher interactions based on the past.

SEI pupils conduct a distorted exchange with their environment. The term used is *problem transference.* They use the patterns they have learned in the past and continue with the same behavior even when it is not appropriate. For example, they may have failed in past learning experiences and developed the response, "I can't do it." You give them an obviously easy task. They will still say, "I can't do it." When it is clear they can, then: "It's baby stuff. Who cares about doing that?" In fact, this only proves their point that they are not able to do what they should, only those tasks that "don't count." SEI children may have learned to get help from the adult rather than working themselves, or they may believe adults won't help or don't care. They try to make us fit their unconscious mental image, even when we take great care to be objective. As we say, they know how to get to a person—it is their greatest talent.

Usually teachers fall into the trap. It is exasperating, to say the least. We point out, then argue, and then become angry. When we have done the right and appropriate thing, we are especially prone to defend ourselves. We may lose our cool. The reasons for spontaneous positive and negative reactions to particular children lie in our own case histories. It is not our purpose to go into details about these matters here, but it can be pointed out how different we are in our sensitivities. The more insight we have about our own sensitivities, the better our control. Some of the common sensitivities are those for the child who simulates "trying hard" with no production, is overdependent, is hostile, sad, alienated, lonely, uninterested, and so on. The behavior of these children is personal and psychological "bad news" to the teacher. We counterreact. When our unfinished life business generates an oversensitivity and we act it out, this is countertransference.

When we reach out to a pupil, which is a point of beginning, it does not mean that the SEI pupil will respond in kind. Often teachers who care most are tested most because the concern is felt by the pupil, even though the pupil cannot deal with his or her feelings in an appropriate manner. Adults have to break the negative cycle produced by the pupil's behavior by controlling their half of the interactions. Often this means not responding with typical teacher behavior that would be useful to the normal pupil.

Our first goal is to cultivate the positive transferences we already have and guard against expecting the pupil to change when we have given a quart of our psychological blood. It is easy to express "justified" rejection after all we have done!

The second goal is to expand our capacity for positive transferences by

recognizing the child's human dilemma behind the facade and symptomatic behavior that bothers us. Pupils who provoke us usually get rejection from us, which is the opposite of what they need. When we feel guilty over our behavior, we overcompensate with positive responses. This alternation results in a confused teacher-pupil relationship and impedes academic effort as well. It is not academics *or* relationship: how we handle one is intertwined with the other at the same time. In fact, the relationship overtones present while we are focusing on an academic task often contain negative feelings of countertransference.

2. *Overcoming our label prejudice.* The disturbed individual differs in degree, not in kind, from children and from adults who consider themselves normal. Characteristics are on a continuum, not in discrete categories with the normal here, the abnormal there. As we recognize our common human bonds with the special pupils, the pupils' behavior becomes less mysterious. The distance between us as human beings is reduced. Who has not felt periods of guilt or anxiety in common with the neurotic? Or fear of failure and defeat? Most of us have known periods of depression, often with inscrutable causes. We have known anger. Or take the value-deficient pupils, who help us remember how thin is the veneer of socialization in ourselves as well. And although we hope never to be far enough extreme to require institutionalization, the behavior of even the psychotic has some normal counterparts. The denial of reality, the suspicion, the idiosyncratic beliefs or combinations of incompatible beliefs—do we not share these too, to a degree? There are even times when we are preoccupied and live in a world of our own, obsessed with certain rituals in temporary autistic behavior. Thus it is that we recognize our oneness whatever the labels. Such awareness encourages us to forge bonds of human relationship.

3. *Avoiding becoming symptom reactive.* Reacting to symptoms without recognizing their meaning oftentimes causes an intervention that exacerbates the problem. We need to appreciate possible causes. How many reasons might be behind a pupil's outburst of anger? It may be triggered by something we have done or it may be from what happened at home this morning or last week. The helping strategy follows the cause, not the symptom. Sometimes we ignore, or we tolerate, we sympathize, we reassure, we give support to deal with the same behavior. Not that we can always home in on the best or reasonable thing to do, but we can have an exploratory openness to the variety of possible motivating factors for behavior. *How* we do what we do will be colored by our understanding. For example, we may have to ask a boy to leave because the classroom is not a useful place for him right now, but he is free to return when he feels ready. We may see that he is testing our limits and we may thus require extensive negotiations prior to considering a return. He may be expected to finish an assigned task, even though to do so seems to make doing a few problems a federal court case.

But we do it because we recognize that compliance is a lesson high on the agenda for this child. Or, we may know that he is likely to come around on his own if ignored, and so we ignore him.

To help us be more confident as we work out plans to meet problematic behavior, we devoted considerable attention to underlying patterns of disturbance.

4. *Recognizing nonpersonal conditions.* No matter what the pupil is like or what the nature of deviance is, behavior is always a consequence of two factors: the person and the particular forces in a given situation. For example, even a distractible student may be able to concentrate on the arithmetic task when alone or when being tutored. But the stimulation of a classroom group may result in distraction galore, a situation that produces attention-getting behavior. Classroom groups are sometimes the primary source of environmental input, even stronger than the pupil-teacher relationship. Classroom climates differ. Some are work minded and supportive to members; others are competitive and hostile. In one group, a special pupil may have a useful role; in another class, she or he may be a scapegoat. In general we know that SEI pupils will have less favorable roles, the "slowest" or most rejected, which will produce defensive behavior. Sometimes pairs of pupils "eat on each other," or negative interacting subgroups form. What happened in the hall before class may condition the behavior in the classroom. The ecological aspect, as assessed by Moos (1979), may go beyond the classroom to the climate of the total school. In short, pathological behavior is a result of the person-environment interface at any given time. We ask what might be altered in the peer or authority relationship that may be provoking undesirable behavior. It is interesting that in a good institutional education program when the environmental conditions have been tuned to the needs of disturbed pupils, the classrooms for the most part operate within the norms of reasonable behavior. But stay around awhile and two things will be evident. There will be individual pupils who break through from time to time and require the teacher's intervention. Second, there will be periods when groups get out of hand. If this becomes chronic, a total reassessment is necessary. But do not expect that disturbed children will never show disturbing behavior, no matter how well the ecology is planned. As one youngster put it, "I'm a special because I lose my temper too often. Don't say, 'Don't lose your temper.' " The disturbed pupil has a birthright to some expression of her or his problem.

5. *Awareness of appropriate leadership style.* It is not enough that the teacher studies and works through group-climate problems. The leadership style of the teacher must also be examined. On the one hand, SEI pupils need the security of routines, and this implies teaching with understood requirements. On the other hand, blatant authoritarianism may touch off cer-

tain youngsters already afraid or angry about authority. Many teachers give much correction for errors and little praise for success. Directions are confused. Expectations can be too rigid. Neither compulsive teaching nor laissez faire approaches will suit. Some of us are afraid that if a pupil once gets away with something, all is lost. Thus it behooves us as teachers to look at our specific classroom presence.

6. *Learning to talk with SEI children.* Somehow, many teachers think only a special education professional can talk to the SEI pupil. Some of us are afraid, some are unskilled, and some won't spend the time. As we indicated previously, we can learn effective ways to interact and we can use them from the first day. They will provide more knowledge to us than many a test or file report. The procedure for teachers is called Life Space Interviewing and is described in *Conflict in the Classroom.* (Long, Morse, & Newman, 1980). It is useful for normal as well as disturbed pupils.

In Summary

Unfortunately, there is no simple counsel to give the teacher in dealing with SEI children. One must seek out and discover. There are two major domains to dealing with these special pupils. The first is the understanding of the various emotionally and socially impaired patterns of the self and the exploration of the unique attributes of the given pupil. The other domain is creative, individualized teaching that avoids adding to the problem conditions and, better yet, becomes a vital part of the restorative process. Fortunately, neither of these two domains is foreign to regular teaching. We need only to step up our skills.

Consideration may be given to "social maladjustment," "emotional disturbance," "behavior disorders," and the like from a variety of points of view (e.g., Kauffman, 1977; Kauffman & Lewis, 1974; Morse, 1975; Pappanikou & Paul, 1977; Rhodes & Paul, 1978). Hallahan and Kauffman (1978), in fact, have identified five approaches to educating disturbed children, which are characterized in Table 4.1. Certain of these approaches, or combinations thereof, may apply to other classes or categories of exceptional children, such as the learning disabled (e.g., Gardner, 1977, 1978; Hallahan & Kauffman, 1976; Kauffman, 1975; Leitenberg, 1976; Thoresen, 1973).

The approach taken in this chapter is neither psychoanalytic nor behavioral (in any "pure" sense). Rather, the approach reflects several points emphasized by Morse (1977) when interviewed by the editor of *Exceptional Children:*

> I would say that the biggest thing that has happened [in the area of behavior disorders during the last five years] is the broadening of the concepts of intervention, that is, basically moving from a rather restrictive dynamic

Table 4.1
Approaches to Educating Disturbed Children

	Psychoanalytic Approach	Psycho-Educational Approach	Humanistic Approach	Ecological Approach	Behavioral Approach
The problem	A pathological imbalance among the dynamic parts of the mind (id, superego, ego).	Involves both underlying psychiatric disorders and the readily observable misbehavior and underachievement of the child.	The disturbed child is out of touch with his own feelings and can't find self-fulfillment in traditional educational settings.	The child interacts poorly with his environment; child and environment affect each other reciprocally and negatively.	The child has learned inappropriate responses and failed to learn appropriate ones.
Purpose of educational practices	Use of psychoanalytic principles to help uncover underlying mental pathology.	Concern for unconscious motivation/underlying conflicts *and* academic achievement/positive surface behavior.	Emphasis on enhancing child's self-direction, self-evaluation, and emotional involvement in learning.	Attempt to alter entire social system so that it will support desirable behavior in child when it is withdrawn.	Manipulation of child's immediate environment and the consequences of his behavior.
Characteristics of teaching methods	Reliance on individual psychotherapy for child and parents; little emphasis on academic achievement; highly permissive atmosphere.	Emphasis on meeting individual needs of the child; reliance on projects and creative arts.	Use of nontraditional educational settings in which teacher serves as resource and catalyst rather than as director of activities; nonauthoritarian, open, affective, personal atmosphere.	Involves all aspects of a child's life, including classroom, family, neighborhood, and community, in teaching the child useful life and educational skills.	Involves measurement of responses and subsequent analyses of behaviors in order to change them; emphasis on reward for appropriate behavior.

(*Note.* Reprinted from Hallahan & Kauffman, 1978, p. 209.)

point of view to an inclusion of behavioristic and other learning approaches and to a greater appreciation of the ecological factors that tell us why some of the interventions that we try do not have long term permanence. I think this has probably been the biggest change in the way we have looked at things. We did not really have an ecological point of view before. Now we expect less to happen on the basis of how the individual changes and more on the basis of environmental input. (p. 158)

Actually, I would say the big movement is the blending relationship between the psychodynamic approach, which is the recognition of the inner life, the emotional life, the motivations, the goals, the aspirations, the drives, and needs that the individual has, and the behavioristic approach. This side has emphasized the external contingencies that are just as real as the internal ones, and it is always the mediation of these two that we have to deal with. The external reality, with its rewards and gratifications, is on the outside. What gets rewarded or gratified is on the inside.

The leaders in the field have finally gotten around to realizing that the human being behaves in a more diverse way than either of these positions alone. Both positions imply things about human nature and about learning. The psychodynamic position certainly has had to expand its horizons about human nature and how behaviors change, and I think the same thing is true in behaviorism. . . .

There is a synthesis in the air, but it seems to be starting pretty far at the top. The problem lies in the proper assimilation, a more complete knowledge of children, an awareness of the complexity of man, and a more astute understanding of how we use behavioristic or learning techniques. (p. 164)

In this chapter we seek suitable balances involving the psychological, sociological, and logical curriculum sources identified by Glennon in chapter 2. We say "balances,"—plural—because there is no *one* balance that is equally suitable and effective for *all* subclasses of socially and emotionally impaired children and youth.

SOCIALLY AND EMOTIONALLY IMPAIRED PUPILS AND MATHEMATICS INSTRUCTION

It is very much in order to ask at the outset, What has *research* to say about the teaching and learning of mathematics with regard to socially and emotionally impaired pupils? In order to answer this question, let us first go back in time and note several things about research on SEI pupils more generally.

In 1966 Balow mentioned that recent "yearly reviews of selected literature on exceptional children" (see Kvaraceus & McInnis, 1963; Kvaraceus & Blatt, 1964, 1965) included "more than 80 articles on the emotionally disturbed and delinquent, but not more than 15 of these can be called research reports" (p. 120).

Three years later Glavin and Quay (1969) indicated that "numerous

publications have appeared recently on the subject of emotionally and socially maladjusted children. The majority of the articles, however, have been descriptions of projects, clinical case studies, or suggested methodologies without supporting data'' (p. 83).

More recently, the Council for Exceptional Children's 1977, 1978, and 1979 topical bibliographies (Emotionally Disturbed—Teaching Methods and Programs) seem to include a somewhat higher proportion of research references.

But within all the preceding works, relatively little can be identified as explicit to mathematics, to say nothing of focusing principally on mathematics. For instance, in 1968 Glennon and Callahan cited only *two* references (Graubard, 1964; Schroeder, 1965) in connection with their discussion of the question, Is there a relationship between emotional disturbance in students and arithmetic disability (at the elementary school level)? According to Glennon and Callahan (1968):

> Evidence would suggest a definite relationship between students with emotional problems and those with arithmetic disabilities. No evidence has been gained, however, on whether arithmetic disabilities are a causal factor in emotional disorders or vice versa. Also, the teacher should be aware that students cannot be collected into one "emotionally disturbed" class and be expected to reflect the same learning disabilities. (p. 56)

When 7 years later Callahan and Glennon (1975) addressed the same question, six additional references were cited (Feldhusen, Thurston, & Benning, 1970; Glavin, 1973; Glavin & Annesley, 1971; Glavin, Quay, & Werry, 1971; Stone & Rowley, 1964; Tamkin, 1960), and conclusions were extended slightly in some instances and reworded slightly in others:

> Evidence generally suggests a definite relationship between students with emotional problems and those with arithmetic underachievement. The underachievement is often more marked in arithmetic than it is in reading. The evidence does not shed light, however, on whether arithmetic disabilities are a causal factor in emotional disorder, or vice versa. Classroom settings that are humanely structured and reward academic performance may be beneficial to the academic performance of students with emotional problems. However, the teacher should be aware that students cannot be collected into one "emotionally disturbed" class and be expected to reflect the same disabilities, or growth, under a single treatment. (p. 67)

More Recent Investigations

Findings and implications (if any) from more recent investigations can be considered in several broad categories.

Piagetian research. Brekke and Williams (1975), citing conflicting research findings (e.g., Filer, 1972, & Howell, 1972), sought "to investigate whether an emotional disability has any relationship to the acquisition of

conservation" (p. 118) of weight. Basing their study on data from 45 "normal" subjects (CA's 10-5 to 14-11; IQ's 84 to 137) and 45 institutionalized emotionally disturbed children (CA's 10-7 to 19-5), they concluded the following:

> It would appear that much of the relationship that exists between emotional disturbance and conservation is due to the lower intelligence scores of the younger children labeled emotionally disturbed. In that mental retardation has previously been shown to cause a deficit in attaining conservation [Brekke & Williams, 1974], it would seem reasonable to conclude that emotional disturbance, insofar as this disturbance is manifested in a hospitalized population, does not contribute to a cognitive deficit in Piagetian conservation. (p. 119)

Working with children of the same chronological age (approximately 12-0) and without controlling for IQ, Jepsen (1975) found that on six conservation tasks 20 children chosen from three residential treatment centers for emotionally disturbed persons "had a statistically significant lower level of conservation performance" (p. 2134A) than 20 "normal" children.

Working with children of the same chronological age (approximately 14-0) whose "level of intellectual functioning was within the average range as measured by performance on Standarized Tests of Intelligence" (p. 6344B), Phillips (1976) found that on four Piagetian conservation tasks there was a "significant difference [.05 level] between the levels of formal thought acquisition for normal adolescents and institutionalized emotionally disturbed adolescents . . . when group mean scores were compared" (p. 6344B).

It remains to be seen whether such lines of research are at all profitable with respect to implications for mathematical learning among emotionally disturbed persons, since implications for mathematical learning among "normal" persons are far from clear.

Behavior modification (and similar concerns). It is not surprising to find that more reports of investigations fall into this category than into any other.

Murry (1977) observed the classroom behavior of 69 fifth-grade pupils during 10 arithmetic class sessions and sought to investigate the relation of that behavior to overachievement and underachievement based on calculating for each subject a score that "was the discrepancy between observed math achievement and achievement predicted by the regression of achievement on IQ. *Classroom behavior was found to have little relationship to over- and underachievement because there was little range of the discrepancy scores* [italics added]" (p. 7156A).

Fontana-Durso (1975) "investigated the effect of behavior modification classroom techniques including a token economy system on locus of control, self-concept, reading achievement, math achievement, and

behavior in second graders. There were 85 children in four classes. Two were experimental classes and two were controls" (p. 4197B). The following impossible finding can likely be attributed to an unfortunate typo: "The math achievement score of the *control* group was significantly higher than that of the *control* classes [italics added]" (p. 4198B). It likely was for other reasons, however, that the investigator indicated that "a more sensitive measure of math achievement [than the math section of the Wide Range Achievement Test (WRAT)] should be used" in further research (p. 4198B). Over all, "It was concluded that the treatment, behavior modification, only had a significant effect on the experimental children's behavior which improved" (pp. 4197B–4198B).

Simmons (1976) "investigated the effects on learning achievement in reading, English, and mathematics among [18] individuals enrolled in a day school for emotionally disturbed boys that was part of a children's psychiatric center of a children's hospital when a level system was removed from a token economy" (p. 6409A). It was observed that "mathematics was the subject that was least effected [*sic*] when the level system was removed. Very few of the subjects declined in their work productivity in mathematics when the level system was discontinued" (p. 6410A). However, there was some evidence that "suggested that differences in response to the experimental treatment seemed to be related to specific psychiatric diagnoses across the basic subject matter areas" (p. 6410A).

At this point the reader is referred to Sternberg's (1976) discussion of her experience with a token economy and reward system for mathematics and other instruction, Grades K–6, from which she concluded that "a reward system is a never-ending trip. Once it is started, it is virtually impossible to stop—the child's goal has become the acquisition of rewards, not the acquisition of knowledge" (p. 459).

Friedman (1976) compared for two groups of "upper elementary aged children, 18 of whom attended classes for Behaviorally Disordered (BD) children and 18 of whom were based in Regular Classes, . . . the effects of Teacher-Applied Reinforcement and Pupil-Applied Reinforcement on academic responding" (p. 725A) involving "addition problems":

> The results indicated that Behavior Disordered children obtain higher [response] rates with Pupil-Applied Reinforcement than with Teacher-Applied Reinforcement. . . . It is possible that the BD children in the Teacher-Applied Reinforcement condition were required to perform at a level inappropriate to the amount of reinforcement they were given. . . . All groups were found to inflate their scores during reinforcement conditions. Since students reported their own scores without teacher supervision, the contingencies may have been more effective in increasing the reporting of inflated scores than in improving actual performance. (p. 725A)

Walker and Hops (1976) questioned the generalizability of findings

from their own investigation of differential reinforcement procedures, since (1) "the treatments may interact strongly with curricula different from the one employed in this study" (p. 224); (2) "observation data sampled reading and math activities only in the experimental classroom, whereas a variety of academic activities were sampled in the regular classroom setting. Thus treatment as well as observational conditions differed for experimental and control subjects" (p. 224); and (3) "finally, there may be some grade differences among subjects in this sample in terms of their response to the various treatments" (p. 224).

Hundert, Bucher, and Henderson (1976) suggested that

> it is possible that the effect of a contingency imposed on either academic achievement or appropriate behaviour may not be confined to that behaviour but may influence other behaviours as well. That is, a child who is reinforced for correctly answering arithmetic problems may also spend more time working quietly in his seat. Similarly, if a child is reinforced for appropriate classroom behaviour, his correct arithmetic work may improve. (p. 195)

Basing their conclusions on data from 22 15-minute sessions involving a two-page arithmetic assignment for five boys (CA's 9-3 to 12-1) who composed one class of a psychiatric hospital school, the investigators found that

> strengthening the appropriate behavior of a class of disruptive children does not necessarily produce an increase in arithmetic performance; whereas an arithmetic performance contingency alone is sufficient to not only increase the level of correct arithmetic work, but also maintain a high rate of appropriate behavior as well. These findings indicate a one-way dependency between arithmetic performance and appropriate behavior. . . . [It should be noted that] the arithmetic assignments that were administered in the present study measured the subjects' application of arithmetic principles they had previously learned. A somewhat different finding might have resulted if the subjects' performance were measured during the process of learning these principles. . . . [Also,] all of the subjects were characterized by low academic proficiency and high disruptiveness in the classroom. Nonhospitalized students of larger classes may not respond in the pattern found in the present study. (p. 200)

Ross (1976) investigated the premise that "an operant-counterconditioning program utilizing the Premack principle and free time as a reinforcer is . . . effective for increasing the rate of correctly completing arithmetic problems while decreasing the rate of disruptive behavior" (p. 3093B). Data were gathered from "six problem students in each of two arithmetic classes taught by the same teacher," for which "ten observers were trained and recorded time-sampled occurrences of on-task and five off-task behaviors for 39 school days," during which time "Modern School Mathematics (MSM) texts and Sullivan program math workbooks were alternate sources of arithmetic problems" (p. 3093B), with these results:

There was a significant increase in the rate of solving MSM but not Sullivan problems between the initial baseline and intervention. The teacher was unsuccessful in increasing the rate of arithmetic problems solved between the withdrawal and retest phases. However, the rate of total off-task behavior decreased during each intervention phase, relative to baseline measures. . . . It is suggested that the teacher reinforced low rates of off-task behavior instead of problem solving. (p. 3093B)

Page and Edwards (1978) investigated "the effectiveness of two group-oriented contingency systems" using as subjects the 52 sixth- to eighth-grade students "in the five classes of a Title I math teacher at an urban middle school" (p. 413):

It was concluded that for junior high [math] students: (a) Free-time is an effective reinforcer. (b) Reinforcing academic behavior is an effective method of reducing disruptive classroom behavior. (c) Both independent and interdependent group contingencies are effective techniques for changing classroom behavior. (d) The teacher can effectively implement a behavior change program with little or no training in behavior analysis. (p. 413)

Program evaluation. In recent years there have been sundry reports describing or evaluating programs in which mathematics was of concern—solely or along with some other academic area(s).

Clary (1975) described a program of diagnosis and prescription for L.D. problems of E.D. adolescents within a residential treatment center.

Kennedy, Mitchell, Klerman, and Murray (1976) described "a day school for aggressive adolescents [CA 13 to 19], organized cooperatively by a school system, a youth guidance center, and a state hospital, [that] is providing an effective alternative to institutionalization" (p. 712).

O'Leary and Schneider (1977) reported that

highly disruptive first graders who spent 8 months in a special class placement did no better upon their return to their regular classes than similar children who attended regular classes for the entire year, with the exception of higher reading achievement scores for the special class group. Second, both groups of children showed significant improvement in their classroom behavior as viewed by both teachers and independent observers. (p. 27)

It also was asserted that

accumulating information raises serious questions about whether and how special class placement should be continued. Without question, a certain small percentage of highly disruptive and severely handicapped children require separation from the mainstream of education. For less disruptive students, the possibility remains, *although not supported by research,* that detrimental effects on the rest of the regular class children outweigh the cost and labeling concerns related to placing these children in special classes [italics added]. (p. 29)

Romeo (1975) investigated the effect of three treatments on the arithmetic achievement scores of 53 emotionally disturbed children in six public school classes. "The two classes in Treatment Group A were taught by teachers using the Directive Teaching Method set into a data retrieval system. Treatment B consisted of two classes taught by teaching using the Directive Teaching Method which was not set into a data retrieval system. Treatment Group C consisted of two classes taught by teachers using a psychoeducational eclectic teaching approach" (p. 222A). Based on changes in WRAT (Level II) raw scores over a 10-week intervention period, "the hypothesis that Treatment Group A will have significantly higher arithmetic scores than Treatment Group B or C had to be rejected. The hypothesis that Treatment Group B would have significantly higher scores than Treatment Group C also had to be rejected" (pp. 222A–223A).

Griggs (1976) concluded that a "mathematics laboratory approach is a very successful intervention in terms of significantly improving the mathematics achievement level of selected subjects, who were at least two years retarded in mathematics and attended special schools for the socially maladjusted and emotionally disturbed" (p. 380).

From the Office of Educational Evaluation of the Board of Education of the City of New York, at least four reports of special programs involving SEI students identified significant achievement gains in mathematics (see Curtis, n.d.; Gottlieb, n.d.; Hicks, n.d.; Schwartz, n.d.).

In contrast with reports that cite statistical evidence in support of program evaluation, there are informal reports of units of mathematics work and the like that are "evaluated" quite subjectively without any supporting statistical evidence (e.g., Pile, 1977).

Distinguishing characteristics. Investigations continue to show both similarities and differences on sundry characteristics among traditional classifications of exceptionality such as ED (Emotionally Disturbed), EMR (Educable Mentally Retarded), and LD (Learning Disabled) individuals. In one investigation (Gajar, 1977) it was reported that although all three "groups exhibited underachievement in . . . arithmetic[,] . . . "ED subjects were distinguished from the other groups by low arithmetic achievement, high scores on the conduct disorder and personality problem measures, and from the EMR group on the immaturity-inadequacy measure" (p. 4091A). Certain of Gajar's findings seemed to be at odds with the broad picture portrayed by Hallahan and Kauffman (1976) in Figures 4.1 through 4.5.

Hallahan and Kauffman (1977) further contend that

> no behavioral characteristics can be found that are associated exclusively with any one of the three areas. Children who are usually identified as learning disabled, mildly disturbed, or mildly retarded reveal more similarities than differences. Consequently, successful teaching techniques do not differ among the three areas. . . . (p. 139)

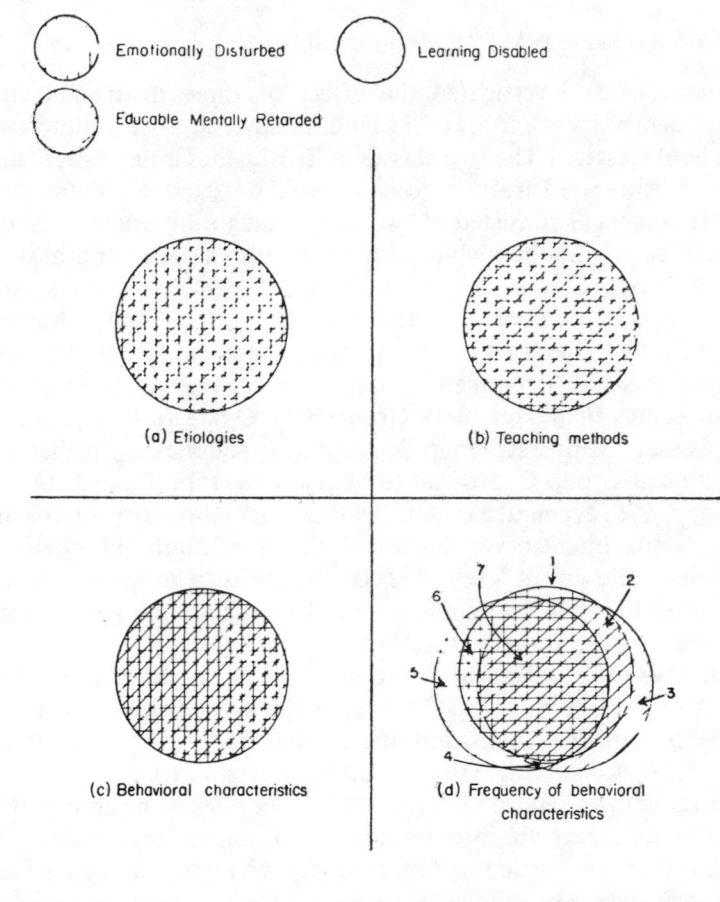

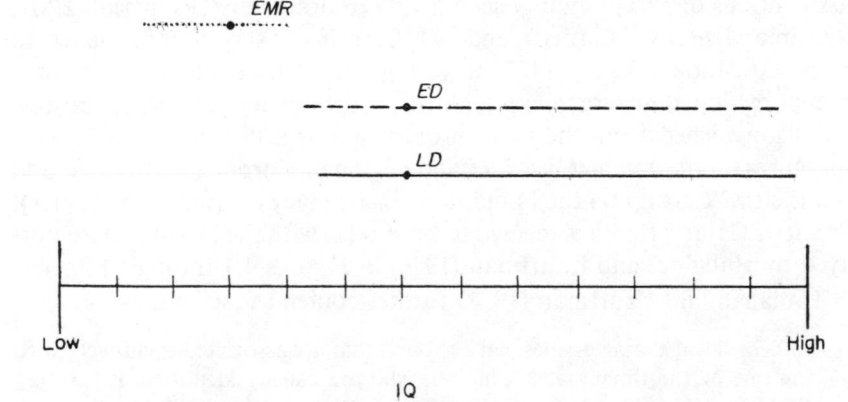

Figure 4.1. Venn diagrams illustrating the similarities and differences among the conditions of emotional disturbance, learning disabilities, and educable mental retardation. (From Hallahan & Kauffman, 1976, p. 37, Fig. 3.1.)

Figure 4.2. Comparison of IQ among educable mentally retarded, emotionally disturbed, and learning disabled populations. (From Hallahan & Kauffman, 1976, Fig. 3.2.)

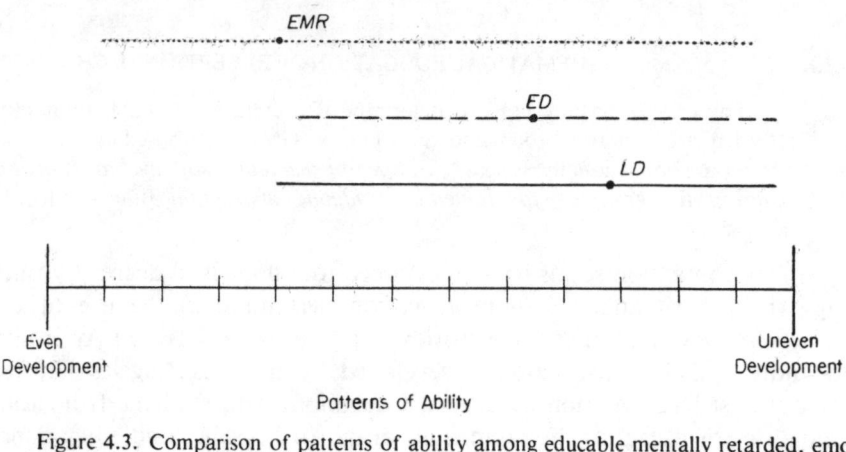

Patterns of Ability

Figure 4.3. Comparison of patterns of ability among educable mentally retarded, emotionally disturbed, and learning disabled populations. (From Hallahan & Kauffman, 1976, p. 39, Fig. 3.3.)

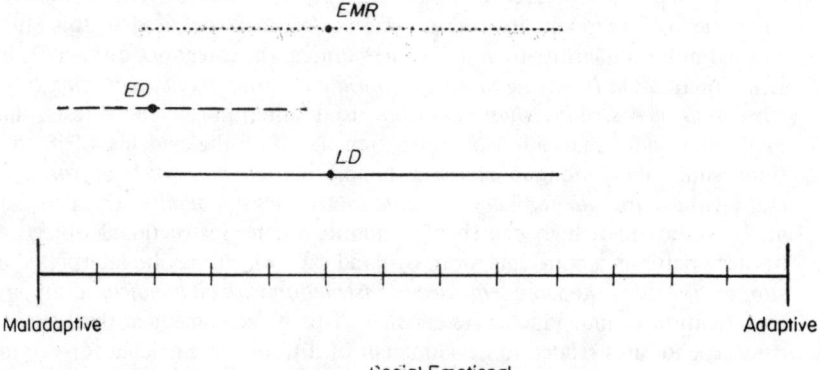

Social Emotional
Development

Figure 4.4. Comparison of social-emotional development among educable mentally retarded, emotionally disturbed, and learning disabled populations. (From Hallahan & Kauffman, 1976, p. 40, Fig. 3.4.)

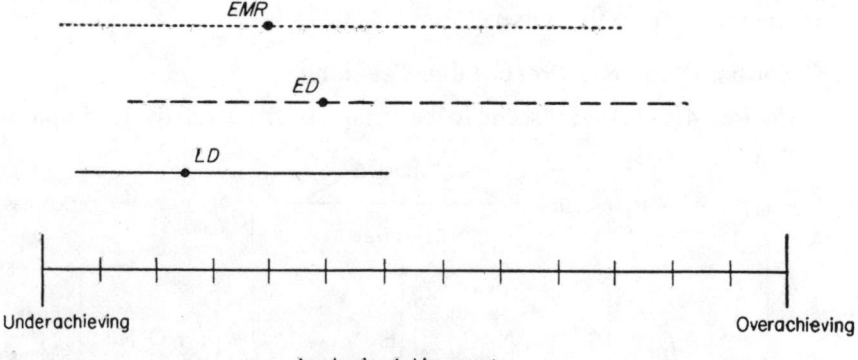

Academic Achievement

Figure 4.5. Comparison of academic achievement among educable mentally retarded, emotionally disturbed, and learning disabled populations. (From Hallahan & Kauffman, 1976, p. 40, Fig. 3.5.)

The criteria usually used to determine if a child is LD, ED, or mildly retarded are just too broad and amorphous. Groupings based upon these criteria are educationally useless. . . . *Specific academic skill level must be the criterion for grouping for remedial academic instruction* [italics added]. (p. 146)

This contention seems to be reinforced to a nontrivial degree by findings from Tashjian's (1976) investigation pertaining to the use of the *"Mathematics* Assessment Inventories" of "System FORE, an Approach to Individualizing Instruction" (developed by the Los Angeles Unified School District's Division of Special Education) with students from four categories of exceptionality: "mental, aural, orthopedic, and educational handicaps" (p. 5750A), leading to these conclusions:

> Although norm-referenced tests reportedly show clear differences between categories of exceptionality, the criterion-referenced test used in this study showed more similarities than differences among the categories on specific instructional tasks. *It may be more appropriate to group pupils according to instructional needs rather than handicap,* using criterion-referenced tests, thus facilitating individualization of instruction. (2) With the evidence of instructional similarities among categories of handicap, *there may not be any need for differential curricula for varying categories of exceptionality.* (3) The data analysis showed a high degree of similarity in the instructional objectives mastery patterns among categories of handicap, which may be interpreted as *support for using the same sequence of instruction with all handicaps,* but paying attention to individual differences. . . . [It is recommended that] significant expenditures related to development of differential curricula for varying categories of exceptionality should be curtailed until these tentative results can be verified or discredited [italics added]. (p. 5751A)

Although research findings will continue to have some bearing on our considerations in this chapter, we shall turn now to a second principal section of this part of the chapter—a section in which some crucial concerns must be raised from the outset.

Differential Diagnosis–Prescriptive Teaching

Figures 4.6–4.9 may seem to be versions (from relatively simple to

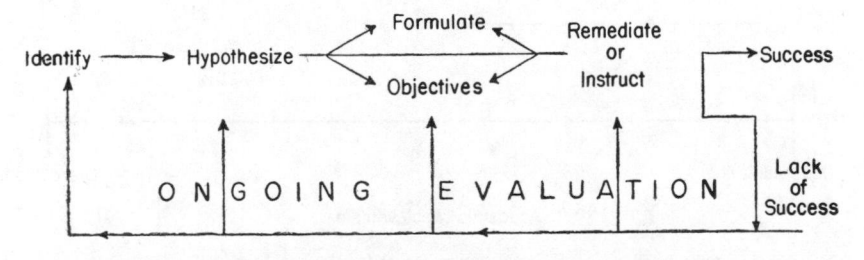

Figure 4.6. Diagnostic teaching cycle. (From Reisman, 1978, p. 7.)

more complex, but with some features in common) of what Arter and Jenkins (1979) term "the dominant instructional model in special education, Differential Diagnosis–Prescriptive Teaching" (p. 517). All versions of the model are augmented or supplemented in one way or another, of course. Johnson (1979), for instance, summarizes his version of the model (Figure 4.7) in terms of these seven steps:

1. Looking for signs of problems in regular classroom work.
2. Using material designed to elicit behavior for diagnostic analysis.
3. Searching for non-arithmetic examples of deficit behavior in areas to which the problem may have generalized.
4. Deciding on whether or not to seek outside help.

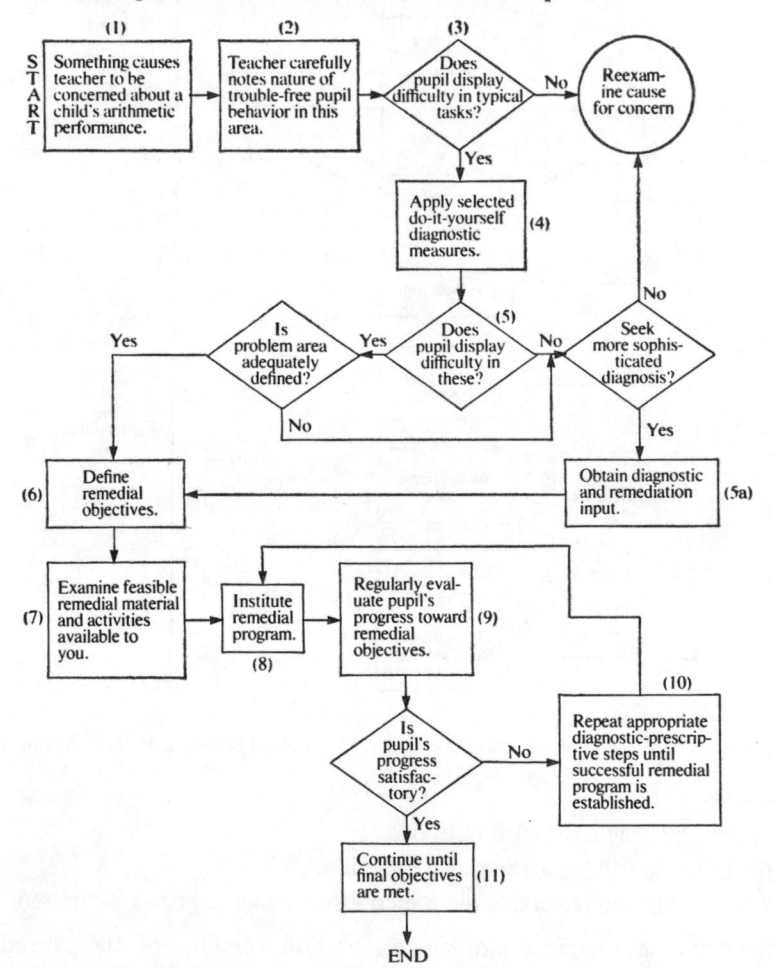

Figure 4.7. Flowchart of prescriptive diagnostic strategy. (From Johnson, 1979, p. 70, Fig. 5.4.)

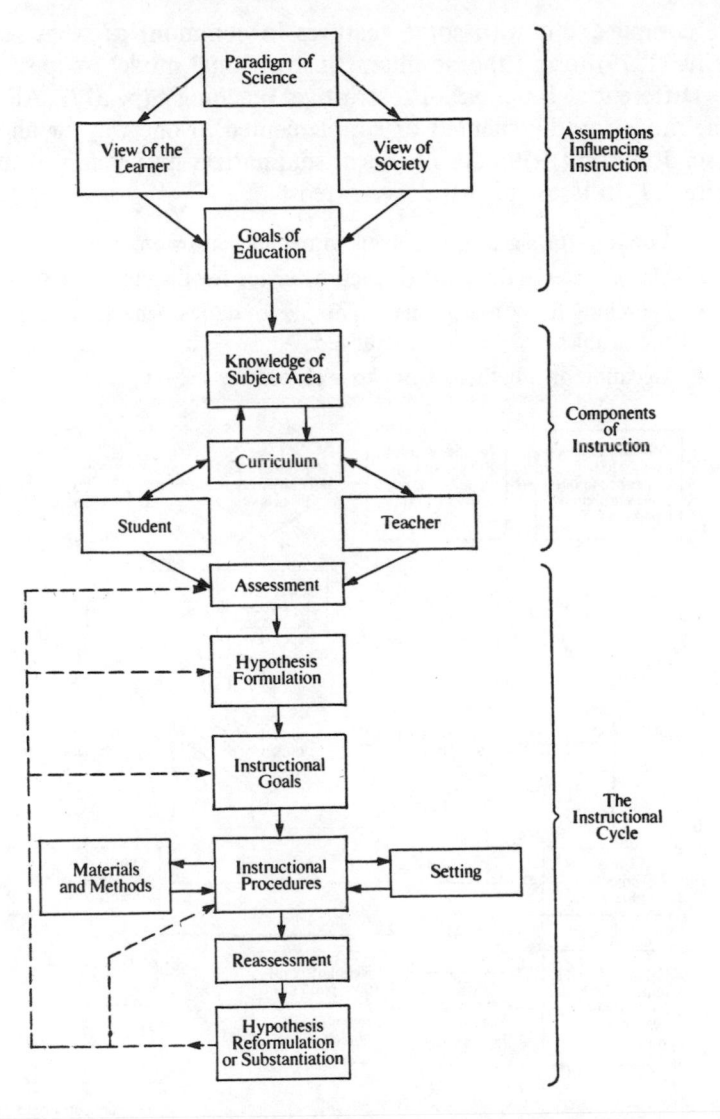

Figure 4.8. Instructional sequence model. (From Hammill & Bartel, 1978, p. 3, Fig. 1-1.)

5. Establishing a remedial objective.

6. Preparing and using remedial materials.

7. Revising and reworking the prescriptive diagnostic processes. (p. 69)

Despite some surface similarities, certain versions of the preceding model differ in a substantial, consequential way, as we shall see.

Arter and Jenkins (1979) indicate that

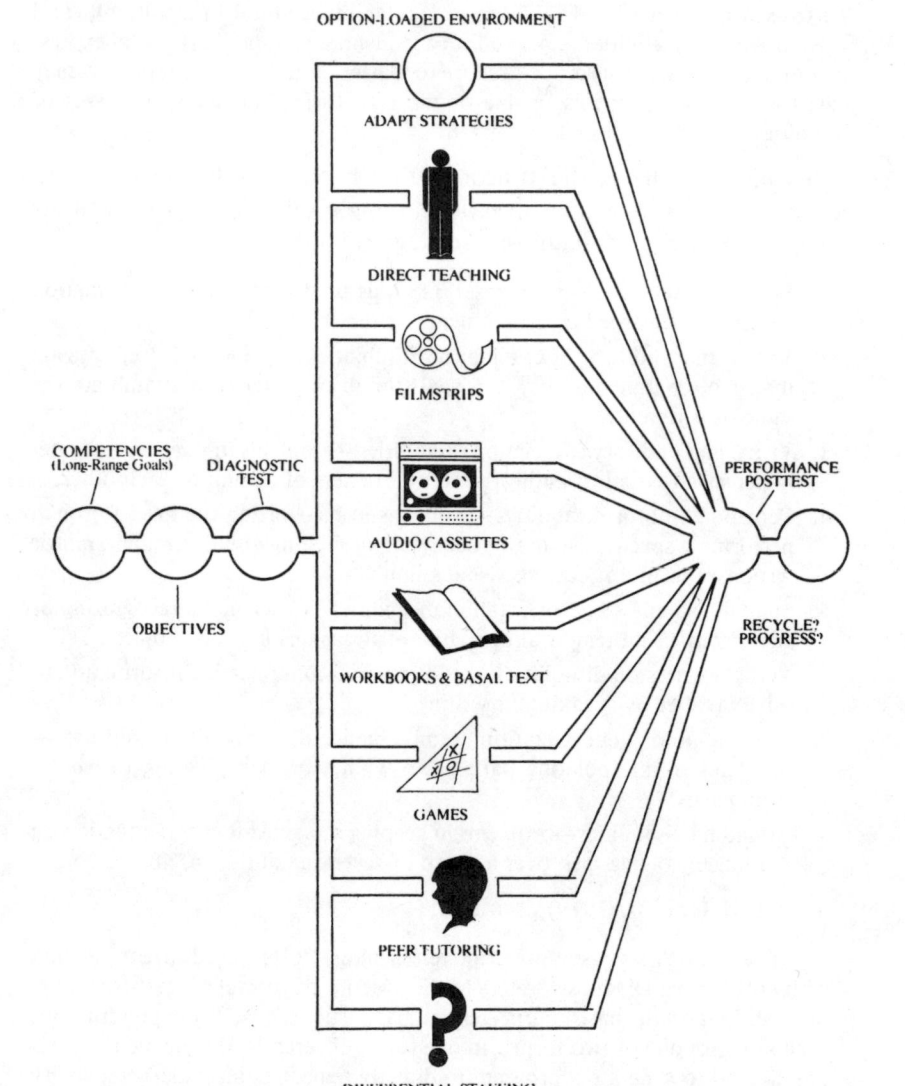

Figure 4.9. ADAPT assessment model. (From Farrald, Gonzales, & Masters, 1979, p. 25.)

the term "differential diagnosis" refers to the process of assessing the learning characteristics of a child so that instruction can be matched to individual learning needs. Although, in theory, this could include any procedure that attempts to delineate a child's specific strengths and weaknesses, it has traditionally referred to those practices that attempt to diagnose abilities that presumably are prerequisite for or underline academic learning. Such general psychological processes include auditory abilities (e.g., auditory discrimination and memory), visual abilities (e.g., visual discrimination and spatial relationships),

cross-sensory perceptual abilities (e.g., auditory-visual integration), and psycholinguistic abilities (e.g., auditory sequential memory and verbal expression). According to this model, failure to master basic academic skills . . . may be traced to impairments in one or more of these underlying processes or abilities. (p. 517)

This undoubtedly is the "theory" that prompts Johnson (1979) to associate the following eight "specific learning disabilities types" with his flowchart of prescriptive diagnostic strategy (Figure 4.7):

1. Memory disabilities—problems in recalling on demand bits of information perceived or learned a few moments before.
2. Visual and auditory discrimination disabilities—problems in recognizing that two separate auditory or visual stimuli or patterns of stimuli are the same or different.
3. Visual and auditory association disabilities—problems in relating separately perceived visual or auditorial stimuli or sets of stimuli to each other.
4. Perceptual-motor disabilities—problems in recognizing the need for or in performing specific eye-motor behaviors or relating visual stimuli to motor responses or motor cues to visual stimuli.
5. Spatial awareness and orientation disabilities—problems in recognizing or adequately using temporal or spatial relationships between objects.
6. Verbal expression disabilities—problems in communicating information to others (either by speaking or writing).
7. Closure and generalization (convergence-divergence) disabilities— problems in interpolating parts from wholes or extrapolating to wholes from parts.
8. Attending disabilities—problems in keeping sustained focus of attention on a problem solving task over a space of several minutes. (p. 48)

Arter and Jenkins (1979) continue:

The term "diagnostic-prescriptive teaching," often used in conjunction with Differential Diagnosis, refers to the practice of formulating instructional prescriptions on the basis of differential diagnostic results. These prescriptions generally take one of two forms. In one form, differential diagnostic information is used to generate a program to directly remediate an underlying ability weakness. In the second form, weak abilities are not remediated; rather, the focus is on academic targets, such as reading or mathematics, for which instructional programs are devised that capitalize upon the child's pattern of underlying strengths and weaknesses, as identified in the course of diagnosis. (p. 518)

"Learning styles" often are associated with emphases on pupils' strengths, even to the following degree emphasized by Hopkins (1978) in her discussion of mathematics instruction: "Unless a teacher is aware of the child's preferred learning style (tactile, visual, auditory, and so on) ap-

propriate experiences resulting in the most efficient learning happen only by accident" (pp. 48–49).

For Arter and Jenkins (1979),

> The terms differential diagnosis and diagnostic-prescriptive teaching are combined as Differential Diagnosis–Prescriptive Teaching (DD-PT) and refer to the psychometric practice of assessing underlying abilities and devising subsequent instruction in accord with ability strengths and weaknesses. . . . The DD-PT label encompasses a number of "process" models which are fundamentally equivalent but which have gone by a variety of names. (p. 518)

In contrast with the preceding emphases, Crenson (n.d.) has indicated that

> mathematics educators traditionally lean toward a task analysis model while those involved in special education are more usually advocates of perceptually oriented models.
>
> A task analysis model is content or discipline oriented. It attempts to assess a child's mathematics strengths and weaknesses by utilizing a content hierarchy, emphasizing component skills and integrating them into more complex terminal tasks. Instruction, then, is geared to strengthening the academic weaknesses indicated in the child's hierarchy.
>
> With perceptually oriented models, the prime concern of initial assessment is to identify ability (process) strengths and weaknesses. Generally, learning modality (auditory, visual, kinesthetic, etc.) dominance or weakness is assessed in order to prescribe appropriate remediation. The primary concern is the identification of perceptive and/or psycholinquistic abilities or processes which are presumed to cause inadequate skill development. (p. 43)

The frequently investigated pros and cons of the Key Math Diagnostic Arithmetic Test and the arithmetic sections of the WRAT (Wide Range Achievement Test) and PIAT (Peabody Individual Achievement Test) (e.g., Baum, 1975; Heil, 1977; Kratochwill & Demuth, 1976; Webster & Schenk, 1978) stem from the use of such instruments in connection with "perceptually oriented" models, which seem to have little or no place for instruments such as the Stanford Diagnostic Mathematics Test (4 levels), the Adston Diagnostic Instruments, the Reisman Sequential Assessment Mathematics Inventory (SAMI) (4 levels), the Piagetian diagnostic activities suggested by Copeland (1979), and so on.

Arter and Jenkins (1979) further discussed the distinctions between the DD-PT and task analysis models:

> In the DD-PT model, the practice of analyzing academic skills into their components bears a strong resemblance to task analysis. . . . According to Resnick, Wang, and Kaplan (1973), in the task analysis model "specific behavioral components are identified and prerequisites for each are determined. The strategy is to develop learning objectives such that mastery of objectives in the hierarchy (simple tasks) facilitates learning of higher objectives

(more complex tasks)" (p. 679). [Farrald, Gonzales, & Masters (1979) make much of the Resnick-Wang-Kaplan "procedure" in connection with their paradigm of Figure 4.9 (assessment model), going so far as to suggest that "Resnick, Wang and Kaplan (1973) describe a method of systematic task analysis that those concerned with creating the Individual Implementation Plan [of an IEP, or Individual Educational Program] would do well to emulate" (p. 16).] Similarly, the DD-PT model holds that academic tasks must be analyzed into basic components. Here though, the basic components consist of underlying abilities or psychological processes. If weaknesses are discovered at the foundational or ability level, they must be remediated before proceeding to higher order skills.

Although the task analytic and DD-PT models appear to be similar, we believe that the similarities are quite superficial and that serious differences exist between the two. *The differences between the models lie both in their level of analysis and in their implications for instruction* [italics added]. With reference to the level of analysis, the task-analytic model breaks down larger general tasks into sets of small specific tasks. These latter tasks are significant only insofar as they are directly related to the next higher task. In contrast, the DD-PT model analyzes academic tasks into abilities or processes (e.g., visual memory) that are seen as significant for a wide variety of higher level tasks.

With reference to instructional implications from the two models, the task-analytic approach maintains that a teacher needs only help the child master specific tasks in the hierarchy that have not been mastered. In the DD-PT model the teacher is faced with a far more serious challenge: to remediate or strengthen an entire process. This requires that the teacher demonstrate improvement or "mastery" of a large number of specific tasks, each of which is thought to depend upon or tap that particular process.

As an illustration of the different instructional implications of these models: Suppose that a child encounters difficulty in learning to count objects. A task-analytic teacher may determine that one prerequisite for counting objects is recitation of numerals in order. In contrast, a DD-PT teacher may formulate the same problem more generally as an auditory-sequential memory deficit. While the task-analytic teacher can satisfy the immediate teaching objective by helping the student learn rote counting, the DD-PT teacher, to satisfy the immediate teaching objective, must improve the child's ability to recite lists of spoken events which are arbitrarily ordered (e.g., color names, animal names, articles of clothing, and perhaps numbers). Thus, in the DD-PT model the teacher is viewed as teaching general abilities; in the task-analytic model the teacher is seen as teaching specific components of academic tasks. Clearly, these two models, although they appear to be similar, lead to very different types of instruction. (pp. 518–519)

Arter and Jenkins (1979) then proceed to bring extensive experimental evidence (almost entirely from the area of reading instruction) to bear on an examination of the validity of "several assumptions regarding psychological abilities and their relationship to academic skills, the

measurement of these abilities, and their susceptibility to modification through training" which underlie the DD-PT model (p. 521.) They say:

> In summary, it is not surprising that DD-PT has not improved academic achievement, since most ability assessment devices have inadequate reliability and suspect validity. Moreover, abilities themselves have resisted training, and . . . it is not surprising that modality-instructional matching has failed to improve achievement.
>
> The repeated failure to support the basic assumptions underlying the DD-PT model casts doubt on the model's validity. We do not intend to suggest that the model is theoretically untenable, or that it may not one day be effectively implemented. Rather, we believe that with the current instructional programs and tests, this model is not useful. . . .
>
> We believe that until a substantive research base for the DD-PT model has been developed, it is imperative to call for a moratorium on advocacy of DD-PT, on classification and placement of children according to differential ability tests, on the purchase of instructional materials and programs which claim to improve these abilities, and on coursework designed to train DD-PT teachers. (pp. 549–550)

Tying Loose Ends Together

Johnson (1979) recognizes a distinction that is important but not always easy to determine:

> Distinguishing between learning disabilities and emotional disturbances is sometimes difficult, particularly in those cases where a child has experienced so much long-term frustration and failure as to begin to develop emotional reaction patterns to them. The discriminating basic differences seem to be twofold. First, emotional problems in reaction to learning disabilities do not seem to be of any particular deep-seated or involved types, and seldom if ever are portrayed along classic neurotic-psychotic syndromes. This is not to say that they are never intense, for learning frustrations can be powerful, long-lasting, and permeating to the personality structure. But, such problems tend to be specifically related to the learning context, and thus perhaps generalize to other situations less frequently, less easily, and more obviously than more basic personality difficulties.
>
> Secondly, although the emotional problems which emerge from learning disabilities may yield to a wide range of typical therapeutic strategies, they also are commonly remitted relatively quickly and easily once the learning difficulty itself is alleviated. They are seen, therefore, to be rather clearly related to the failure to accomplish in the learning environment, and as such are a legitimate, fairly predictable reaction to the frustration-failure lowered self-concept experience. Since they are apt to be less basic than more involved personality pattern problems, they tend to be more easily and quickly removed, and often spontaneously remit once the deficit learning behavior is removed.
>
> In some cases, more involved personality deterioration is observed. But most often, this is found to be an interaction of a learning disability and a more

basic personality problem. Had the learning disability not been present, the problem would have emerged using some alternate route. In these cases, treatment must proceed along two lines: (1) removal of the emotional problem behavior, and (2) removal of the learning deficit as well. And, though the two cannot be said to be independent of each other, they are not necessarily parallel problems with removal of one directly affecting or alleviating the other. (pp. 15–16)

Our concern in this chapter is with persons who are in fact socially and emotionally impaired and who very likely are also experiencing learning *difficulties* or learning *problems* in the area of mathematics, regardless of whether such problems or difficulties are associated with learning *disabilities* in the sense in which that term is commonly defined and used today.

The first part of this chapter has suggested a position, a tone of approach as it were, that may guide us in the selection and application of suitable procedures for coping with, and helping individuals cope with, social/emotional impairments. Also, after a person's initial identification as SEI by a "multidisciplinary team" or whatever, teachers may find useful more informal checklists, such as the one reproduced as Table 4.2.

Table 4.2

Teacher-Made Checklist for Measuring Problems in
Social and Emotional Development

Teacher Checklist: This measure was designed to be used by teachers in any classroom to make them more aware of their students' behavior. This list might help identify behavior that otherwise might be overlooked or misunderstood. From here the teacher might want to take frequency counts of identified behavior, or in some other way further analyze the situation.

	Frequently	*Not Frequently*
1. Self-Image		
A. Makes I can't statements		
B. Reacts negatively to correction		
C. Gets frustrated easily		
D. Makes self-critical statements		
E. Integrity: cheats		
tattles		
steals		
destroys property		
F. Makes excessive physical complaints		
G. Takes responsibility for actions		
H. Reacts appropriately to praise		
2. Social Interaction		
A. Seeks attention by acting immaturely: thumbsucking, babytalking, etc.		
B. Interacts negatively		

C. Fails to interact
D. Initiates positive interaction
E. Initiates negative interaction
F. Reacts with anger, verbally
G. Reacts with anger, physically

3. Adult/Teacher Relationships
A. Seeks attention by acting immaturely
B. Excessively demands attention
C. Reacts appropriately to teacher requests
D. Inappropriately reacts to authority figures

4. School-Related Activities
A. Attends to task
B. Exhibits off-task behavior
C. Interferes with the other students' learning
D. Shows flexibility to routine changes

(*Note.* Reprinted from Brown, 1978, pp. 223–224, Fig. 6-3.)

The handling of learning difficulties, of learning problems, may be effected through what Arter and Jenkins (1979) and Crenson (n.d.) identified as task analysis models. Such an approach is evidenced in Figure 4.10, for instance, and is implicit in Figure 4.11. It is extended by Romberg (n.d.) in

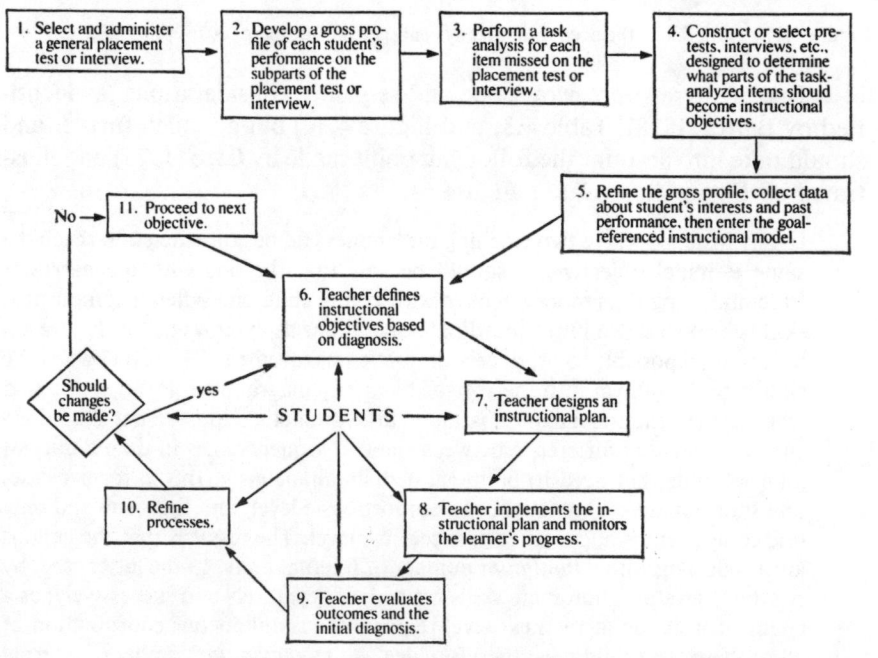

Figure 4.10. A model for goal-referenced diagnosis. (From Trueblood, 1976, p. 122, Fig. 1.)

his discussion of "second level diagnosis," which deals with the problem of discrepancy between observed and expected performances observed in connection with "first level diagnosis."

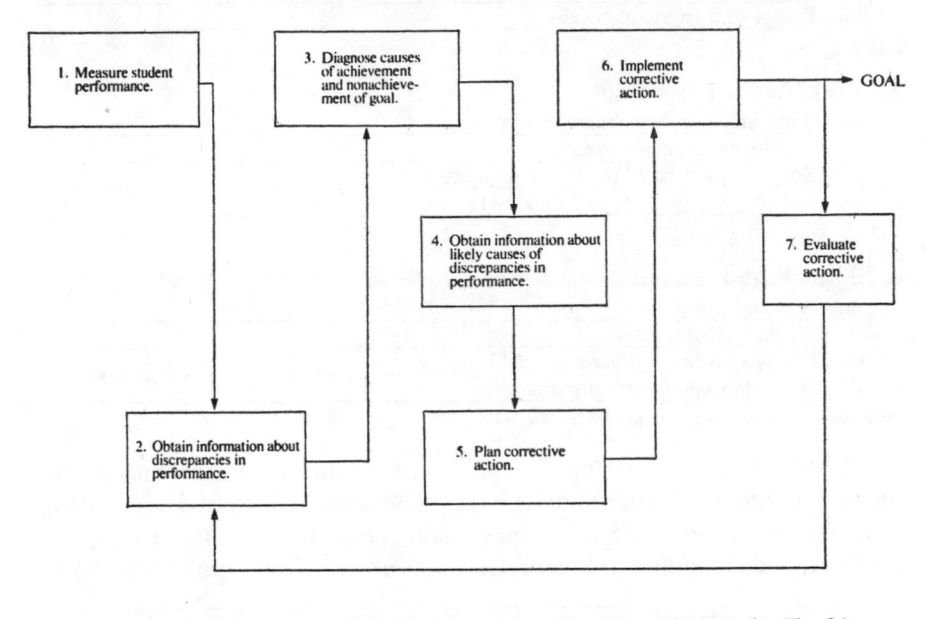

Figure 4.11. A model of the accountability system. (From Romberg, 1976, p. 85, Fig. 2.)

Task analyses *start with* scope-and-sequence considerations (as identified by Bartel (1978), Table 4.3, and Figure 4.12) but go much further and should take into account the following point made by Case (1975) and illustrated by Figure 4.13 (Case's Figure 6):

> In any instance where two teaching hierarchies can be constructed to reach the same terminal objective, it should be true that the one with the narrower "hierarchy span" is more effective with young children. When a complicated skill is broken down into subordinate operations as diagrammed in Figure 6a, it should be possible to produce a dramatic improvement. However, when the skill is broken down into the sort of hierarchy diagrammed in Figure 6b and when each of these is taught separately, little dramatic improvement should occur. The essential difference between the two sequences lies in the number of internal units that need to be integrated simultaneously. In the former case, one subordinate skill is taught at the most basic level, and then one and only one component is added at each successive level. The result is that the child is always dealing with a *minimum* number of internal units. In the latter case, by contrast, several subordinate skills are trained separately and successively; as a result, instruction at the next level requires the simultaneous coordination of all of these. The child must therefore deal with a *maximum* number of internal units in order to effect the required integration. (pp. 75, 77)

Table 4.3
Typical Scope and Sequence of Elementary Mathematics

		K	1	2	3	4	5	6
I.	**Readiness for Mathematics**							
	Classification	•	•	•	•	•	•	•
	One-to-one correspondence	•	•	•	•	•	•	•
	One-to-many correspondence				•	•	•	•
	Seriation or ordering	•	•	•	•	•	•	
	Space and spatial representation	•	•	•	•	•	•	•
	Flexibility and reversibility	•	•	•	•	•	•	•
	Conservation	•	•	•	•	•	•	
II.	**Mathematical Concepts**							
	Same, equal, as much as	•	•	•	•	•	•	•
	More than, greater, greatest, larger, largest	•	•	•	•	•	•	•
	Bigger, biggest, longer, longest	•	•	•	•	•	•	•
	Less than, fewer, fewest, smaller, smallest	•	•	•	•	•	•	•
	Shorter, shortest, most, least	•	•	•	•	•	•	•
	Enough, not enough, more than enough	•	•	•	•	•	•	•
	Left, right		•	•	•	•	•	•
	Above, below, up, down, next to, between		•	•	•	•	•	•
	Putting together, add, plus		•	•	•	•	•	•
	Take apart, take away, subtract, minus		•	•	•	•	•	•
	How many in all? How many are left?	•	•	•	•	•	•	•
	Odd, even			•	•	•	•	•
	Open, closed		•	•	•	•	•	•
	=, □, ©		•	•	•	•	•	•
	Factors, primes, multiples							•
III.	**Sets**							
	Definition	•	•	•	•	•	•	•
	Elements of sets	•	•	•	•	•		•
	Kinds of sets							
	Identical	•	•	•	•	•		•
	Equal and equivalent	•	•	•	•	•	•	•
	Unequal and nonequivalent						•	•
	Empty set				•	•	•	•
	Union of sets (addition)		•	•	•	•	•	•
	Subset (subtraction)	•	•	•			•	•
	Intersection of sets						•	•
IV.	**Whole Numbers**							
	Abstracting idea of cardinal number from equivalent set	•	•	•	•	•	•	•
	Counting: one through ten	•	•	•	•	•	•	•
	Concepts and counting: numbers above ten		•	•	•	•	•	•
	Concept of zero	•	•	•	•	•	•	•
	Skip counting by twos, threes, fives, tens		•	•	•	•	•	•
V.	**Operations on Whole Numbers: Addition and Subtraction**							
	Properties							
	Closure and nonclosure			•	•	•	•	•
	Commutativity and noncommutativity			•	•	•	•	•
	Associativity and nonassociativity			•	•	•	•	•
	Inverse relation of addition and subtraction			•	•	•	•	•
	Ways of conceptualizing							
	Union of sets or forming of subsets		•	•	•	•	•	•
	Number Line		•	•	•	•	•	•
	Addition and subtraction with zero		•	•	•	•	•	•
	Addition and subtraction with horizontal notation		•	•	•	•	•	•
	Addition and subtraction with vertical notation	•	•	•	•	•	•	•
	Addition and subtraction without regrouping							
	One-place numbers	•	•	•	•	•	•	•
	Two-place numbers		•	•	•	•	•	•
	Three-place numbers			•	•	•	•	•

Table 4.3—Continued

	Grade						
	K	1	2	3	4	5	6
Numbers with more than three digits				•	•	•	•
Addition and subtraction with regrouping							
Two-place numbers			•	•	•	•	•
More than two-place numbers				•	•	•	•
Column addition		•	•	•	•	•	•
VI. Operations on Whole Numbers: Multiplication and Division							
Properties							
Commutativity of multiplication			•	•	•	•	•
Associativity of multiplication				•	•	•	•
Distributive property of multiplication and division over addition					•	•	•
Inverse relation of multiplication and division			•	•	•	•	•
Ways of conceptualizing							
Union of sets or partitioning into equivalent sets		•	•	•	•	•	
Repeated addition or successive subtraction		•	•	•	•	•	•
Arrays		•	•	•	•	•	
Number line			•	•	•	•	
Multiplication and division with horizontal notation		•	•	•	•	•	
Multiplication and division with vertical notation		•	•	•	•	•	
Use of zero in multiplication and division		•	•	•	•	•	
"One" as the identity element		•	•	•	•	•	
Multiplication and division with 10's, 100's, etc.				•	•	•	•
Computation without regrouping							
One-place factor or divisor, one-place sums, dividend			•	•	•	•	•
One-place factor or divisor, two-place sums or dividends			•	•	•	•	•
Computation with regrouping							
One-place factor or divisor, two- or three-place sums or dividends				•	•	•	•
Two-place factors or divisors, any number sums or dividends					•	•	•
Three- or four-place factors or divisors							•
Multiple multiplication				•	•	•	•
VII. Fractions							
Definition		•	•	•	•	•	•
Ways of conceptualizing							
Number line				•	•	•	•
Arrays or subsets				•	•	•	•
Geometric figures		•	•	•	•	•	•
Computation							
Addition and subtraction of simple fractions with common denominators				•	•	•	•
Addition and subtraction of simple fractions with mixed denominators					•	•	•
Addition and subtraction of mixed fractions with common denominators				•	•	•	•
Addition and subtraction of mixed fractions with mixed denominators					•	•	•
Multiplication and division							•
Decimal fractions							•
VIII. Measurement							
Measurement of length (inch, foot, yard, mile, metric)		•	•	•	•		•
Measurement of area (English and metric units)						•	•
Measurement of weight (ounce, pound, ton, metric units)					•	•	•
Measurement of liquids (cup, pint, quart, metric units)	•	•	•	•	•	•	•
Dry measures (quart, peck, bushel, metric units)				•	•	•	•
Measurement of quantity (dozen, gross)				•	•	•	•
Measurement of temperature (Fahrenheit, Celsius)				•	•	•	•

Table 4.3—Continued

		Grade						
		K	1	2	3	4	5	6
	Measurement of time (clock, calendar)	•	•	•	•	•	•	•
	Measure of money (coins, paper bills)		•	•	•	•	•	•
IX.	*Geometry*							
	Geometric shapes (circle, square, rectangle, triangle)	•	•	•	•	•	•	•
	Geometric shapes (pentagon, hexagon, octagon, parallelogram)				•	•	•	•
	Spatial relationships	•	•	•	•	•	•	•
	Point, line, line segment, ray, intersection					•	•	•
	Parallel line, curved line, straight line						•	•
	Radius, diameter					•	•	•
	Angles, arc degrees							•
	Closed-line plane, open-line plane						•	•
	Area and perimeter						•	•
	Three-dimensional shapes (sphere, cube, cone)						•	•

(*Note.* From Bartel, 1978, pp. 110–113, Table 3-4.)

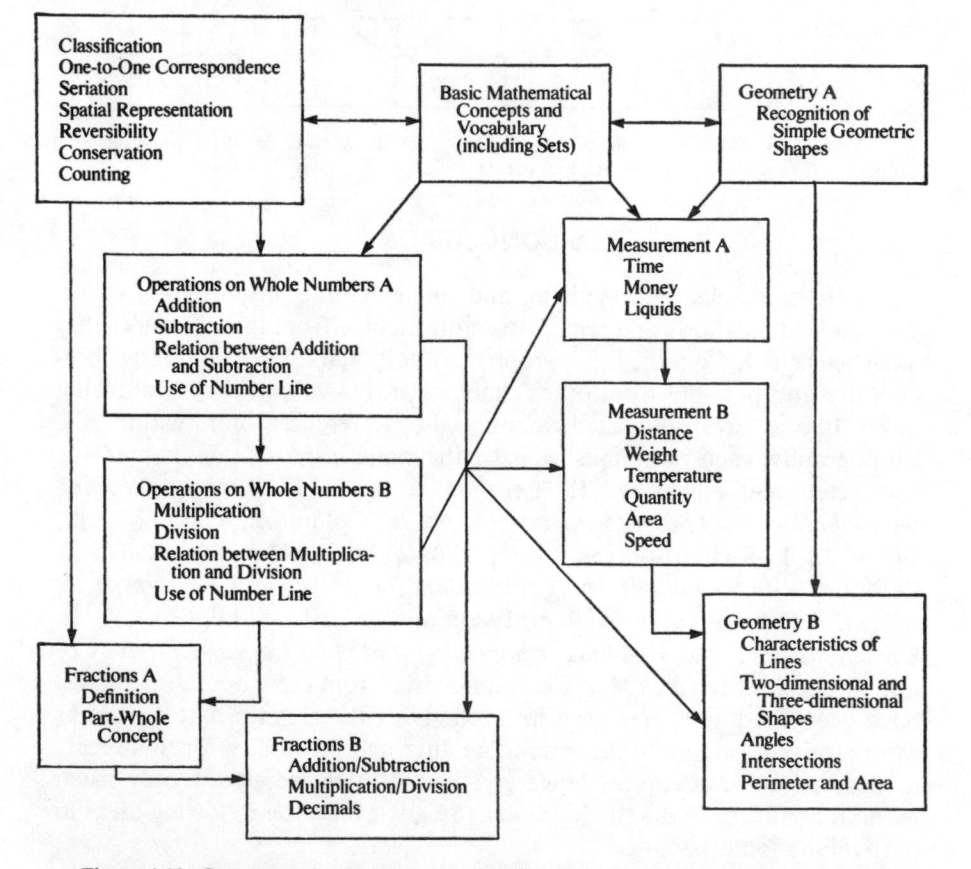

Figure 4.12. Summary of scope and sequence in typical elementary mathematics. Scope-and-sequence analyses similar to Table 4.3 and Figure 4.12 can be developed, of course, for postelementary mathematics programs. (From Bartel, 1978, p. 114, Fig. 3-2.)

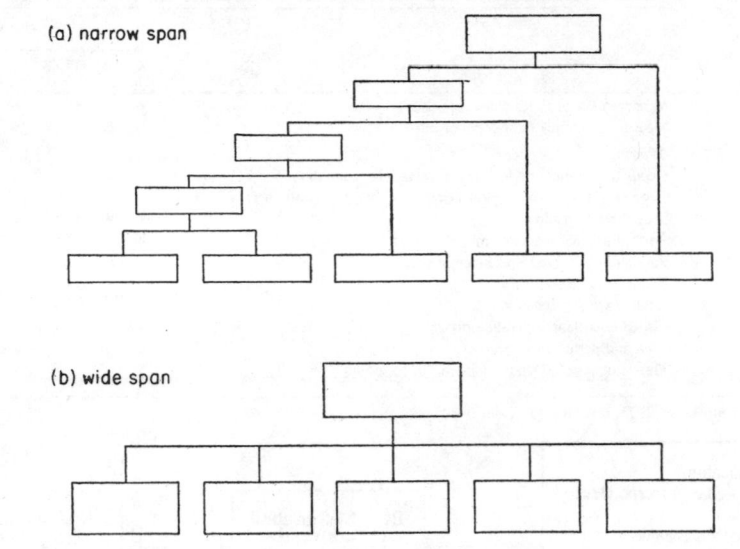

Figure 4.13. Different forms of teaching hierarchy designed to reach the same terminal objective. (From Case, 1975, p. 76, Fig. 6.)

IN CONCLUSION

Further details of organizing and implementing any program of individualized diagnosis and remediation must come from the references that have been cited, from the Bibliography of additional references listed subsequently, and possibly from other chapters in this volume. (The following three books are *not* listed among the References nor within the Bibliography; each was published *after* the manuscript for this chapter was completed and edited: F. K. Reisman & S. H. Kauffman, *Teaching mathematics to children with special needs* [Columbus, Ohio: Merrill, 1980]; L. I. Richardson, K. L. Goodman, N. N. Hartman, & H. C. LePique, *A mathematics activity curriculum for early childhood and special education* [New York: Macmillan, 1980]; and R. G. Underhill (Ed.), A. E. Uprichard, & J. W. Heddens, *Diagnosing mathematical difficulties* [Columbus, Ohio: Merrill, 1980]. Certain material from these books might well have been cited and referenced in the body of the chapter, but the books were received too late to accommodate any such possibility. Each appears to deserve more attention, however, than it might receive if only listed without comment in the Bibliography.) In any event, the following ideas in particular should be noted:

1. The diagnosis-remediation plan necessitates diversity and variety—in assessment procedures as well as in all facets of the instructional process.

2. Although a task-analytic model has been suggested, this does not exclude from consideration certain information commonly associated with perceptually oriented models—information that will be used in a different way from a different frame of reference.

3. We must avoid unwarranted generalizations across SEI individuals. Consider, for instance, Copeland's (1976) assertions:

> Emphasis in the development of mathematical skills must be on the functional. Many of these children are struggling for emotional or social survival and are concerned with those things that are useful to them. They should be taught math skills which have immediate use and, as such, motivational value.
>
> For children significantly below grade level, particular care must be taken in the selection of materials. Children get bored with material they have seen over and over again, and older children resent material they consider to be babyish. For these reasons, it is sometimes helpful to introduce completely new materials that do not have the connotation of failure and to which the child does not relate as being chronologically beneath him. Math instruction incorporated in core curriculum or unit activities is useful with these children. (p. 213)

It was indicated clearly in the first part of this chapter that the "functional" curriculum is not necessarily motivating for all SEI subclasses and that "core curriculum" or "unit activities" is not necessarily the organizational pattern to use with all SEI individuals. ("Unit activities," if used, must be correlated with a task-analytic model.)

4. Finally, let us not shortchange SEI children and youth by interpreting their mathematics programs *too narrowly* in terms of an unfortunate myopic interpretation of "basic skills." Our planning of mathematics programs should be done *in full cognizance of* a more enlightened interpretation of what is "basic," such as that taken by the National Council of Supervisors of Mathematics (1978) in its position paper on basic mathematical skills, sections of which are reprinted below, coupled with a recognition of the limitations (if any) that may be placed on SEI individuals owing to an interaction with other exceptionalities.

INTRODUCTION

The currently popular slogan "Back to the Basics" has become a rallying cry of many who perceive a need for certain changes in education. The result is a trend that has gained considerable momentum and has initiated demands for programs and evaluations which emphasize narrowly defined skills.

Mathematics educators find themselves under considerable pressure from boards of education, legislatures, and citizens' groups who are demanding instructional programs which will guarantee acquisition of computational skills. Leaders in

mathematics education have expressed a need for clarifying what are the basic skills needed by students who hope to participate successfully in adult society.

The narrow definition of basic skills which equates mathematical competence with computational ability has evolved as a result of several forces:

1. Declining scores on standardized achievement tests and college entrance examinations;
2. Reactions to the results of the National Assessment of Educational Progress;
3. Rising costs of education and increasing demands for accountability;
4. Shifting emphasis in mathematics education from curriculum content to instructional methods and alternatives;
5. Increased awareness of the need to provide remedial and compensatory programs;
6. The widespread publicity given to each of the above by the media.

This widespread publicity, in particular, has generated a call for action from governmental agencies, educational organizations, and community groups. In responding to these calls, the National Institute of Education adopted the area of basic skills as a major priority. This resulted in a Conference on Basic Mathematical Skills and Learning, held in Euclid, Ohio, in October, 1975.

The National Council of Supervisors of Mathematics (NCSM), during the 1976 Annual Meeting in Atlanta, Georgia, met in a special session to discuss the Euclid Conference Report. More than 100 members participating in that session expressed the need for a unified position on basic mathematical skills which would enable them to provide more effective leadership within their respective school systems, to give adequate rationale and direction in their tasks of implementing basic mathematics programs, and to appropriately expand the definition of basic skills. Hence, by an overwhelming majority, they mandated the NCSM to establish a task force to formulate a position on basic mathematical skills. This statement is the result of that effort.

RATIONALE FOR THE EXPANDED DEFINITION

There are many reasons why basic skills must include more than computation. The present technological society requires daily use of such skills as estimating, problem solving, interpreting data, organizing data, measuring, predicting, and applying mathematics to everyday situations. The changing needs of society, the explosion of the amount of quantitative data, and the availability of computers and calculators demand a redefining of the priorities for basic mathematics skills. In recognition of the inadequacy of computation alone, NCSM is going on record as providing both a general list of basic mathematical skills and a clarification of the need for such an expanded definition of basic skills.

Any list of basic skills must include computation. However, the role of computational skills in mathematics must be seen in the light of the contributions they make to one's ability to use mathematics in everyday living. In isolation, computational skills contribute little to one's ability to participate in mainstream society.

Combined effectively with the other skill areas, they provide the learner with the basic mathematical ability needed by adults.

DEFINING BASIC SKILLS

The NCSM views basic mathematical skills as falling under ten vital areas. The ten skill areas are interrelated and many overlap with each other and with other disciplines. All are basic to pupils' development of the ability to reason effectively in varied situations.

This expanded list is presented with the conviction that mathematics education must not emphasize computational skills to the neglect of other critical areas of mathematics. The ten components of basic mathematical skills are listed below, but the order of their listing should not be interpreted as indicating either a priority of importance or a sequence for teaching and learning.

Furthermore, as society changes our ideas about which skills are basic also change. For example, today our students should learn to measure in both the customary and metric systems, but in the future the significance of the customary system will be mostly historical. There will also be increasing emphasis on when and how to use hand-held calculators and other electronic devices in mathematics.

BASIC SKILLS AND THE STUDENT'S FUTURE

Anyone adopting a definition of basic skills should consider the "door-opening/door-closing" implications of the list. The following diagram illustrates expected outcomes associated with various amounts of skill development.

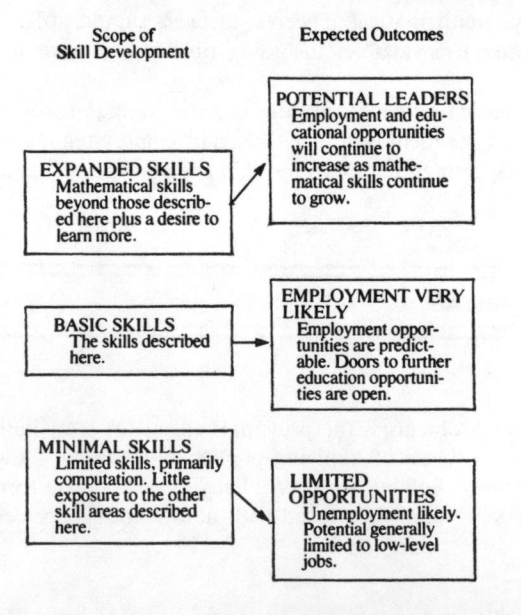

MINIMUM ESSENTIALS FOR HIGH-SCHOOL GRADUATION

Today some school boards and state legislatures are starting to mandate mastery of minimum essential skills in reading and mathematics as a requirement for high-school graduation. In the process, they should consider the potential pitfalls of doing this without an appropriate definition of "basic skills." If the mathematics requirements are set inordinately high, then a significant number of students may not be able to graduate. On the other hand, if the mathematics requirements are set too low and mathematical skills are too narrowly defined, the result could be a sterile mathematics program concentrating exclusively on learning of low-level mathematical skills. This position paper neither recommends nor condemns minimal competencies for high-school graduation. However, the ten components of basic skills stated here can serve as guidelines for state and local school systems that are considering the establishment of minimum essential graduation requirements.

DEVELOPING THE BASIC SKILLS

One individual difference among students is style or way of learning. In offering opportunities to learn the basic skills, options must be provided to meet these varying learning styles. The present "back-to-basics" movement may lead to an emphasis on drill and practice as a way to learn.

Certainly drill and practice is a viable option, but it is only one of many possible ways to bring about learning and to create interest and motivation in students. Learning centers, contracts, tutorial sessions, individual and small-group projects, games, simulations and community-based activities are some of the other options that can provide the opportunity to learn basic skills. Furthermore, to help students fully understand basic mathematical concepts, teachers should utilize the full range of activities and materials available, including objects the students can actually handle.

The learning of basic mathematical skills is a continuing process which extends through all of the years a student is in school. In particular, a tendency to emphasize computation while neglecting the other nine skill areas at the elementary level must be avoided.

TEN BASIC SKILL AREAS

Problem Solving

Learning to solve problems is the principal reason for studying mathematics. Problem solving is the process of applying previously acquired knowledge to new and unfamiliar situations. Solving word problems in texts is one form of problem solving, but students also should be faced with non-textbook problems. Problem-

solving strategies involve posing questions, analyzing situations, translating results, illustrating results, drawing diagrams, and using trial and error. In solving problems, students need to be able to apply the rules of logic necessary to arrive at valid conclusions. They must be able to determine which facts are relevant. They should be unfearful of arriving at tentative conclusions and they must be willing to subject these conclusions to scrutiny.

Applying Mathematics to Everyday Situations

The use of mathematics is interrelated with all computation activities. Students should be encouraged to take everyday situations, translate them into mathematical expressions, solve the mathematics, and interpret the results in light of the initial situation.

Alertness to the Reasonableness of Results

Due to arithmetic errors or other mistakes, results of mathematical work are sometimes wrong. Students should learn to inspect all results and to check for reasonableness in terms of the original problem. With the increase in the use of calculating devices in society, this skill is essential.

Estimation and Approximation

Students should be able to carry out rapid approximate calculations by first rounding off numbers. They should acquire some simple techniques for estimating quantity, length, distance, weight, etc. It is also necessary to decide when a particular result is precise enough for the purpose at hand.

Appropriate Computational Skills

Students should gain facility with addition, subtraction, multiplication, and division with whole numbers and decimals. Today it must be recognized that long, complicated computations will usually be done with a calculator. Knowledge of single-digit number facts is essential and mental arithmetic is a valuable skill. Moreover, there are everyday situations which demand recognition of, and simple computation with, common fractions.

Because consumers continually deal with many situations that involve percentage, the ability to recognize and use percents should be developed and maintained.

Geometry

Students should learn the geometric concepts they will need to function effectively in the 3-dimensional world. They should have knowledge of concepts such as point, line, plane, parallel, and perpendicular. They should know basic properties of simple geometric figures, particularly those properties which relate to measurement and problem-solving skills. They also must be able to recognize similarities and differences among objects.

Measurement

As a minimum skill, students should be able to measure distance, weight, time, capacity, and temperature. Measurement of angles and calculations of simple areas

and volumes are also essential. Students should be able to perform measurement in both metric and customary systems using the appropriate tools.

Reading, Interpreting, and Constructing Tables, Charts, and Graphs

Students should know how to read and draw conclusions from simple tables, maps, charts, and graphs. They should be able to condense numerical information into more manageable or meaningful terms by setting up simple tables, charts, and graphs.

Using Mathematics to Predict

Students should learn how elementary notions of probability are used to determine the likelihood of future events. They should learn to identify situations where immediate past experience does not affect the likelihood of future events. They should become familiar with how mathematics is used to help make predictions such as election forecasts.

Computer Literacy

It is important for all citizens to understand what computers can and cannot do. Students should be aware of the many uses of computers in society, such as their use in teaching/learning, financial transactions, and information storage and retrieval. The "mystique" surrounding computers is disturbing and can put persons with no understanding of computers at a disadvantage. The increasing use of computers by government, industry, and business demands an awareness of computer uses and limitations.

REFERENCES

Arter, J. A., & Jenkins, J. R. Differential diagnosis–prescriptive teaching: A critical appraisal. *Review of Educational Research,* 1979, *49,* 517–555.

Balow, B. The emotionally and socially handicapped. *Review of Educational Research*, 1966, *36*, 120–133.

Bartel, N. R. Problems in mathematics achievement. In D. D. Hammill & N. R. Bartel (Eds.), *Teaching children with learning and behavior problems* (2nd ed.). Boston: Allyn & Bacon, 1978.

Baum, D. D. A comparison of the WRAT and the PIAT with learning disability children. *Educational and Psychological Measurement,* 1975, *35,* 487–493.

Brekke, B., & Williams, J. Conservation of weight with the mentally retarded. *Journal of Genetic Psychology*, 1974, *125*, 225–231.

Brekke, B., & Williams, J. D. Conservation of weight with the emotionally disturbed. *Journal of Educational Research*, 1975, *69*, 117–119.

Brown, L. L. Teaching strategies for managing classroom behaviors. In D. D. Hammill & N. R. Bartel (Eds.), *Teaching children with learning and behavior problems* (2nd ed.). Boston: Allyn & Bacon, 1978.

Callahan, L. G., & Glennon, V. J. *Elementary school mathematics: A guide to current research* (4th ed.). Washington, D.C.: Association for Supervision and Curriculum Development, 1975.

Case, R. Gearing the demands of instruction to the developmental capacities of the learner. *Review of Educational Research*, 1975, *45*, 59–87.

Clary, S. *Diagnosis and prescription for L.D. problems of E.D. adolescents within a residen-*

tial treatment center. Paper presented at the International Federation of Learning Disabilities, Brussels, Belgium, January 1975. (EDRS No. ED 126 627)

Copeland, R. W. *Mathematics and the elementary teacher* (3rd ed.). Philadelphia: Saunders, 1976.

Copeland, R. W. *Math activities for children: A diagnostic and developmental approach.* Columbus, Ohio: Merrill, 1979.

Council for Exceptional Children. *Emotionally disturbed—Teaching methods and programs: 1977 topical bibliography* (Exceptional Child Education Resources Topical Bibliography Series, No. 704). Reston, Va.: CEC ERIC Clearinghouse, n.d.

Council for Exceptional Children. *Emotionally disturbed—Teaching methods and programs: 1978 topical bibliography* (Exceptional Child Education Resources Topical Bibliography Series, No. 804). Reston, Va.: CEC ERIC Clearinghouse, n.d.

Council for Exceptional Children. *Emotionally disturbed—Teaching methods and programs: 1979 topical bibliography* (Exceptional Child Education Resources Topical Bibliography Series, No. 904). Reston, Va.: CEC ERIC Clearinghouse, n.d.

Crenson, J. Modality: Importance to diagnosis and prescription. In T. Denmark (Ed.), *Issues for consideration by mathematics educators* (Selected papers presented at the fourth and fifth RCDPM annual conferences). Research Council on Diagnostic and Prescriptive Mathematics, n.d.

Curtis, R. C. *Improving instruction and services in schools for socially maladjusted, emotionally disturbed children: Evaluation period, school year 1975–1976*. New York: Board of Education of the City of New York, Office of Educational Evaluation, n.d. (EDRS No. ED 142 653).

Farrald, R. R., Gonzales, F. M., & Masters, B. F. *A diagnostic and prescriptive technique (ADAPT), Handbook II—Disabilities in arithmetic and mathematics: Approaches to diagnosis and treatment*. Sioux Falls, S. Dak.: ADAPT Press, 1979.

Feldhusen, J., Thurston, J., & Benning, J. Aggressive classroom behavior and school achievement. *Journal of Special Education,* 1970, *4,* 431–439.

Filer, A. A. Piagetian cognitive development in normal and in emotionally disturbed children (Doctoral dissertation, University of Rochester, 1972). *Dissertation Abstracts International,* 1972, *33,* 2342B. (University Microfilms No. 72-28,749).

Fontana-Durso, B. The effects of behavior modification on locus of control, self-concept, reading achievement, math achievement, and behavior in second grade children (Doctoral dissertation, St. John's University, 1975). *Dissertation Abstracts International,* 1976, *36,* 4187B–4188B. (University Microfilms No. 76-2984)

Friedman, P. C. The effects of teacher vs. pupil applied reinforcement of arithmetic response rates in upper elementary behavior disordered and regular class children (Doctoral dissertation, University of New Mexico, 1976). *Dissertation Abstracts International,* 1977, *38,* 725A. (University Microfilms No. 77-16,097)

Gajar, A. H. Characteristics and classification of educable mentally retarded, learning disabled and emotionally disturbed students (Doctoral dissertation, University of Virginia, 1977). *Dissertation Abstracts International,* 1978, *38,* 4090A–4091A. (University Microfilms No. 77-28,644)

Gardner, W. I. *Learning and behavior characteristics of exceptional children and youth: A humanistic behavioral approach*. Boston: Allyn & Bacon, 1977.

Gardner, W. I. *Children with learning and behavior problems: A behavior management approach* (2nd ed.). Boston: Allyn & Bacon, 1978.

Glavin, J. Followup behavioral research in resource rooms. *Exceptional Children,* 1973, *40,* 211–213.

Glavin, J., & Annesley, F. Reading and arithmetic correlates of conduct—Problem and withdrawn children. *Journal of Special Education,* 1971, *5,* 213–219.

Glavin, J. P., & Quay, H. C. Behavior disorders. *Review of Educational Research,* 1969, *39,* 83–102.

Glavin, J., Quay, H., & Werry, J. Behavioral and academic gains of conduct problem children in different classroom settings. *Exceptional Children*, 1971, *37*, 441–446.

Glennon, V. J., & Callahan, L. G. *Elementary school mathematics: A guide to current research* (3rd ed.). Washington, D.C.: Association for Supervision and Curriculum Development, 1968.

Gottlieb, J. *Transitional classes program: School year 1975–1976*. New York: Board of Education of the City of New York, Office of Educational Evaluation, n.d. (EDRS No. ED 136 465)

Griggs, S. A. An experimental program for corrective mathematics in schools for the socially malajusted [*sic*] and emotionally disturbed. *School Science and Mathematics,* 1976, *76,* 377–380.

Graubard, P. S. Extent of academic retardation in a residential treatment center. *Journal of Educational Research*, 1964, *58*, 78–80.

Hallahan, D. P., & Kauffman, J. M. *Introduction to learning disabilities: A psycho-behavioral approach*. Englewood Cliffs, N.J.: Prentice-Hall, 1976.

Hallahan, D. P., & Kauffman, J. M. Categories, labels, behavorial characteristics: ED, LD, and EMR reconsidered. *Journal of Special Education*, 1977, *11*, 139–149.

Hallahan, D. P., & Kauffman, J. M. *Exceptional children: Introduction to special education*. Englewood Cliffs, N.J.: Prentice-Hall, 1978.

Hammill, D. D., & Bartel, N. R. (Eds.). *Teaching children with learning and behavior problems* (2nd ed.). Boston: Allyn & Bacon, 1978.

Heil, E. S. Correlational study of the Wide Range Achievement Test, Peabody Individual Achievement Test, and the Key Math Diagnostic Arithmetic Test with learning disabled children with a modality deficit (Doctoral dissertation, Texas Woman's University, 1977). *Dissertation Abstracts International*, 1978, *38*, 5394A. (University Microfilms No. 7801760)

Hicks, J. S. *Individualized instructional program for emotionally disturbed children unable to participate in formal educational programs (Title VI): School year 1974–1975*. New York: Board of Education of the City of New York, Office of Educational Evaluation, n.d. (EDRS No. ED 136 464)

Hopkins, M. H. The diagnosis of learning styles in arithmetic. *Arithmetic Teacher,* 1978, *25*(7), 47–50.

Howell, R. W. Evaluation of cognitive abilities of emotionally disturbed children: An application of Piaget's theories (Doctoral dissertation, Southern Illinois University, 1971). *Dissertation Abstracts International*, 1972, *32*, 5037A–5038A. (University Microfilms No. 72-10,259)

Hundert, J., Bucher, B., & Henderson, M. Increasing appropriate classroom behavior and academic performance by reinforcing correct work alone. *Psychology in the Schools*, 1976, *13*, 195–200.

Jepsen, M. L. Comparison of conservation performance of normal and institutionalized emotionally disturbed children (Doctoral dissertation, University of Oklahoma, 1975). *Dissertation Abstracts International*, 1975, *36*, 2134A. (University Microfilms No. 75-21,806)

Johnson, S. W. *Arithmetic and learning disabilities: Guidelines for identification and remediation*. Boston: Allyn & Bacon, 1979.

Kauffman, J. M. Behavior modification. In W. M. Cruickshank & D. P. Hallahan (Eds.), *Perceptual and learning disabilities in children: Research and theory* (Vol. 2). Syracuse, N.Y.: Syracuse University Press, 1975.

Kauffman, J. M. *Characteristics of children's behavior disorders*. Columbus, Ohio: Merrill, 1977.

Kauffman, J. M., & Lewis, C. D. (Eds.). *Teaching children with behavior disorders: Personal perspectives*. Columbus, Ohio: Merrill, 1974.

Kennedy, J., Mitchell, J. B., Klerman, L. V., & Murray, A. A day school approach to aggressive adolescents. *Child Welfare*, 1976, *55*, 712–724.

Kratochwill, T. R., & Demuth, D. M. An examination of the predictive validity of the Key

Math Diagnostic Arithmetic Test and the Wide Range Achievement Test in exceptional children. *Psychology in the Schools*, 1976, *13*, 404–406.

Kvaraceus, W. C., & Blatt, B. Selected references from the literature on exceptional children. *Elementary School Journal*, 1964, *64*, 341–347.

Kvaraceus, W. C., & Blatt, B. Selected references from the lite rature on exceptional children. *Elementary School Journal*, 1965, *65*, 222–228.

Kvaraceus, W. C., & McInnis, I. M. Selected references from the literature on exceptional children. *Elementary School Journal*, 1963, *63*, 351–355.

Leitenberg, H. (Ed.). *Handbook of behavior modification and behavior therapy*. Englewood Cliffs, N.J.: Prentice-Hall, 1976.

Long, N. J., Morse, W. C., & Newman, R. G. *Conflict in the classroom: The education of children with problems* (4th ed.). Belmont, Calif.: Wadsworth, 1980.

Moos, R. H. *Evaluating educational environment*. San Francisco: Jossey-Bass, 1979.

Morse, W. C. The education of socially maladjusted and emotionally disturbed children. In W. M. Cruickshank & G. O. Johnson (Eds.), *Education of exceptional children and youth* (3rd ed.). Englewood Cliffs, N.J.: Prentice-Hall, 1975.

Morse, W. C. Serving the needs of individuals with behavior disorders (Editor's interview with W. C. Morse). *Exceptional Children*, 1977, *44*, 158–164.

Murry, M. D. The relationship of classroom behavior to academic achievement and aptitude (Doctoral dissertation, University of Tennessee, 1977). *Dissertation Abstracts International*, 1978, *38*, 7156A. (University Microfilms No. 7807711)

National Council of Supervisors of Mathematics. Position paper on basic mathematical skills. *Mathematics Teacher*, 1978, *71*, 147–152.

O'Leary, S. G., & Schneider, M. R. Special class placement for conduct problem children. *Exceptional Children*, 1977, *44*, 24–30.

Page, D. P., & Edwards, R. P. Behavior change strategies for reducing disruptive classroom behavior. *Psychology in the Schools*, 1978, *15*, 413–418.

Paluszny, M. J. *Autism: A practical guide for parents and professionals*. Syracuse, N.Y.: Syracuse University Press, 1979.

Pappanikou, A. J., & Paul, J. L. *Mainstreaming emotionally disturbed children*. Syracuse, N.Y.: Syracuse University Press, 1977.

Phillips, G. D. An investigation of predicted differences in the acquisition of formal operational thought between normal and institutionalized emotionally disturbed adolescents (Doctoral dissertation, University of Oklahoma, 1976). *Dissertation Abstracts International*, 1977, *37*, 6344B. (University Microfilms No. 77-12,756)

Pile, S. Using CB lingo to develop communication skills. *Teaching Exceptional Children*, 1977, *9*, 110–111.

Reisman, F. K. *A guide to the diagnostic teaching of arithmetic* (2nd ed.). Columbus, Ohio: Merrill, 1978.

Rhodes, W. C., & Tracy, M. L. (Eds.). *A study of child variance* (Vols. 1–5). Ann Arbor: University of Michigan Press, 1972–1976.

Rhodes, W. C., & Paul, J. L. *Emotionally disturbed and deviant children: New views and approaches*. Englewood Cliffs, N.J.: Prentice-Hall, 1978.

Romberg, T. A. The diagnostic process in mathematics instruction. In J. L. Higgins & J. W. Heddens (Eds.), *Remedial mathematics: Diagnostic and prescriptive approaches* (Papers from the First National Conference on Remedial Mathematics). Columbus, Ohio: ERIC Center for Science, Mathematics, and Environmental Education, 1976.

Romberg, T. A. Second-level diagnosis: Assessing underlying processes, not just objectives. In T. Denmark (Ed.), *Issues for consideration by mathematics educators* (Selected papers presented at the fourth and fifth RCDPM annual conferences). Research Council on Diagnostic and Prescriptive Mathematics, n.d

Romeo, D. J. The effectiveness of the directive teaching method and a data retrieval system on

the arithmetic achievement scores of emotionally disturbed children (Doctoral dissertation, University of Pittsburgh, 1975). *Dissertation Abstracts International*, 1975, *36*, 222A–223A. (University Microfilms No. 75-5152)

Ross, J. M. The effect of a free-time contingency on arithmetic and problem behavior in the classroom (Doctoral dissertation, North Texas State University, 1976). *Dissertation Abstracts International*, 1976, *37*, 3093B. (University Microfilms No. 76-29,166)

Schroeder, L. B. Study of the relationship between 5 descriptive categories of emotional disturbance and reading and arithmetic achievement. *Exceptional Children*, 1965, *32*, 111–112.

Schwartz, L. J. *Transitional classes program: School year 1974–1975*. New York: Board of Education of the City of New York, Office of Educational Evaluation, n.d. (EDRS No. ED 139 896)

Simmons, J. B. Effects on school work productivity among emotionally disturbed boys with the removal of a level system from a token economy (Doctoral dissertation, University of Utah, 1976). *Dissertation Abstracts International*, 1977, *37*, 6409A–6410A. (University Microfilms No. 77-7405)

Sternberg, B. J. Will tokens and trophies teach mathematics? *Arithmetic Teacher*, 1976, *23*, 456–459.

Stone, F., & Rowley, V. Educational disability in emotionally disturbed children. *Exceptional Children*, 1964, *30*, 423–426.

Tamkin, A. A survey of educational disability in emotionally disturbed children. *Journal of Educational Research*, 1960, *53*, 313–315.

Tashjian, K. S. Differences among categories of exceptional pupils in mastery of mathematics behavioral skills as measured by criterion-referenced tests (Doctoral dissertation, University of Southern California, 1976). *Dissertation Abstracts International*, 1977, *37*, 5751A.

Thoresen, C. E. (Ed.) *Behavior modification in education* (72nd Yearbook, Pt. 1). Chicago: National Society for the Study of Education, 1973.

Trueblood, C. R. Reaction paper [to] Remediation of learning difficulties in school mathematics: Promising procedures and directions. In J. L. Higgins & J. W. Heddens (Eds.), *Remedial mathematics: Diagnostic and prescriptive approaches* (Papers from the First National Conference on Remedial Mathematics). Columbus, Ohio: ERIC Center for Science, Mathematics, and Environmental Education, December 1976.

Walker, H. M., & Hops, H. Increasing academic achievement by reinforcing direct academic performance and/or facilitative nonacademic responses. *Journal of Educational Psychology*, 1976, *68*, 218–225.

Wang, M. C., Resnick, L. B., & Boozer, R. F. The sequence of development of some early mathematics behaviors. *Child Development*, 1971, *42*, 1767–1778.

Webster, R. E., & Schenk, S. J. Diagnostic test pattern differences among LD, ED, EMH, and multi-handicapped students. *Journal of Educational Research*, 1978, *72*, 75–80.

BIBLIOGRAPHY

(Additional references for further reading)

Ardi, D. B. The relationship of functional academic achievement to the clinical categories of brain injury and emotional disturbance (Doctoral dissertation, Boston College, 1978). *Dissertation Abstracts International*, 1978, *39*, 806A. (University Microfilms No. 7813771)

Arena, J. *How to write an I. E. P.* Novato, Calif.: Academic Therapy Publications, 1978.

Ashlock, R. B. *Error patterns in computation: A semi-programmed approach* (2nd ed.). Columbus, Ohio: Merrill, 1976.

Backman, C. A. Analyzing children's work procedures. In M. N. Suydam (Ed.), *Developing computational skills* (1978 Yearbook). Reston, Va.: National Council of Teachers of Mathematics, 1978.

Brown, V. Learning about mathematics instruction. *Journal of Learning Disabilities*, 1975, *8*, 476–485.

Cawley, J. F., & Vitello, S. J. Model for arithmetical programming for handicapped children. *Exceptional Child*, 1972, *39*, 101–110.

Coble, C. R., Hounshell, P. B., & Adams, A. H. *Mainstreaming science and mathematics: Special ideas and activities for the whole class.* Santa Monica, Calif.: Goodyear, 1977.

Cox, L. S. Systematic errors in the four vertical algorithms in normal and handicapped populations. *Journal for Research in Mathematics Education*, 1975, *6*, 202–220.

Flinter, P. F. Educational implications of dyscalculia. *Arithmetic Teacher*, 1979, *26*(7), 42–46.

Focus on Learning Problems in Mathematics. Published quarterly by the Center for Teaching/Learning Mathematics, Framingham, Mass.

Glennon, V. J., & Wilson, J. W. Diagnostic-prescriptive teaching. In W. C. Lowry (Ed.), *The slow learner in mathematics* (35th Yearbook). Reston, Va.: National Council of Teachers of Mathematics, 1972.

Guyer, B. L., & Friedman, M. P. Hemispheric processing and cognitive styles in learning-disabled and normal children. *Child Development*, 1975, *46*, 658–668.

Harmer, W. R., & Williams, F. The Wide Range Achievement Test and the Peabody Individual Achievement Test. *Journal of Learning Disabilities*, 1978, *11*, 667–670.

Hynes, M. C. (Ed.). *An annotated bibliography of periodical articles relating to the diagnostic and prescriptive instruction of mathematics.* Research Council for Diagnostic and Prescriptive Mathematics, 1979.

Hynes, M. E. (Ed.). *Topics related to diagnosis in mathematics for classroom teachers* (Selected papers presented at the fourth and fifth annual diagnostic and prescriptive mathematics conferences). Research Council for Diagnostic and Prescriptive Mathematics, n.d.

Inskeep, J. E., Jr. Diagnosing computational difficulty in the classroom. In M. N. Suydam (Ed.), *Developing computational skills* (1978 Yearbook). Reston, Va.: National Council of Teachers of Mathematics, 1978.

Magne, O. The psychology of remedial mathematics. *Didakometry* (Malmo, Sweden, School of Education), No. 59, February 1978.

Mauser, A. J. *Assessing the learning disabled: Selected instruments* (2nd ed.). Novato, Calif.: Academic Therapy Publications, 1977.

McSpadden, J. V., & Strain, P. S. Memory thresholds and overload effects between learning disabled and achieving pupils. *Exceptional Children*, 1977, *44*, 35–37.

Merrill Area Public Schools. *Emotionally disturbed program.* Merrill, Wis.: Merrill Area Public School District, 1974. (EDRS No. ED 116 389)

Moroz, S. W. Mathematical problem solving ability in learning disabled children as a function of memory capacity and memory organization (Doctoral dissertation, Rutgers University The State University of New Jersey, New Brunswick, 1978). *Dissertation Abstracts International*, 1978, *39*, 2871A. (University Microfilms No. 7820336)

Moyer, J. C., & Moyer, M. B. Computation: Implications for learning disabled children. In M. N. Suydam (Ed.), *Developing computational skills* (1978 Yearbook). Reston, Va.: National Council of Teachers of Mathematics, 1978.

Myers, A. C., & Thornton, C. A. The learning disabled child—Learning the basic facts. *Arithmetic Teacher*, 1977, *25*(3), 46–50.

Vacc, N. A., & Kirst, N. Emotionally disturbed children and regular classroom teachers. *Elementary School Journal*, 1977, *77*, 309–317.

Wilson, J. W. Diagnosis and treatment in mathematics. In P. Knoblock (Ed.), *The teaching-learning process in educating emotionally disturbed children.* Syracuse, N.Y.: Syracuse University Press, 1967.

5

Teaching Mathematics
to Slow-Learning
and Mentally Retarded Children

Leroy G. Callahan
State University of New York at Buffalo

Donald L. MacMillan
University of California, Riverside

Dr. Leroy G. Callahan is professor and chairman, Department of Elementary and Remedial Education, State University of New York at Buffalo. He is a member of the Association of Mathematics Teachers of New York State, Association for Supervision and Curriculum Development, National Council of Teachers of Mathematics, National Association for the Education of Young Children, Phi Delta Kappa, and the Research Council for Diagnostic and Prescriptive Mathematics. He has been listed in Who's Who in the East *and* Leaders in Education.

Dr. Donald L. MacMillan, University of California, Riverside, is a fellow in AAMD and Division 33 of the American Psychological Association. He is associate editor of the American Journal of Mental Deficiency, *author of* Mental Retardation in School and Society, *and has published over 60 articles. A former consultant to federal agencies in the United States and Venezuela, he currently serves on national advisory committees for large-scale projects on early intervention with handicapped children.*

NO OTHER category of exceptional children requires quite the same modification in instruction that is required by mentally retarded children. For the deaf or blind child, techniques are required that bypass the impaired modality, and special teaching techniques have been developed for children with impaired perceptual processes. However, the mentally retarded child requires modifications not only in *how* a subject will be taught but also in terms of *what* should be taught. Extending this point to

This study was supported in part by Grants No. HD-04612 and HD-05540 from the National Institute of Child Health and Human Development.

mathematics, one must consider the relative importance of mathematics vis-à-vis other subject-matter areas; moreover, one must consider what particular mathematical concepts are essential for independent or semi-independent functioning as an adult. To achieve the latter goal, one must decide on the teaching strategies and materials that will most efficiently promote the generalization of these concepts and skills to everyday living. Therefore, the essence of special education for the mentally retarded entails adaptations in both *how* and *what* mathematical concepts and skills are to be taught—a dual modification no other exceptionality requires.

The changes that have occurred over the years in special education in the schools emerged almost exclusively in the area of mental retardation (MacMillan, 1977). The exclusion of the most patently disabled from public education was addressed in *Pennsylvania Association for Retarded Children (PARC)* v. *Commonwealth of Pennsylvania* (1972), and the process for identifying mildly handicapped learners was challenged in *Diana* v. *State Board of Education* (1970) and *Larry P.* v. *Riles* (1972) on behalf of children of ethnic minorities. Such cases have had a direct impact on federal and state legislation pertaining to the rights of all handicapped children (Meyers, MacMillan, & Zetlin, 1978), such as Public Law 94-142. As will be developed subsequently in this chapter, the changes resulting from litigation and legislation make it virtually impossible to specify the population parameters of those children classified mentally retarded in the public schools. First, however, let us consider the definition of *mental retardation* and attempt to describe the children of concern in this chapter.

MENTAL RETARDATION

The most widely used definition of mental retardation is that of the American Association on Mental Deficiency (AAMD):

> Mental retardation refers to significantly subaverage general intellectual functioning existing concurrently with deficits in adaptive behavior, and manifested during the developmental period. (Grossman, 1973, p. 5)

"Significantly subaverage general intellectual functioning" refers to a score on an individual test of intelligence that is two or more standard deviations below the population mean. The concept of impairments in adaptive behavior has proved elusive to measure (Clausen, 1972); however, it attempts to address the fact that at different stages of development a mastery of certain tasks is expected. In the preschool years, the child is expected to develop communication skills, self-help skills, and socialization; during the school years, a mastery of academic skills and the ability to apply them to daily living are expected. Furthermore, during school years the child is expected to develop reasoning and judgment skills and additional social skills.

In adulthood adaptive behavior refers to vocational and social responsibilities and performances.

What is essential to realize is that for an individual to be classified mentally retarded there must be evidence of both low IQ *and* impaired adaptive behavior. Mental retardation is not synonymous with low IQ—the dual criteria must be met. Moreover, the AAMD definition stresses the current level of functioning and does not presuppose that individuals classified retarded at one time in their life should remain indefinitely in that status.

It is also important to recognize that those individuals meeting the definition are by no means a homogeneous group; in fact, they are quite heterogeneous. Therefore, most persons working in the field find it useful to classify the mentally retarded into somewhat more homogeneous subgroups (MacMillan, 1977). These classification schemes tend to emphasize one of the following:

1. *Degree* of retardation (mild, moderate, severe, or profound)
2. *Form*, which tends to dichotomize the population into those where there is some pathological condition versus those who are simply at the lower end of the normal distribution of intelligence (e.g., exogenous vs. endogenous)
3. *Etiology*, schemes that have gained more attention from medical personnel (e.g., infections and intoxications, metabolism and nutrition, chromosomal anomalies, etc.)

The classification scheme employed in educational circles subdivides the mentally retarded according to the educational program deemed most appropriate for meeting the special educational needs of the child. This corresponds rather closely with the level of retardation and could be considered a classification system that is based on the degree of retardation. Historically, there were two such categories. First, programs for the educable mentally retarded (EMR) served children having IQs roughly between 50 or 55 and the upper limit of the mentally retarded range. Second, programs for the trainable mentally retarded (TMR) were designed to serve children whose IQs ranged from as low as 25 up to 55 or so and usually required for enrollment that the child be toilet trained and able to communicate basic needs. With court cases like PARC and the passage of PL 94-142, education departments have been forced to serve children functioning below the TMR level, the severely and profoundly retarded (PMR), thereby creating a three-tiered educational classification scheme.

Two Distinct Groups of Retarded Children

Authors have tended to distinguish between the more seriously impaired mentally retarded (now classified educationally as TMR and PMR) and the more mildly retarded. The introduction of mental testing permitted

the addition of the latter group as a mild and unspecific type of impairment to the previously identified special clinical types, which as a rule had more severe impairments. It was the custom of writers to preserve the contrast with the use of different labels. Kanner (1948) argued that there was a need to distinguish the "absolute" condition from one that is relative to normalcy, but Masland, Sarason, and Gladwin (1958) preferred the contrasting labels *mentally deficient* and *mentally retarded* to differentiate the former, or "defect," group, composed of those marked by bodily stigmata and specific biomedical syndromes of symptoms, from the "retarded" group, who possessed normal bodies and generally demonstrated no sufficient single biomedical causality for their lowered ability. The battle to maintain the distinction was lost during the so-called Kennedy era, when all such children became "mentally retarded" at one level or another.

The adoption of a common rubric to subsume two distinct types of retarded children did nothing to remove the inherent distinction. Dingman and Tarjan (1960) provided a useful demographic contrast of the two. Whereas the mildly retarded could be represented as occupying a space on the lower end of the probability curve of normal IQs, the more severely retarded occurred in numbers far greater than could be found by prediction from the Gaussian distribution, that is, from about minus two and one-half standard deviations down, leading these investigators to conclude that the lower group had its own distribution of psychometric scores, thereby constituting a type of difference in Kanner's sense from the main body of people. Zigler (1967) developed this distinction further with his major contributions to the complex psychology of the mildly impaired and his convincing arguments that the deficit or difference concepts contributed little to our understanding of the behavior of this group. More recently he argued for a return to separate labeling, with the mildly handicapped no longer being called "retarded" (Zigler, 1977).

Slow-Learning Children

In this chapter the term *slow learner* refers to children whose academic progress is significantly below age/grade expectation and is associated with general intellectual functioning between one and two standard deviations below the population mean. Moreover, these children exhibit general academic retardation across subject-matter areas, as contrasted to children with specific learning disabilities or perceptual process problems that delimit their academic deficits to certain areas of school learning.

This working definition reflects an attempt to acknowledge in our schools the presence of a group of children whose general intellectual functioning is too high to qualify for EMR programs but whose academic functioning is sufficiently deviant to warrant some "special" educational provision if optimal progress is to be made. MacMillan and Meyers (in press)

observed that many such children participate in compensatory education programs as a means of providing supplemental help without labeling the children with one of the disability labels required for special education servicing. However, many others receive no special help and are allowed to wallow in regular classes unaided, achieving social promotions and often dropping out of school before graduation.

The presence of slow-learning children in regular grades reflects the shift from the Kennedy era, where services were provided for "all who need them" and the AAMD definition (Heber, 1961) was inclusive, to the present era of a more restrictive AAMD definition (Grossman, 1973) and the provisions of PL 94-142, which provides for labeling only the clear-cut cases EMR. Meyers and Lombardi (1974) recognized that with the shift in definition came the loss of advocacy for the thousands of children made "normal" by associations like AAMD. Moreover, the change in definition did nothing to alleviate the learning problems that precipitated the referral process.

The children who fit the slow-learner designation herein include many of the pre-1970 higher functioning EMR population who would have been classified EMR had they gone through the school system prior to the litigation and legislation described earlier. These are academic casualties whose academic careers are marked by too much failure academically and socially. It is our firm belief that these children *do* need special educational provision but that they should not be categorized mentally retarded in order to qualify for needed services.

Prevalence

In 1975, the Bureau of Education for the Handicapped of the U. S. Office of Education estimated that 2.3% of the child population *should be* mentally retarded. No demographic data have been published since the revision of the AAMD revision in 1973 or since the enactment of PL 94-142 with its stringent procedural guidelines for the assessment process. In addition, one cannot begin to estimate the number of children who fit the slow-learner designation. Epidemiological data are crucial to those making decisions about the allocation of resources—it is the only way to judge how many children need services of one type or another. Let us examine the older data to the extent that they provide insights into the magnitude of the problem.

Despite the earlier claims of a 3% rate of prevalence for retardation (President's Task Force on the Mentally Handicapped, 1970; President's Committee on Mental Retardation, 1962), the number of people classified mentally retarded at a given point in time has actually hovered closer to 1% (Tarjan, Wright, Eyman, & Keeran, 1973; Mercer, 1973b). Table 5.1 displays the rates of prevalence for mental retardation in a prototypical

community of 100 000 people. Given the current recommended IQ cutoff (Grossman, 1973) of the American Association on Mental Deficiency, the figures for the IQ ranges 0–19, 20–49, and 50–69 are of interest. The actual data count of Mercer (1973b) corresponds much more closely to Tarjan's 1% model except that she found only about half as many cases in the 50–69 range as would be predicted from the 1% model of Tarjan.

Table 5.1

Theoretical Distributions Comparing Tarjan's 3% and 1% Prevalence Models with Mercer's Data for a Prototype Community of 100 000

	0–19	20–49	50–69	70+	Total
3% (Tarjan)	100	400	2500	-	3000
1% (Tarjan)	50	200	750	-	1000
Mercer's Data	42	137	387	404	970

Reprinted from MacMillan (1977, p. 64).

The rates of prevalence for the profoundly and the severely retarded were estimated at 0.5 per 1000 and 0.8 per 1000 respectively by Eyman and Miller (1978), or a total of 1.3 per 1000 (using an IQ of 35 as the upper limit). Abramowicz and Richardson (1975) found a slightly higher prevalence for severe retardation of 4 per 1000; however, they used an IQ of 50 as the upper limit for severe mental retardation. What seems evident from the foregoing is that epidemiological evidence collected in the past can be used for cases of profound, severe, and probably moderate retardation. As will be discussed, evidence on mild mental retardation (EMR) and slow learners is sorely needed.

The identification process for EMR children in the public schools has been drastically overhauled in response to court actions and legislation (MacMillan & Meyers, in press), with one obvious consequence being a radical reduction in the number of EMR children identified. Meyen and Moran (1979) reported that the number of mildly retarded children reported by BEH is far below expectation, as the implementation of PL 94-142 proceeds. Specifically, they attributed the low rates of prevalence to the fact that regular class teachers are not referring problem cases because—

1. the student will remain their responsibility;
2. if the child is certified, the teacher will have to participate in numerous conferences, develop individualized education programs, and perform extensive record-keeping operations;
3. regardless of the certifiability of the child, responsibility for instruction will remain with the regular class teacher, and furthermore, these teachers have a negative impression of the support services they would receive.

Further support for the belief that identification of the mildly retarded has been reduced drastically comes from contrasting Mercer's (1973a) data with current enrollments in the Riverside Unified School District, where Mercer's research was conducted in the mid-1960s. Mercer (1973a, p. 104) reported a total EMR enrollment of 271 students, with 71 EMR children identified in a single academic year. Since 1975, the EMR enrollments in the same district have never been more than 58 EMR pupils (a reduction of 213). Although one cannot estimate precisely the total impact of the reduction in the numbers of retarded children of IQ 50 to 70, it is apparent that enrollments have been reduced drastically.

MacMillan (1977) also pointed out that an *average* rate of prevalence of 1% cannot be uncritically applied to any community, since prevalence is found to vary according to age, sex, community, and race or socioeconomic status. Higher prevalence rates are found during the school years, in males, in rural communities, and among blacks and Spanish-surnamed groups.

Causation

The etiology of mental retardation is multidimensional and far too complex to explain in these limited pages. It is important for the reader to recognize that mental retardation describes a phenotype—one that results from numerous possible causes. The public hears of a medical finding that claims that mental retardation is one of the sequelae of some biochemical or chromosomal anomaly. A recent such example is fetal alcohol syndrome. However, in over 75% of all cases of mental retardation no specific cause can be established (MacMillan, 1977). At this point it seems appropriate to reintroduce the notion of two subgroups of retarded individuals. In the lower functioning group there is usually demonstrable organic pathology, even when the precise cause of that pathology cannot be pinpointed. In the higher functioning group the degree of retardation is milder, there is no sign of pathology, and children tend to come from homes of lower social status. It is important to recognize that the pattern of causation differs dramatically in the two groups of mentally retarded persons. The pathological condition present in the lower IQ range overrides the genetic information, and although the specific agent that causes the pathology cannot be ascertained, in most cases the presence of pathology is frequently apparent.

The AAMD manual (Grossman, 1973) suggests the following as additional descriptors to the degree of retardation when a diagnosis can be made:

1.　Infection and intoxication
2.　Trauma or physical agent
3.　Disorders of metabolism or nutrition
4.　Gross brain disease

5. Diseases and conditions due to unknown prenatal influence
6 . Chromosomal abnormality
7. Gestational disorders
8. Psychiatric disorder
9. Environmental influences

The vast majority of cases of IQ 50 or above do not exhibit signs of pathology; however, such cases come from families in the lower strata of society and ethnic minority homes in disproportionately high numbers. Although there are any number of factors associated, or correlated, with low socioeconomic status (e.g., poor language models, crowded living conditions, poorer prenatal and postnatal medical care) that could depress intellectual functioning, they have not been shown to be causal factors in any empirical fashion. Moreover, the vast majority of children coming from these sociolinguistically deprived environments are not mentally retarded. MacMillan (1977) reviewed correlates of low social class hypothesized to affect IQ detrimentally as well as the major contrasting positions of Bloom (1964) and Jensen (1969) concerning the dynamics of postnatal environmental effects.

Suffice it to say here that mental retardation is a term descriptive of phenotypic functioning, the underlying causes of which can only infrequently be established. In cases of IQ below 50, the probability of some organic pathology is reasonably high, whereas above IQ 50 the causes are most likely other than pathological. Let us turn our attention now to the diagnostic process whereby the condition of mental retardation is established.

Diagnosis of Mental Retardation

The identification process for the two groups of retarded persons differs in terms of the developmental stages at which diagnosis is made, the professionals involved in the diagnosis, and the symptom pattern that leads to the diagnosis. Generally, the more severe the degree of retardation, the earlier in a child's life the diagnosis of mental retardation is made. For purposes of organization we shall consider diagnosis in the preschool years and diagnosis made after the child is enrolled in public school.

Diagnosis during the preschool years. Persons exhibiting most obvious physical symptoms or gross developmental lags are frequently diagnosed mentally retarded during the first year of life. For example, a child with Down's syndrome is commonly diagnosed at, or soon after, birth, given the physical characteristics associated with that condition. Other cases where there is a prolonged absence of oxygen accompanied by seizures once the child is born will alert the pediatrician to the possibility of brain damage,

which can be confirmed in the initial examination. Although such a child would not be diagnosed mentally retarded at this time, the pediatrician would alert the parents to watch for signs of motor delays and would keep the infant under surveillance for later developmental lags.

Another set of circumstances surrounds the diagnosis of children who appear normal at birth. They may score in the marginal range in early neurological exams, but as the first two or three years pass, they do not master the developmental tasks of sitting, talking, or walking within the normal time frame. Such delays sensitize the parents that "something is wrong"; however, the parents often focus on a narrow aspect of development (e.g., they claim the child is shy, or they may suspect a hearing loss when the child is slow to speak). Friends and family reassure the parents that the child will "grow out of it" (MacMillan, 1977).

When the parents seek professional help, the physician (the usual professional contact) is usually cautious in ruling out other possible explanations for the slower than normal development. Symptoms that are quite similar, such as delayed speech or poor ambulation, could result from visual or hearing problems, cerebral palsy, or emotional disorders as well as mental retardation. Therefore, a careful diagnosis is essential (Gardner, Tarjan, & Richmond, 1965). The pediatrician confronted with a child slow to develop should do a complete workup including (a) a developmental, social, and medical history; (b) a physical examination to compare the child's current functioning against developmental norms; and (c) a psychological and sociocultural evaluation to ascertain intellectual development and sociocultural factors that might depress performance.

The diagnostic process of cases identified before entrance into public school is primarily performed by physicians who rely on medical evidence to make the diagnosis; psychological evidence (e.g., IQ) may be used to confirm or supplement the medical data. Generally speaking, this diagnostic process is more typical of the children classified later as having profound, severe, or moderate cases of mental retardation.

Diagnosis after enrollment in school. Cases of mild mental retardation are diagnosed in an altogether different process. The children who find their way into EMR programs go through the preschool years with no one suspecting they are anything but normal. The public schools are the principal labeling agency of EMR children (Mercer, 1973a) in a well-documented sequence of events. These children exhibit "mental retardation" only in the context of the school and were typically undetected prior to attending school.

The diagnostic process for EMR has been described in detail elsewhere (MacMillan, 1977; Mercer, 1973a; Meyers, Sunstrom, & Yoshida, 1974). The common pattern is as follows:

1. Academic failure in comparison to the child's sociocultural age peers occurs in regular grades, in the majority of cases after the child has repeated one grade. The teacher then makes this determination, and the child is sometimes placed in grades where the modal achievement of the class is well below grade level. In other words, the reference group for this initial screening step is the sociocultural age peers, not national norms.

2. The next step after referral by the teacher is a psychological assessment, which consists of far more than the administration of a test of intelligence. The child's academic history is examined, teachers are interviewed, and testing is conducted. The testing is often a state-legislated requirement. The IQ can serve, and has served, to prevent the proper placement (Ashurst & Meyers, 1973) of children, particularly ethnic minority children. It is crucial to realize that low IQ and mental retardation are not, and have never been, synonymous.

3. If the psychological assessment reveals that the child is *eligible* for EMR placement, a committee meets to ascertain whether EMR placement is the most appropriate placement. Ashurst and Meyers (1973) found that 63 referred children who were found eligible for EMR were *not* placed in an EMR class whereas 86 eligible cases were placed in EMR classes, the point being that eligibility and placement do not follow automatically.

The diagnostic process for EMR has been challenged (*Diana*, 1972; *Larry P.,* 1972) and this process altered significantly by PL 94-142 in terms of its due process provision, protections in evaluation procedures (PEP), and parental involvement. At this time it is impossible to ascertain the direct impact of these procedural safeguards on the number of children diagnosed or the validity of the diagnostic process. It is clear that the total number of EMR children has been reduced, but this could also be due, in part, to the shift in definition (Grossman, 1973), the trepidation among school personnel to certify any but the most obvious cases (MacMillan & Meyers, in press), and the reluctance on the part of teachers to refer cases (Meyen & Moran, 1979). Whatever the reason, the EMR totals have been reduced, with the resultant swell in the number of slow learners either to be served under some other "compensatory education" rubric or to go on with no supplemental help. Given the findings of Congress, the latter option seems risky. PL 94-142 includes the following finding:

> There are many handicapped children throughout the United States participating in regular school programs whose handicaps prevent them from having successful educational experience because their handicaps are undetected. (Section 601)

Only time will tell whether the reduction in EMR enrollments is a politically expedient step that further swells the ranks of the unserved mildly handicapped beyond the condition alluded to in the quote above.

Let us now turn to consider behavioral characteristics germane to the mathematics performance of the children diagnosed mentally retarded, as described above.

BEHAVIORAL CHARACTERISTICS

Mentally retarded children are not a homogeneous group; they exhibit a wide range of individual differences on any number of learning and motivational traits. The interested reader must consult textbooks (e.g., MacMillan, 1977; Robinson & Robinson, 1976) that develop more fully the range of individual differences found in mentally retarded children. In this chapter we attempt to highlight those learning and motivational characteristics that would be hypothesized to alter performance in mathematics.

The most directly relevant research is that which relates child characteristics to arithmetic skills. In terms of arithmetic *computation*, mildly retarded children achieve close to what one would expect based on their mental age (Cruickshank, 1948b, 1948c; Dunn, 1954); however, in arithmetic *reasoning*, retarded children perform significantly lower than their normal mental age peers. Apparently when the information necessary for the solution of the problem is embedded in superfluous information, the retarded have difficulty, possibly due in part to the reading problems associated with low IQ. Cruickshank (1948a) also noted a number of primitive work habits (e.g., counting on their fingers) and careless mistakes by retarded students.

Beyond the very limited research base using mathematics per se as the dependent measure, one must turn to more basic research on learning characteristics, keeping in mind that the learning task employed in a study may differ markedly from mathematical problem solving, the focus of this chapter. Let us consider those learning and motivational characteristics of mentally retarded children that have *implications* for the teaching of mathematics.

General Observations

Retarded children with IQs above 50 or so seem to learn in the very same fashion as their nonretarded peers do, albeit a little less efficiently. Zigler (1969) described this group of retarded children as representing a downward extension of the normal curve, but certainly a portion of the normal distribution of the normal curve. As such, the principles of learning apply to them; however, the differences in learning are differences of *degree* rather than *kind*. Applying Bloom's (1976) notion of mastery learning, one would argue that the major difference in learning between the mildly retarded and slow learner and the more able child would be differences in the *time*

required for the retarded or slow-learning child to reach a level of mastery. For the teacher of these children, the implications of the foregoing are that unique materials or instructional strategies are not required; rather, a greater period of time will be required in order for the child to achieve mastery.

This position does not imply that nothing special need be done for mildly retarded or slow-learning children. Rather, it suggests, not that the modifications need entail different materials or instructional strategies, but instead the instruction must be more *intense* and specific steps taken to promote generalization or transfer of training. Moreover, the teacher must make instruction explicit, since these children do not learn as much incidentally.

Although these children are capable of learning much of the school curriculum, there are certain inefficiencies that have been shown in learning research to which the teacher should be sensitive. We shall briefly consider some of these characteristics and later discuss how they can be accommodated.

Learning

Attention. One inefficiency exhibited by retarded children is found in their attending to the dimensions of a problem crucial to the solution of the problem (Zeaman & House, 1963). In discrimination learning, there was a greater period of time and amount of practice before the learning curve ascended, which the investigators attributed to the difficulty these children had attending to the relevant stimulus dimensions. Zeaman and House have suggested several remedial procedures for the attention deficit found in retarded subjects such as using three-dimensional objects and emphasizing the relevant dimensions by tracing. Possibly the discrimination of numerical symbols (9 and 6) would be facilitated by means of such techniques.

Turnure (1970) challenged the position that retarded children exhibit an attention deficit. He summarized a series of research studies suggesting that children who fail excessively learn to seek cues from the environment rather than attending to the cues inherent in the task itself. The reason for the reliance on external cues is the distrust of their own abilities resulting from excessive failure.

Attending to the task seems to be a problem, regardless of the reason, and yet it is a necessary prerequisite to the solution of the task. Teachers will have to be sure such attention is present before instructing, and when it is not, techniques such as those described by Hewett (1968) should be employed. A second level of attention that warrants consideration is the active focusing on the essential elements necessary for the solution of the problem (Zeaman & House, 1963) noted above in discrimination learning. The relative difficulty encountered by the retarded in solving mathematical

reasoning problems (Dunn, 1954) may represent a similar dynamic. If so, some of the remedial procedures of Zeaman and House would appear worthy of testing.

Input organization. Another area of difficulty exhibited by the retarded is in imposing some organizational structure on incoming stimuli, a necessary and efficient strategy when bombarded by many stimuli. Spitz (1966) referred to this as input organization and in a series of studies demonstrated that the performance of retarded subjects was improved by structuring or organizing the input for the subject; such organization did not promote better performances by nonretarded subjects, who spontaneously employed their own organizational strategy.

Much of the research on input organization (Harris, 1972; Jensen, 1965; MacMillan, 1972; Spitz, 1966) has used digit span as the experimental task. The strategies imposed on the subjects included *spatial grouping* of digits (e.g., 72 86 as contrasted with 7286) and spatial grouping paired with calling the grouped digits couplets (e.g., 72 86 called "seventy-two" and "eighty-six"). These organizational strategies, when provided the EMR child, can be used to improve recall. Efforts to teach the retarded to generate their own strategies spontaneously have not demonstrated long-term benefits but have been of very short duration.

Another type of strategy has been studied with retarded subjects using verbal stimuli—verbal mediators. Mediators are the psychological activity that mediates between the stimuli and the responses, and they facilitate learning, retention, and understanding. Although mediators can be in the form of imagery, the vast majority of work has been done with verbal mediation (e.g., Jensen & Rohwer, 1963a, 1963b; Milgram, 1967; Turnure & Thurlow, 1975). The results of these investigations are very similar to those described with digit span—mildly retarded children increase in performance when provided with verbal mediators. For example, in paired-associate learning a child is told that when presented with DOG, she is to recall HAT. When the experimenter provides a sentence connecting the words (e.g., "The DOG ate the HAT"), the association is made more readily. Experimenter-provided verbal mediators assist the mildly retarded but do not benefit their nonretarded peers, for whom the mediators seem to compete with self-generated mediators. We can summarize the findings on input organization as follows:

1. A certain level of cognitive development (around MA 9 or 10) is required before imposed strategies can be used by EMR children.

2. Such strategies, if experimentally provided, can be used to advantage by mildly retarded children.

3. Mildly retarded children do not spontaneously organize input

unless specifically instructed to do so, and then their "strategies" tend to be rather primitive.

Memory. The retention of previous experience is essential if a child is to generalize to new situations, and the comparative research suggests the retarded perform significantly below their nonretarded peers. Most recent work (e.g., Atkinson & Shiffrin, 1968; Ellis, 1970) in memory research and theory distinguishes between short-term and long-term retention. In the former, information is retained for very short periods of time (seconds). However, for it to be retained for longer periods of time, it is necessary for some strategy (e.g., rehearsal) to be employed; otherwise, the information quickly decays.

The major area of weakness found in retarded subjects is in short-term memory (Ellis, 1970). However, training the retarded to use rehearsal strategies has been shown to provide some increments in performance (Belmont & Butterfield, 1971; Brown, Campione, & Murphy, 1974). If the retarded "overlearn" material, their long-term memory seems comparable to that of the nonretarded (Vergason, 1962). It should be noted that it takes the retarded longer to learn the material initially; however, if they do learn it, they retain it reasonably well.

For the teacher, it is necessary to ascertain what material requires memorization and to be prepared to spend the time required for the EMR child to master the initial learning. This initial learning will require more trials than taken by nonretarded children, but it is essential that mastery occur. Even then, the likelihood is reduced that this material or information will be transferred to new situations (Shif, 1969).

Motivation

Despite the fact that mentally retarded and slow-learning children are considered to differ from the nonretarded primarily in the intellectual sphere, the instructional adaptations made for these children must consider the motivational sphere as well as the intellectual (MacMillan, 1971). These children simply experience too much failure, which leads to several motivational characteristics that can be detrimental to their problem solving. It is important to realize that these characteristics are not the result of lowered intellect but rather the result of the failure experienced typically by these children in their academic and social careers.

Expectancy for failure. Because of a succession of failure experiences when presented with new tasks to be learned, these children approach new learning with trepidation—before even trying the task, the child expects to fail. Heber (1964) described the vicious circle that results: Failure leads to lowered expectancies, which lowers effort and performance, thus insuring failure, which in turn lowers expectancies for success on future tasks. The result of this high expectancy for failure is that the child behaves defensively

in an effort to avoid failure (or at least a sense of failure) rather than trying to achieve success.

Success experiences, so often discussed in educational circles, must be programmed by the teacher. The use of extrinsic consequences, prompting, and other techniques that permit the child to exert a maximum effort and break the cycle of recurrent failure are in order. The successes must be on challenging tasks and not merely a trivial problem the child does not perceive as a challenge.

Reaction tendencies. Zigler (1966) described institutionalized retarded persons as desiring to interact with approving adults (*positive reaction tendency*) while at the same time being somewhat wary of adults (*negative reaction tendency*) because of numerous negative experiences with adults in the past. The desire to interact results from having been deprived of such social experiences. These constructs were extended by Zigler (1968) to children from socially disadvantaged backgrounds.

If children are using social interactions with teachers and aides primarily to satisfy their need for attention and approval, then their energy is not being focused on the learning tasks being presented them. This serves to depress academic performance below the levels one would expect based on the child's ability.

Teachers should also be sensitive to their own behavior as being a determinant of whether the positive or negative reaction tendency will predominate. If the child perceives the teacher as approachable and receptive, the positive reaction tendency is promoted. Then the key to successful instruction depends in part on the teacher's contingent use of attention and approval.

Outerdirectedness. When children fail excessively, they come to distrust their own abilities and seek cues to "proper responses" from the environment (which includes teachers). Turnure and Zigler (1964) initially demonstrated that retarded children rely excessively on cues external to the task itself—a problem-solving approach that grows out of repeated failure. Obviously, everyone uses environmental cues when not able to solve a problem, but this becomes dysfunctional for retarded children because they do so when they are capable of solving the problem without the aid of such cues.

Teachers must recognize that whereas outerdirectedness can help an inefficient learner get the right answer, it is not in the child's interest to rely heavily on external cues. Such a problem-solving style does not promote cognitive growth; in fact, it inhibits such growth. Teachers should be careful, not to provide cues (e.g., smiling when child is on the right track) on which the child can rely, but rather to focus further attention on the task itself.

The following sections will consider the mathematical tasks that form the curriculum content for slow and mentally retarded students. Consideration will also be given to some principles to guide methods of instruction as well as evaluating the mathematics learning of these students.

MATHEMATICS INSTRUCTION

As indicated previously, the research base for formulating mathematics programs and practices for slow and mentally retarded students is very limited. The following discussion of mathematics content, methods, and assessment procedures attempts to follow sensibly—if not scientifically—from general observations of the learning characteristics of slow and mentally retarded students. The discussion is predominantly concerned with mathematics instruction for those students who are most likely to need special educational provisions within the regular school program. Before content, methods, and assessment procedures are considered, a few very broad beliefs about school mathematics, teaching, and responsibility to students will be presented, since these beliefs affect the orientation of the ensuing discussion of program practices.

The teaching act has an artistic and creative dimension as well as a scientific dimension. The competent teacher draws on research, scientific evidence, and authoritative thought to develop guiding principles to make knowledgeable decisions on what to teach and how best to teach. At that dynamic point of interaction between teacher and student in the classroom, however, there is a creative, artistic component at play. Knowledge guides the teacher in making decisions at that point, but the dynamic learning climate is created.

The total school mathematics program cannot be reduced to a set of minute cognitive atoms, described in terms of overt behaviors, arranged in prescribed linear order, and then presented atom by atom for mastery. As compelling as that analytic, reductionistic approach may be, it deprives students of the opportunity to glimpse the power of mathematics in developing the ability to go beyond the information given. In discussing the early work of Spearman, Bruner (1973b) writes, "The most characteristic thing about mental life, over and beyond the fact that one apprehends the events of the world around one, is that one constantly goes beyond the information given" (p. 218). Schools and their programs should nurture the independence of cognitive process in their students, not cognitive dependence.

The premise that there is an artistic and creative dimension to teaching and that the body of knowledge of mathematics cannot be totally reduced to a large number of discrete behavior objectives suggests that the ideal being sought in programming mathematics for slow and mentally retarded

students is *not* a static, teacher-proof program with prescribed procedures. Rather, the ideal is a dynamic, teacher-prone program. Rising, Brown, and Meyerson (1977) state that in mathematics instruction, the teacher is the central figure in planning and interpreting curricular materials, in interacting with and among students, in orchestrating classroom activities, and in maintaining a positive classroom atmosphere. And regarding instruction of mentally retarded students, Blatt (1977) states that "teachers must be creators of learning environment. . ." (p. 30).

One general and pervasive principle that comments on the school's responsibility to students should also be mentioned at this point. Its essence is captured in the Latin *primum non nocere,* "first, do no harm" (Glennon, 1975). For the slow learner or mentally retarded students, the statement might be slightly qualified to, "first, do no further harm." For students who already reflect subaverage general intellectual functioning *and* deficits in adaptive behavior, the principle suggests that an appropriate mathematics program should involve the attainment of a sensitive "mini/max" equilibrium between student and school mathematics: the chances of increasing anxiety, fears, and failures through inappropriate programming or pacing must be *minimized,* since this could lead to further deficits in adaptive behavior, while the opportunities to learn essential mathematical knowledge and strategies for problem solving must be *maximized* in order not to further compromise deficits in intellectual functioning.

Sources of the Mathematics Curriculum

When appropriate mathematics for the slow or mentally retarded student is considered, the merit of the three sources of the mathematics curriculum presented by Glennon in an earlier chapter should be examined. These sources flow from three different perspectives of the locus of control of mathematics for school learning. The first perspective suggests that the locus of control is inherent in the expressed needs of the student. This is the clinical-personality point of view, which places primacy on the importance of the affective aspects of human development.

A second perspective suggests that the locus of control for curriculum decisions in mathematics exists within the social milieu. That mathematics that is most good and valuable is that which is pressed on us by society and which must be mastered if a healthy socialization is to be achieved. It places a primacy on the mathematics needed for life skills in the given society.

The third perspective suggests that the locus of control exists within the logical and systematic structure of the discipline of mathematics. Mathematics is perceived as a system of abstract, related ideas. This perspective places a primacy on using the structure, relationships, and logical organization of mathematics in promoting productive thinking.

The merit of the clinical-personality perspective will be examined initially, then the logical and sociological views will be examined jointly in considering appropriate mathematics content for the curriculum of the slow or mentally retarded student.

The expressed-needs-of-the-individual perspective. The extreme stream of thought for this theory holds that what comes from within the student is the most important aspect of development. The only honest source of content must and can only eventuate out of the expressed needs of the student. Advocates often use the metaphor of "health," equating optimal physical development with bodily health and optimal mental development with mental health (Kohlberg & Mayer, 1972). There is an unequivocal belief that when provided with an appropriately free environment, optimal growth, development, and learning will result. The pedagogical environment should be permissive enough to allow the inner "good" to unfold and the inner "bad" to come under self-control. To advocates of this position, such as Neill was (1960), the aim of education is to be able to work joyfully and to find happiness. And how can this come about? "Abolish authority. Let the child be himself. Don't push him around. Don't teach him. Don't lecture him. Don't elevate him. Don't force him to do anything" (p. 297).

How appropriate is this perspective in making decisions on what mathematics is most appropriate for the slow or mentally retarded? Certainly, as Glennon points out, the psychoeducational match is a fairly simple matter for the teacher. It involves creating a psychologically open environment and then responding to the expressed quantitative or spatial needs of students as they spontaneously arise. If a student becomes aware of the need for a specific arithmetic skill, measuring the width of a window, say, then the teacher responds by satisfying that expressed need by teaching that measurement skill. The skill is not satisfying in and of itself but is only a means to enhance inner awareness, happiness, or mental health. If no expressed need for mathematics skills arises, then none are taught.

But the slow learner and especially the mentally retarded student have often developed emotional and personality blocks to a healthy coping by the time teachers meet them in the school situation. Many have already experienced crippling unhappiness, anxiety, hostility, rejection, and feelings of unworthiness. In turn, they have already developed and use a variety of self-defeating techniques to handle these feelings and their confusion about the world around them (Robinson & Robinson, 1976). They have already established tendencies to depend on external guides to action, "outer-directedness" (Turnure & Zigler, 1964), rather than depend on their own internal resources. Further, when responding in a problem situation in the environment, the expressions of these students often are quite impulsive and do not reflect the development of a strategy or course of action prior to making a response.

For these, and other, reasons the practice of taking the lead from the expressed needs of the slow learner or mentally retarded student as the sole source of the mathematics curriculum seems especially questionable. Waiting for such expressions of need with these students may be somewhat akin to withholding physical therapy from a child that has cerebral palsy until he or she expresses a need for such therapy. Few would argue the ethics of such a practice.

To question the appropriateness of the expressed needs of slow or retarded students as the sole source of their mathematics curriculum does not imply an unconcern for affective outcomes of the mathematics curriculum. From a clinical point of view, the relationship between feelings about self and the content of the mathematics program is a two-way street. Appropriate mathematics content in a school intervention program may have salutory effects on feelings about the self—for example, it may satisfy a need for acceptance, achievement, competence, and so on. This, in turn, may contribute to some dismantling of inappropriate defense mechanisms that the students have developed and ultimately make the expressed needs of the students a more valid source of mathematical content for school and social living.

The needs-of-society and the needs-of-the-discipline-of-mathematics perspective. The extreme streams of thought that flow from these sources suggest, respectively, that the locus of control of mathematics content for school learning resides in society and the discipline of mathematics. Their influences have ebbed and flowed during the past century. To gain a perspective on the contributions of these two lines of thought, it would be useful to consider their development.

Mathematics was closely associated with, and affected by, the particular needs of early cultures. It generally was perceived as a tool that not only facilitated the development of a culture but was itself more or less shaped by the culture. Much of the mathematics knowledge of early Babylonian and Egyptian cultures was concerned with astronomical and calendar questions, with the construction of buildings, and with land measurement and surveying. The mathematics was closely tied to social need. However, there was the beginning of an incorporation of mathematical ideas that went beyond immediate social need. The generalized extension of the system of natural numbers was at least anticipated if not concisely fashioned, and from the measurement there grew some awareness of the notion of the mathematical infinite (Schaaf, 1961).

Greek civilization greatly influenced western mathematical thought in the ensuing centuries. The Greeks distinguished between two aspects of knowledge about numbers; one was referred to as *logistica* and the other as *arithmetica* (in the Latin form). *Logistica* was generally concerned with the techniques of computation to be used in social utilitarian situations;

arithmetica dealt with the theory of numbers detached from any utilitarian applications. The former was considered beneath the dignity of mathematicians and philosophers, and they devoted their attention to the latter. This bifocal way of looking at numbers was enhanced by the Greeks and continued for centuries.

Arithmetic from about 1850 to the present may be said to play a dual role in the history of civilization. The more familiar role is that of tool subject, closely associated with social applications. The other role, in the tradition of Peano, Cantor, Dedekind, and 19th-century mathematicians, views arithmetic as a catalyst in the examination of the logical foundations of all mathematics. The search for essential "structure" of mathematics was under way. In commenting on this latter role, Schaaf (1961) wrote:

> Contemporary mathematics is to be distinguished from all previous mathematics in two vital respects: (1) the intentional study of abstractness, where the important considerations are not the things related, but the relations themselves; and (2) the relentless examination of the very foundations—the fundamental ideas—upon which the elaborate superstructure of mathematics is based. (p. 9)

School mathematics has not been immune from the press of the social and structural views of number and arithmetic. Proponents of the sociological perspective argue that the only appropriate mathematical content is that directly associated with a student's social needs in life. The view is manifested in discussions of curriculum for mentally retarded students. White (1976) writes:

> Too much emphasis is being placed on academics and too little attention to the needed skills for realization of the ultimate goal of education (the production of a reasonably happy, well adjusted, contributing member of our society). . . . Academics should be utilized as *tools* [italics added] to achieve these goals rather than the goals themselves. (p. 295)

Proponents of the needs-of-mathematics point of view assert that the validity of mathematical reasoning cannot be ascribed to the nature of things; it is due to the very nature of thinking. The important aspect is not the things related but the relations themselves. The *process* of thinking shares importance with the *product* of the thought. Again, manifestations of the view can be glimpsed in discussions of curriculum strategies for the mentally retarded. Winschel (1977) writes:

> The retarded are defeated inevitably by the multitude of specific skills necessary to minimal functioning in society. The efforts are laudable but the central objective, increased problem-solving behavior, is largely ignored. Clearly, we need to develop educational approaches which, in addition to teaching children to know more, help them to think better. (p. 26)

The position taken here, and the reason for discussing these two strands of thought jointly, is that they must be viewed as two mutually inclusive considerations when determining the mathematics content for slow or retarded learners. It would be difficult to imagine that anyone would promote an extreme logical/structural view of mathematics as appropriate for these students. That would be inappropriate. The mathematics program should be predominantly sensitive to the social needs, the life skill needs, of the slow or retarded student; but the value of mathematics as a systematic and sequential system of related ideas—even though greatly restricted in its cognitive range—should not be ignored.

In considering the contributions of the two sources of curriculum for these students, it may be helpful to use the analogy of a spider's web. The students are the spiders; the mathematics curriculum is the web. The students have a life space—very limited initially—that will continuously expand, although at a slower rate than that of normal students. The life space is anchored to the home and school, or their appropriate surrogates. These are the window sills, sidewalls, or sturdy plant stalks that form the anchorage for the analogous spider web.

As the life space expands, needs arise that pose problems requiring arithmetic solutions, for example, "How many plates are needed for everyone at the table?" The student may have developed a simple strategy serum needed to spin the solution—counting. As the life space expands, many "How many . . ." problems are posed in different contexts and different settings, but the strategy of counting accommodates each problem. There is a "spread," or generalization, of the use of the counting strategy. The web becomes more dense.

Somewhat different problems may arise in the expanding life space that simple counting will not accommodate. Piaget (1973) would suggest that this creates some disequilibrium. "If there were nine students to have lunch and three have already eaten, how many still must eat?" Now the potency of the counting-strategy serum must be increased so that the student can count on from a number other than one, or reverse the counting procedure in order to count down from a number to a given number. The web spreads to new areas of the life space but relates back to the already spun network—for example, the counting strategy is still employed, but there are new refinements that create the potential for addressing new, but related, problems. The web grows in area and density.

The spider web analogy is a much oversimplified model of the interplay between the contributions of mathematics as a process of thinking and as a product for social use in the school curriculum. Still it is useful in caricature to make the point of interrelationship between the two perspectives of school mathematics. The network is made up of *points* of intersection and *segments* connecting the points. Socially significant quantitative problems

are posed in the student's life space. These are the points in the network. A simple counting strategy was used in finding solutions to quantitative problems in different social contexts. The strategy of counting related the points in the growing network and formed the segments in the network. As life space expands, there may be need to increase the potency of the strategy. Simple counting may be extended to counting by tens, or reverse counting may be needed to accommodate new life space situations. But each new expansion of the network builds from the old. Systematic, frequent traversing of the segments in the network gives meaning *to* numbers and arithmetic as a system of related ideas; systematic, frequent stops at points in the network gives meaning *for* mathematics as a socially useful tool (Brownell, 1947).

Both points and segments are indispensable for the web's structural existence. Analogously, both views of mathematics are needed in developing the school mathematics curriculum. With overemphasis on thinking processes associated with the structure of mathematics and underemphasis of opportunities for social applications, the curriculum network will be fragile because the points of intersection that give significance to the study will be poorly developed. With overemphasis on the discrete social applications of numbers and underemphasis of structural relationships, the network will be fragile because the segments that give meaning to the mathematics will be weak.

Principles for Selecting the Content

Some guiding principles for choosing appropriate mathematical content can be discerned from the consideration of the sources of curriculum. First, it is imperative to develop mathematics intervention programs for the slow and retarded learners. It would be highly questionable to base a curriculum on responses to the expressed needs of these students. This does not imply that the affective needs of the students are ignored. The mathematics curriculum should be sensitive and responsive to affective needs but not solely determined by those needs.

The web analogy used in discussing the contributions of the social utility view and the logical view suggest other guiding principles in choosing mathematics content. The mathematics content web of slow and mentally retarded students will be smaller in area than that of the normal student. As stated in the initial paragraph of this chapter, the mentally retarded child requires a modification of what mathematics is to be taught. An examination of the behavior characteristics of these students led to the conclusion that the major difference in learning between the mildly retarded and slow learner and the more able child would be in the *time* required to reach a level of mastery learning. The pace of presentation of the mathematics must be

slowed, with the result that there will be some curtailment in the content covered when compared with a typical program. The content curtailment would be severe for the more seriously retarded and less curtailed for the mildly retarded or slow learner. The form and pattern of the content curriculum web would not differ significantly from that of the normal student, however.

The form and pattern of the analogous web suggests some further principles in mathematics content selection. First is the centrality of problem solving for the program. Rich and varied opportunities must be provided for posing socially significant problems. The density of these points in the curriculum web are critical to the sturdiness of the content web. In the current "back to basics" scramble it may be overlooked that problem-solving skills are the most essential life skills. The National Council of Supervisors of Mathematics (NCSM) (1977) placed problem solving at the top of its list in presenting basic skills in mathematics needed by students. The NCSM group stated, "Learning to solve problems is the principal reason for studying mathematics" (p. 19).

A second implication suggests the development of simple, but potent, strategies that can be learned and that address a broad range of quantitative situations. These were the interrelationships, the connecting segments, in the curriculum web. The enhancement of learning and retention by learning a few generalizable strategies rather than a large number of discrete rules of thumb has a long history of empirical support (McConnell, 1941). This position seems consonant with the learning behaviors of the slow and mentally retarded student.

The development of a minimum number of strategies to respond to a maximum number of social situations can contribute to learning by helping the slow or retarded learner impose some organizational structure on incoming stimuli. Also, since the strategy is employed over and over in response to many and varied situations, opportunities for overlearning and for developing proficiency and feelings of confidence in applying the strategy are increased. This proficiency and competence can allow the learner to direct more attention to the problem task and less attention to the cognitive skill involved with the strategy. For example, a poor counter may have to divert the majority of his or her attention to the process of counting rather than attending to the socially significant situation to which the counting strategy is addressed. The use of few strategies in many situations also contributes to the mastery and overlearning of a strategy that aids retention and is necessary if it is to be generalized to new but related situations.

Applying curriculum principles to content selection. The centrality of providing opportunities for socially significant problem solving must be in the forefront of concern in the selection of mathematics content for the

slow and mentally retarded student. Arithmetic and geometric needs in life situations associated with general consumer skills, vocational skills, and recreational skills will be of central concern. Specific measurement skills will be an important component within each of these general areas. For as pointed out by Sanders (1977), the world as we know it is possible because of measurement. Measurement is necessary if we are to have the things we wish to have and do the things we wish to do. Many of the simple tasks we all perform and take for granted are made possible or easier through measurement.

Measurement skills involving money, length, area, weight, volume, and time will be needed in responding to problems posed in the socially significant areas. Each of the measurement areas will require explicit and intensive instructional time in developing essential vocabulary, concepts of the units of measurement most commonly used, and the application of number and arithmetic skills needed in response to the "How many?" and "How much?" types of questions.

In considering number and arithmetic skills for these students, the previous section suggested the principle of a few simple, but potentially powerful, strategies that can be applied to a variety of social situations arising in the student's life space. A few such strategies will be presented to illustrate the application of the principle.

One strategy that can be applied to many situations in life and also used in developing meaning for other arithmetic processes is counting. Counting is a very primitive skill. A number of participants in the Conference on Basic Mathematical Skills and Learning (National Institute of Education, 1975) commented on the importance of counting. Buchanan (1975) stated that no system can afford to fail in developing this skill at a rather early point in the child's learning experience. Gelman and Gallistel (1978) assert that the counting principles they identified with young children constitute a scheme in the Piagetian sense. They go on to state that children cannot reason about numbers without reference to representatives of specific numerosities. These representations are obtained by counting. The judgment of equivalence, order, the applications of the operations of addition, subtraction, and identity, and the process of solving all depend on counting.

Normally developing students have generally mastered many, if not all, of the component principles of counting by the time they enter first grade, but this may not be true of the slow or mentally retarded student. As pointed out by Robinson and Robinson (1976), the mentally retarded may exhibit a "viscosity," which retards progress in cognitive development. And if Zigler (1969) is accurate in his contention that the retarded progress from lower to higher cognitive development levels in the same sequence as normal students and the only differences are the rates at which the individuals progress, then much specific and explicit work on the principles of counting

may have to be undertaken by teachers during the early school years. Analyses of the cognitive components involved with rational counting have been carried out by a number of researchers (Beckwith & Restle, 1966; Gelman & Gallistel, 1978; Ginsburg, 1977; Wang, Resnick, & Boozer, 1971) and should be examined in choosing content and a sequence of instruction that focuses on the development of counting ability.

Along with the development of the counting strategy, the significance of its use should be promoted by providing a variety of socially useful counting experiences. Incidental occurrences in the classroom can provide some opportunities for counting in response to problem situations. Many counting opportunities must be explicitly planned, however, often in association with measurement activities: How many nickels does John have? How many of Sue's footprints does it take to cover the distance from front to back in the room? How many squares will it take to cover the top of a desk? How many gram weights does it take to balance the scale when there is a candy bar in the pan on one side of the balance? How many glasses of water will it take to fill the quart pitcher? Can you count clockwise by ones from the origin (12) on a clockface to determine the number of minutes past an hour? (For a discussion of the measurement of time and the counting of frequencies to indicate duration, see Reisman, 1971.)

As counting skill increases and rich and varied opportunities are provided to apply counting strategies to socially significant problems, an associated "feel" or "sense" of number may develop. Often when teachers discuss low achievers in mathematics, they indicate that there is a lack of sense or feeling for number. Ogletree, Rackauskas, and Buergin (1970) suggest that the rhythmic nature of oral counting experiences may contribute to a feel or sense of number, as well as being a strategy for finding solutions to quantitative problems.

Quantitative problems in the students' emerging life space will continue to become more complex. Primitive counting strategies become cumbersome, and operations of arithmetic (e.g., addition, subtraction, multiplication, and division) are needed as shortcuts for counting. In directly solving these more complex problems or in solving story problems in school programs that indirectly represent these problems, deciding which operation to perform (addition, subtraction, multiplication, or division) is the major stumbling block to successful problem solving (Zweng, 1979). Is there a strategy that could be taught that would address a wide variety of problems? Wilson (1967a, 1967b) found it effective to train students to seek wanted-given structure in problem situations. On face, this strategy appears quite abstract; however, the low mental age group in the study evidently found it effective as a strategy in choosing correct operations. The attraction of the strategy is its potential power. All one-step problems are in one of four major categories. In unsophisticated language:

1. If what is *wanted* is the "size of the total (sum)" and what is *given* is the "size of each part (addends)," then add.

2. If what is *wanted* is the "size of a part" and what is *given* is the "size of the total and the size of one part," then subtract.

3. If what is *wanted* is the "size of the total (product)" and what is *given* is the "size of equal parts (factor) and the number of equal parts (factor)," then multiply.

4. If what is *wanted* is the "size of the equal parts" or "how many parts of equal size" and what is *given* is the "size of the total," then divide.

As with opportunities to associate counting strategies with a rich variety of simple quantitative situations, a rich variety of more complex problem situations should be provided to develop and master a strategy for choosing the correct arithmetic operation that will lead to a correct solution.

Once the operation for finding a solution to a problem is chosen, there is still a need to carry out the required computation. It does little good to develop proficiency in using a strategy for deciding if addition, subtraction, multiplication, or division is called for in a problem situation if skill in computing is then lacking. This is the point where demand on curriculum time by the computation program comes into conflict with the time demands of the problem-solving program. This is especially true for the slow or retarded learner because the rate of learning is so much slower. It is difficult to keep problem solving at a central point in curriculum content if significant amounts of instructional time are taken to develop paper-and-pencil computational proficiency. Something must "give," and very often it is the problem-solving part of the program.

Two general alternatives would seem to be defensible within the reality of given time constraints and the principle of the centrality of problem solving in the curriculum. One would involve the teaching for mastery of a greatly curtailed, socially essential, paper-and-pencil computational program. A second is to introduce the hand-held electronic calculator as a prosthesis for the paper-and-pencil computational part of the program.

The curtailed, socially essential, computation program would strip all but the absolutely essential computational procedures from the curriculum. If a procedure could not pass the test of social usefulness, it would not be included in the program. How often will a student, for living and vocational needs, be required to add five four-digit numbers using paper-and-pencil procedures? How often will a student need to subtract a five-digit number from a six-digit number using paper-and-pencil procedures? How often will a student be required to divide by a two-digit number? If the answer to these questions is that these skills will be called for relatively few times for addressing socially significant problems, then they should not take up precious

time in the curriculum. Generally the most useful form of an algorithm should be determined and then directly taught. In this essential paper-and-pencil computation program, the goal would be the mastery of the basic combinations and their use in developing proficiency with a significantly curtailed set of paper-and-pencil algorithms. (For a discussion of "low stress" algorithms, see Hutchins, 1977.)

The prosthesis alternative is a contemporary alternative and is based on the ease of accessibility to the electronic hand-held calculator. In supporting the use of calculators with mentally retarded students, Gallery (1978) cited the following statement from the Conference Board of Mathematical Sciences, National Advisory Committee on Mathematics Education (1975):

> Arithmetic proficiency has commonly been assumed as an unavoidable prerequisite to conceptual study and application of mathematical ideas. This practice has condemned many low achieving students to a succession of general mathematics courses that begin with and seldom progress beyond drill in arithmetic skills. Providing these students with calculators has the potential to open a rich new supply of important mathematical ideas for these students . . . at the same time breaking down self-defeating negative attitudes acquired through years of arithmetic failure. (pp. 41–42)

The use of the calculator would keep problem solving and the application of a strategy (or strategies) to determine correct operations for solving problem situations as the prime consumer of curriculum time. As consumer and other life skill problems are posed that involve the use of money, the measurement of time, length, volume, and weight, or other socially significant aspects of the mathematics program and as the computational demands go beyond counting strategies for solution, electronic calculator use could be directly taught to students.

Counting skills developed early in the program would continue to be used in either of the computational alternatives. The use of some form of counting when adding or subtracting numbers is widely prevalent. Cruickshank (1948) observed this with retarded students, but it goes well beyond that category of students. Sauls and Beeson (1976), for example, found that over 60% of the fourth graders in their study resorted to some form of counting to calculate in addition and subtraction. Beattie (1979) described various counting procedures used by fifth- and sixth-grade students in their subtraction computing and encouraged teachers to ensure that the procedures were used correctly. Rathmell (1978) has demonstrated the efficiency of counting strategies in learning some of the basic addition and multiplication facts.

The development of fairly sophisticated counting procedures might be especially useful for students who have been given calculators as a prosthesis for paper-and-pencil computations. Given a situation where 34 and 25 are to be added, students might be taught to use counting by tens and ones

to find the sum. The 34 would be counted onto 25 in the following way, using the bars placed above the 25 as a crutch to assist short-term memory in determining when to stop counting by tens and when to stop counting by ones. In subtraction, reverse counting skill could be brought into play:

— •
— •
— •   Count (while touching each bar, then each dot):
    •   *"Twenty-five—*thirty-five, forty-five, fifty-five—
                    fifty-six, fifty- seven, fifty-eight,
34 + 25 = ____   fifty-nine."

34 − 25 = ____

— •
    •   Count (while touching each bar, then each dot):
    •   *"Thirty-four—* twenty-four, fourteen—thirteen,
    •   twelve, eleven, ten, nine."
    •

Results of the counting procedures could be associated with results from pressing appropriate keys on an electronic calculator in order to give some rational association with the workings of the calculator. If a calculator was unavailable, the student would have some recourse for solution by using the more primitive counting procedures. Also, some students could be encouraged to test the reasonableness of the calculator outcome periodically by using a gross counting check.

The discussion of mathematics content for slow and mentally retarded learners to this point has not been meant as a complete and exhaustive coverage. Rather, it was meant to illustrate the form that content might take within a certain segment of the curriculum when the guiding principles developed in the previous section were applied. Emphasis was given to the segment of the curriculum dealing with the development of whole numbers. No consideration was given to the content in the domain of rational numbers.

The curriculum principles would again be applied in determining program content with fractions, decimals, and percent. Opportunities for socially relevant problem solving would again be central to that segment of the program. Certainly a significant number of applications would involve

carefully planned experiences with the measurement of money, distance, area, volume, weight, and time. There would be need to develop explicitly the concepts for frequently used rational number ideas such as one-half, one-third, and one-fourth. With increasing use of SI (the metric system) in measurement, more experiences will be needed in work with tenths and hundredths but less with such fractional parts as twelfths or sixteenths. And it will be increasingly common to name parts of units using decimal numerals rather than fractional numerals. Opportunities to apply strategies in choosing correct operations in responding to problem situations with rational numbers should build on, and be consistent with, the strategies developed with whole numbers. Serious thought would again have to be given to whether to have the students master a minimum number of socially essential paper-and-pencil algorithms with fractions and decimals or develop the use of electronic processing procedures.

Opportunities should also be provided for some geometry experiences. Concepts and associated vocabulary for common two- and three-dimensional shapes should be developed. These shapes can then be used to explore space, for example, which shapes will cover an area without gaps or overlaps and which will not. The shapes can also be used in exploring symmetry in space and balance in arrangements that appear aesthetically pleasing. Relationships such as congruence and similarity may also be appropriate for some students. Informal explorations of geometric ideas can serve as a nice change of pace from arithmetic work and also provide opportunities to develop a more sensitive awareness of the geometric world that surrounds the student.

Teaching Mathematics to Slow and Mentally Retarded Students

Glennon pointed out in an introductory section of this book that teachers have three general sources of methodology: teaching by telling, teaching by guided discovery, and teaching as an educational therapist. The latter is primarily the teaching response directed to concern for the affective development of the student; the former two are teaching responses directed to concerns for the cognitive development of the student. But cognitive and affective development interact in highly complex ways, and at the classroom level these sources of method swirl together in complex ways in the stream of classroom instruction.

This section will primarily be concerned with general principles for guiding classroom instructional practice in mathematics learning—a cognitive matter. This does not reflect a disregard for the importance of affect in learning mathematics but of viewing that instructional component as a state of being in the classroom atmosphere. For the slow and retarded learner it is surely important for the teacher to be warm, to be supportive, to be trusted so that students develop positive feelings about themselves in

relation with the world around them—especially the quantitative and spatial aspects of the world. The more maladaptive behaviors manifested by these students, the more importance the affective dimension assumes. This is a necessary, but not sufficient, dimension to consider for attaining a good psychoeducational match between the slow and retarded learner and the methods of teaching mathematics. Beyond what it is desirable for teachers to *be*, there is considerable importance to what they can *do* in the classroom to optimize learning. The following section presents some general instructional principles that may assist and enhance mathematics learning for these students.

Instructional pace and patterning. One of the most fundamental ways in which retarded children differ from normal children at the same age lies in the slowness and inefficiency with which they acquire knowledge and skills (Robinson & Robinson, 1976). Connally (1973) indicated that the typical retarded student will tend to progress at the rate of approximately one-half grade a year. The importance of curtailment in content was discussed previously, but adjustment must also be made in the pace of instruction. Each framed learning activity must be carefully arranged and "held" a little longer, and the transition to the next instructional frame must be carefully planned and explicitly presented. The cognitive leaps that the more able students make through their active and spontaneous organization of incoming stimuli are seldom experienced by the slow or retarded learner. Instead, organizational responsibility rests more on the teacher, who must provide explicit instructional steps that are often passively received by these students.

In spite of these students' more passive responding and poor organizational ability, teachers may be able to help them make some cognitive steps on their own. Opportunities for using the potential of patterning should be encouraged. Consider an instructional procedure for introducing simple multiplication ideas. A problem may be posed that requires finding how many students there are in all if there are two students in a row and five rows. Representational manipulative materials (number strips) could be arranged to model the situation (Figure 5.1). The symbolic record of the situation should be closely associated with the display. A counting strategy may be employed to find the solution. The teacher may then continue the modeling and symbolic record with four 2s, three 2s, two 2s, one 2, taking care to promote the pattern in the perceptual field. At that point a review of what has been presented can be undertaken, examining what has been found out about one, two, three, four, and five rows of two people. The teacher may then pose a "What would happen if . . ." problem. "What would happen if there were six rows of two people? Could you show me with number strips? Could you write it? How many people would there be?"

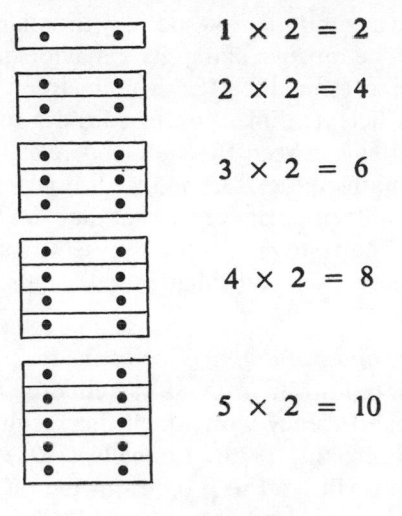

$$1 \times 2 = 2$$

$$2 \times 2 = 4$$

$$3 \times 2 = 6$$

$$4 \times 2 = 8$$

$$5 \times 2 = 10$$

Figure 5.1.

The compelling nature of the pattern in the perceptual field may allow slow or retarded students to make a small cognitive step on their own in response to the "What would happen if . . ." problem. This may be a small, insignificant step for a more normal student, but perhaps the feeling of a giant leap by a retarded or slow student who has seldom experienced success on a cognitive step on his or her own. The orderly and elegant structure of the number system lends itself nicely to patterned presentations in the perceptual field of the learner and may assist and compel the learner to make measured steps beyond the information given. Junge (1972) has suggested a variety of instructional techniques for emphasizing number patterns in teaching mathematics to slow-learning students.

Instructional material. The stage theories of mental development developed by Bruner (1973a) and by Piaget (1973) place considerable importance on student activity on or with concrete materials. Such activity at early stages of development helps develop thinking schemes that are indispensably tied to later internalized symbolic and logical thought. Lovell (1966) found that by ages 13 to 15 only some mildly retarded young persons had attained the stage of concrete operations. He maintained that almost all adolescents with IQs roughly 75 to 85 eventually reach this stage but do not succeed to the next step of formal operations. It would seem that the vast majority of the slow and mentally retarded students for whom the schools are responsible have not developed intellectually to the point that they depend on internalized thought processes but instead are greatly dependent on mental actions on external objects.

As important as the use of concrete and pictorial materials are to these students—in fact, *because* the students are so dependent on these exter-

nals—great care must be used in choosing and using concrete manipulative materials in framing instructional episodes. Many students are still at a preoperational stage of development and thus tend to focus their attention on the most compelling attribute of the material. If care isn't taken, an instructional frame using manipulatives to develop a number idea may not be doing so at all—and in fact may be distracting—since the student may be centering attention on some other, more compelling attribute such as the color, length, or texture of the materials. Teachers of the slow and mentally retarded must be especially aware of the paradox that is faced in developing and using concrete or pictorial materials in mathematics instruction. To make the materials interesting, unessential (to mathematics) attributes are often incorporated. These details may heighten interest but at the same time detract attention from the essential attribute needed for learning. Normal students are often able to filter out the unessential from the essential; slow and retarded students are less able to observe selectively.

It would seem that concrete mathematics materials such as natural wood blocks that have been "engineered" precisely so that they are constant in size and shape and have attributes that reflect the base ten numeration system would be especially appropriate for teaching early number and numeration ideas. If such materials are unavailable, homemade number strips like those in Figure 5.1 may be useful. Such materials allow the student to count or measure in determining number or the relations between numbers. After careful early development, systematic instruction can be undertaken to develop the idea that number is conserved through a variety of physical arrangements and across various contexts of a display.

A "mixed blessing" problem arises with materials in many compensatory programs in schools. As indicated earlier, many of the slow and mildly retarded students in a school system may be serviced by compensatory programs. Schools that were nearly void of any mathematics materials beyond a textbook have, since the late 1960s, been inundated with a variety of instructional materials. "Math labs" or "resource rooms" are filled with attractive materials. Many different materials can be used in different instructional settings to develop mathematical skills, concepts, and understandings. But such diversity may be quite inappropriate for the slow or retarded student. With their difficulty in flexibly using such mediators in transfer and generalization of learning, it would seem more appropriate to use fewer types of concrete materials that have comprehensive use for learning mathematics over a wide range of content.

Print materials used in mathematics instruction should also be chosen or prepared with much care so that both in format and in content a premium is placed on the clarity of the presentation. Friedlander (1968) reported that it is quite clearly established that retarded children have more problems and more serious problems of a perceptual nature than other

children. When learning materials for special education use are not carefully designed to eliminate perceptual difficulties, the pupils not only have difficulty with the intended content of their learning tasks but also have difficulty attaining a well-organized sense of what they are supposed to be seeing and doing. Normal and superior children can often figure out what an author, a publisher, or a teacher intends even when the material is not clearly presented, but the retarded are helpless victims of such carelessness.

Coordination and articulation of instruction. Consistency in instructional procedures is a very important consideration in teaching the slow and retarded student. The previous section suggested that consistent use of a few concrete materials with comprehensive potential for modeling mathematics ideas may be better than using different materials at every turn. But consistency in instruction is not limited to materials. Words and sentences also affect learning and therefore require consistency. It is desirable to use a consistent language in mathematics instruction with all students, but it is particularly important with the slow and retarded. Normal and bright students may be able to cognitively rise above the clutter of having instructional language associate the minus sign sometimes with "subtracting," other times with "taking away," and still other times with "minusing." But for slower students such inconsistency can contribute more inefficiency to an already inefficient cognitive processing.

Getting "comfortable" with mathematics words and materials that are used consistently and regularly over a period of time may help create a certain expectancy for what is to come in an instructional frame. This, in turn, may lead to a rehearsal of what is to come in the frame and improve the retention of what is taught. Transfer of learning may also be enhanced. Robinson and Robinson (1976) have indicated that although the long-lasting effect of training (on transfer) is somewhat discouraging (given existing empirical evidence), it has been obtained in some instances in which the training has been both extensive and consistent.

Communication among those people involved with the mathematics instruction of slow and retarded students is critical if consistency is to be achieved. This is especially important at the point of instruction where a student may be "passed on" to a teacher at the next grade level or where more than one person is involved with mathematics instruction during the year. As indicated earlier, many of the slow and mildly retarded students may be serviced through compensatory instruction programs in a school system. They may leave the classroom teacher for supplementary help in mathematics. Parents, aides, or volunteers may also assist students with their mathematics work. Communication about mathematics materials and the use of the language used in instruction should be encouraged among all these people in order to achieve consistency. To use an analogy from the

world of sports, most coaches encourage their team players to talk to one another so each knows what the other is doing at all times. The team of teachers, aides, and parents involved with teaching mathematics to slow and retarded students should also constantly use such talk to insure consistency in language and procedures.

Practice and maintenance in instruction. Providing systematic practice of a mathematics skill, concept, or strategy is a very important component of the instructional sequence for slow and mentally retarded students. In regard to students retaining what they have learned, Smith (1971) stated that in general retarded youngsters are able to remember material as well as normal subjects if (a) they have overlearned the fact or concept beyond a minimum criterion level and (b) they have had an opportunity to reinforce this learning through constant use. Very serious consideration must be given to the mathematics content that requires overlearning, and then specific and systematic practice provided.

Burton (1972) asserts that practice has two essential phases, the *integrative* phase, in which perception of the meaning is developed, and the *repetitive* phase, in which precision is developed. These two dimensions of practice interrelate in the development of mastery and precision in the use of mathematics skills and abilities.

Suppose a two-dimensional array of number strips, like those shown in Figure 5.1, was used in the initial teaching of multiplication combinations. It may be that a student will initially use a primitive counting process to determine that 5×2 is 10. Systematic integrative practice can be provided so the learning will "spread" to situations other than number strips. "How many chairs are in this 5 by 2 array?" "How many square feet in this 5 by 2 array?" A further spread of the idea to one-dimensional situations can be undertaken. "How long a pole can I make with 5 sticks, each 2 yards long?" A further spread to duration of time can be considered. "How long will it take to boil 5 2-minute eggs one at a time?" The spread can continue to a variety of appropriate social situations that can be mathematically modeled by 5×2. Students who are counting by ones can be encouraged to find a faster way of processing, for example, counting by twos. The various social situations may be revisited again using this higher level of processing. Ultimately it is desirable to recall the fact that 5×2 is 10. As each successive higher level of processing is attained, some repetitive practice may be needed to fix the learning at that level.

Because of the amount of time that is required for these students to master the initial learning, not only is it important to choose the content to be mastered with extreme care, but it is also important to use class time efficiently. Every possible opportunity should be grasped to work on primary and secondary mathematics objectives in a single lesson. If the primary objective of a particular lesson involves integrative practice with multiplica-

tion combinations in the area of linear measurement, the teacher should also be alert to the opportunities for providing incidentally (though systematically) planned maintenance opportunities for previously mastered vocabulary concepts or skills in the linear measurement area. Likewise, if the primary objective of the lesson is work with linear measurement, every possible opportunity should be grasped to incidentally furnish appropriate maintenance work in the area of numbers.

Task complexity awareness. Few things in mathematics teaching are as simple as they may at first appear. There is a tendency, for example, to pass off $2 + 2 = 4$ as a "simple fact." Brownell and Hendrikson (1950), however, suggest that such facts are "ideational learning tasks which are heavily freighted with meaning . . . involving as it does, not only the idea 'two', the idea 'four', an understanding of the equivalence ($=$) of '2 + 2' on the one hand and of '4' on the other" (p. 194). The implications of complexity awareness by the teacher of typical students is important; to the teacher of the slow and retarded it is much more important, since more of the input structuring and sequencing for effective student learning falls on the teacher.

An example of a group addressing this principle in a particular area of mathematics is found in the work of Cawley and Goodman (1969) and Cawley and Vitello (1972) in mathematics word problems. Research was undertaken over the years to apprehend more clearly the network of variables at play in the successful solving of word problems. It led to an awareness of the effect that conditions such as sentence structure, vocabulary level, information-processing demands, and complexity of computations have on the successful solving of word problems by mentally retarded students.

What the principle suggests to the teacher is not to be taken in by what may appear to be deceptively simple tasks of mathematics. In teaching essential mathematics to the slow and mentally retarded students, few things are simple. Friedlander (1968) pointed out that teachers must develop greater respect for the difficulty of what we expect young children to perform when we try to teach them the "easiest" part of learning their numbers. The learning of a single number concept, a simple addition combination, or a solution to a simple word problem are all incredibly complex psychological undertakings for these slower students. Learning prospects can be enhanced if there first is an awareness of the psychological requirements mathematics tasks impose on the learner and then explicit instruction is framed in accordance with that awareness.

Assessment of Learning

The development and evaluation of individualized education programs (IEPs) for students with handicapping conditions requires sensitive assess-

ment procedures both in formulating appropriate programs and in judging the degree of success of the programs. Summative evaluation is directed toward the degree to which program outcomes have been attained as a result of a particular unit of work or a more extensive program. Summative assessment procedures are carried out after learning or instruction has taken place. Formative evaluation involves assessment procedures used in ascertaining the next steps in the instructional sequence. Unlike summative evaluation, which is carried out after learning or instruction has taken place, formative evaluation is an integral part of instruction and assists the teacher in determining the next steps in instruction.

A teacher's evaluative judgments in either formative or summative situations are typically related either to the degree of learning attainment on certain mathematical content (criterion referenced) or to other students' performance in learning that same mathematical content (norm referenced). In using criterion-referenced procedures, the teacher evaluates performance strictly in terms of content attainment. For example, if the focus was on learning basic addition combinations, an objective criterion level for mastery on an assessment procedure would be set—95% of the items must be correct to indicate mastery. Judgments are made relative to a student's performance on particular content. How other students perform on that particular content does not enter into or influence the judgment. In norm-referenced evaluation, the student's performance is judged in relation to the performance of other students on the content of assessment tasks. School-wide or statewide standardized achievement testing programs are examples of norm-referenced assessment. Results can then be used to make gross comparisons of performance between and among comparable groups.

Extensive use of norm-referenced evaluation procedures with the slow and mentally retarded students is not particularly profitable. The intellectual development of these students is generally marching to a different developmental drumbeat from that of the normal population. Their performance on standardized achievement tests is little more than a yearly reminder of the cumulative achievement deficit being experienced relative to the norming population on the test. It is of little value or consolation to know that a particular student's performance on basic addition combinations is at the 65th percentile relative to other students' performances if she or he responded accurately to only 10 out of 20 tasks on an assessment tool.

Criterion-referenced assessment appears to be a compatible evaluation procedure for slow and mentally retarded students. They need to develop feelings of accomplishment and competence on highly focused and delimited segments of the curriculum. This should come from mastering learning tasks, not from mastering their peers. What does it profit a student to "do best" in his or her group if that "best" is far from the mastery of an essential skill? Systematic use of criterion-referenced assessment procedures

can help both student and teacher set attainable instructional goals and contribute some awareness to reasonable time schedules for the mastery of particular units of work.

Criterion-referenced evaluation, and the concept of mastery learning, is probably more important and appropriate for slow and mentally retarded students than for the typical or superior student population. Ebel (1971) indicated that arguments for mastery learning are compelling when applied to basic intellectual skills that everyone needs to exercise almost flawlessly in order to live effectively in modern society but that these basic skills make up only a small fraction of what schools teach. Proportionately, these basic intellectual skills take significantly more of the instructional time for the slow and retarded student and thus make the mastery-learning procedure more attractive for these students.

The mastery-learning procedure, even with slow and mentally retarded students, must be used sensibly. It would appear to be most effectively applied in teaching the skill parts of the mathematics curriculum, for example, counting, basic combinations, telling time, and so on. However, common sense must be used with the procedure. There have been times when students have spent unreasonable amounts of time on a particular task because they have not achieved "mastery." The teacher was unwilling to go to anything else until such mastery occurred. As a result, students were seriously deprived of opportunities to learn other important aspects of the curriculum.

It was pointed out in an earlier section that the school mathematics program could not be reduced to thousands of linearly arranged behavioral objectives for learning. This is important to remember when using mastery procedures. It must be kept in mind that problem solving is a central consideration in the mathematics curriculum. Arithmetic skills are mastered so that they can be used in solving problems, not as something to be mastered for their own sake. If all the mathematics time is taken to achieve a mastery of skills in isolation and no opportunities are provided for solving problems using these skills, then such mastery is a bad bargain for these youngsters. Also, it must be kept in mind that problem solving and proficiency in the skill areas create a two-way street. Success in applying skills in problem solving can contribute to increased mastery and the overlearning of those skills; mastery and the overlearning of skills can contribute to improved problem-solving ability.

Valid evaluation requires a congruence between assessment procedures and the content of the mathematics curriculum. Earlier comment on content suggested that two broad, interrelated aspects of arithmetic and number be included in the curriculum: arithmetic as a tool subject and arithmetic as a thinking process. Both characteristics of arithmetic should be taken into account in the evaluation program. The tool aspect em-

phasizes the "product" ends of mathematics learning; the thought aspect emphasizes the "process" means used in mathematics functioning.

Consider an arithmetic task such as 9 + 3 in examining process and product aspects of learning and evaluation. A student is faced with this task on a paper-and-pencil test. She makes hatch marks on her hand,

/ / / / / / / /   / / /,

counts the marks, and records the "product" of her thought—12. The teacher in turn makes inferences about the student's knowledge on the basis of the paper-and-pencil response to the task. The learning "products" are typically judged on the basis of speed and accuracy of response. But the thinking "process" aspect is much more difficult to judge, especially from responses to paper-and-pencil assessments. These judgments require the teacher to be skilled in informal assessment procedures. Both incidental observations of student performance on mathematics tasks and planned informal interviews (Weaver, 1955) are needed for insights in "process" evaluation.

A simple Cartesian model might be used in illustrating the value of taking both "process" and "product" learning into account in mathematics assessment. For the student mentioned in the previous paragraph (Student A), the hand marking and rudimentary counting "process" may become fixed and continue for a long period of time. The marks may be made faster, the arrangement clearer, and the counting less error prone, so that strictly on the basis of product outcomes on paper-and-pencil assessments there may be some growth in proficiency from a speed and accuracy point of view. Student A's growth curve on such tasks is shown in Figure 5.2.

Another student (B) may respond to the addition combination task in the same way. However, at a particular point a teacher intervenes and suggests a better way of processing. Perhaps a strategy for 9 + 3 would be to choose the "bigger" number and count on by the indicated amount of the other number. Initially it may be necessary to make three hatch marks in order to remember when to stop counting; with practice this crutch may be discontinued. It may well be that at the point where this student is weaned from the rudimentary counting process to the more sophisticated, "choose the bigger and count on" process, some regression in proficiency (speed and accuracy) with the tasks will appear. However, with practice, proficiency will return, and the student with the more mature thinking "process" will ultimately outperform the student with the immature process on product outcomes. Student B's growth curve on such tasks is also presented in Figure 5.2.

Evaluation of the learning product is typically carried out through paper-and-pencil assessment procedures. The curriculum content is sampled

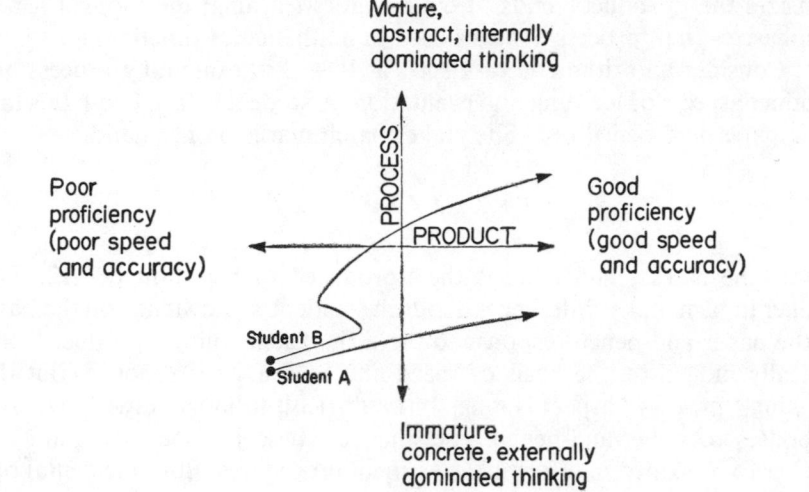

Figure 5.2.

by test item tasks; students respond by recording answers on paper or choosing an answer from multiple options. Teachers then infer the degree of product learning on the basis of the test.

Evaluation of the learning process is much more subtle, sensitive, and difficult. Sometimes an examination of scrap paper of doodles on paper-and-pencil tests can give clues to the thinking process being used. A teacher's direct observations of students working on mathematics tasks in the classroom can give insight into the thinking processes being used. Such incidental observations may not give a thorough insight into thinking processes, however, and more systematic procedures may have to be used.

The structured informal interview can provide a useful means of assessing process, as well as product, outcomes of instruction. To complement incidental observations, teachers may present arithmetic tasks that sample content in an informal, but structured, interview situation. This procedure can provide a maximum amount of information from a minimum amount of visual stimuli. So often paper-and-pencil tests, especially diagnostic tests, appear overwhelming to the slow or mentally retarded student because of the great number of tasks needed to ascertain strengths and weaknesses. The well-conducted informal interview allows the teacher to make some intensive and extensive probes of thinking without an overwhelming number of mathematics tasks in the visual field.

Most tests capture student performance on paper. Indirect inferences about mathematics learning are then made from the paper. Alternatives to recording performance on paper are becoming more available in the highly developed electronic era in which we are living. It has become a relatively

easy matter to capture student performance on electronic tape. Videotaping can become a particularly useful complement of the structured informal interview for assessing student learning. This medium allows for more direct inferences about mathematics learning on the basis of the direct performance of students captured on videotape. The modern teacher now has available the means not only to "show" parents, colleagues, and others how a student performs on a paper-and-pencil test but also to show a very direct and dynamic performance on mathematics tasks through this electronic medium. For years highly successful football coaches have spent hours analyzing the performance of their players in order to improve that performance. This is also a useful means for teachers to use for assessing mathematics performance of students and then planning appropriate instructional experiences.

The development of sensitive and sensible IEPs will require insight into the strengths and weaknesses of students on various curriculum content areas of mathematics. This involves assessing not only the speed and accuracy with which they perform tasks in the content areas but also the mental processes they employ in achieving those ends.

SUMMARY

This chapter initially described the general classifications of mentally retarded and slow-learning students. Particular attention was given to court cases, public laws, and shifting definitions of professional organizations that have tended to define the populations of these handicapped students in the public schools. Evidence from various research and authoritative sources was summarized in presenting a few key concepts regarding causation and diagnosis in these areas of exceptionality.

Behavioral characteristics of slow-learning and mentally retarded children were examined. Emphasis was given to those behavioral characteristics that appeared to be germane to mathematics performance. Aspects of learning and motivational characteristics that differentiate the slow-learning and mentally retarded students from the more typical student population and that implied the need for adaptations in mathematics instruction for these students were presented.

Mathematics instruction for these students was examined in light of the general perspectives developed by Glennon in chapter 2 and the characteristics of mentally retarded and slow-learning students presented in the initial sections of this chapter. Curriculum suggestions included a curtailment of the scope of the mathematics program; emphasis on fewer, but cognitively potent, strategies and skills that could be used to address a broad spectrum of socially relevant problems; and the centrality of problem-solving activities. Classroom procedures pointed to the importance

of instructional pace and patterning; the use of a few comprehensibly applicable types of concrete instructional materials; the consistent and correct use of language in mathematics instruction; the importance of overlearning and providing for appropriate practice and maintenance procedures; and awareness by teachers of the complexity of the simple appearing mathematics learnings.

The importance of assessment of mathematics learning in the development of IEPs was examined. The contributions of both product and process assessment in both formative and summative evaluation were considered. The use of paper-and-pencil tests and informal interviews was suggested in developing the teacher's insight for evaluation purposes.

An awesome amount of hard work and rigorous research is required to develop a base of knowledge that is needed in order to put forward a defensible mathematics program for slow-learning and mentally retarded students. The few broad suggestions for instruction made in this chapter are tentative and generally untested, but they seem sensible at this time. Teams of researchers, including both mathematics and special educators, are needed to develop cooperatively rigorous research and development programs in mathematics for these exceptional students. By building on the few things we think we know and developing procedures to discern the things we need to know, we can develop more comprehensive and specific procedures for teaching mathematics in the years ahead. There is much work to be done.

REFERENCES

Abramowicz, H. K., & Richardson, S. A. Epidemiology of severe mental retardation in children: Community studies. *American Journal of Mental Deficiency*, 1975, *80*, 18–39.

Ashurst, D. I., & Meyers, C. E. Social system and clinical model in school identification of the educable retarded. In R. K. Eyman, C. E. Meyers, & G. Tarjan (Eds.), Sociobehavioral studies in mental retardation. *Monographs of the American Association on Mental Deficiency*, 1973, No. 1, pp. 150–163.

Atkinson, R. C., & Shiffrin, R. M. Human memory: A proposed system and its control processes. In K. W. Spence & J. T. Spence (Eds.), *The psychology of learning and motivation: Advances in research and theory* (Vol. 2). New York: Academic Press, 1968.

Beattie, I. D. Children's strategies for solving subtraction-fact combinations. *Arithmetic Teacher*, 1979, *27*(1), 14–15.

Beckwith, M., & Restle, F. Process of enumeration. *Psychological Review*, 1966, *73*, 437–444.

Belmont, J. M., & Butterfield, E. C. Learning strategies as determinants of memory deficiencies. *Cognitive Psychology*, 1971, *2*, 411–420.

Blatt, B. Teach children and teachers to be. *Education and Training of the Mentally Retarded*, 1977, *12*, 29–31.

Bloom, B. S. *Human characteristics and school learning.* New York: McGraw-Hill, 1976.

Bloom, B. S. *Stability and change in human characteristics.* New York: Wiley, 1964.

Brown, A. L., Campione, J. C., & Murphy, M. D. Keeping track of changing variables: Long term retention of a trained rehearsal strategy by retarded adolescents. *American Journal of Mental Deficiency*, 1974, *78*, 446–453.

Brownell, W. A. The place of meaning in the teaching of arithmetic. *Elementary School Journal*, 1947, *47*, 256–265.

Brownell, W. A., & Hendrikson, G. How children learn information, concepts, and generalizations. In *Learning and instruction* (Forty-ninth Yearbook of the National Society for the Study of Education, Pt. I). Chicago: University of Chicago Press, 1950.

Bruner, J. S. The course of cognitive growth. In J. M. Anglin (Ed.), *Beyond the information given*. New York: Norton, 1973. (a)

Bruner, J. S. Going beyond the information given. In J. M. Anglin (Ed.), *Beyond the information given*. New York: Norton, 1973. (b)

Buchanan, A. D. Some notes on basic mathematical skills and learning. In *Conference on basic mathematical skills and learning* (Vol.1). Washington, D.C.: National Institute of Education, 1975.

Burton, W. H. *The guidance of learning activities: A summary of the principles of teaching based upon the growth of the learner*. New York: Appleton-Century-Crofts, 1972.

Cawley, J., & Goodman, J. Arithmetic problem solving: A demonstration with the mentally handicapped. *Exceptional Children*, 1969, *36*, 83–88.

Cawley, J., & Vitello, S. Model for arithmetical programming for handicapped children. *Exceptional Children*, 1972, *39*, 101–110.

Conference Board of the Mathematical Sciences, National Advisory Committee on Mathematical Education. *Overview and analysis of school mathematics, grades K–12*. Reston, Va.: National Council of Teachers of Mathematics, 1975.

Connally, A. Research in mathematics education and the mentally retarded. *Arithmetic Teacher*, 1973, *20*, 491–497.

Cruickshank, W. M. Arithmetic ability of mentally retarded children, I. *Journal of Educational Research*, 1948, *42*, 161–170. (b)

Cruickshank, W. M. Arithmetic ability of mentally retarded children, II. *Journal of Educational Research*, 1948, *42*, 279–288. (c)

Cruickshank, W. M. Arithmetic work habits of mentally retarded boys. *American Journal of Mental Deficiency*, 1948, *52*, 318–330. (a)

Dingman, H. F., & Tarjan, G. Mental retardation and the normal distribution curve. *American Journal of Mental Deficiency*, 1960, *64*, 991–994.

Dunn, L. M., & Capobiance, R. J. A comparison of the reading processes of mentally retarded and normal boys of the same mental age. *Monographs of the Society for Research in Child Development*, 1954, *19*, 7–99.

Ebel, R. L. Criterion-referenced measurements: Limitations. *School Review*, 1971, *79*, 282–288.

Ellis, N. R. Memory processes in retardates and normals. In N. R. Ellis (Ed.), *International review of research in mental retardation* (Vol. 4). New York: Academic Press, 1970.

Eyman, R. K., & Miller, C. A demographic overview of severe and profound mental retardation. In C. E. Meyers (Ed.), Quality of life in severely and profoundly mentally retarded people: Research foundations for improvement. *Monograph of the American Association on Mental Deficiency*, 1978, No. 3, pp. ix–xii.

Friedlander, B. Z. Psychology and the third R in special education. *Education and Training of the Mentally Retarded*, 1968, *3*, 80–89.

Gallery, M. E. Teaching calculator use and checking account skills to the mildly handicapped (Doctoral dissertation, Utah State University, 1978). *Dissertation Abstracts International*, 1978, *39*, 2866A. (University Microfilms No. 78-21,130)

Gardner, G. E., Tarjan, G., & Richmond, J. B. *Mental retardation: A handbook for the primary physician*. Chicago: American Medical Association, 1965.

Gelman, R., & Gallistel, C. R. *The child's understanding of number*. Cambridge, Mass.: Harvard University Press, 1978.

Ginsburg, H. *Children's arithmetic: The learning process*. New York: D. Van Nostrand, 1977.

Glennon, V. J. Elementary school mathematics: Alternatives and imperatives. In A. D. Roberts (Ed.), *Educational innovation: Alternatives in curriculum and instruction*. Boston: Allyn & Bacon, 1975.

Grossman, H. J. (Ed.). *Manual on terminology and classification in mental retardation*. Washington, D.C.: American Association on Mental Deficiency, 1973.

Harris, G. J. Input and output organization in short-term serial recall by retarded and nonretarded children. *American Journal of Mental Deficiency*. 1972, *76*, 423–426.

Heber, R. F. A manual on terminology and classification in mental retardation (Rev. ed.). *American Journal of Mental Deficiency Monograph*, 1961 (Supp. 64).

Heber. R. F. Personality. In H. A. Stevens & R. Heber (Eds.), *Mental retardation: A review of research*. Chicago: University of Chicago Press, 1964.

Hewett, F. M. The emotionally disturbed child in the classroom. Boston: Allyn & Bacon, 1968.

Hutchings, B. Low-stress algorithms. In D. Nelson (Ed.), *Measurement in school mathematics* (1976 Yearbook of the National Council of Teachers of Mathematics). Reston, Va.: The Council, 1976.

Jensen, A. R. How much can we boost IQ and scholastic achievement? *Harvard Educational Review*, 1969, *39*, 1–123.

Jensen., A. R. Rote learning in retarded adults and normal children. *American Journal of Mental Deficiency*, 1965, *69*, 828–834.

Jensen, A. R., & Rohwer, W. D., Jr. The effect of verbal mediation on the learning and retention of paired-associates by retarded adults. *American Journal of Mental Deficiency*, 1963, *68*, 80–84. (b)

Jensen, A. R., & Rohwer, W. D., Jr. Verbal mediation in paired-associate and serial learning. *Journal of Learning and Verbal Behavior*, 1963, *1*, 346–352. (a)

Junge, C. W. Adjustment of instruction (Elementary school). In *The slow learner in mathematics* (Thirty-fifth Yearbook of the National Council of Teachers of Mathematics). Reston, Va.: The Council, 1972.

Kanner, L. Feeblemindedness, absolute, relative, and apparent. *Nervous Child*. 1948, *7*, 365–397.

Kohlberg, L., & Mayer, R. Development as the aim of education. *Harvard Educational Review*, 1972, *42*, 449–496.

Lovell, K. The developmental approach of Jean Piaget: Open discussion. In M. Garrison, Jr. (Ed.), *Cognitive models and development in mental retardation. American Journal of Mental Deficiency*, 1966, *70*, 84–95. (Monograph Supplement)

MacMillan, D. L. Facilitative effect of input organization as a function of verbal response to stimuli in EMR and nonretarded children. *American Journal of Mental Deficiency*, 1972, *76*, 408–411.

MacMillan, D. L. *Mental retardation in school and society*. Boston: Little, Brown & Co., 1977.

MacMillan, D. L. The problem of motivation in the education of the mentally retarded. *Exceptional Children*, 1971, *37*, 579–586.

MacMillan, D. L., & Meyers, C. E. Educational labeling of handicapped learners. In D. Berliner (Ed.), *Review of research in education*. Washington, D.C.: American Educational Research Association, in press.

Masland, R. L., Sarason, S. B., & Gladwin, T. *Mental subnormality*. New York: Basic Books, 1958.

McConnell, T. R. Recent trends in learning theory: Their application to the psychology of arithmetic. In *Arithmetic in general education* (Sixteenth Yearbook of the National Council of Teachers of Mathematics). New York: Bureau of Publications, Teachers College, Columbia University, 1941.

Mercer, J. R. *Labelling the mentally retarded*. Berkeley: University of California Press, 1973. (a)

Mercer, J. R. The myth of 3% prevalence. In R. K. Eyman, C. E. Meyers, & G. Tarjan (Eds.), Sociobehavioral studies in mental retardation. *Monographs of the American Association on Mental Deficiency*, 1973, No. 1. (b)

Meyen, E. L., & Moran, M. R. A perspective on the unserved mildly handicapped. *Exceptional Children*, 1979, *45*, 526–530.

Meyers, C. E., & Lombardi, T. Definition of the mentally retarded: Decision time for AAMD. *Mental Retardation*, 1974, *12*, 43.

Meyers, C. E., MacMillan, D. L., & Zetlin, A. Education for all handicapped children. *Pediatric Annals*, 1978, *7*(5), 348–356.

Meyers, C. E., Sundstrom, P. E., & Yoshida, R. K. The school psychologist and assessment in special education. *School Psychology Monographs*, 1974, *2*(1), 3–57.

Milgram, N. A. Retention of mediation set in paired-associate learning of normal and retarded children. *Journal of Experimental Child Psychology*, 1967, *5*, 341–349.

National Council of Supervisors of Mathematics. Position statement on basic skills. *Arithmetic Teacher*, 1977, *25*(1) 19–22.

National Institute of Education. *Conference on basic mathematical skills and learning* (Vol. 1). Washington, D.C.: Author, 1975.

Neill, A. S. *Summerhill*. New York: Hart, 1960.

Ogletree, E. J., Rackauskas, J. A., & Buergin, T. F. Teaching number sense through rhythmical counting. *Elementary School Journal*, 1970, *70*, 11–17.

Piaget, J. Comments on mathematics education. In A. G. Howson (Ed.), *Developments in mathematical education* (Proceedings of the Second International Congress on Mathematical Education). London: Cambridge University Press, 1973.

President's Committee on Mental Retardation. *Report to the president: A proposed program for national action to combat mental retardation*. Washington, D.C.: U.S. Government Printing Office, 1962.

President's Task Force on the Mentally Handicapped. *Action against mental disability*. Washington, D.C.: U.S. Government Printing Office, 1970.

Rathmell, E. C. Using thinking strategies to teach the basic facts. In M. N. Suydam (Ed.), *Developing computational skills* (1978 Yearbook of the National Council of Teachers of Mathematics). Reston, Va.: The Council, 1978.

Reisman, F. K. Children's errors in telling time and a recommended teaching sequence. *Arithmetic Teacher*, 1971, *18*, 152–55.

Rising, G. R., Brown, S. I., & Meyerson, L. N. The teacher-centered mathematics classroom. In F. J. Crosswhite (Ed.), *Organizing for mathematics instruction* (1977 Yearbook of the National Council of Teachers of Mathematics). Reston, Va.: The Council, 1977.

Robinson, N. M., & Robinson, H. B. *The mentally retarded child* (2nd ed.). New York: McGraw-Hill, 1976.

Sanders, W. J. Why measure? In D. Nelson (Ed.), *Measurement in school mathematics* (1976 Yearbook of the National Council of Teachers of Mathematics). Reston, Va.: The Council, 1976.

Sauls, C., & Beeson, B. F. The relationship of finger counting to certain pupil factors. *Journal of Educational Research*, 1976, *70*, 81–83.

Schaaf, W. L. Mathematics as a cultural heritage. *Arithmetic Teacher*, 1961, *8*, 5–9.

Shif, Z. I. Development of children in schools for the mentally retarded. In M. Cole & I. Maltzman (Eds.), *A handbook of contemporary Soviet psychology*. New York: Basic Books, 1969.

Smith, R. M. *An introduction to mental retardation*. New York: McGraw-Hill, 1971.

Spitz, H. H. The role of input organization in the learning and memory of mental retardates. In N. R. Ellis (Ed.), *International review of research in mental retardation* (Vol. 2). New York: Academic Press, 1966.

Tarjan, G., Wright, S. W., Eyman, R. K., & Keeran, C. V. Natural history of mental retarda-

tion: Some aspects of epidemiology. *American Journal of Mental Deficiency*, 1973, *77*, 369–379.

Turnure, J. E. Distractibility in the mentally retarded: Negative evidence for an orienting inadequacy. *Exceptional Children*, 1970, *37*, 181–186.

Turnure, J. E., & Thurlow, M. L. Effects of structural variations in elaboration on learning by EMR and nonretarded children. *American Journal of Mental Deficiency*, 1975, *79*, 632–639.

Turnure, J. E., & Zigler, E. Outerdirectedness in the problem-solving of normal and retarded children. *Journal of Abnormal and Social Psychology*, 1964, *69*, 427–436.

Vergason, G. A. *Retention in educable retarded and normal adolescent boys as a function of amount of original learning*. Unpublished doctoral dissertation, George Peabody College, 1962.

Wang, M., Resnick, L., & Boozer, R. The sequence of development of some early mathematical behaviors. *Child Development*, 1971, *42*, 1767–1778.

Weaver, J. F. Big dividends from little interviews. *Arithmetic Teacher*, 1955, *11*, 40–47.

White, R. Education of the retarded: A point of view. *Education and Training of the Mentally Retarded*, 1976, *11*, 295.

Wilson, J. W. The role of structure in verbal problem solving. *Arithmetic Teacher*, 1967, *14*, 486–496. (a)

Wilson, J. W. What skills build problem-solving power? *Instructor*, 1967, *76*, 79–81(b).

Winschel, J. F. Teach children to learn. *Education and Training of the Mentally Retarded*, 1977, *12*, 26–28.

Zeaman, D., & House, B. J. The role of attention in retardate discrimination learning. In N. R. Ellis (Ed.), *Handbook of mental deficiency*. New York: McGraw-Hill, 1963.

Zigler, E. Dealing with retardation. *Science*, 1977, *196*, 1192–1194.

Zigler, E. Developmental versus difference theories of mental retardation and the problem of motivation. *American Journal of Mental Deficiency*, 1969, *73*, 536–556.

Zigler, E. Familial mental retardation: A continuing dilemma. *Science*, 1967, *155*, 292–298.

Zigler, E. Research on personality structure in the retardate. In N. R. Ellis (Ed.), *International review of research in mental retardation* (Vol. 1). New York: Academic Press, 1966.

Zigler, E. *Training the intellect versus development of the child*. Paper read at the annual meeting of the American Educational Research Association, Los Angeles, April 1968.

Zweng, M. The problem of solving story problems. *Arithmetic Teacher*, 1979, *27*(l), 2–3.

Teaching Mathematics to the Talented and Gifted

H. Laurence Ridge
University of Toronto

Joseph S. Renzulli
University of Connecticut

Dr. H. Laurence Ridge has worked with the talented and gifted in mathematics and their teachers as an instructor in mathematics at the University of Toronto Schools; instructor for the Ministry of Education, Ontario; advisor and instructor in a program for exceptional children in the Borough of Scarborough (Metropolitan Toronto); conference and professional development speaker and workshop leader; designer and instructor of courses in recreational mathematics and problem solving, University of Toronto; and contributor to the periodical literature.

Dr. Joseph S. Renzulli is professor of educational psychology and director of the Teaching the Talented Program, University of Connecticut. He is a former president of the Association for the Gifted and serves on the editorial boards of Exceptional Children *and the* Gifted Child Quarterly. *He has been a consultant to school districts and agencies including the Office of Gifted and Talented (U.S. Office of Education) and the White House Task Force on the Education of the Gifted.*

We Americans are justly proud of our egalitarianism, of our demand for equal education for all, but we are equally proud of our goal of individualization to fit the program to the child's needs. We have moved far toward providing access to education for all, but we are less effective in meeting the differing needs and abilities of individual children. For those children at the extremes—the handicapped and the gifted—the commitment to individualization has been halting and incomplete. Failure to help the handicapped child reach his potential is a personal tragedy for him and his family; failure to help the gifted child reach his potential is a social tragedy, the extent of which is difficult to measure but which is surely great. How can we measure the sonata unwritten, the

curative drug undiscovered, the absence of political insight? They are the difference between what we are and what we could be as a society.

James J. Gallagher
Teaching the Gifted Child

WHAT MAKES GIFTEDNESS: REEXAMINING A DEFINITION

THROUGHOUT recorded history and undoubtedly even before records were kept, people have always been interested in persons who have displayed superior ability. As early as 220 B.C. the Chinese had developed an elaborate system of competitive examinations to select outstanding persons for governmental positions (DuBois, 1970), and down through the ages almost every culture has had a special fascination about its most able citizens. Although the areas of performance in which one might be recognized as a "gifted" person are determined by the needs and values of the prevailing culture, scholars and lay persons alike have debated, and continue to debate, the age-old question, What makes giftedness? This general concern, coupled with the more practical responsibilities of formal education systems, has caused psychologists and educators to raise two related questions:

1. How can we identify persons who have the highest potential for superior performance?

2. What types of learning experiences can we provide to develop this potential?

Within the field of special education for the gifted, more attention has probably been devoted to the topics of identification and characteristics than all other areas combined. And yet a great deal of disagreement still remains about the definition of giftedness and the specific procedures that should be used to select students for participation in special programs. Although this disagreement is an obviously healthy aspect of a dynamic field, it has also hampered the efforts of practitioners who are faced with

Many thanks are due the following individuals who permitted interviews and gave access to much useful material: Ruth Banks, Supervisor, Gifted Programs; Jim Fencott, Coordinator of Mathematics; and Paul Zolis, Peter Crippin, and Larry Rice of Woburn Collegiate—all in the Borough of Scarborough, Metropolitan Toronto. We also thank Doug Mabee, Northern Secondary School, Toronto; Al Fleming, University of Toronto Schools; Henry Courtney, Mathematics Consultant, Halton Board of Education; and Steven Conrad, Benjamin N. Cardozo High School, Bayside, New York. Especially helpful in gathering literature were Mary Shortt, Sophie Kaszuba, and the staff of the Faculty of Education Library at the University of Toronto and Anne McLellan of the Canadian Educational Association. The largest debt of gratitude is due the many students with whom we have had the pleasure of working, in cooperation with whom many of these ideas have been developed, and without whom the undertaking of this task would have been impossible.

the Monday morning realities of identifying students and implementing school programs for gifted and talented youngsters.

The purposes of our initial discussion are these: First, we shall attempt to analyze some of the past and present definitions of giftedness. Second, we shall review some studies that deal with the characteristics of gifted individuals. Finally, we shall present a definition of giftedness that is operational—that is, useful to school personnel—and defensible in terms of research findings.

An operational definition of giftedness is considered an essential part of any special program because it gives direction both to identification systems and to practices that become the major focus of special educational efforts. A definition may not provide all the answers to our identification needs, but if it is defensible in terms of logic, previous research, and a generally agreed-on set of values, then it can give us direction in the selection and development of instruments rather than allowing the availability of instruments to determine the definition.

The Definition Continuum

One way of analyzing existing definitions of giftedness is to view them along a continuum ranging from "conservative" to "liberal" in the degree of restrictiveness that is used to determine who is eligible for special programs and services.

Restrictiveness can be expressed in two ways. First, a definition can limit the number of *specific performance areas* (defined later) that are considered in determining eligibility for special programs. A conservative definition, for example, might limit eligibility solely to academic performance and exclude other areas such as music, art, drama, leadership, public speaking, social service, and creative writing; it might also specify the degree or level of excellence one must attain to be considered gifted.

At the conservative end of the continuum is Terman's (1926) definition:

> [Giftedness is] the top 1 percent level in general intellectual ability, as measured by the Stanford-Binet Intelligence Scale or a comparable instrument. (p. 43)

This definition is restrictive in terms of both the type of performance specified (i.e., how well one scores on an intelligence test) and the level of performance one must attain to be considered gifted (top 1%). At the other end of the continuum can be found more liberal definitions such as the following one by Witty (1958):

> There are children whose outstanding potentialities in art, in writing, or in social leadership can be recognized largely by their performance. Hence, we have recommended that the definition of giftedness be expanded and that we

consider any child gifted whose performance, in a potentially valuable line of human activity, is consistently remarkable. (p. 62)

Although liberal definitions have the obvious advantage of opening up our conception of giftedness, they have also opened up two additional cans of worms by introducing (a) a values issue (What are the "potentially valuable" lines of human activity?) and (b) the age-old problem of subjectivity in measurement.

In recent years the values issue has been largely resolved. Few educators cling tenaciously to a purely academic definition of giftedness based solely on IQ. *Multiple talent* and *multiple criteria* are almost the bywords of the present-day gifted-student movement, and most reasonable persons would probably accept a definition that includes almost every socially useful area of human endeavor.

The problem of subjectivity is not as easily resolved. As the definition of giftedness is extended beyond academic abilities, educators must rely on less precise estimates of performance and potential and place more emphasis on the opinions of qualified human judges. If some degree of subjectivity cannot be tolerated, then our definition of giftedness and the resulting programs will, of course, be limited to abilities that can be measured only by objective tests.

The USOE Definition

In recent years the following definition set forth by the U.S. Office of Education (USOE) (Marland, 1972) has grown in popularity, and numerous states and school districts throughout the nation have adopted it for their programs:

Gifted and talented children are those . . . who by virtue of outstanding abilities are capable of high performance. These . . . children . . . require differentiated educational programs and/or services beyond those normally provided by the regular school program in order to realize their (potential) contribution to self and society.

Children capable of high performance include those who have demonstrated any of the following abilities or aptitudes, singly or in combination:

1. general intellectual ability
2. specific academic aptitude
3. creative or productive thinking
4. leadership ability
5. visual and performing arts
6. psychomotor ability (p. 10)

The USOE definition has served the useful purpose of calling attention to a wider range of abilities; however, it has also presented some major

problems. The first lies in its failure to include nonintellective (motivational) factors. The importance of these factors is borne out by an overwhelming body of research, which we shall consider later.

A second and equally important problem relates to the nonparallel nature of the categories. Two of the six (*specific academic aptitude* and *visual and performing arts*) call attention to general performance areas in which talents and abilities are manifested. The remaining four are qualities, or processes, that can be brought to bear on such performance areas. For example, the process of creativity can be brought to bear on a specific aptitude (e.g., chemistry) or a visual art (e.g., photography). Or the processes of leadership and general intelligence might be applied to such a performance area as choreography or the management of a high school yearbook. In fact, it can be said that processes such as creativity and leadership do not exist apart from a performance area to which they can be applied.

A third problem is that the definition tends to be misinterpreted and misused. It is not uncommon to find educators developing entire identification systems based on the six USOE categories and, in the process, treating them as if they were mutually exclusive. It is equally distressing that many people talk a good game about using the categories but continue to rely on a relatively high intelligence or aptitude score as a requirement for entering a special program. Although both aspects of this problem result from misapplication rather than the definition itself, the definition is not entirely without fault, since it fails to give the kind of guidance necessary to avoid such pitfalls.

Toward a Definition of Giftedness

An operational definition of giftedness has been elusive because of the many concepts and vague terms that have been used within statements of definition. From platform rhetoric to policy statements, such psychological concepts as *ability, capacity, aptitude, potential, intelligence, achievement,* and *creativity* seem to abound. Added to these concepts is an ever-growing list of such educational terms as *academically talented, creatively gifted, productive thinker,* and *kinesthetically gifted.* Thus it is little wonder that after more than 75 years of relatively intensive study the biggest single question in this field is still, "Who are the gifted?"

Three Important Terms

Before we analyze existing definitions, it might be helpful to clarify three important terms that will be used. These terms are not being offered as definitions of giftedness but rather as concepts that will facilitate communication in the discussion that follows.

1. General abilities. This term refers to areas of ability (including general intelligence) that are typically measured by tests of intelligence, ap-

titude, creativity, or primary mental abilities. Examples of such abilities are verbal and numerical reasoning, spatial relations, ideational fluency, and originality. It should be emphasized, however, that many areas of general ability—such as the arts, leadership, and social relations—are *not* easily measured by tests. General abilities are those that can be brought to bear on certain specific types of performance.

2. Specific performance areas. This term will be used to describe the numerous ways and means through which human beings express themselves in real-life (nontest) situations, such as chemistry, sculpture, poetry, photography, and landscape architecture. Each area can be further subdivided into even more specific areas, such as portrait photography, astrophotography, news photography, and microphotography. As we move toward a definition of giftedness, the important role played by specific performance areas will become apparent.

3. Creative-productive. This term will describe the output aspects of performance. Creative writing, for example, consists of the learning (input) and the doing (output). The two types of involvement are not mutually exclusive or even necessarily sequential. But it is important to keep in mind that the doing is the important goal of the learning that takes place in special education. In other words, we teach young people basic techniques in creative writing because we expect and, indeed, encourage them to apply the techniques in their own original creative writing. The term, then, will describe advanced involvement in any specific performance area. Furthermore, as we move toward a definition of giftedness, we shall attempt to show that high levels of creative-productive accomplishment are, in fact, synonymous with the term *gifted*.

An operational definition must give direction and be logically related to programming practices. If such practices are to include and, indeed, emphasize creative-productive applications, then it is important that our definition embrace specific performance areas as well as general abilities. If teachers of the gifted are serious about transcending the training-exercise level and going on to creative-productive applications, then they must go beyond teaching exercises in, say, spatial relations and provide opportunities for such general abilities to be applied to specific performance areas.

But what are the general abilities that should be included in our definition, and how do we make provisions for a multitude of specific performance areas?

The Three-Ring Conception of Giftedness

Research on creative-productive people has consistently shown that although no single criterion can be used to determine giftedness, those who

have achieved recognition because of their unique accomplishments and creative contributions possess a relatively well defined set of three interlocking clusters of traits. These clusters consist of above-average, though not necessarily superior, general abilities, task commitment, and creativity (see Figure 6.1). It is important to point out that no single cluster "makes giftedness." Rather, the interaction among them has been shown by research to be the necessary ingredient for creative-productive accomplishment. This interaction is represented by the shaded portion of Figure 6.1. It is also important to point out that each cluster is an equal partner in contributing to giftedness. This point must be stressed. One of the major errors that we continue to make in identification procedures is to overemphasize superior abilities at the expense of the other two clusters of traits.

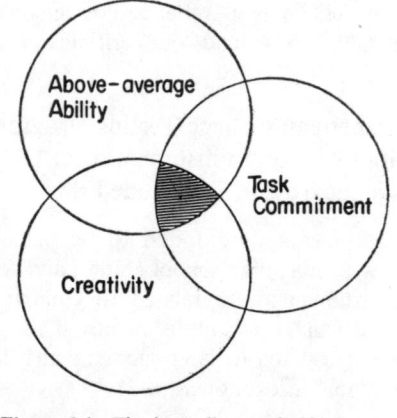

Figure 6.1. The ingredients of giftedness.

Above-average General Ability

Many researchers have found that creative accomplishment is not necessarily a function of measured intelligence. In a review of several research studies dealing with the relationship between academic aptitude tests and professional achievement, Wallach (1976) concluded that

> above intermediate score levels, academic skills assessments are found to show so little criterion validity as to be a questionable basis on which to make consequential decisions about students' futures. What the academic tests do predict are the results a person will obtain on other tests of the same kind.   (p. 57)

Wallach goes on to point out that academic test scores at the upper ranges—precisely the levels that most often qualify students for special programs—do not necessarily reflect the potential for creative-productive accomplishment. He suggests that test scores be used to screen out those who score in the lower ranges and that beyond this point decisions should be based on other indicators of potential.

Numerous research studies support Wallach's finding. Parloff, Datta, Kleman, and Handlon (1968) found that the novelty and effectiveness of high school students' research projects conducted independently of course work were unrelated to intellectual aptitude, tests, or grades. Similar findings were reported by Mednick (1963), who found that when college faculty evaluated independent research projects for imaginativeness and the degree to which they represented contributions to knowledge, the ratings bore no relationship to the students' course grades or scores on the Miller Analogies Test. In a study dealing with the prediction of different dimensions of achievement among college students, Holland and Astin (1962) found that

> getting good grades in college has little connection with more remote and more socially relevant kinds of achievement; indeed, in some colleges, the higher the student's grades, the less likely it is that he is a person with creative potential. So it seems desirable to extend our criteria of talented performance. (pp. 132–133)

A study by the American College Testing Program (Munday & Davis, 1974) entitled "Vanities of Accomplishment after College: Perspectives on the Meaning of Academic Talent" concluded that

> the adult accomplishments were found to be uncorrelated with academic talent, including test scores, high school grades, and college grades. However, the adult accomplishments were related to comparable high school non-academic (extra curricular) accomplishments. This suggests that there are many kinds of talents related to later success which might be identified and nurtured by educational institutions. (p. 2)

The pervasiveness of this general finding is demonstrated by Hoyt (1965), who reviewed 46 studies dealing with the relationship between traditional indications of academic success and postcollege performance in various careers. From this extensive review, Hoyt concluded that traditional indications of academic success have no more than a very modest correlation with various indicators of success in the adult world. Hoyt further concludes that

> there is good reason to believe that academic achievement (knowledge) and other types of educational growth and development are relatively independent of each other. (p. 73)

These studies raise some basic questions about the use of tests in making decisions about selection. There is a clear indication that vast numbers and proportions of our most productive persons are not those who scored at the 95th percentile or above on standardized tests, nor were they necessarily staight-A students who discovered early how to play the lesson-learning game. In other words, more creative-productive persons come from below the 95th percentile than above it, and if we use such cutoff scores to deter-

mine qualification for special programs, we may be guilty of actually discriminating against youngsters who have the greatest potential for high levels of accomplishment.

Task Commitment

A second cluster of traits that has consistently been found in creative-productive persons is a refined or focused form of motivation known as *task commitment*. Whereas motivation is usually defined in terms of a general energizing process that triggers responses in organisms, task commitment represents energy that is brought to bear on a particular problem (task) or specific performance area.

The argument for including this nonintellective cluster of traits in a definition of giftedness is nothing short of overwhelming. From popular maxims and autobiographical accounts to research findings, one of the key ingredients that has characterized the work of gifted persons is their ability to involve themselves totally in a specific problem or area for an extended period of time.

The legacy of both Sir Francis Galton and Lewis Terman clearly indicates the importance of task commitment. Although Galton was a strong proponent of the hereditary basis for what he called "natural ability," he nevertheless subscribed heavily to the belief that hard work was part and parcel of the making of a gifted person.

> By natural ability I mean those qualities of intellect and disposition, which urge and qualify a man to perform acts that lead to reputation. I do not mean capacity without zeal, nor zeal without capacity, nor even a combination of both of them, without an adequate power of doing a great deal of very laborious work. But I mean a nature which, when left to itself, will, urged by an inherent stimulus, climb the path that leads to eminence and has strength to reach the summit—on which, if hindered or thwarted, will fret and strive until the hindrance is overcome, and it is again free to follow its laboring instinct. (Galton, 1869, p. 33, as quoted in Albert, 1975, p. 142)

Terman's monumental studies undoubtedly represent the most widely recognized and frequently quoted research on the characteristics of the gifted. However, he may have unintentionally left us a mixed legacy, since most persons have dwelt on "early Terman" rather than on the conclusions he reached after several decades of intensive research. It is important to consider the following conclusion, reached after 30 years of follow-up studies on the same population:

> [A] detailed analysis was made of the 150 most successful and 150 least successful men among the gifted subjects in an attempt to identify some of the non-intellectual factors that affect life success. . . . Since the less successful subjects do not differ to any extent in intelligence as measured by tests, it is clear that notable achievement calls for more than a high order of intelligence.

The results [of the follow-up] indicated that personality factors are extremely important determiners of achievement. . . . The four traits on which [the most and least successful groups] differed most widely were *persistence in the accomplishment of ends, integration toward goals, self-confidence,* [emphasis added] and freedom from inferiority feelings. In the total picture the greatest contrast between the two groups was in all-round emotional and social adjustment, and in *drive to achieve* [emphasis added]. (Terman, 1959, p. 148)

Although Terman never suggested that task commitment should replace intelligence in our conception of giftedness, he did state that "intellect and achievement are far from perfectly correlated" (p. 148).

Several more recent studies support the findings of Galton and Terman and have shown that creative-productive persons are far more task oriented and involved in their work than the general population. Perhaps the best known of these studies are those of Roe (1952) and MacKinnon (1964, 1965). MacKinnon (1964) pointed out traits that were important in creative accomplishments—enthusiasm, determination, and industry. Extensive reviews of research carried out by Nicholls (1972) and McCurdy (1960) found patterns of characteristics that were consistently similar to the research reported by Roe and MacKinnon. Although task commitment is not as easily and objectively identified as general cognitive abilities, it is, nevertheless, a major component of giftedness and should therefore be reflected in our definition.

Creativity

The third cluster of traits that characterizes the gifted consists of factors that have usually been lumped together under the general heading of "creativity." A review of the literature in this area reveals that the terms *gifted, genius,* and *eminent creators* or *highly creative persons* are used synonymously. In many of the research projects cited, the subjects ultimately selected for intensive study were, in fact, recognized because of their creative accomplishments. In MacKinnon's (1964) study, for example, panels of qualified judges (professors of architecture and editors of major American architectural journals) were asked to nominate and later to rate an initial pool of nominees using the following dimensions of creativity:

1. Originality of thinking and freshness of approaches to architectural problems,

2. constructive ingenuity,

3. ability to set aside established conventions and procedures when appropriate, and

4. a flair for devising effective and original fulfillments of the major demands of architecture, namely: technology (firmness), visual form

(delight), planning (commodity), and human awareness and social purpose. (p. 360)

It is important to consider the problems researchers have encountered
in establishing relationships between creativity tests and more substantial
accomplishments. Do tests of divergent thinking actually measure true
creativity? Although some validation studies have reported limited relationships between measures of divergent thinking and creative performance
criteria (Dellas & Gaier, 1970; Guilford, 1964; Shapiro, 1968; Torrance,
1969), the research evidence for the predictive validity of such tests has been
limited. Unfortunately, very few tests have been validated against real-life
criteria of creative accomplishment, and where such studies have been conducted, the creativity tests have done poorly (Crockenburg, 1972). Thus,
although divergent thinking is indeed a characteristic of highly creative persons, caution should be exercised in the use and interpretation of tests
designed to measure this capacity.

Nicholls (1972), among others, suggests that an analysis of creative
products is preferable to the trait-based approach in making predictions
about creative potential (p. 721). Wallach's (1976) extensive review of
creativity studies resulted in a similar conclusion. He suggests that work
samples and verifiable signs of creative potential should be assessed by
qualified judges. The procedure should involve having candidates for
special programs submit examples or reports of their best work (p. 60).
Wallach feels that such reports are sufficiently accurate to provide a usable
source of data.

The conclusions and recommendations discussed above once again
raise the haunting issue about subjectivity in measurement. Thus, our problem is not so much in the area of defining creativity but rather in offering
guidelines for identifying creative potential.

Practitioners of the arts have for years relied on sample products and
performances. In view of questions research raises about the reliability of
more objective measures of divergent thinking, perhaps the time has come
for specialists to develop more careful procedures for evaluating the work
of candidates for special programs.

Discussion and Generalizations

The best available research points, then, to certain basic generalizations that can be used to develop an operational definition of giftedness.
The first is that giftedness consists of an interaction among three clusters of
traits—above-average, but not necessarily superior, general abilities, task
commitment, and creativity.

Related to this generalization is the need to distinguish between traditional indicators of academic proficiency and creative productivity. A sad

but true fact is that special programs have favored proficient lesson learners and test takers at the expense of students who may have somewhat lower test scores but who more than compensate by having high levels of task commitment and creativity. Research has shown that members of this group ultimately make the most creative-productive contributions to their respective fields of endeavor.

A second generalization is that an operational definition should be applicable to all socially useful performance areas. The one thing that the three elements of giftedness have in common is that each can be brought to bear on a multitude of specific performance areas. Since giftedness does not exist in a vacuum, our definition must reflect yet another interaction—the interaction between the overlap within the cluster and the performance area to which the overlap might be applied. This interaction is represented by the large arrow in Figure 6.2.

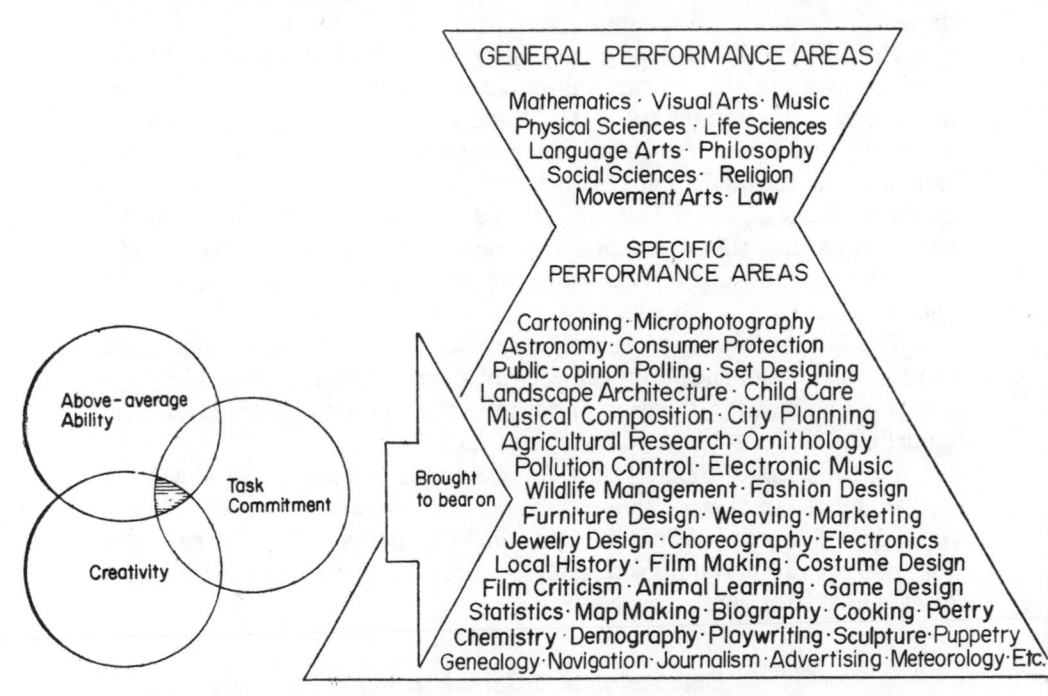

Figure 6.2. Graphic representation of the definition of giftedness.

It is important to place general abilities and specific performance areas in proper perspective. If a definition is to be operational in terms of what teachers teach and the ways human beings express themselves, the target of the three rings must be a specific performance area. We do not offer courses or college majors in IQ, nor do people pursue careers or avocations in idea-

tional fluency or semantic transformations. These are general abilities to be brought to bear on specific areas of human expression.

A third and final generalization is concerned with the types of information that should be used to identify superior performance in specific areas. Test developers have thus far devoted most of their energy to the development of measures of general ability. Checklists, rating scales, and self-reports of interests and accomplishments are obviously more subjective than hard-data instruments such as aptitude tests. So we must ask: How much of a trade-off are we willing to make on the objectivity-subjectivity continuum? Should we assume that the objective test approach is equally appropriate for all performance areas? Does a prize-winning painting or a smoke-detection device invented by a child score at the 67th or the 94th percentile? The absurdity of this last question highlights the way in which we have traditionally been pursuing the identification of giftedness in many of our special programs.

A second concern is that some of the checklist and self-report studies were carried out with high school and college students. These procedures may not be easily adaptable for younger children; however, the fact that some research has already been carried out with younger populations (Renzulli et al., 1976) lends support to the feasibility of conducting similar studies in other specific performance areas. It behooves us to think that specialists in every area of human performance could at least give some guidance about indicators of superior performance in their respective fields.

The last generalization raises yet another problem. Checklists, guidelines, or expert opinion that would help us spot talent in specific areas would not guarantee the appropriate use of such procedures. Sometimes our efforts to assure an egalitarian atmosphere in the classroom result in a reluctance to recognize, let alone to foster, high-level performance. If a teacher or specialist in some performance area is to make knowledgeable judgments about a youngster's potential, we must be willing to provide opportunities for various types of expression and also to make critical judgments about such expression. Otherwise we may inappropriately apply specific talent-recognition procedures to traditional lesson-learning behaviors and find ourselves falling backward into the same dilemma of focusing our identification procedures on general abilities only.

A Definition of Giftedness

Although no single statement can effectively integrate the many ramifications of the research studies described above, the following definition of giftedness attempts to summarize the major conclusions and generalizations resulting from this review of research.

The definition, represented in Figure 6.2, is an operational one because it meets three important criteria. First, it is derived from the best available

research studies dealing with characteristics of gifted and talented individuals. Second, it provides guidance for the selection and development of instruments and procedures that can be used to design defensible identification systems. Finally, it provides direction for the programming practices that will capitalize on the characteristics that bring gifted youngsters to our attention as learners with special needs.

Giftedness consists of an interaction among three basic clusters of human traits: above-average general abilities, high levels of task commitment, and high levels of creativity. Gifted and talented children are those possessing or capable of developing this composite set of traits and applying them to any potentially valuable area of human performance. Children who manifest or are capable of developing an interaction among the three clusters require a wide variety of educational opportunities and services beyond those ordinarily provided through regular instructional programs.

Guidelines Underlying Identification Systems

Although procedures for identifying gifted and talented students will vary from program to program, certain general guidelines can be applied to almost all programs. A comprehensive and systematic plan should attempt to take account of as many of the following guidelines as possible. They are adapted from an unpublished paper prepared by Marshall Sanborn, Research and Guidance Laboratory for Superior Students, University of Wisconsin, and are used with permission.

A . An adequate plan for the identification of gifted and talented individuals requires the use of a variety of techniques over a long period of time.

    1. The gifted and talented express themselves in many ways.

    2. Gifted and talented performances may emerge at certain times in life and under certain opportune conditions.

B. Identification of gifted and talented individuals should be based on a knowledge of the individual, the cultural-experiential context in which the individual has developed, and the fields of activity in which he or she performs.

    1. At least some methods of identification should be individualized, yielding case-study data unlikely to be obtained by standardized group methods.

2. Identification techniques can be locally developed with methods and criteria that are appropriate for the particular population to be studied.

3. The identification process should call for systematic involvement of those professionals who are acquainted with the individuals through direct observation of behavior and performances.

4. The identification process should call for the involvement of those persons best qualified to judge the quality of a performance or product. This is especially important in areas such as the visual and performing arts.

5. The identification process should involve persons best qualified to understand the culture and the specific circumstances of individuals whose performances are being assessed.

C. Both self-chosen and required performances should be assessed.

D. Considerable freedom of expression of response should be allowed.

E. The adequacy of the identification program should be continually reassessed.

1. Follow-up study should involve both those who were identified as gifted or talented and those who were not.

2. Methods and procedures for identification should be modified by refining, adding, and deleting on the basis of evidence obtained.

3. Those individuals who have been misclassified can be appropriately reclassified on the basis of evidence.

F. Evidence obtained during the identification process should provide a primary basis for programming experiences and opportunities.

Types of Information Used in Identification Systems

The comprehensive approach suggested by the foregoing definition and guidelines requires a wide variety of case-study information for selecting youngsters for special programs. Just how much information should be gathered and the specific instruments and procedures to be used should depend on two major concerns. The first is programmatic: There should be a logical relationship between the aims of a special program and the instruments and procedures used to assess a student's eligibility for the program. In other words, if a program offers advanced training opportunities in drama or the movement arts, then above-average ability, task commitment,

and creativity in this performance area should be major considerations for our identification procedures.

Similarly, if a special program consists mainly of advanced-level course work in a traditional academic area and such course work does not emphasize (or even allow for) such creative applications as self-initiated research activity, then it is reasonable simply to use scores from appropriate ability tests for identification. Although we do not advocate this approach (i.e., advanced courses without an emphasis on creative-productive applications), research has shown that traditional tests do, in fact, predict proficiency in traditional lesson-learning situations. (For a detailed discussion of the programming approach advocated by the writers, see Renzulli, 1977. This model, as it can be related to the teaching of mathematics, is discussed later in the chapter.) For this reason, the same principle applies. For example, there is a logical and empirical relationship between advanced scores on mathematics aptitude tests and the ability to earn high grades in advanced mathematics courses. Thus, a straight test-score approach appears to be warranted in this situation because the basic programmatic experience consists of skill and concept learning in advanced mathematics. (In partial agreement with this point of view, SMPY uses a battery of tests, specified later in the chapter, to identify candidates but then examines other criteria to determine the type of accelerated program most suitable for the individual.)

A second concern is purely practical. The time, money, and resource persons available for screening and selection must obviously be taken into account as we begin to develop identification systems for particular programs. Unfortunately, little research has been conducted about the cost effectiveness or efficiency of different approaches. When such studies have been carried out, the ultimate criterion measure for judging the efficiency and effectiveness of alternative identification has almost always been individual intelligence tests. This approach presumes that an individual IQ score is the only valid way of determining if a person is really gifted and thus ignores the validity of such considerations as task commitment and creativity.

A study by Renzulli and Smith (1977) compared traditional test-score methods of identification with various case-study approaches that used several types of identification information. In this study the criterion for effectiveness consisted of follow-up evaluations of the students' success in their respective programs and the degree to which teachers in regular and special programs rated the appropriateness of student placement. Time and cost analyses were also carried out.

The results indicated that the two approaches were equally effective from the classroom teachers' perspective. However, the case-study approach had the following advantages:

1. Teachers in special programs showed significantly higher ratings of effectiveness.

2. It was more sensitive to identifying academically able students in schools that serve populations of minority groups.

3. Contrary to popular belief, it was far more economical than the traditional method, costing only about a third as much and requiring approximately half as much professional time for each student selected.

In view of these findings and the research studies summarized earlier, it is recommended that identification systems include a balanced combination of the following four families of identification information:

A. Preschool and developmental information
   1 . Advanced expressions of interest or talent in a given area or areas
   2. Precocity in physical or intellectual development, such as early walking, talking, or reading
   3. Evidence of social and emotional maturity

B. Psychometric information
   1. Standardized tests of intelligence, aptitude, achievement, creativity, and other cognitive processes
   2. Interest inventories
   3. Self-ratings and teacher ratings of past accomplishments in particular performance areas
   4. Peer ratings of unusual accomplishments in particular areas

C. Performance information
   1. Summaries and analyses of work completed
   2. Actual samples of highly creative products such as stories, paintings, projects, or inventions
   3. Descriptions of outstanding performances in areas such as music or drama or in situations that require advanced leadership ability

D. Motivational information
   1. Written or verbal expressions of aspirations, interests, ambitions, and plans for the future
   2. Expressions of insights, self-understanding, and commitments to particular areas of creative endeavor
   3. Evidence, from performance, of intensive and sustained interest in a particular hobby, topic, activity, or cause

GIFTEDNESS AND MATHEMATICS

The Three-Ring Conception and Mathematical Talent

Mathematical giftedness is well accommodated by the three-ring conception. It is appropriate that the graphic demonstration (Figure 6.2) be an application of a mathematical concept—namely, a Venn diagram that illustrates a three-way intersection.

Above-average General Ability

Although a high IQ does indicate a high learning potential, it provides little information about specific subject achievement or about the relationship between verbal and quantitative skills or, indeed, about a student's special interests (Fox, 1976). Conversely, however, mathematical talent does imply high general intelligence (Aiken, 1973; Moredock, 1961). Hence, above-average general ability is necessary but not sufficient for mathematical giftedness.

Creativity

The place of creativity in mathematical ability was reviewed by Ridge (1977) in discussing the nature of mathematical aptitude with high school students interested in mathematics from a career standpoint.

> Early in this century, the great French mathematician, Henri Poincare, analysed the nature of the mental ability of the creative mathematician, the person who is able to succeed at the highest (open-search) level of thinking. The real key to creative ability in mathematics appears to be a sort of intuition which brings about solutions by placing all the pertinent ideas in the right order; the ability to see through a problem and experience a solution as a sudden illumination. [This often subconscious stage can be referred to as "incubation" and is preceded by a period of "preparation" that involves deep involvement and concentration—a mathematical form of commitment to task; the "illumination" must be followed by a "verification," that is, the cleaning up, or elaboration and refinement, of an insightful solution (Aiken, 1973).] Even a person without a particularly good memory who is endowed with some degree of this gift has the ability to understand and create mathematics. Poincare felt that a mathematician doesn't need the power of memorization which is required by a good chess player, and he hastened to point out that most chess players would become lost in difficult mathematical reasoning. However, if you have an exceptionally good memory and a longer-than-usual attention span, even mere traces of intuition will allow you to understand higher mathematics and apply it to a certain extent. But the ability to create will be missing.
>
> In secondary school mathematics memory is the factor which accounts for most achievement. [Krutetskii (1969) describes mathematical memory in a

mathematically gifted individual thus: "The typical indications of problems, generalized methods of solving typical problems, basic schemes of reasoning and proofs, and logical schemes are remembered and well preserved" (pp. 96–97).] Besides the obvious memorization of definitions and some formulas through constant use, the key to a solution is usually the recalling of an appropriate technique (algorithm) for a particular situation. New situations which involve an open search and require more reasoning ability than memory are rarely encountered.

Most people lack this special intuition, and if they also don't have much of a memory or attention span, then the understanding of higher mathematics becomes an utter impossibility for them. Although computational ability is extremely important in writing solutions to problems and in communicating mathematics, Poincare has shown that facility with computation is not necessary for understanding the reasoning of mathematics and in no way implies creative ability in mathematics. This is the reason why some students who get high marks on the basis of computational skill become totally dismayed when they are no longer able to maintain their previous achievement in mathematics courses requiring higher-level thinking. . . . Your degree of prowess in mathematics is directly proportional to the distance between the types of problems you can solve and the types of problems which are already familiar to you. (pp. 16–17)

Michael (1977) reported that mathematicians classified by their peers as "highly creative" had been found not to differ in intelligence from mathematicians not so classified. The creative mathematicians scored significantly lower on "neatness and orderliness in habits of work" but scored significantly higher on "confidence and mathematical sociability," "initiative and inventiveness in research," "role of critical leadership in one's field," and very significantly higher on an art-scale measure. They preferred asymmetrical and complex designs. This picture is not surprising; it is almost stereotypic.

Task Commitment

Task commitment as a facet of giftedness is clearly evident in the tenacity of any mathematical problem solver or researcher. It could be argued that such people have little choice in the matter because of the incubation factor, which operates in an involuntary if not subconscious state until the light dawns. Collins (1969) noted the amazing tenacity of a group of gifted 8- and 9-year-olds in the Brentwood Experiment. Even though it appeared that they had given up on a purposely difficult problem, it turned out that the wheels had been turning all the while the youngsters were apparently idle. As a result, success became theirs. "Less able children," Collins remarked, "when appearing to have given up a problem, have usually stopped working on it altogether, and seldom return to it" (p. 91).

Identifying Mathematically Adept Students

In order to identify students of extreme mathematical talent (of the order of the top 0.5%), the Study of Mathematically Precocious Youth (SMPY) has developed an extensive identification procedure that considers early adolescents in the 95th percentile of a standardized in-grade test (or the 98th percentile of a verbal or numerical subtest or a combination of both criteria). Students nominated by more than one teacher who are not below the 85th percentile overall are also considered. Scores on PSAT-V (verbal) and PSAT-M (mathematical) in a second stage of screening determine those to be considered for placement in special programs of various degrees of acceleration (Fox, 1976).

Although creativity is not mentioned as a criterion, it is inherent in the problem-solving aspect of mathematics. (Creative thinking is not inherent in traditional, computationally oriented mathematics programs.) To be considered for placement in a fast-paced course, candidates must also have exhibited a keen interest in mathematics and good study habits, including a desire for independent study—in other words, task commitment.

Remarks were made earlier regarding the limitations of psychological testing. Yet, Stanley (1976) continues to advocate the use of tests as the principal instrument for preliminary identification of high-level achievement or aptitude. (Stanley hastens to point out that no wise measurement specialist would base a judgment solely on test scores. He also makes the point that tests such as SAT-M have a talent-finding aspect and are important for disadvantaged groups as well as those whose abilities have developed to a high level early.) It is extremely important that a test have a sufficient "ceiling" for the individual. This is the reason that tests designed for 11th- or 12th-grade students or even college freshmen are necessary for highly precocious 7th- and 8th-grade students. One of the problems of testing procedures in general is that the additional validity indicated by very high scores is not used. For example, neither of two students in the 90th and 99th percentiles would find a regular Grade 8 course at all stimulating, but the student in the 90th percentile would have difficulty in a course appropriate for the student in the 99th percentile.

The late sixth or early seventh grade is considered the most opportune time for the selection and placement of these youngsters (Fox, 1976) as they move from an elementary to a more senior school setting. Up to this point they have had little formal instruction in any mathematics beyond arithmetic. The timing is also in deference to Piaget's theory of development in that these students should be moving into the "stage of formal operations" and hence be capable of more abstract thought. (The Brentwood Experiment (Collins, 1969) and the personal experience of one of the authors give evidence that it is not unusual for gifted children of the age of 8

or even younger to explain solutions or game strategies in terms of "adult logic.")

The technique of selection through testing really does fit the four-part model recommended earlier in the chapter. The case-study approach is very much in evidence after the dual screening procedure has identified potential candidates. The heavy emphasis in the initial stages on psychometric information from standardized testing (granted, of a very specific and specialized nature) is incorrectly inferred by some observers to mean a denigration of other criteria.

Identifying Mathematical Talent in Younger Children

Ashley (1973) has pointed out some of the characteristics of younger children having mathematical potential. The very young have an interest in numbers, clocks, and calendars. They love to measure—anything. They exhibit exceptional mathematical reasoning, good memory, and persistence (all of which harks back to the three-ring conception of giftedness). Their IQ scores relating to mathematical prowess are usually about 120, and they are ahead of their classmates in mathematics. Collins (1969) corroborates the reasoning ability and interest in measurement as observed in British children. From experience with another British program for mathematically gifted children from ages 4 to 16, Hayman et al. (1976) note concentration spans of 3 to 4 hours and beyond. Preschoolers' interest in numbers is cited even to the point of personal relationships with numbers. As well as displaying a kind of "Pythagorean attitude" (p. 244) in their like or dislike of certain numbers, the younger children appeared to contradict the theory of Piaget by their well-established abstract conception of number and operation.

Krutetskii (1969) identified outward signs of mathematical ability in children through experimentation with highly precocious children. The extent and clarity of these signs will, of course, vary with individuals.

1. A clear interest (sometimes even a keen interest) in mathematics (arithmetic, algebra, geometry). The tendency to work with mathematics with pleasure and without compulsion.
2. Mastery of definite mathematical skills and habits at an early age.
3. Fast mastery of mathematics.
4. Attainment of a comparatively (by age) high level of mathematical development. (pp. 115–16)

Gallagher (1976) comments on the difficulty that teachers have in identifying gifted youngsters, often because they are looking for the wrong kinds of behavioral indicators. For example, to expect that gifted children should be models of enthusiasm and cheerfulness is frequently to be misguided. Some gifted children are even considered slow and difficult

because of their lack of response to standard classroom stimuli; yet their lack of response is occasioned by boredom and the fact that they indeed are not being stimulated. Peer pressure can also be a factor in the behavior of gifted children. Unfortunately, the greatest need for special help lies in those who are the most difficult to identify.

Giftedness in Unexpected Places

The gifted underachiever is surely an enigma. Even when the potential is unearthed by a testing procedure (or other means), it might be that no amount of stimulation on the part of the teacher will succeed in drawing out the talent. The cause may be attitudinal or emotional, as detailed by Gallagher (1976)—often the result of broken or emotionally debilitating home situations (Havighurst, 1976). Although it is incumbent on teachers to encourage top performance, they should not be loath to seek psychological assistance for such students. (The National/State Leadership Training Institute on the Gifted and the Talented has produced a number of publications dealing specifically with the "disadvantaged gifted." Write in care of Ventura County Superintendent of Schools, 535 E. Main St., Ventura, CA 93009.)

The three-ring conception of giftedness has been criticized for its apparent exclusion of the gifted underachiever on the basis of a lack of task commitment. (In fact, the definition calls for the inclusion of those who are *capable of developing* the composite set of traits.) Some educators oppose such a stance, claiming that a system that helped turn these youngsters off should do all it can through special programs to turn them on. (Whether the system can be blamed in light of the previous paragraph is a moot point.) The press recently championed the case of a 15-year-old youth of exceptional ability who could not be reached because of his relative inability to read or write (90% of gifted underachievers are male). It was claimed that the system just could not help him even though he was about to leave school a very disillusioned young man.

Mabee (Note 1) tells of a youngster who was identified as a slow learner because of a perceptual problem in writing and speaking but who was doing integral calculus at age 7. A research paper written when this student was in Grade 10 evidences that the writing difficulties have still not been entirely overcome, but the mathematical content is unquestionable, and the diagrams (dealing with the four-dimensional tesseract) are extremely well done, even to the inclusion of a color-coding system to clarify concepts.

It is unusual that a person be multitalented, that is, extremely precocious in more than one field. Banks (Note 2) recounts the case of an 11-year-old girl who had been recognized as a linguistic prodigy (later achieving a very high standing in a second-year university course in French at age 13) but who had apparently played the "girls aren't good at math"

game so successfully that no one suspected any special mathematical talent. It was only when she volunteered a project for a math display that the truth became known. She had produced an original "theory of theorems," a university-level treatise. The flexibility of the program she was in permitted individual work with mathematics specialists. (The discussion on methodology later in this section suggests procedures that can encourage giftedness in mathematics to become overt.)

A real assist in assessing potential task commitment and creative productivity could accrue from a student's keeping some form of log, diary, or portfolio of mathematical activities (aside from the regular class routine). In the spirit of the "Performance information" aspect of the four-part identification model, such a dossier might include a record of successes, abortive attempts, conjectures, and even some notes of thoughts and questions as the student worked through the material. The recording of all one's thoughts in the process of attempting to solve a problem has been identified as a significant procedure in developing skill as a problem solver (Mason, 1978).

Program Organization

Mirman (1971) has voiced the spirit of the movement for special education for the gifted:

> Capacity alone is not enough to ensure the actualizing of giftedness. There must be nurture to maximize nature. (p. 219)

This is certainly so in the case of mathematical giftedness (Jaffar, 1976; Krutetskii, 1969).

Syphers (1972) sees such nurture from a more general point of view:

> A program for the gifted is simply one phase of providing for individual differences in children and not an arrangement giving special privileges or rewards to a select few. (p. 21)

Fremont (1969) concurs. It is not really what can be done for any particular classification of students but rather

> what we can do to help each and every child realize his (or her) own potential as a student of mathematics. (p. 510)

The individualization within the SMPY program of Julian Stanley and his colleagues has been commended by Anastasi (1975):

> Within this highly selected group . . . there was considerable differentiation of abilities. . . . One feature of the intervention program that I vigorously applaud is its deliberate and explicit recognition of individual differences among the highly talented pupils. Unlike most previous efforts at special education for the gifted, there is no recommendation for the establishment of special classes,

special schools, or even special programs for the telescoping of high school, college, and graduate education. Instead, the educational counselling and implementation programs are individually tailored to each pupil in terms of his (or her) unique ability pattern, past history, interests, emotional maturity, motivation, and even his (or her) geographical circumstances—a picture which should truly gladden the heart of any differential psychologist! (pp. 95, 101–102)

The SMPY program may be laudable, but one must remember that it caters only to students of extremely high mathematical ability. For less able, albeit gifted, students in mathematics, more traditional—even if psychologically less acceptable—program organizations may be more appropriate. In addition to all the discussion and controversy regarding the pros and cons of grouping and mainstreaming among educational researchers, psychologists, and sundry other experts, the voice of the front-line teacher should be heard. Tilsley (1979) has analyzed a survey of teacher attitudes and opinions regarding gifted children and their education. Responses (49%) represented elementary- and secondary-level teachers in five countries. The summary of opinion regarding program organization is as follows:

Of the general organizational principles . . . streaming was strongly rejected. Setting [grouping by ability/attainment in specific subjects], approved by a majority [of teachers] at all age levels was progressively more favoured as children became older and as [teacher] attitude score increased. . . . The converse held for full time mixed ability grouping which was accorded majority support only by teachers of the 5–9 age group. However, part time mixed ability grouping coupled with part time [setting] . . . was the most favoured form of organization amongst teachers of the two younger age groups [5–9, 7–13] and those with low or middle attitude scores. Secondary teachers and those with high attitude scores also gave majority approval though ranking it second to setting in desirability. (p. 36)

This point cannot be emphasized too strongly. Whatever form of organization is used, it will serve gifted students well only if it is sufficiently flexible to permit real individualization—not just everyone doing the same stencils at a different rate. It could be argued that the extent to which both flexibility and individualization are effected varies directly with teacher attitude and ability. Banks et al. (1978) state that the same teaching strategies apply with an entire class of gifted students or with one gifted student in a regular classroom setting.

Content and methodology will be discused more fully, but let's stop here for a moment to take up the challenge of the one gifted student in a regular classroom setting—the "mainstreaming" motif. Figure 6.3 shows an example of one type of activity that could be used for the whole class but that contains features for different ability levels in mathematical reasoning.

Estimate; then find the sum.

1.	358	2.	5362	3.	25948
	261		6241		60132
	738		3758		39867

4.	825	5.	6379	6.	46703
	574		5341		35067
	425		4658		64932
	312		6025		78421
	687		3974		21578

7.	638	8.	7984	9.	31825
	142		2135		23458
	361		9002		40563
	555		7864		68174
	857		2015		59436

Figure 6.3.

Students could be asked to find the sums on the basis that there is a hidden pattern. Should a straight drill situation be deemed necessary for some students, then so be it—the same exercise still suffices. (Some may object that the ubiquitous calculator has made the manual addition of such figures obsolete. Then this material can be used as an exercise in estimation or in gauging the reasonableness of answers in conjunction with calculator work. There is still a pattern well worth looking for.)

Some students, regardless of grade level, will see no pattern whatever but will at least have had some practice in estimating sums and checking those estimates. Some may see a pattern as relating only to the top number in questions 1–6 and nothing at all in questions 7–9. Others will see that the sum is related to one of the addends in every question but won't be aware of the necessary structuring of the other addends. Only students with high ability in mathematical reasoning will appreciate the structure of the pattern to the point of being able to explain how it works and, further, to make up their own examples and even create similar patterns of their own. In an entire group or class of gifted students, this same basic exercise could initiate individual extensions as suggested above, perhaps for all students.

In this type of activity every student has a chance to exercise his or her full potential. With astute questioning and guidance, the teacher might urge individuals a little beyond the point they have reached on their own. From the practical side, the overall time spent by students of different ability

levels would probably work out to be about the same. The time not used in the operations, calculator-assisted or otherwise, would be spent in pattern analysis.

Acceleration and Enrichment

The mathematics education community seems to consider that a program based on radical overall acceleration may be working out well for SMPY's exceptionally precocious students but that the great majority of young people recognized as gifted in mathematics are found elsewhere. There are many forms of less radical acceleration involving mathematics separately. Some gifted high school students (who are not necessarily geniuses) do take university mathematics courses; many more take advantage of advanced placement programs. Less formally, individuals do take regular mathematics courses early, sometimes through a telescoping plan, especially at the junior high school level (three years' work in two).

Renzulli (1977) cites acceleration in the form of taking advanced courses early (à la SMPY) as the simplest kind of enrichment. Even though such an arrangement lacks curricular reconstruction (a benefit in the eyes of its proponents), it may be appropriate for such subjects as mathematics, physics, and computer science, which are highly structured and sequential. Regardless, such plans relate only to the advanced ability of the student without taking into account such dimensions as specific individual interests and preferred styles of learning. "Everyone ends up marching to the tune of the same drummer, albeit at a faster beat" (p. 16).

Varying proportions of acceleration and enrichment are found in situations such as the following:

- Highly rigorous programs such as the Secondary School Mathematics Curriculum Improvement Study (SSMCIS) and the Comprehensive School Mathematics Program (CSMP) at the secondary level
- More theoretical or comprehensive treatment of regular course content at any level, whether for individuals or specially formed groups or classes
- Extensions both in breadth and depth at any level through clubs or preparation for competition and independent study (with no formal classes) done either under the aegis of a school program or strictly independently, perhaps by correspondence or supported by a personal study of the literature and occasional interviews
- Saturday morning programs, usually sponsored by school boards or area jurisdictional groups
- Summer institutes such as that offered by the University of Chicago. (Information is available from the Assistant Director, Student Science Training Program, Department of Mathematics, University of Chicago, Chicago, IL 60637.)

The mix-and-match possibilities are considerable.

A wide range of opinion exists on the best overall approach for those gifted students for whom radical acceleration is not appropriate. Tilsley (1979) reports in the teacher-opinion survey described previously that 81% of the respondents support some form of special provision. The types of provision surveyed (with variants of each type) were segregation, withdrawal, acceleration, enrichment, and extended working time. (Note that in British usage *enrichment* includes accelerated, or earlier, placement of content, whereas *acceleration* denotes placement with an older age group.)

> The types of such provision which were regarded as desirable by a majority of the sample as a whole were:
>
> Enrichment—deeper and wider study of topics normally studied by the child's own age group.. 97%
>
> Enrichment—work on topics normally studied by older children..... 79%
>
> Withdrawal—for work with a special group within the school........ 78%
>
> Enrichment—study of topics not normally encountered in the school curriculum.. 66%
>
> Extended working time—special programs of homework during term time 59%
>
> Acceleration—part time placement with an older age group for appropriate curriculum areas....................................... 50%
>
> The remaining types of provision did not receive majority support. . . . Withdrawal to a special group within the school . . . received strong support, except amongst secondary teachers and those with low attitude scores. The same groups also gave majority approval to part time acceleration. In addition, special programmes of homework during term time were supported by teachers of the 7–13 and 11–18 age groups and those with middle and high attitude scores. (pp. 32, 36)

Tilsey also points out that

> enrichment . . . [is] regarded as a necessary policy within the class or group whatever form of organization is implemented. . . . [An] advantage of implementing enrichment programs . . . [is the] beneficial effect on the whole class not only the gifted, perhaps because of the introduction of new materials and ideas into the class. (p. 25)

The latter concept is a basis for mainstreaming the gifted, still a controversial point of view in the United States for all forms of special education. Rising and Harkin (1978) share the following view:

> As experience is accumulated, teachers realize that mathematics appropriate to a given grade is far broader than what they will ever have time to cover except with truly gifted students. They must *always* choose a program somewhat less than the full content of the figure:

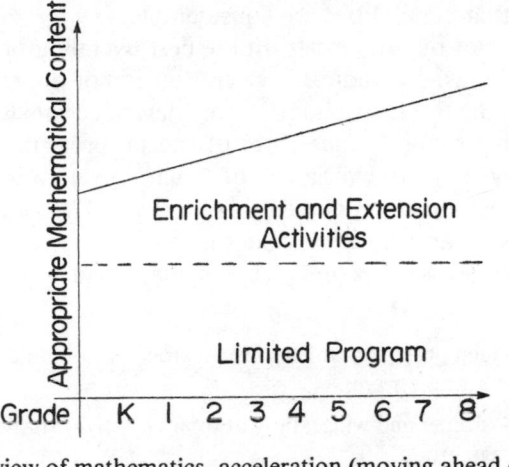

Given this view of mathematics, acceleration (moving ahead of the curriculum sequence) is usually inappropriate. What should be emphasized is the development of strong enrichment activities that support and extend the basic program.

Time is a key factor here. Too much valuable school experience is lost because "there just wasn't enough time.". . . So any "surplus" time is of great value, and should not be lost by moving ahead too rapidly to the next topic. (From p. 280 of *The Third "R", Mathematics Teaching for Grades K–8*, by Gerald R. Rising and Joseph B. Harkin. © 1978 by Wadsworth Publishing Co., Inc., Belmont, CA 94002. Reprinted by permission of the publisher.)

Most teachers feel that no matter how much enrichment material is made available for gifted youngsters, these students have the desire, if not the need, to "get on with it" and will pursue more advanced curricular material on their own if not as part of their school program. Fleming (Note 3) has found that the best approach to the enrichment-acceleration dilemma is through the brisk pacing of regular course material (not unlike some of the early SMPY work) with individualization effected through special projects. The net effect is the telescoping of five years' work (Grades 9–13) into four. This program, in a school for the gifted, includes many students of high general ability who are not particularly talented in mathematics. (Information is available from Mr. G. A. Fleming, University of Toronto Schools, 371 Bloor Street West, Toronto, ON M5S 2R7.)

The Enrichment-Triad Model

The development of this model (Renzulli, 1977) was spurred by a number of concerns:

- Many so-called enrichment programs for the gifted are little more than collections of kits, puzzles, trips, and games used in a somewhat random fashion with little or no developmental thread.

- The great majority of students involved in such programs are enjoying the experience much as one would enjoy recess, so that much potential is not being realized.
- Enrichment is viewed as not the unique purview of the gifted, but if it is to be appropriate for the gifted, it needs to be qualitatively differentiated from enrichment for other students.
- Many programs for the gifted have developed a preoccupation with the taxonomic process as an end in itself rather than as a path to learning. The taxonomic approach is not that used by professionals and scholars in investigating problems in their own fields.

The enrichment-triad model has been designed to fulfill two main objectives (Renzulli, 1977):

> For the majority of time spent in . . . gifted programs, students will have an opportunity to pursue their own interests to whatever depth and extent they so desire; and they will be allowed to pursue these interests in a manner that is consistent with their own preferred styles of learning. . . . The primary role of each teacher in . . . [a] program for gifted and talented students will be to provide each student with assistance in (1) identifying and structuring realistic solvable problems that are consistent with the student's interests, (2) acquiring the necessary methodological resources and investigative skills that are necessary for solving these particular problems and (3) finding appropriate outlets for student products. (pp. 5, 10)

The three types of enrichment in the model have been characterized by Renzulli (1977) as follows:

Type I: General exploratory activities to stimulate interest in specific subject areas. "Type I Enrichment consists of those experiences and activities that are designed to bring the learner into touch with the kinds of topics or areas of study in which he or she may have a sincere interest" (p. 17). Typical of this level would be interest centers in the classroom stocked with all manner of attention-getting stimuli. Visitations and visitors would also be suitable at this level so long as students were not relegated to a strictly observational role. This would be a chance for enthusiastic, creative professionals to influence the development of significant student interests and for students to delve into the actual workings of various procedures in the professional or scientific world. (Such experiences are being made available through children's museums and science centers in the larger metropolitan areas.) Another important aspect of this interest-generating level of enrichment is that students are free to choose, explore, and experiment without the threat of having to prepare a report or provide any sort of formal recapitulation.

Such open types of activities must have purposeful objectives in guiding students to make decisions about areas of further study. The

teacher is also availed of the opportunity for subjective observation and assessment of characteristics that may indicate creative-productive potential. Students who show an unusual interest in a particular Type I experience should be given the opportunity to select and follow through on a specific topic or subtopic. Teachers should note that not every student can, wants to, or should follow up on a particular Type I experience.

Type II: Group training activities to develop processes related to the areas of interest developed through Type I experiences. Type II activities can be characterized as training exercises preparatory to Type III enrichment; they are analogous to physical exercises practiced by athletes. The content of these sessions is made up of "processes or operations (the 'powers of mind') that enable him or her to deal more effectively with content" (p. 25). Typical of these thinking and feeling processes are "critical thinking, problem solving, reflective thinking, inquiry training, divergent thinking, sensitivity training, awareness development, and creative or productive thinking" (p. 25). (Problem solving applies to (a) the application of mathematics to the solution of problems in other fields, (b) the solution of puzzles or logically oriented problems, and (c) the solution of mathematical problems requiring specific mathematical content and processes. All these forms of problem solving can benefit from experiences in the various types of thinking outlined above.) It is important that the processes dealt with at this stage be based on a logical outgrowth of the interests of the group generated through Type I experiences and do not simply represent a potpourri of "neat" activities chosen on the basis of availability or teacher interest.

According to Mirman (1971), part of a Type II program should also include

> training in the acquisition of work habits which will contribute to his (or her) success in school and in later professional or business activities. . . . As well as the acquisition of disciplined thinking in logical problem solving, this would involve specific how-to skills, such as:
> a) using library systems to aid his researching;
> b) outlining, abstracting, synthesizing;
> c) classification experiences as a basis for primitive organizational structures;
> d) being exposed to and taught simple computer languages. (p. 221)

Both Type I and Type II enrichment are appropriate for most students. For the gifted student they serve as preparation for Type III enrichment in the form of logical input and support systems. Type III is the only level considered suitable mainly for the gifted. The relationship among the three types that forms a total enrichment model is shown in Figure 6.4.

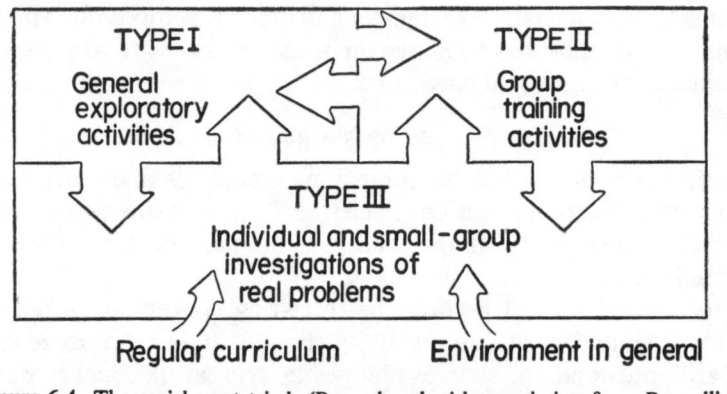

Figure 6.4. The enrichment triad. (Reproduced with permission from Renzulli, J. S., *The Enrichment Triad Model*. Mansfield Center, Conn.: Creative Learning Press, 1977, p. 14.)

Type III: Individual and small-group investigations of real problems. Giftedness becomes manifest in certain students as a result of their willingness to go beyond Type I and Type II experiences and to engage in more complex, self-initiated investigative activities. The essence of Type III enrichment is that students become problem finders as well as problem solvers and that they investigate a real problem using methods of inquiry appropriate to the nature of the problem. Since impact on an audience is one of the main characteristics of a Type III experience, we must use our own imagination to steer students toward identifying relevant audiences and bringing their work to bear on such audiences. For example, if a student has developed a series of mathematical puzzles, we might encourage him or her to contact the editor of a local newspaper, the school newspaper, or a mathematics club newsletter. Some of the outlets for students' work and the audiences on which we might attempt to have an impact may be relatively contrived; however, the main purpose of this approach is to help youngsters see the difference between structured exercises and real problems.

An example of a contrived audience might be teachers and other students in a particular school. Students with an unusual interest in mathematics might be asked to survey teachers for information about possible teaching aids (e.g., probability teaching devices, visual aids for teaching computer programming, etc.). And, of course, teaching other youngsters is a bona fide Type III activity that can readily be used when youngsters develop specific interests and creative approaches for instructional presentations and written assignments.

Gifted students who experience Type I and Type II activities but who are excluded from those in Type III are akin to actors and actresses or musicians who continually rehearse but are deprived the fruition of a performance in front of a live audience. Similarly, school athletes would not be

subjected to a regimen of development and practice without the opportunity of applying all they have learned in a real game with real opponents, sometimes in front of real spectators.

The Many Faces of Mathematical Ability

Before considering suitable content, methodology, and other aspects of a theory of instruction as set out in chapter 2, it would be wise to consider the variables inherent within the concept of mathematical talent so that our response is not simplistic.

First, as mentioned before, the three-ring concept of giftedness includes task commitment and creativity along with above-average (but not necessarily outstanding) general abilities as criteria of equal importance. This conception requires some rethinking of recommendations that might be made within a more traditional setting. The related enrichment-triad model, which is designed to encourage and develop the creative-productive mode in gifted students to the point of investigating or solving problems of real significance, requires a great deal of flexibility both in content and methodology.

Second, even very high general ability does not imply any particular level of mathematical ability or interest. (A majority of fifth-grade students of high general ability who were screened as candidates for a program for the gifted exhibited comparatively mediocre mathematical ability. It turned out that this phenomenon was attributable more to a lack of nurture than to an omission of nature (Banks, Note 2). Recall that the converse does hold. Above-average general ability is necessary for high mathematical ability (Aiken, 1973).) Even more disconcerting, substantial mathematical ability is neither necessary nor sufficient for keen interest in the subject (Krutetskii, 1969).

Third, mathematical ability can be manifest in a number of forms. Krutetskii (1969) speaks of a mathematical turn of mind (p. 102) possessed by people who infer mathematical or logical meaning in the reality about them. (A prominent American mathematics educator has a phone number the first three digits of which have half-turn symmetry and the last four of which have vertical bilateral symmetry. A former student with a "mathematical turn of mind" requested a mathematical telephone number and got one—a palindrome!) Exceptional mathematical ability, however, is generally viewed as encompassing a number of components such as "generalization of mathematical material 'on the spot' " (p. 82). (The other components identified, logically rather than through factor analysis, are (a) "to think in 'curtailed' structures" [i.e., shortcuts in operations and reasoning], (b) "flexibility of mental processes," (c) "economy of thought . . . clarity, simplicity, and 'elegance' of solutions" (pp. 87–93).) Aiken (1973) comments on two basic types of mathematical mind—the slower, logical,

formal type (sometimes associated with analysts) and the quicker, intuitive type (sometimes associated with geometers).

Another consideration is the brain-hemisphere theory. Right-hemisphere mathematical ability relates to physical manipulation (as in tactile geometric and topological puzzles) and art-related concepts (such as geometric design). Left-hemisphere mathematical talent relates more to analytic considerations—the great majority of the content in school mathematics courses at all levels. Right-hemisphere talent often lies unearthed, and, should analytic talent be lacking, valuable potential can be lost. (One of the authors has met youngsters who have excelled in spatial perception and in solving manipulative puzzles but who have verged on the inept in matters of calculation or algebraic manipulation.)

A question that cuts across all four of these matters involves the extent to which a student should be permitted to pursue, in an enrichment setting, previously developed interests and remain strictly within his or her current style of mathematical operation as opposed to being encouraged to widen content interests and develop forms of mathematical thought and process not yet firmly within his or her repertoire. For young people still in a mathematically formative stage, at least some if not considerable emphasis should be placed on the latter approach, regardless of the freedom of choice inherent in Type I enrichment.

An advantage of the enrichment-triad model is that it can be implemented in any classroom and exploited to the extent appropriate to each individual in the class. Everyone has the opportunity to exercise his or her full potential, a situation that is rare for gifted children in their particular areas of talent. In mathematics the triad model permits (indeed requires) the flexibility necessary to respond to the many faces and facets of mathematical talent.

FORMING A THEORY OF INSTRUCTION

The remainder of this chapter deals with the variables in a theory of instruction: content, methodology, motivation, consolidation, students' strengths and weaknesses, and developmental characteristics. Although content and methodology are considered in separate sections, all the variables are treated through a synthesis based on the three-ring concept of giftedness and on the enrichment-triad model. The intent is to provide an underlying structure and a better defined rationale for those activities referred to loosely by mathematics teachers as enrichment. Thinking of an activity as representative of enrichment of Type I, II, or III serves to place it in a more long-range, meaningful perspective. Renzulli (1977) points out that the triad approach is for the teacher who is willing to wrestle with a somewhat different approach to programming for the gifted.

Mathematical Content

General Consideration

What type of content is most suitable for gifted and talented students? Gallagher (1960) refers to the "talented" as the top 14.0% of the population in general ability, "gifted" as the top 2.0%, and "highly gifted" as the top 0.1%. ("Talented" can refer to giftedness in a specific performance area (Banks et al., 1978) rather than to a degree of general ability.) In chapter 2 Glennon refers to the "increasingly rigorous interpretation of the logical structure of mathematics as the primary source of . . . curricula" for those same "talented" (*T* in Figure 6.5), "gifted" (*G*), and "highly gifted" (*HG*) students. For such students at the junior high school level, "modern" content stressing major abstract principles, as opposed to "traditional" content, was found to be superior (Gallagher, 1975), as was acceleration to enrichment.

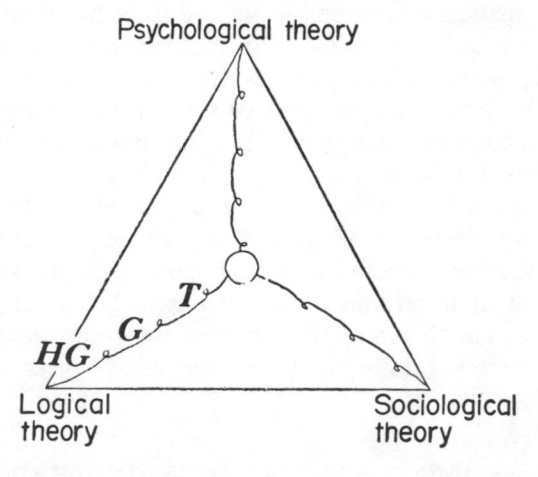

Figure 6.5. Major sources of the curriculum.

The keynotes of "abstraction" and "rigor" have been well exploited by two major curriculum projects designed for very able mathematics students. The Secondary School Mathematics Curriculum Improvement Study (SSMCIS) is a highly abstract approach to mathematics for gifted junior and senior high school mathematics students. (SSMCIS is directed by Howard Fehr, Teachers College, Columbia University and sponsored by the university jointly with the U.S. Department of Education.) The content treatment reflects the considerable influence of European mathematicians (Johnson & Rising, 1976). This influence is seen in the integrated or unified approach to mathematical concepts cutting across and combining topics of algebra and geometry, for example, much in opposition to the American

tradition of algebra I, algebra II, geometry, and so on. (A more integrated approach to mathematics is also found in Canadian textual materials for most ability levels.)

The Comprehensive School Mathematics Project (CSMP) is aiming for "implementation of the Cambridge report today" (Johnson & Rising, 1976, p. 22). (CSMP is directed by Burt Kaufman and sponsored jointly by the Central Midwestern Regional Educational Laboratory (CEMREL) and Southern Illinois University, Carbondale, Illinois. See "A Program for the Gifted," *Mathematics Teacher,* Feb. 1979, p. 154.) In fact, it even exceeds those recommendations in its treatment of modern algebra in the Elements of Mathematics (EM) series of textual material, which represents the most rigorous approach to mathematics yet devised for high school students' consumption. (The elementary school material, very much influenced by Frédérique Papy of Belgium, is packaged in individualized units and is designed for a more universal audience of students.)

The programs referred to so far are very course oriented. One of the main objectives of such programs has to be the passing of, or excelling in, fixed courses—the strength of "lesson learners" but often the bane of creative-productive students. (SMPY might be criticized for this reason.) An outstanding exception is CSMP's EM problem book (see Appendix 4 for a full bibliographic reference), which reflects the creativity aspect of mathematical giftedness as indicated by the three-ring concept discussed earlier. It is also an excellent example of Type II enrichment in providing development and practice in problem solving through 200 "nonroutine and nontrivial . . . problems requiring no special prerequisites beyond the most basic mathematical skills for their solution. They will give you the opportunity to do mathematical research on a level which is tailored to your maturity and your mathematical horizon" (Engel, 1975, p. 1). (Problems are rated on a five-point scale of difficulty; hints and solutions are available as necessary. One set of problems is based on Dirichlet's "pigeon hole," or "mail box," principle, another on two-person and solitaire game strategies—refreshingly removed from the standard fare of the mathematics curriculum.)

There is something of a trend under way in university mathematics problem-solving courses for "amateurs," including teachers, to use content collectively referred to as "recreational mathematics," a field that has gained considerable respectability over the last several years through the efforts of such stalwarts as Martin Gardner, Charles Trigg, J. A. H. Hunter of Canada, and Roger Penrose and John Conway of Great Britain. (See Appendix 1 for a brief reference list of recreational or intriguing mathematics.)

For mathematically gifted students in elementary school, the determination of game strategies, solution of puzzles, and explanations of

number tricks (not to mention the creation of one or more) are most appropriate cultivators of creative problem solving. Through such activities can come the ideas, interests, and questions that lead to problem creation. (The extent to which educators are missing the boat in this regard is made appallingly clear in a recent article in a large-circulation magazine in which an elementary school principal extolls the virtues of the current system whereby "we try to make school a happier experience. For example, we used to select the brightest ones to play in the band. Now we take a youngster who may not be so bright in math and teach him an instrument. *In years to come no one will be doing math problems for fun* [emphasis added]—but that youngster may be sitting at the end of a dock enjoying playing the clarinet. So we give him something to look forward to. It can turn him on to school and make it a better place" (Solway, 1979, p. 12). Such an attitude guarantees the self-fulfillment of the prophesy.) It is important that students be encouraged to express and pursue their original ideas in order to break the mind set of concentration on accuracy, correctness, and fidelity to authority (Passow, 1976).

Here are three such ideas that have recently been communicated to one of the authors:

1. A girl in a rural school came up with a novel test for divisibility by 11. This is her method applied to 6783:

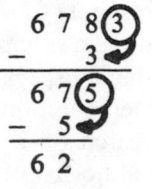

Because 62 is not divisible by 11, neither is 6783.

For 42 669:

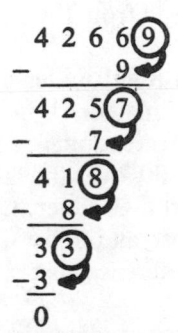

33 is divisible by 11. Hence, 42 669 is also divisible by 11. If the pro-

cedure is continued until a zero remainder occurs, the quotient, 42 669 ÷ 11, is given by the circled numbers in reverse order—namely, 3879.

Out of this discovery came some interesting questions: Why does the method *always* work? (Note that she was sure that it did.) Are there any other numbers that have a similar divisibility test? Why are you able to read off the quotient from the subtracted numbers? The key to solving this student-created problem is in the computation below. (For further information, see Rosen, D. A., "An Uncommon Divisibility Test," *Mathematics Teaching,* No. 76, Sept. 1976, pp. 32–33; Ridge, H. L., "Divisibility Dilemma Defused," *Ontario Mathematics Gazette,* Vol. 17, No. 2, Dec. 1978, pp. 55–57; or write to H. L. Ridge, Faculty of Education, University of Toronto, 371 Bloor Street West, Toronto, ON M5S 2R7.)

$$
\begin{array}{r}
4\ 2\ 6\ 6\ 9 \\
-\ \ \ \ \ \ 9\ 9 \\
\hline
4\ 2\ 5\ 7\ 0 \\
-\ \ \ \ \ 7\ 7\ 0 \\
\hline
4\ 1\ 8\ 0\ 0 \\
-\ \ \ 8\ 8\ 0\ 0 \\
\hline
3\ 3\ 0\ 0\ 0 \\
-3\ 3\ 0\ 0\ 0 \\
\hline
0
\end{array}
$$

2. The configurations of five contiguous squares known as Pentominoes have become the darlings of recreational mathematics since their inception in 1954. (Pentominoes is a registered trademark of Solomon W. Golomb.)

    Figure 6.6 shows 2 of the 12 different Pentominoes. The variations are usually referred to by letter—for example, Z and P in Figure 6.6, for obvious reasons. The others are T, U, V, W, X, Y, F, L, I, and N.

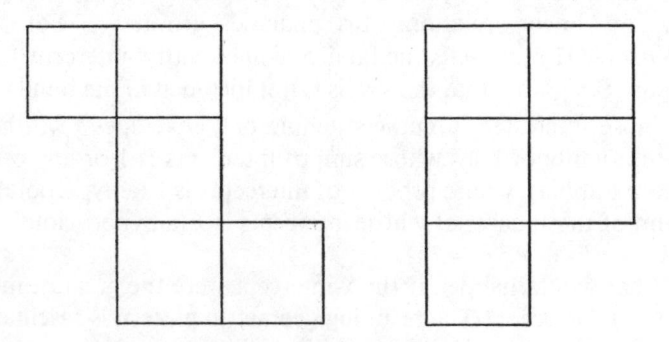

Figure 6.6. Sample Pentominoes.

One young man thought of making numerals out of sets of four Pentominoes. The configuration for "1" is shown in Figure 6.7. He claimed there were 39 different ways of filling that outline with four Pentominoes. How many can you find? How can you be sure there aren't any more? (For more information, write to H. L. Ridge at the address given earlier.)

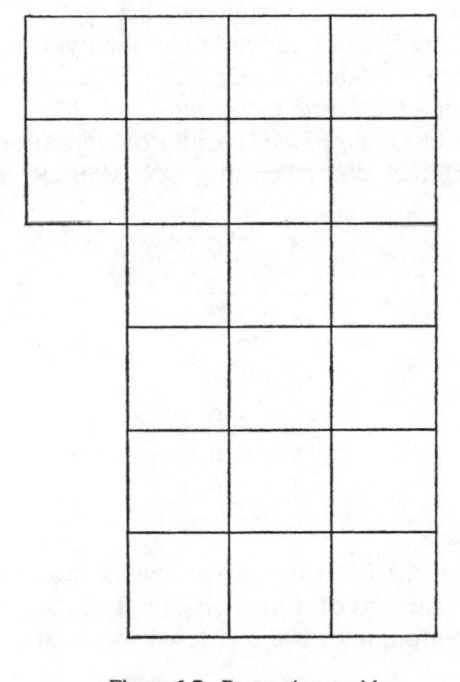

Figure 6.7. Pentomino problem.

3. A consideration of families of lines is standard fare in the high school study of linear relations or analytic geometry. For example, $y = mx + 1$ represents the family of lines with y-intercept 1 as shown in Figure 6.8. (Note that the y-axis is not included in the family of lines.)

Those interested in curve stitching or "envelopes" will have dealt with the family of lines whose sum of intercepts is 1 or any other constant (a parabola); whose product of intercepts is 1 (a hyperbola); or even the sum of the squares of whose intercepts is 1 (a hypocycloid—its equation is $x^{2/3} + y^{2/3} = 1$).

What would happen if the x-intercept were the greatest integer less than the y-intercept? The resulting geometric pattern is fascinating. The entire plane is covered by this family except for two infinte sequences of triangular regions and a "three-sided parallelogram" region (to coin a

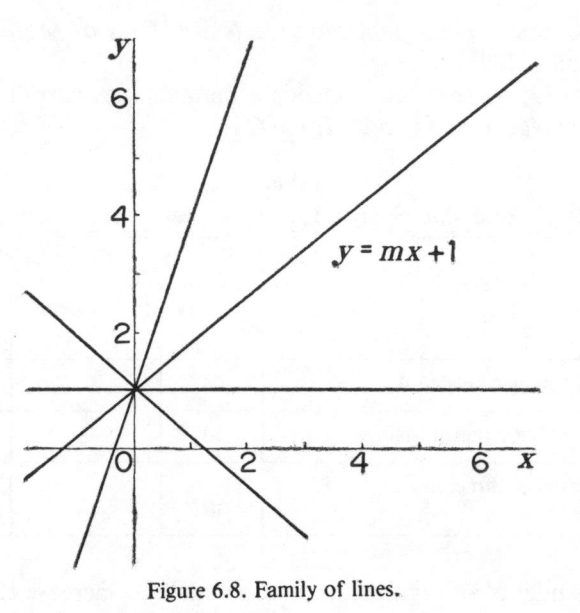

Figure 6.8. Family of lines.

phrase). You have to try it to appreciate it! Then it's your turn to exercise your creativity and make up your own exotic families of lines.

All these examples involve activities of Types I and II in that they accrued from some sort of open investigation in which an individual had some interest (Type I) that led, by the creation of related questions, to a consideration of processes or problem-solving techniques for establishing answers and, no doubt, generating more questions. The dimensions of reality, product, and audience necessary for Type III qualification has occurred quite by chance through their publication for a real audience made up of the readers of this book. There was no intent in the minds of the creators beyond the stimulation of self-interest followed by a desire to share and discuss ideas.

A Shift toward Application

Gifted students have a penchant for abstract thought, often to the virtual exclusion of the practical. Collins (1969) noted the initial uneasiness registered by 8- and 9-year-olds when they were confronted with drawing mathematical relationships from physical apparatus. Such a trait is certainly one that should not be aided and abetted. The whole dimension of mathematics developed from, and applied to, practical considerations is one to which gifted students need considerable exposure if they are to grasp the concept of mathematical modeling and simulation—the very heart of the mathematics of today's and tomorrow's business and industrial pro-

cedures. (A most topical publication is *Newer Uses of Mathematics* (New York: Penguin, 1978).)

Post (1979, p. 168) recommends a mathematics curriculum balanced among the categories shown in Table 6.1.

Table 6.1

Percentages of Total Mathematics Time to Be Devoted to Various Alternatives

Category	Grade Level		
	Primary	Intermediate	Junior High School
A: Structured Number-Related Activities	40	30	20
B: Environmental or Applied Mathematics	50	50	50
C: Logic-Oriented or Structural Mathematics	10	20	30

For gifted students an argument could be made to increase the proportion of logic-oriented or structural mathematics. However, environmental or applied mathematics should remain a strong component.

If mathematically talented students are encouraged to deepen a consuming interest in pure mathematics to the utter exclusion of any knowledge of applied mathematics, they run the distinct risk of joining the glut of Ph.D.s with nowhere to go but behind the wheel of a cab and, hence, are being done a real disservice.

Mason (1978) gives an example of a real problem, in the applied sense, that has appeal for young people because of its subject of application.

> Between the two reels of a tape cassette there are marks which can be used to give some measure of the tape still unplayed. The marks are uniformly spaced. Is this sufficiently accurate or could the marks be improved? (p. 34)

Interestingly, Mason anticipates Type III enrichment by noting at the end of his solution and discussion that

> the main thing that has been omitted from this problem is a final report addressed to the manufacturer pointing out the problem, the solution and, as an appendix, the reasoning. (p. 36)

The concept of mathematical modeling is characterized, albeit simplistically, by an approximation of a real situation by a mathematical construct, usually one or more equations, followed by a working of the mathematics and an interpretation of the result in terms of the real situation. For students interested in biology and, in particular, animals, Collins (1977) has presented a fascinating mathematical explanation of the com-

parative abilities and behaviors of certain animals. "Why does a running mouse take more steps per minute than a horse?" (p. 52). An easily accessible work for gifted students and a good introduction to the breadth of the applications field is Bernice Kastner's *Applications of Secondary School Mathematics* (Reston, Va.: National Council of Teachers of Mathematics, 1978), as is *A Sourcebook of Applications of School Mathematics*, prepared by a Joint Committee of the MAA and the NCTM (Reston, Va.: National Council of Teachers of Mathematics, 1980).

The modules produced by the Undergraduate Mathematics and Its Applications Project (UMAP) provide a very comprehensive appropriate treatment of applied mathematics, even though they are intended for university undergraduates. The modules are written by experts in their respective fields and can be purchased at nominal cost. They deal with a remarkable variety of applications, from "Prescribing Safe and Effective Dosage" to "The Geometry of the Arms Race" to "A Linear Programming Model for Scheduling Prison Guards." (Information is available from the Project Director, EDC/UMAP, 55 Chapel St., Newton, MA 02160.)

A Need for Basics

It cannot be overemphasized that, in conjunction with any consideration of enrichment material, attention must be paid to the mastery of basic mathematical operations. (Banks (Note 2) tells of problems that arose in a program for the gifted because of a naive assumption by all in charge that a mastery of basics could be assumed.) Mirman (1971) states that preparation in the basics should

> also include, at least on the elementary and junior high school level, appropriate and sufficient drill on spelling, handwriting, grammar, and arithmetic computation. . . . Gifted children . . . [should] be able to communicate with others and . . . be able to compute correctly. We do not think it inhibits their creativity, but rather that it helps provide a foundation of skills on which they may build. (p. 221)

In his introduction to *The Creative Process* (New York: New American Library, 1952), Brewster Ghiselin has this to say:

> A great deal of the work necessary to equip and activate the mind for the spontaneous part of invention must be done consciously and with an effort of will. Mastering accumulated knowledge, gathering new facts, observing, exploring, experimenting, developing technique and skill, sensibility, and discrimination, are all more or less conscious and voluntary activities. The sheer labor of preparing technically for creative work, consciously acquiring the requisite knowledge of a medium and skill in its use, is extensive and arduous enough to repel many from achievement. Discipline and hard work are essential for the creative process. High and sustained achievement demands even more, the concentration of a life. (Mirman, p. 221)

Addressing the basics is no mean task because of the utter disdain in which gifted students hold drill exercises. In an effort to exact such practice painlessly, some teachers resort to recreationally oriented drill packages such as the *Mathimagination* series (Palo Alto, Calif.: Creative Publications, 1973), the kind of material more often associated with programs for low achievers. Such material can fulfill a need for gifted students but should not be construed as enrichment. It can be used, however, as a necessary, sweetened preliminary to enrichment activities.

Content for Type I Enrichment, Stimulating Interest

Because of the need to kindle interest even in some able youngsters, special attention is given to this level of enrichment, which calls for freedom of student choice among subject areas and among topics or items within a subject. This philosophy is in keeping with the right of the gifted to "exposure to large bodies of knowledge" (Mirman, 1971, p. 219). We can respond to this spirit at any level of the elementary-secondary continuum. At the elementary level we try to encourage interest in the overall subject of mathematics. Regardless of the age or ability level of our students, their interest does require nurturing. For students in secondary-level mathematics courses, we must continue to stimulate their overall interest as well as turn them on to various areas of mathematics.

It is perhaps surprising that many items of mathematical interest can be used over a wide range of grade levels. The differentiation lies in the kind and depth of treatments. However, discretion should be used as to whether it is more appropriate to expose students to an entire book or kit of stimulating items or whether individual items should be used a few at a time—as the basis for activity cards, for example. At some point students should be permitted to delve into the complete collection in order to make their own selections and gain whatever additional benefit might derive from working with the original form. (Supply and demand often determine the only practical solution. School librarians and resource-center personnel are usually very cooperative in providing suitable material if they are made aware of your class's needs sufficiently in advance.)

Professional journals (such as the *Arithmetic Teacher, Instructor, Learning,* and *Teacher* at the elementary level, and later on, the *Mathematics Teacher* as well as student journals such as the *Mathematics Student*) provide ready and renewable sources of ideas. Because student choice and the whetting of interest are essential to Type I enrichment, teachers should not try to predetermine all these areas of interest. Students should be encouraged to bring in magazines, other media, and objects that relate to their own interests. Such an approach permits the realistic and natural integration of mathematics with other subject areas. (A recent such eye-opener for one of the authors was the magazine *Skateboarder*, brought

into class by a gifted seventh-grade student. Skateboarding is rife with content that relates to Type II and Type III enrichment. For example, there are at least four different types, or shapes, of skateboard. What are the advantages or purposes of each type?) Collins (1969) comments on the heightened interest potential when an enrichment activity is based on ideas or materials provided by the students rather than by the teacher. We are also reminded by Collins that it is the unusual that especially stimulates gifted youngsters. *A New Twist* (Reading, Mass.: Addison-Wesley, 1979) offers some interesting treatments, including alternative basic-operation algorithms.

Just as Type I enrichment is not to be prescriptive for students, neither is this chapter intended to create a course by listing all possible items of input. Rather, the character and thrust of the enterprise is what we are seeking to communicate. However, some of the following recent additions to the classroom mathematical literature could be useful. *Mathemagic: The 1978 Childcraft Annual* (Chicago: World Book—Childcraft International, 1978) might be considered a junior-league analogue of the long-established Time-Life *Mathematics* (New York, 1963, rev. ed. 1967). *Project-a-Puzzle* (Reston, Va.: National Council of Teachers of Mathematics, 1978) is a collection of time-honored puzzle situations set in an attention-getting cartoon motif and produced for the easy making of overhead-projector transparencies. (The material has much more promise for follow-up of Types II and III than the comments that accompany each item suggest.) *Mathematical History: Activities, Puzzles, Stories, and Games* (Reston, Va.: National Council of Teachers of Mathematics, 1978), like *Mathemagic*, includes items *about* mathematics that can help stimulate further appreciation of the subject by gifted students whose main talents or interests lie in other subject areas. Both these publications give some attention to a multicultural point of view appropriate for gifted children whose social concerns often encompass such interests.

There is a plethora of books *about* mathematical topics in children's literature. At the primary level, the MacDonald Educational *Starters Series* (London, 1974) contains 70 general-interest topics and several subseries, among them *Starters Maths*. (The titles in this subseries are (a) *Kitchen Maths*; (b) *Garage Maths*; (c) *Circus Maths*; (d) *Seaside Maths*; (e) *Toyshop Maths*; (f) *Playground Maths*; (g) *Farm Maths*; (h) *Building Maths*; (i) *Clothes Maths*; and (j) *Going Places Maths*.) Somewhat more sophisticated is the Crowell *Young Math Book* series of five titles: *Estimation; Weighing and Balancing; Straight Lines, Parallel Lines; Perpendicular Lines*; and *What Is Symmetry? Mathematical Games and Puzzles* (London: Batsford, 1973) is an excellent "how to" book for the construction and enjoyment of mathematical pursuits by older elementary school youngsters. A comprehensive extension of some of these recreational pastimes for students and fanciers is the profusely and beautifully illustrated *Creative Puzzles of*

the World (New York: Abrams, 1978). The comprehensive *Mathematics Resource Project* (Palo Alto, Calif.: Creative Publications, 1977) contains almost anything that junior high school students and teachers might desire in the way of resources for mathematical stimulation.

Another first-rate collection of stimulators, well tested with gifted junior high school students, is the Canadian publication *Mathematics Enrichment for Grades Seven to Ten* (Toronto: Copp Clark, 1966). The historical vignettes are a real find—brief, readable accounts of 17 great creators in mathematics, from Euclid to Maria Agnesi to Nicholas Bourbaki. In fact, bibliographies and pictures of renowned mathematicians could be featured within displays of mathematical instruments, posters, charts, and assorted interest-catching "mathemabilia." For more mature students, readings from the *Scientific American* have been compiled in *Mathematics: An Introduction to Its Spirit and Use* (San Francisco: Freeman, 1979), reviewed in the *Mathematics Teacher* (vol. 72, Sept. 1979, p. 473).

The ubiquitous calculator should not be overlooked as a source of almost endless pleasure and intrigue with numbers. For young children, and many not-so-young ones, preprogrammed machines such as Dataman (Texas Instruments) make for fascinating learning. The stimulation of some calculator games, for example, can be carried over into activities of Types II and III, in addition to strengthening basic operations and number sense. (The marketplace abounds with publications of games and activities for use with calculators. Among others, those authored by Wallace Judd provide lots of good material.) Also, the potential of microprocessors is just beginning to be tapped.

Mathematical devices, such as the pantograph (Figure 6.9) for drawing similar figures, the planimeter (Figure 6.10) for measuring the area of irregular figures by tracing the boundary, the hypsometer (Figure 6.11) and the clinometer (Figure 6.12) for measuring remote angles and distances, and models of all kinds, including various forms of packaging, provide Type II content for studying mechanical processes or analyzing the reasons for certain packaging procedures. (Pantographs have even been offered as premiums in boxes of cereal. To quote the star of "Donald in Mathmagic Land" (Walt Disney, 1960), the ultimate mathematical film turn-on, "You find mathematics in the darnedest places." Your local drafting supplies merchant may be willing to lend you a planimeter for classroom demonstration and student participation. Next question—"How does it work?") Again, academically gifted youngsters do not take well to concrete materials or practical situations (Collins, 1969), but such experiences should be present in deference to the three-ring concept of giftedness and also as an opportunity for students to widen their horizons. If gifted students are to become involved at the real level in Type III enrichment, then Types I and II

as preparatory stages should at least encourage interest in the mathematical aspects of the real world.

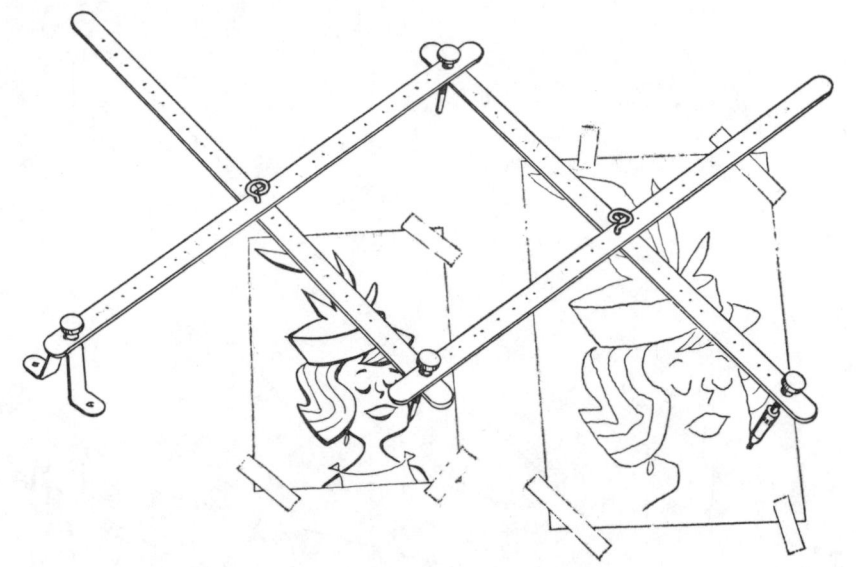

Figure 6.9. Pantograph.

In conjunction with displays of scientific equipment and other applications of mathematics, great benefit can derive from visitations by or to individuals whose careers involve related mathematics. Meteorologists, actuaries, urban planners, engineers, and systems analysts are among a myriad of possibilities. The key here is contact with a "turned on" professional, the kind of person who thinks the world would fall apart tomorrow

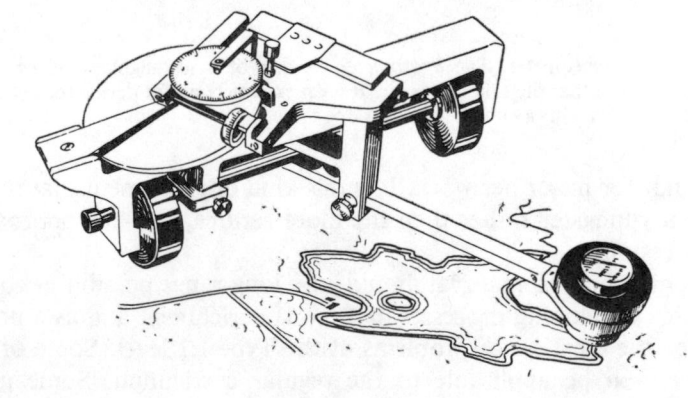

Figure 6.10. Planimeter.

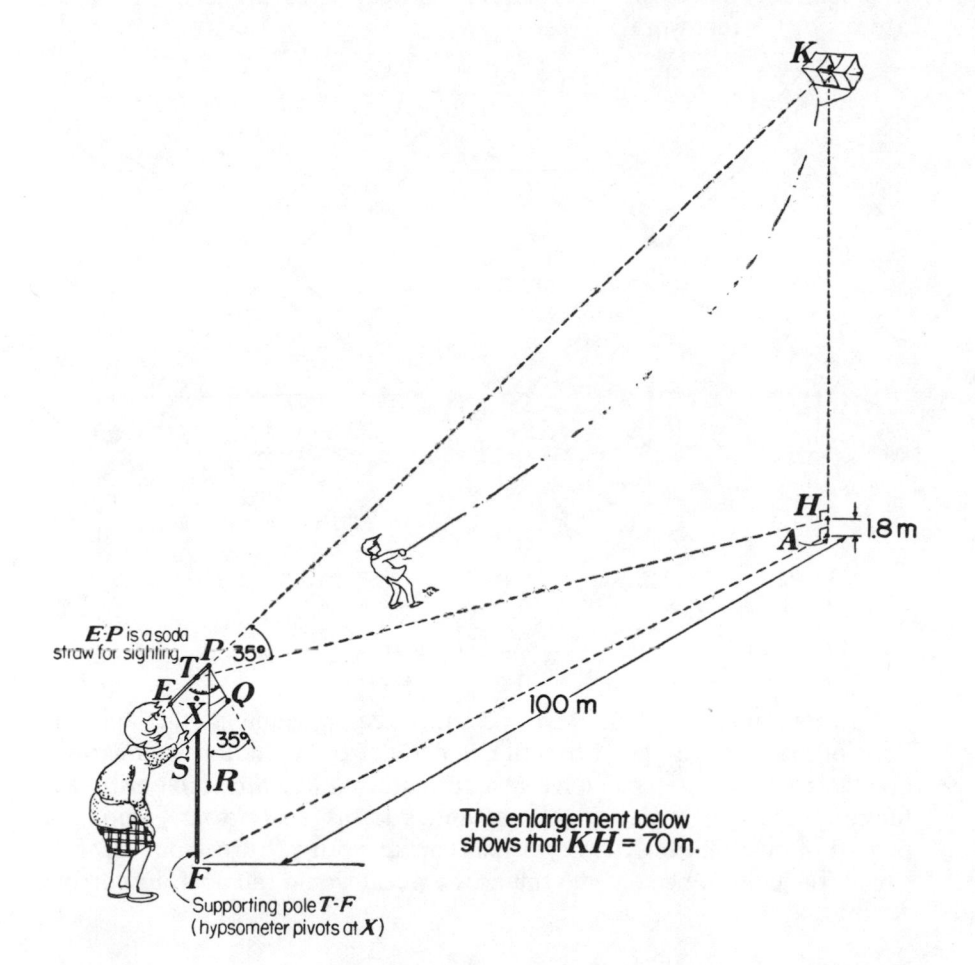

Figure 6.11. Hypsometer. The *hypsometer* consists of a rectangular grid on a plate, fastened to a pole so that the grid can pivot. It is an extremely useful device for determining heights when coupled with a clinometer and slope table.

if it were not for his or her work. It is this kind of excitement that tends to stimulate a youngster rather than the more serious, low-key approach of some professionals.

Most high-interest material should have long-range possibilities both as a vehicle for developing processes in Type II enrichment and as a possible context for the creation of problems at the Type III level. Some of these ideas may even be applicable to the regular curriculum. Some games, puzzles, and so-called recreational materials have just such potential. (The

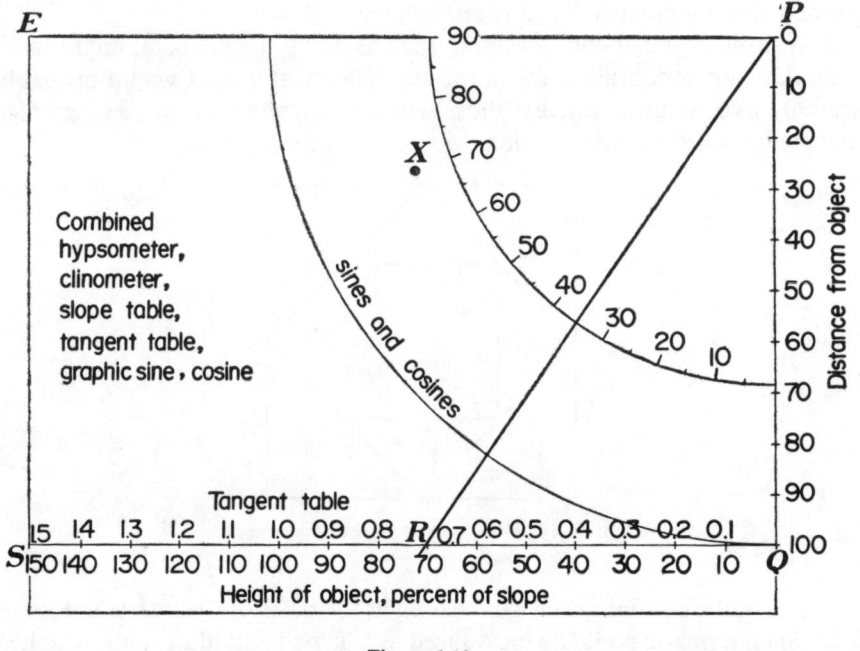

Figure 6.12.

pejorative mention of such items earlier in the chapter referred to their indiscriminate, nondevelopmental use as entertaining ends in themselves.) These materials also allow teachers to observe student behavior that may be indicative of hidden talent.

Here is a case in point. Krutetskii (1969) has used the puzzle motif shown in Figure 6.13 as a gross dividing line between lesser and greater mathematical abilities, at least in terms of perception. Those of lesser mathematical ability answer "four"; the more able answer "eight."

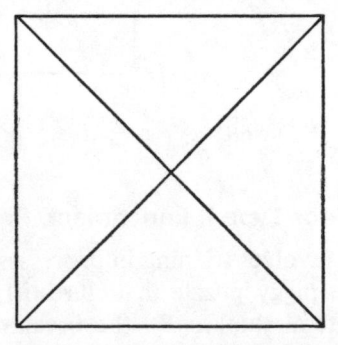

Figure 6.13. How many triangles do you see?

Anything in between shows promise and should be pursued as a part of the process development in Type II enrichment.

A similar type of configuration, such as that in Figure 6.14, might serve a similar purpose. Students with less mathematical insight would probably see only two squares, whereas those with more acute perception or greater knowledge of geometric relations would see three squares.

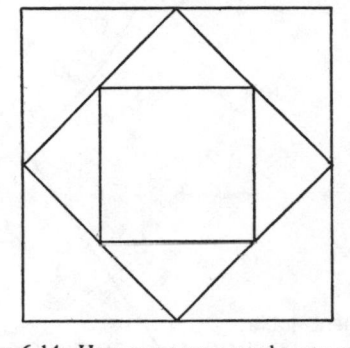

Figure 6.14. How many squares do you see?

This same configuration can be used as the basis of the puzzle in Figure 6.15. Such a puzzle could be introduced as a Type I stimulator, but whether a correct solution is given or not the situation lends itself to Type II analysis.

Nine piggies live in a square pen. Add 2 more squares so that each piggy has its own pen.

Figure 6.15. A piggy puzzle.

Content for Type II Enrichment, Process

Type II enrichment involves training in processes related to Type I exploratory activities. The piggy puzzle in Figure 6.15 can be used to introduce some basic "lateral thinking"—the breaking of a mind set, or *einstellung. Lateral thinking* is a term attributed to DeBono in referring to a

restructuring of thought, a kind of flanking move or "end run," when the usual analytic or logical pattern of direct thinking produces an impasse. DeBono calls it a "de-patterning process in a patterning system" (Mason, 1978, p. 42). Those who have trouble solving the puzzle may assume that each pig must have a square pen or that all the pens must be the same size—that is, have equal area. Such adherence to balance is a block to creativity. (Recall the mention earlier that the more creative mathematicians relate better to asymmetric and irregular complex design.) Some people, regardless of age, have a mental block that a square is not a square unless its sides are horizontal and vertical. No one speaks of a "baseball square," for example. To break down this block it may be necessary to have students make a square and rotate it so they can see that *all* the properties of a square are preserved under this transformation.

The process being illustrated is part of a very useful problem-solving technique—that of recording all your thoughts as you try to solve a problem. As you think of an assumption ("The pens must be square") or wonder, even momentarily, about a condition ("Do the pens have to be the same size?"), *write it down!* This has somewhat the same effect as conversing with, or bouncing ideas off, another person—a technique that can often produce a flash of insight that may clarify a problem.

Another often-neglected process in problem solving that should become routine especially for gifted students is that of trying to generalize the situation. This, of course, calls for a recognition of the underlying mathematical concept. In the piggy puzzle, the concept is that the line segments terminated by the midpoints of successive sides of a square also form a square. A generalization might be made in the form of a conjecture or of a question. Two possibilities come to mind:

1. What kind of figure is formed by the line segments terminated by the midpoints of successive sides of a quadrilateral?

2. What kind of figure is formed by the line segments whose endpoints divide (a) the successive sides of a square in the same ratio? (b) the successive sides of a quadrilateral in the same ratio?

Each of these questions gives rise to another problem-solving procedure—inductive investigation through a ·systematic examination of various cases. Prior to such an investigation, each student involved should make a written conjecture or educated guess about the nature of the outcome.

As the results of such an investigation are compiled and organized so that patterns can be readily abstracted—yet another problem-solving technique—considerable opportunity arises for the creation and solution of new problems, even if only special variations on the original questions. The inclusion of deductive proof will depend on the students' mathematical

maturity. Such an activity is a most appropriate challenge for gifted students. In fact, it verges on a Type III enrichment activity—creating and solving a real problem. (Problems on this topic that have actually been created by a group of students working with one of the authors involve the investigation of the sufficient conditions for the formation of specific figures such as a square, rhombus, or rectangle by joining the midpoints or other points of section of successive sides of a quadrilateral.) Problems formed through student activity and then investigated, if not ultimately solved, are no doubt very real to those students, whether or not the result has a significant real-world application. The only dimension missing for Type III inclusion is that of a real audience. The additional challenge of writing an article based on the investigation for submission to a student mathematics journal or to a mathematics education journal would certainly elevate the proceedings to Type III status.

Before submitting such an article for publication, students can be encouraged to engage in an extra dimension of the problem-solving process at a professional level, namely, searching the literature to see what work has been done on the topic. Such a procedure is really a Type II activity in that there is a definite routine to be followed and a knowledge to be developed of what kinds of information can be found where. Consultation with a librarian, a visit to a nearby college library, and assistance from a practicing mathematician would be advantageous and perhaps even necessary. These latter experiences could be classified as Type I enrichment. The interrelationship of all three types, as shown in Figure 6.4, is evident in any project that becomes sufficiently consequential.

Methodology

In chapter 2, Glennon presented a model for the sources of a teacher's methodologies and a model for the sources of the curriculum and discussed the interaction between them. We made several methodological inferences in our section on content. Content will play a similar role in this section.

Gifted students prefer methodologies that lie at two extremes. They are somewhat impatient with guided discovery. "Just *tell* us how it goes, and we'll do it," they say. The problem here is that although their responses may be rapid and correct, adequate understanding is lacking, and the net effect is one of a peripheral treatment. Even worse, some gifted students are so quick in their responses that they make mechanical slips and often produce illegible work. Although a messy page could be a promising sign, some emphasis should be placed on clear, concise communication.

At the other extreme is the desire to work totally independently with input through the printed word rather than through physical experiment. (Experimental strategy in problem solving is a most important technique often overlooked or, indeed, avoided by very bright mathematics students who

feel that they can do everything in their heads.) Hence, gifted students need to be involved in dialogues about mathematics and in the development of ideas. Research claims that little creativity is gained through a group approach to problem solving. However, much is to be gained affectively—that is, in group cooperation, listening to and appreciating the ideas of others, developing self-concept, and so on—by encouraging a sharing and discussion of mathematical thinking. One way is to offer a challenge that is sufficiently difficult to require mutual consultation. Collins (1969) cites one such situation in which a combination of individual and consultative work brought about a solution to a problem that less able students would have given up in utter frustration in much less time.

Time for thinking and creating is imperative. If gifted youngsters are to be given challenges appropriate to their ability, they must be afforded the time to do necessary research, either in class or in lieu of class meetings. We have previously noted Passow's (1976) remark that a considerable amount of sweat is involved in creativity before that flash of illumination or inspiration can be triggered.

The detailed example that follows is an attempt to react to some of these considerations. We do not suggest that all material should be taught in the manner described but do present a model that has been shown to be particularly effective with gifted students.

The model recognizes the ability of gifted students to deal with the abstract and make generalizations. It also relates, albeit to a lesser extent, their need to work with and appreciate the mathematics associated with concrete items and more practical concerns (Collins, 1969). Again, students need to see that work with the concrete or enactive mode relates to a mathematical idea or structure; otherwise, work with materials may well be regarded negatively. Collins (1969) reports that some gifted youngsters regarded the use of concrete materials in regular lessons as unnecessary and, in fact, irrelevant. (Surprisingly, perhaps, work with colored rods, for example, was seen as an exercise based on color, not on number concepts.)

The investigations presented on the following pages involve a variety of materials for generating data and suggest a wide range of media for recording and reporting the data. (Much of this package was developed by one of the authors on the basis of ideas expressed by Zalman Usiskin as a consultant to the Ontario Ministry of Education, 1970.) Some of the activities could be used at the Type I level to stimulate an interest in things mathematical. The fact that operations on physical things could generate a "table" of results not unlike those for addition or multiplication would be surprising. Novel approaches and unexpected results are the stuff of interest to the gifted. Rather than being confused, they are intrigued and curious to delve more deeply into what is going on.

Various organizational strategies can be used in a Type II procedure.

Small-group interaction is preferable to solo development but certainly not mandatory. At whatever stage results are shared, interaction and discussion should be encouraged in a natural way.

Plan 1

These investigations can be introduced as exercises in data gathering, organization, and analysis—all part of Type II enrichment. In fact, at the outset students might be given only a set of elements and operation within each context and be asked to gather and organize data to find out all they can about each of these finite little systems.

Each small group or individual works through Investigation 1 and then, over an extended period of time, deals with all the other investigations in any order.

Should students not be sufficiently familiar with, say, matrix multiplication, they should be encouraged to consult readily available reference material as another aspect of Type II enrichment. Becoming familiar with reference literature, which includes anything beyond course textbooks, is a prerequisite to Type III activity.

Another feature of such a "demand learning" situation is the strong and natural motivation of needing information in order to accomplish a worthwhile task. The immediate application of the information to the task at hand helps the student to assimilate the ideas more readily.

Information seeking also encourages individualization to the extent that any one student or small group seeks only the information they need. Some decision making—another Type II activity—could determine whether it is more advantageous to work something out or to go to another source, be that another student, group of students, print resources, or other media. The teacher, of course, is also a resource who should assist with search procedures and discuss difficulties that may arise in the reference material but who should stop short of acting as the purveyor of information. Two points should be made about gifted students in this connection. The first is that confidence and competence as independent researchers must be encouraged. The second, and more basic for some individuals, is that they need to break the notion that asking questions or seeking assistance is a slur on their giftedness. Developing a sense of efficient use of time and ability both for short-term and long-range objectives is part of the maturing process that should be aided and abetted at every opportunity. Type II enrichment, after all, is intended to develop techniques and processes applicable especially to areas of student interest.

As students work through these investigations, the teacher has an excellent opportunity to gauge the degree of abstraction, generalization, and making and testing of conjectures of which they are capable at the time. How many entries will they calculate individually before spotting and ex-

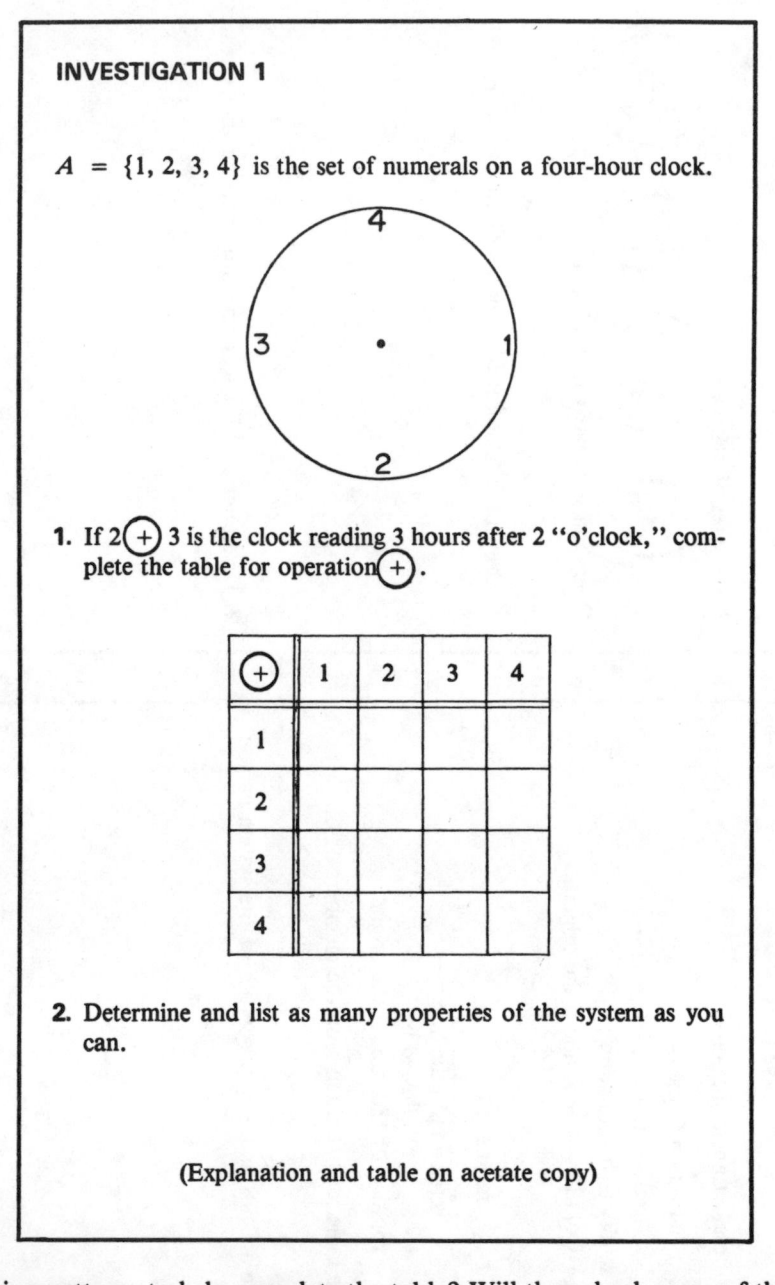

INVESTIGATION 1

$A = \{1, 2, 3, 4\}$ is the set of numerals on a four-hour clock.

1. If 2 (+) 3 is the clock reading 3 hours after 2 "o'clock," complete the table for operation (+).

(+)	1	2	3	4
1				
2				
3				
4				

2. Determine and list as many properties of the system as you can.

(Explanation and table on acetate copy)

ploiting patterns to help complete the table? Will they check some of these conjectured entries or just be satisfied with the assumed pattern? What structural properties will they abstract in any one investigation? (Closure, identity, inverse, and commutativity can be inferred directly from the

INVESTIGATION 2

C is the set of plane transformations

$r_{y=x}$ (reflection in the line $y = x$);
$r_{y=-x}$ (reflection in the line $y = -x$);
I (identity transformation);
$R_{180°}$ (rotation of 180° about the origin).

1. If $R_{180°} * r_{y=x}$ means

reflection in the line $y = x$
"followed by"
rotation of 180° about the origin.

draw up a table for operation $*$ on the members of C.

2. Determine and list as many properties of the system as you can.

(Table on large sheet; illustrations on pegboard)

INVESTIGATION 3

B is the set of matrices

$$\begin{pmatrix} 0 & 1 \\ 1 & 0 \end{pmatrix}, \begin{pmatrix} 0 & -1 \\ -1 & 0 \end{pmatrix}, \begin{pmatrix} 1 & 0 \\ 0 & 1 \end{pmatrix}, \begin{pmatrix} -1 & 0 \\ 0 & -1 \end{pmatrix}.$$

Operation $*$ is matrix multiplication.

1. Draw up a table for operation $*$ on the members of B.

2. Determine and list as many properties of the system as you can.

(Table on large sheet; explanation on board)

INVESTIGATION 4

D is the set of motions of a model of rectangle $XYZW$.

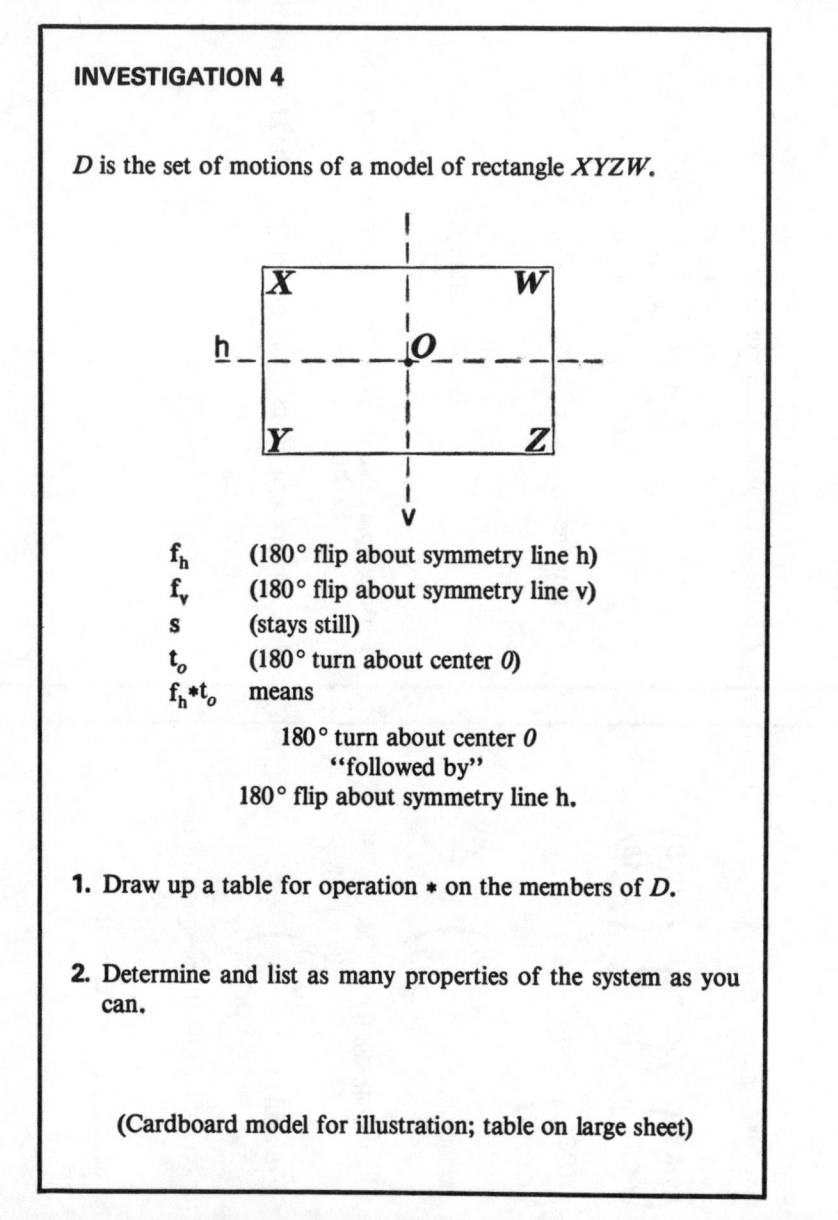

f_h	(180° flip about symmetry line h)
f_v	(180° flip about symmetry line v)
s	(stays still)
t_o	(180° turn about center O)
f_h*t_o	means

180° turn about center O
"followed by"
180° flip about symmetry line h.

1. Draw up a table for operation * on the members of D.

2. Determine and list as many properties of the system as you can.

(Cardboard model for illustration; table on large sheet)

operation table. With only four elements in the system, associativity can be readily checked by examples. Each structure is a commutative, or abelian, group.) Have they determined the structural properties by a consideration of the physical aspects of the materials involved (enactive mode), by a diagrammatic analysis (iconic mode), or by a study of patterns within the operation table (symbolic mode)? It is important that the teacher con-

INVESTIGATION 5

E is the set of permutations

$$\begin{pmatrix} ABCD \\ BADC \end{pmatrix}, \begin{pmatrix} ABCD \\ DCBA \end{pmatrix}, \begin{pmatrix} ABCD \\ ABCD \end{pmatrix}, \begin{pmatrix} ABCD \\ CDAB \end{pmatrix}.$$

1. If $\begin{pmatrix} ABCD \\ DCBA \end{pmatrix} * \begin{pmatrix} ABCD \\ CDAB \end{pmatrix}$ means

permutation $\begin{pmatrix} ABCD \\ CDAB \end{pmatrix}$

"followed by"

permutation $\begin{pmatrix} ABCD \\ DCBA \end{pmatrix}$,

draw up a table for operation * on the members of E.

2. Determine and list as many properties of the system as you can.

(Explanation and table on large sheets)

INVESTIGATION 6

F is the set of plane transformations

$$f: (x, y) \rightarrow (y, x);$$
$$g: (x, y) \rightarrow (-y, -x);$$
$$h: (x, y) \rightarrow (x, y);$$
$$k: (x, y) \rightarrow (-x, -y).$$

$f * g$ means

transformation g
"followed by"
transformation f.

1. Draw up a table for operation * on the members of F.

2. Determine and list as many properties of the system as you can.

(Table on large sheet; explanation on acetate)

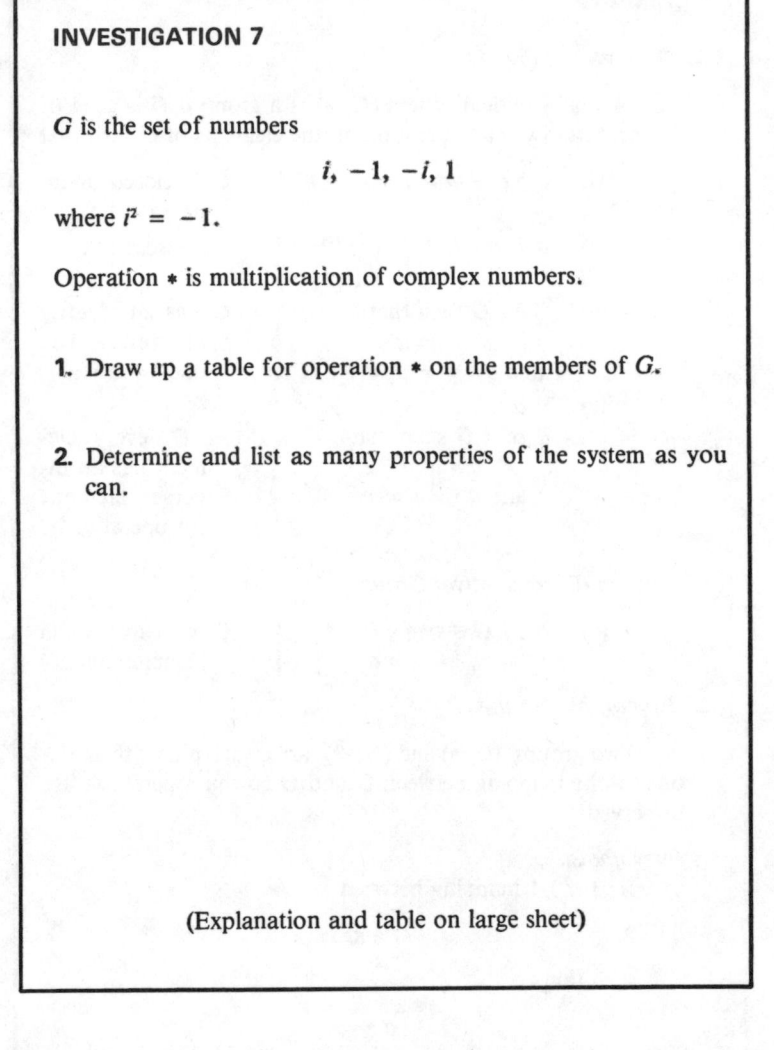

INVESTIGATION 7

G is the set of numbers

$$i, -1, -i, 1$$

where $i^2 = -1$.

Operation * is multiplication of complex numbers.

1. Draw up a table for operation * on the members of G.

2. Determine and list as many properties of the system as you can.

(Explanation and table on large sheet)

solidate students' concepts by discussing the interpretation of symbolic patterns seen in a table in relation to the physical or diagrammatic material that generated the table. The converse is also necessary so that gifted students do not get the impression that the work and role of mathematics involves only the abstract.

The study of the interrelation of the abstract and the physical involves the very essence of mathematical modeling. A physical situation gives rise to a mathematical form, or model, that represents certain relationships—often an equation, but here an operation table. Patterns or properties that might be more easily recognized through this abstract form that is free of physical

SUMMARY

1. *Group Structure*

A mathematical system $(G, *)$ is a group if G is a set of elements and $*$ is an operation on the elements of G such that

(i) $a, b \, \varepsilon \, G \Rightarrow a * b \, \varepsilon \, G$ $\Big\}$ G is closed under operation $*$.

(ii) $a, b, c \, \varepsilon \, G \Rightarrow (a*b)*c$
$= a * (b * c)$ $\Bigg\}$ $*$ is associative.

(iii) $\exists \, e \, \varepsilon \, G$ such that
$a * e = a$
and $e * a = a, \forall \, a \, \varepsilon \, G$ $\Bigg\}$ G has an identity element for operation $*$.

(iv) $\forall \, a \, \varepsilon \, G$
$\exists \, a^{-1} \, \varepsilon \, G$ such that
$a * a^{-1} = e$
and $a^{-1} * a = e$ $\Bigg\}$ In G, every element has an inverse element for operation $*$.

Abelian (Commutative) Group

(v) $a, b \, \varepsilon \, G \Rightarrow a * b$
$= b * a$ $\Big\}$ Operation $*$ is commutative.

2. *Isomorphic Groups*

Two groups, $(G, *)$ and $(H, \#)$, are isomorphic if there is a one-to-one mapping between G and H so that operations are preserved.

In symbols:
If $\exists \, a$ 1-1 mapping between

$$G \text{ and } H$$

such that

$$a \leftrightarrow \alpha$$
$$b \leftrightarrow \beta$$
$$\Rightarrow (a * b \leftrightarrow \alpha \# \beta)$$

then $(G, *)$ and $(H, \#)$ are isomorphic groups.

trappings can then be interpreted to elicit more information about the physical, or less abstract, situation.

As students continue these investigations, to what extent do they appreciate, use, or even look for analogies among the content items in any of the enactive, iconic, or symbolic modes? How is the four-hour clock related

to multiplication by i, for example? How are the arrangements of letters related to certain motions of a rectangular piece of cardboard, and how is each arrangement related to certain transformations on a coordinate plane? Such leading questions may have to be asked if students continue to carry out each investigation independently of the experience of previous investigations. For gifted students, there is a good chance that interrelationships would trigger on their own, "Hey, this result is just like what we got with the . . ." How deeply such an observation is followed up is another matter. The teacher's timing arrangements should be flexible enough to permit a worthwhile follow-up of such a discovery. Students should not be pressured to complete all seven activities for their own sake but should be encouraged to pursue observed relationships and perhaps test conjectures by applying them to yet untried investigations.

As students begin to realize that these investigations are intimately related, some almost disguises for others, they should be challenged to find the relationships or underlying patterns. Such a challenge promotes further student cooperation and interaction in a natural way—again, through need. Teachers may need to curb a natural tendency to intercede when it appears that students have reached a dead end. The ideas must be given a chance to incubate.

Investigations 1 and 7 are isomorphic. Both have the form of table shown below. Both are examples of the cyclic 4-group. One element generates all the other elements as powers. For example, in Investigation 7, $i^2 = -1$, $i^3 = -i$, $i^4 = 1$.

*	A	B	C	D
A	B	C	D	A
B	C	D	A	B
C	D	A	B	C
D	A	B	C	D

Investigations 2–6 are also isomorphic. All have the form of table shown below. All are examples of the Klein 4-group. This and the cyclic group above are the only two 4-groups, and they are both commutative.

*	A	B	C	D
A	D	C	B	A
B	C	D	A	B
C	B	A	D	C
D	A	B	C	D

To consolidate the concept of isomorphism, everyone can be instructed to reproduce their tables using the same set of symbols, say, X, Y, Z, and W. Gifted students will simply translate the entire table into the new symbols. Less able students will probably start recalculating tabular entries. The fact that five of the investigations generate the same table, as do the other two a different table, must be of some practical value—food for further discussion, perhaps even a Type III project. (An immediate consequence is that results in any one of the specific situations can be found by working in the system that is easiest for a particular individual. For some, matrix multiplication is the most direct because it involves only a "how to" instruction. Application of the group concept can be found in theoretical physics and in the symmetries of crystalline structures studied in physical chemistry.)

Plan 2

This is a more sophisticated version of Plan 1. Each group or individual performs Investigation 1 and one other. Each group then displays its findings and reports to the full class on its particular investigation. This procedure demands the development of communication skills including oral presentation and the use of a variety of media. The communication must be understood, since everyone else must use these results to derive the relationships discussed under Plan 1. This arrangement encourages two-way communication among students in terms of questions, clarifications, challenges, refutations, and so on.

As the nature and results of succeeding investigations become known, some students may see on their own that connecting patterns are emerging. When all or a sufficient amount of the evidence is in, students are then challenged to investigate the interrelationships as thoroughly as they can. Then matters can proceed much as they did in Plan 1.

One advantage of seeing the big picture of all the results without having to go through all the details is that one might see more of the forest than the trees. The disadvantage is having less feeling for the specifics involved, especially from the reinforcement that can accrue from carrying out the many repetitive operations necessary for the completion of a table. This is not just a ploy to coerce gifted students into a drill situation; it is just a fruitful spin-off from the processes of data gathering and organization.

Because gifted students can deal with abstraction at an early age and can benefit from a unified approach to mathematics, it is important to give them opportunities to experience and appreciate the integration of mathematical concepts and to sense the power of mathematical abstraction —that one mathematical structure or model can represent many apparently different types of situations. By working within that structure, we can, in effect, operate within all the specific applications simultaneously.

Mathematics teachers might aspire to have all their students develop such insight and understanding, but gifted students have the potential that can make this hope a reality. It puts the ball in our court.

Type III Enrichment Possibilities

This final section recognizes the importance of Type III enrichment as the discriminating feature of a program for the gifted. It serves as a kind of guide to possible activities.

Type III enrichment involves real production for a real audience. It represents the ultimate consolidation for gifted students. Mathematics is a tool of design and analysis in integrated projects involving science, social sciences, language, the arts, business, and technical subjects. Many of the necessary mathematical processes, such as data gathering, could be developed on a "how to" basis as a Type II activity. (Mathematics per se as the basis of Type III activity is quite another matter.)

The Unified Science and Mathematics for Elementary Schools (USMES) program is promoted as being based on the solution of real problems in the sense of responding to a real need for real people and would, at first glance, appear to be a natural candidate for Type III experience. "A 'real' problem connotes a practical, immediate impediment to good, safe, or pleasurable living" (Lomon et al., 1975, p. 54). This interdisciplinary program, however, is designed for general classroom use by all elementary school students regardless of grade or ability level. The philosophy is that in today's complex society everyone has some responsibility for creating his or her own happiness, and hence, "most of us must become good solvers of real problems" (Lomon et al., 1975, p. 53). (For information about USMES write to Moore Publishing Co., P.O. Box 3036, West Durham Station, Durham, NC 27705.)

Does this program and the point of view of its director, quoted above, imply that Type III enrichment is (a) not really enrichment at all because it is basic for the majority of the population and (b) not qualitatively differentiable, and hence not justifiable, as an approach for the gifted? Before we suggest that the whole thrust of the enrichment-triad model has been undermined, some closer scrutiny is necessary.

The USMES guide suggests that teachers adapt students' expressed interests or needs to an appropriate challenge to be taken on as a class project. The apparent contrivance is somewhat dispelled by the list of 26 units, as of 1976, that represent a broad cross section of interests typical to youngsters. (Each USMES unit is based on a real problem expressed in the form of a challenge. For example, in the unit on consumer research, the challenge is "Determine which brand of a product is the best buy for a specific use" (Sampson, S. S., Finstein, L. A., & Keskulla, J. *Consumer Research*, 4th ed. Newton, Mass.: Educational Development Center, 1976, p. 13).) The

program contains a considerable battery of "how to" cards designed to help students develop skills in mathematics, science, and practical design for which a need becomes evident during work on a problem. This is certainly in the spirit of Type II enrichment—procedures on demand occasioned by demonstrated interest. Some individualization is also evidenced in that students use only those "how to" cards that are necessary. In addition, the program provides background papers, written by USMES staffers, that are accessible both to teachers and to students and an extensive bibliography on the topics of geometry, graphing, measurement and approximation, and probability and statistics. To its credit, the bibliography includes a number of Canadian and British titles. (This is, perhaps, in deference to the close relationship that USMES bears to the British Nuffield Project.)

Some may argue that the very practical nature of the real problems in USMES is not appropriate in programs for the gifted, regardless of the problem-solving processes involved. Such a reaction smacks of stereotyping and elitism in a highly pejorative sense. Work with the practical is needed to complement the abstract thinking associated with gifted students. Also, a "market" is needed for the creative productivity that should be fostered in the gifted. Another consideration is the task commitment involved in carrying a solution to fruition in the practical sense of effecting an actual benefit.

Another asset for the gifted in the USMES program is the interdisciplinary approach inherent in solving real problems. Social science and language arts are involved as well as mathematics and science. The uncontrived integration of subject areas is necessary in any such pursuit. Unfortunately, beyond elementary school the logistics of interdisciplinary study become difficult because of the subject specialization of teachers.

Northern Secondary School, Toronto, Ontario, offers, within a regular high school, a program for gifted and talented students that is remarkable in its effective integration of subjects representing the academic, commercial, art, and technical facilities. (Information is available from Northern Secondary School, 851 Mount Pleasant Rd., Toronto, ON M4P 2L5.)

The preceding remarks might be interpreted by some as completing the undermining of the enrichment-triad model with its Type III enrichment for the gifted only. Such is not the case. The features cited above as benefits are, as the program states, benefits for *all* students. For gifted students, adaptations such as the following could create a qualitatively differentiated program.

1. Although gifted students should be expected to work in group situations to develop communication and other social skills (Bell, 1978), they should have more freedom for independent study than what is implied by the whole-class motif of the USMES program.

2. Gifted students require more freedom of choice in Type III enrich-

ment pursuits than what can be provided by the teacher's appeal to a specified list of challenges, especially considering the diverse and more sophisticated interests of the gifted. The program must be sufficiently flexible to permit the encouragement of a student's development as a problem finder in his or her own area of interest.

3. Gifted students should be permitted a narrowed interdisciplinary subject range to encourage creative productivity in their respective areas of greatest strength. It is not enough for them just to "do better" than other students in the same pursuits.

4. Gifted students should be encouraged to dip into reference material of as broad and deep a character as possible, even beyond the USMES background papers and bibliographies.

(These adaptations are in no way intended to cast aspersions on the USMES program. They are suggested only to add a unique dimension for the gifted, not to imply a need for revision in the program as currently constituted. The fact remains, however, that the program is based on pre-planned and administered exercises and therefore cannot be classified as a Type III experience. The USMES guides are examples of excellent Type II material that could help generate ideas that could *lead to* Type III experiences.)

Math Leagues

Type III enrichment for gifted students was compared earlier with school athletics, in which preparation culminates in competition with real opponents in front of real spectators. In the literal spirit of this analogy are the many mathematics leagues across the continent that provide a natural Type III activity.

The format of competition is a tournament style, usually similar to that of a television game show. In some areas the school math teams vie with the athletic, music, or dramatic groups for high profile, overt peer and public recognition, and the development of strong self-images for the individual team members. Flener (1976) has extolled the virtues of such activity in the Chicago area.

Contests and Competitions

Mathematics contests based on written examinations are accessible to various age groups from about Grade 6 and up. (See Appendix 2 for a partial listing of such contests. For further information about contests in the U.S. in particular, contact Stephen R. Conrad, Benjamin N. Cardozo High School, Bayside, NY 11360.) These contests are another source of keen competition, although less overt than math leagues, a condition that may be more inviting to a greater number of competitors. Preparation for such

bouts, either oral or written, has virtually become part of the curriculum for many gifted students, especially in keenly competitive schools.

Preparation for competition demands a good deal of individualization and independent study and in that regard is most appropriate for gifted students. Yet, most contests and competitions require rapid as well as accurate responses under a lot of pressure. Preparation for such a fray is not conducive to the development of necessary long-term work habits in the form of clear but concise communication of ideas and reasoning. Nor are generalization and problem creation part of the preparation for a competition that demands the honing of time-saving techniques such as replacing a general question with a suitable specific case. (For example, to find the percentage increase in the volume of a cube when the sides are increased by 50%, one would be well advised to use a unit cube rather than consider a general cube of, say, side "a" units.) Hence, it is important that high-ability mathematics students have an extensive smorgasbord of curricular activities that encourage them to broaden their repertoire.

Furthermore, success in such competitions is indicative of a particular type of mathematical talent but tells little about the slower, so-called logical or formal type of mathematical mind (Aiken, 1973) that comes to the fore in problem solving that requires the essay style of response. This facet of problem solving is the basis of the National and International Mathematics Olympiads, which are open only to students who have proved themselves in preliminary, objective-style competitions. (See Appendix 2 for details.) Olympiads are intended only for the crème de la crème who can succeed in both the objective-style and essay-style situations.

A column called "The Olympiad Corner" is featured in every issue of the journal *Crux Mathematicorum*. The column is written by Murray Klamkin, one of the coaches of the U.S. Olympiad Team. The following excerpt from the introductory column (Jan. 1979) is reprinted with permission as a matter of information and for the excellent advice it contains, especially regarding work habits.

     This column will provide, on a continuing basis, information about various mathematical contests taking place in Canada, the U.S.A., and internationally. It will also provide from time to time practice sets of problems on which interested students can test and sharpen their mathematical skills and thereby possibly qualify to participate in some Olympiad. "Official" solutions to these problems will be published in a succeeding issue. Teachers are encouraged to go into these solutions and possible extensions more thoroughly with their interested students. They should impress upon the students the importance of having *clear, concise*, and *complete* solutions since *good presentation counts* (in both the Canadian and U.S.A. Mathematical Olympiads). This includes *legibility, good English*, and *mathematical clarity*.

     I will be glad to receive communications on these problems from students

(or their teachers) who have come up with an elegant solution different from the "official" one, and/or a nice extension with proof. Some of these may then be published in this section.

PRACTICE SET I (3 hours)

1-1 If a, b, c, d are positive integers such that $ab = cd$, prove that $a^2 + b^2 + c^2 + d^2$ is never a prime number.

1-2 If two circles pass through the vertex and a point on the bisector of an angle, prove that they intercept equal segments on the sides of the angle.

1-3 a) If a, b, $c \geqslant 0$ and $(1 + a)(1 + b)(1 + c) = 8$, prove that $abc \leqslant 1$.
    b) If a, b, $c \geqslant 1$, prove that $4(abc + 1) \geqslant (1 + a)(1 + b)(1 + c)$.
    (pp. 12–13)

(*Note:* All communications about this column should be sent to M. S. Klamkin, Department of Mathematics, University of Alberta, Edmonton, AB T6G 2G1. Information about the journal is available from F. G. B. Maskell, Mathematics Department, Algonquin College, 200 Lees Ave., Ottawa, ON K1S 0C5.)

Mathematical Research

Mathematical research for the purpose of extending their own frontiers is definitely a possibility for gifted students, especially in the fields of number theory and combinatorics; expertise with readily available computers and programmable calculators could be developed as a Type II activity. (Such devices are neither necessary nor sufficient for research purposes but can be useful aids. Many mathematicians look on computerized exhaustion proofs with disdain, even the recent Haken-Appel proof of the famous four-color conjecture.) One of the authors recently met a student who for several years had kept a notebook of his own interesting number ideas, conjectures, proposed problems, and even theorems with proofs. The student was taking a computer science course for the first time and was generating data to corroborate his theoretical findings and to provide the basis for further conjectures. (One investigation involved numbers that divide the sum of the squares of *all* their factors. They were dubbed "square perfect numbers." Several theorems dealing with their properties have been proved. All the square perfect numbers less than 200 are 1, 10, 60, 65, 84, 130, 140, 150, and 175 (Nyberg, 1976).)

All this became a Type III experience when an instructor assisted the student in initiating a fruitful correspondence with a receptive authority in the field who was willing to advise him of the state of the art in a particular area, to criticize constructively, and generally to offer informed encouragement. It should be noted that the role of the teacher in helping to establish a link with the real world is indispensable for the level of enrichment to become Type III.

Math and Science Fairs

Situations such as the preceding cannot realistically be the norm, but one way for creative-productive students, even in elementary school, to get professional reaction and criticism beyond that of their teacher and hence of Type III caliber is to take part in mathematics fairs or mathematics sections of science fairs. These events encourage submissions from students of a wide age range and provide the opportunity for some face-to-face discussion with judges who are on the lookout for creative talent. It is important that gifted students be in contact with turned-on professionals in their field of interest (Renzulli, 1977).

Essay Contest

A refinement and extension of the math-fair concept is seen in the annual Samuel Beatty Prize Mathematics Essay Contest for students in any elementary or secondary school in Canada. (Information is available from E. J. Barbeau, Secretary, Samuel Beatty Fund, c/o Department of Mathematics, University of Toronto, Toronto, ON M5S 1A1.) The contest is intended to encourage students interested in mathematics to pursue a topic at some length, either through reading or original investigation, and to prepare a report on it.

Talent Search

U.S. students in their last year of high school are invited to submit research papers in mathematics, as well as in scientific fields, to the Westinghouse National Science Talent Search; the awards are substantial scholarships. (Information is available from Science Service, 1719 N St., NW, Washington, DC 20036.) Conrad (Note 4), a teacher whose students have achieved considerable success in this competition, feels that very few mathematics teachers encourage even their highly talented students to enter this competition, perhaps fearing that the research has to be original. The point is that submissions must show originality—quite a different situation. Many more candidates could avail themselves of this excellent opportunity to participate in mathematical investigation.

The Maryland Mathematics Talent Search is a totally different kind of enterprise. It is a statewide administration of the SMPY selection procedure referred to earlier in the chapter (George & Solano, 1976).

Student Articles

For student ideas that teachers deem to be of sufficient merit to share with the immediate mathematics or mathematics education community, if not beyond, journals will print letters to the editor or may even consider an article composed by a student. (An interesting case in point is a recent letter to the editor of the *Arithmetic Teacher* (Jan. 1979) from a group of gifted

Grade 5 students, under their teacher's auspices, setting out the results of investigations they had conducted on properties of Pentominoes. Their investigations had been inspired by an article in a previous issue. For these students, their enterprise was of Type III significance.) Local or regional journals published by associations of mathematics teachers or by college and university mathematics education departments for a teaching readership offer some opportunity for real, even if limited, exposure on a refereed basis. (One reality of life is that products, no matter how creative their development, must stand up to public scrutiny and, hence, run the risk of rejection.)

Problem Solving

A number of journals feature sets of problems for which sample reader solutions are published along with lists of solvers; these problems are complementary to the exercises for rapid-fire mathematical minds found in contests of the objective style. (See Appendix 3 for an annotated listing. See Appendix 4 for a bibliography of books of problems.) It can be a real turn-on to have one of your solutions printed, often a thrill even to see your name listed in the "also solved by" column. *Crux Mathematicorum*, mentioned previously, is a relatively new journal devoted mainly to problem solving. Although a rather high level of sophistication is maintained, some problems are accessible to very talented high school students. The solutions are enhanced by copious comments, including references to the literature on problem solving.

A unique problem-solving activity and mathematical experience is offered to very able senior high school students by the Gelfand Club of Ontario. Participating students are invited to correspond with professors about topic development and problems distributed in monthly communications. Membership has no geographical constraints. (Write to the Gelfand Club of Ontario, Mathematics Department, University of Toronto, Toronto, ON M5S 1A1.)

Postlude

If gifted students are to have the opportunity to exercise their full potential through any Type III level of activity, it is incumbent on teachers to do all they can to cut through the red tape that often precludes the flexibility necessary for the provision of adequate time, environment, and support material. Such arrangements are more easily made within special programs, classes, or schools for the gifted but are not beyond the realm of possibility regardless of organizational format. First the will—then the way!

Even after the groundwork is laid, sustained sincere interest and encouragement of respected adults is an extremely positive catalyst (Collins, 1969).

APPENDIX 1: PUZZLES, PROBLEMS, AND INTRIGUING MATHEMATICS

(In order of authors)

Essays on Mathematics

Martin Gardner, *The Scientific American book of mathematical puzzles and diversions* (New York: Simon & Schuster, 1959).

Martin Gardner, *The second Scientific American book of mathematical puzzles and diversions* (New York: Simon & Schuster, 1961).

Martin Gardner, *More mathematical puzzles and diversions* (Baltimore, Md.: Penguin, 1961).

Martin Gardner, *Martin Gardner's new mathematical diversions from Scientific American* (New York: Simon & Schuster, 1966).

Martin Gardner, *Mathematics magic show* (New York: Knopf, 1967).

Martin Gardner, *The unexpected hanging and other mathematical diversions* (New York: Simon & Schuster, 1969).

Martin Gardner, *Martin Gardner's sixth book of mathematical games from Scientific American* (New York: Scribner, 1975).

Martin Gardner, *Mathematical carnival* (New York: Vintage, 1977).

Martin Gardner, *Mathematical circus* (New York: Knopf, 1979).

Ross Honsberger, *Ingenuity in mathematics* (Washington, D.C.: Mathematical Association of America, NML #23, 1970).

Ross Honsberger, *Mathematical gems* (Washington, D.C.: Mathematical Association of America, 1973).

Ross Honsberger, *Mathematical gems* (Washington, D.C.: Mathematical Association of America, 1976).

Ross Honsberger, *Mathematical plums* (Washington, D.C.: Mathematical Association of America, 1979).

Problems and Puzzles

Mathematical puzzles of Sam Loyd (New York: Dover, 1959).

Henry Ernest Dudeney, *536 puzzles and curious problems* (New York: Scribner, 1967).

Maurice Kraitchik, *Mathematical recreations* (New York: Dover, 1953).

Boris A. Kordemsky, *The Moscow puzzles: 359 mathematical recreations* (New York: Scribner, 1972).

Geoffrey Mott-Smith, *Mathematical puzzles for beginners and enthusiasts* (New York: Dover, 1954).

Dale Seymour, *Eureka* and guide (rev. ed.) (Palo Alto, Calif.: Creative, 1972).

Psychology, Pedagogy, Heuristic, Development of Ideas

Martin Gardner, *The paradox box* (filmstrip and text) (San Francisco: Freeman, 1975).

Martin Gardner, *Aha! Insight* (filmstrip and text) (San Francisco: Freeman, 1978)

Carole E. Greenes et al., *Problem-Mathics* (Palo Alto, Calif.: Creative, 1977).

Richard D. Porter, *Project-a-puzzle* (Reston, Va.: National Council of Teachers of Mathematics, 1978).

Ken Weber, *Think Lab I* and *II* (Chicago: Science Research Associates, 1974, 1976).

General

J. A. H. Hunter & Joseph S. Madachy, *Mathematical diversions* (New York: Dover, 1963, 1975).

APPENDIX 2: MATHEMATICS COMPETITIONS OPEN TO HIGH SCHOOL STUDENTS
(Reprinted with permission from *Crux Mathematicorum*, March 1979)

1. Annual High School Mathematics Examination (Canada and U.S.A.) (March)
This examination is limited to pre-calculus mathematics with emphasis on intermediate algebra and plane geometry. It is a multiple choice type of examination and the time allowed is 80 minutes.

Sample problem (1978): *In a room containing N people, N > 3, at least one person has not shaken hands with everyone else in the room. What is the maximum number of people in the room that could have shaken hands with everyone else?*

(A) 0   (B) 1   (C) $N-1$ (D) N (E) none of these

For information: Dr. Walter E. Mientka, Executive Director
Annual High School Mathematics Examination
917 Oldfather Hall
University of Nebraska
Lincoln, Nebraska 68588

2. Competitions open to all high school students
(a) *Junior Mathematics Contest* (February): For students in Grades 9–11 in Canadian (and some U.S.A.) schools. There are 30 questions. (b) *The Euclid Contest* (April): Aimed primarily at Grade 12 students, it involves both multiple-choice and written solutions. (c) *The Descartes Competition* (April): Designed for students in their last year of secondary school and used to determine scholarship recipients in the Faculty of Mathematics at the University of Waterloo. (Students may not write both (b) and (c).)

For information: Professor R. G. Dunkley
Faculty of Mathematics
University of Waterloo
Waterloo, Ontario N2L 3G1

3. Alberta High School Prize Examination (March)
This examination involves both multiple choice (60 minutes) and written solutions (110 minutes).

Sample problem (1978): *36 points are placed inside a square whose sides have length 3. Show that there are 3 points which determine a triangle of area no greater than ½.*

For information: Professor G. J. Butler
Provincial Exam Chairman
Department of Mathematics
University of Alberta
Edmonton, Alberta T6G 2G1

4. Canadian Mathematical Olympiad (May)
This Olympiad, now consisting of 5 problems to be done in 3 hours, was established in the autumn of 1968 by the Education Committee of the Canadian Mathematical Congress (now the Canadian Mathematical Society). Provincial competitions had already existed for many years in all the provinces and, with these firmly established, it was the right time to start on a national competition. Candidates are chosen by quota for each province from the students who performed well in the provincial competitions. Also, high school principals may nominate candidates who, for some good reason, did not participate in the provincial competition but nevertheless seem to be of Olympiad quality.

Sample problem (1977): *If A, B, C, D are four points in space such that*

$$\angle ABC = \angle BCD = \angle CDA = \angle DAB = \pi/2,$$

prove that A, B, C, D lie in a plane.

For information: Professor John Burry, Acting Chairman
Canadian Mathematical Olympiad Committee
Memorial University of Newfoundland
St. John's, Newfoundland A1C 5S7

5. U.S.A. Mathematical Olympiad (May)

This Olympiad, consisting of 5 problems to be done in 3 hours, was established in the autumn of 1971 by the Olympiad Sub-Committee of the Mathematical Association of America. The purpose of the Olympiad was to attempt to discover secondary school students with superior mathematical talent, students who possessed mathematical creativity and inventiveness as well as competence in computational techniques. Candidates are chosen from the top 100 students in the Annual High School Mathematics Examination (U.S.A. and Canada), plus a small number of students with special recommendations.

Sample problem (1977): *If a, b, c, d, e are positive numbers bounded by p and q, that is,*

$$0 < p \leqslant a,b,c,d,e \leqslant q,$$

prove that

$$(a + b + c + d + e) \left(\frac{1}{a} + \frac{1}{b} + \frac{1}{c} + \frac{1}{d} + \frac{1}{e} \right) \leqslant 25 + 6 (\sqrt{p/q} - \sqrt{q/p})^2$$

and determine when there is equality.

For information: Professor S. L. Greitzer, Chairman
U.S.A. Mathematical Olympiad Committee
350-A Lafayette Road
Metuchen, New Jersey 08840

6. International Mathematical Olympiad (July)

This Olympiad was started by Romania in 1959. It is a two-day examination, with 3 problems to be done in 4½ hours each day. Each year, the host country sends out invitations to various countries which choose an 8-person team based on the results of their national Olympiads.

Sample problem (1977): *In a finite sequence of real numbers, the sum of any seven successive terms is negative and the sum of any eleven successive terms is positive. Determine the maximum number of terms in the sequence.*

We will be glad to receive and publish information about other mathematical competitions. [Write to M. Klamkin at the address on p. 255. An extensive bibliography of competition-related papers has also been published.]

APPENDIX 3: PUBLICATIONS CONTAINING PROBLEM SECTIONS

(Reprinted with permission from *Crux Mathematicorum*, April 1979)

1. The *Mathematics Student* (terminates June 1981)

This slim newsletter is published 8 times a year by the National Council of Teachers of Mathematics and contains a Competition Corner edited by George Berzsenyi. The individual subscription rate is $2 a year for N.C.T.M. members. There are also group subscriptions: MS 5-Packs (5 copies of each issue) at $5 a pack and MS Class Sets (35 copies of each issue) at $30 a set.

Sample problem (1978): *Prove that any subset of 55 numbers chosen from the set (1,2,3, . . . ,100) must contain numbers differing by 9, 10, 12, and 13, but need not contain a pair differing by 11.*

Write to James R. Tewell
      Circulation Manager
      1906 Association Drive
      Reston, Virginia 22091

[Problems in this publication are generally more accessible than those in the other listed publications. More opportunity for younger talented students is provided by the *Ontario Mathematics Gazette*, published three times a year by the Ontario Association for Mathematics Education at a subscription price of $7. The Problems section is edited by D. McKay and J. McKnight. Here is a sample problem for up to Grade 10 (1978): *If 8888^8888 is multiplied out, what is the units digit in the final product?* Write to M. B. McGregor, Secretary-Treasurer, O.A.M.E., 247 Bright Street, Sarnia, ON N7T 4E9.]

2. *Ontario Secondary School Mathematics Bulletin*

The *Bulletin* is published 3 times a year at the University of Waterloo. The subscription rate is $2.50 a year, with a reduction for multiple subscriptions. It has a Problem Section edited by E. M. Moskal.

Sample problem (1978): *A sequence $\{b_n\}$ is defined by requiring that b_n is the number of subsets of $\{1, 2, . . ., n\}$ having the property that any two different elements of the subset differ by more than 1. Show that for all n, $b_{n+2} = b_{n+1} + b_n$, and then determine b_{10}.*

Write to Mr. E. Anderson
      Faculty of Mathematics
      University of Waterloo
      Waterloo, Ontario N2L 3G1

3. *Pi Mu Epsilon Journal*

This journal is published twice a year at the South Dakota School of Mines and Technology. It is the official journal of the Pi Mu Epsilon honorary mathematical fraternity. The subscription rate for two years is $4 for members, $6 for nonmembers. There is an extensive problem section edited by Leon Bankoff.

Sample problem (1978): *Are there examples of angles which are trisectible but not constructible? That is, can you find an angle α which is not constructible with straight edge and compass, but such that when α is given, $\alpha/3$ can be constructed from it with straight edge and compass?*

Write to Pi Mu Epsilon Journal
      South Dakota School of Mines and Technology
      Rapid City, South Dakota 57701

4. *The Pentagon*

This is the official journal of the Kappa Mu Epsilon College Honor Society. It is published twice a year and the subscription price is $5 for two years. There is a Problem Corner edited by Kenneth M. Wilke.

Sample problem (1976): *Each of the three consecutive integers 4, 5, and 6 terminates its own cube. That is, $4^3 = 64$, $5^3 = 125$, and $6^3 = 216$. Find four pairs of larger consecutive integers in which each integer terminates its own cube.*

Write to Douglas W. Nance
      Business Manager, The Pentagon
      Central Michigan University
      Mount Pleasant, Michigan 48859

5. *School Science and Mathematics*

This is the official journal of the School Science and Mathematics Association, Inc. It is published 8 times a year and the subscription price is $9 a year in the U.S.A. ($11 elsewhere). The Problem Department is edited by N.J. Kuenzi and Bob Prielipp.

Sample problem (1979): *The triple (5,12,13) is a primitive Pythagorean triple. So is the triple (15,112,113) formed by affixing the same digit (in this case a 1) to each member of the first*

triple. Prove or disprove that there are no other pairs of primitive Pythagorean triples that are related in this way.

Write to Dale M. Shafer, Executive Secretary
Stright Hall, P.O. Box 1614
Indiana University of Pennsylvania
Indiana, Pennsylvania 15705

6. *Journal of Recreational Mathematics*

This journal is published 4 times a year by the Baywood Publishing Company, Inc. The individual subscription price is $10 per volume (4 issues). It has a Problems and Conjectures Section edited by Friend H. Kierstead, Jr.

Sample problem (1978): *The lengths and widths of two rectangles are chosen randomly in the interval (0,1).*

(a) *What is the probability that one will fit completely within the other?*

(b) *What is the probability that the one with the smaller area has the larger perimeter?*

Write to Baywood Publishing Company, Inc.
120 Marine Street
Farmingdale, N.Y. 11735

7. The *Two-Year College Mathematics Journal*

This is one of three journals published by the Mathematical Association of America (see below for the other two). It is published 5 times a year. Annual dues for members of the M.A.A. (including a subscription to the *TYCMJ*) are $16 for each of the first two years of membership and $20 thereafter. Student membership is available with annual dues of $10. For nonmembers the subscription price is $12. The *Journal* has a Problem Section edited by Erwin Just. . . .

Sample problem (1977): *A 3-brick is a 3 × 1 × 1 rectangular parallelepiped. Assume that a 7 × 7 × 7 cube has been packed with 3-bricks and a single unit cube which is not located on the periphery. Prove that the unit cube must be located at the center.*

Write to TYCMJ Subscriptions Department
The Mathematical Association of America
1529 Eighteenth St., N.W.
Washington, D.C. 20036

8. *Mathematics Magazine*

Another journal published by the M.A.A. There are 5 issues a year for $12. Members of the M.A.A. or of Mu Alpha Theta may subscribe at reduced rates. The Problem Section is edited by Dan Eustice and Leroy F. Meyers.

Sample problem (1977): *A river flows with a constant speed w. A motorboat cruises with a constant speed v with respect to the river, where v > w. If the path travelled by the boat is a square of side L with respect to the ground, the time of traverse will vary with the orientation of the square. Determine the maximum and minimum times for the traverse.*

Write to A. B. Willcox, Executive Director of the M.A.A., at the address given above in 7.

9. The *American Mathematical Monthly*

The *Monthly* is published 10 times a year by the M.A.A. Annual dues for members of the M.A.A. (including a subscription to the *Monthly*) are $21 for each of the first two years of membership and $25 thereafter. Student membership is available with annual dues of $15. For nonmembers the subscription price is $28. The Problem Section is edited by A. P. Hillman.

Sample problem (1978): *Let A_1, A_2, . . ., A_n be distinct non-collinear points in the plane. A circle with center P and radius r is called minimal if $A_k P \leq r$ for all k and equality holds for at least three values of k.*

If A_1, A_2, . . ., A_n vary (n being fixed) what is the maximum number of minimal circles?

Write to A. B. Willcox as in 8.

If the above Problem Sections are not enough, here are a few more for which [M. S. Klamkin will] be glad to supply additional information on request [see p. 255 for address]:

10. *Canadian Mathematical Bulletin*
11. *Delta*
12. *Elemente der Mathematik*
13. *The Fibonacci Quarterly*
14. *Mathematics Association of Two-Year Colleges Journal*
15. *Mathematical Spectrum*
16. *Nabla*
17. *Nieuw Archief Voor Wiskunde*
18. *Scientific American*

APPENDIX 4:
BIBLIOGRAPHY OF MATHEMATICAL PROBLEM SOLVING FOR GIFTED STUDENTS

(In alphabetical order of titles)

Challenging Mathematical Problems (2 vols.), A. M. Yaglom & I. M. Yaglom (San Francisco: Holden-Day, 1967).

The Contest Problem Book: Problems from the Annual High School Contests of the Mathematical Association of America, C. T. Salkind (Ed.) (New York: Random House, 1961).

Elements of Mathematics, Book B, EM Problem Book, A. Engel et al. (St. Louis: CEMREL, 1975).

Famous Problems of Mathematics: Solved and Unsolved Problems from Antiquity to Modern Times, H. Tietze (New York: Graylock, 1965).

International Mathematical Olympiads 1959–1977, S. Greitzer (Washington, D.C.: Mathematical Association of America, 1978).

Hungarian Problem Book, (2 vols.), G. Hajos, G. Heukomm, & J. Suranyi (Eds.) (New York: Random House, 1963).

The MAA Problem Book II: Annual High School Contests of the Mathematical Association of America, 1961–1965, C. T. Salkind (Ed.) (New York: Random House, 1966).

The MAA Problem Book III, C. T. Salkind (Ed.) (New York: Random House, 1974).

Mathematical Challenges: Selected Problems from the Mathematics Student Journal, M. Charosh (Ed.) (Washington, D.C.: National Council of Teachers of Mathematics, 1965).

Mathematical Challenges II—Plus Six, T. Hill (Ed.) (Washington, D.C.: National Council of Teachers of Mathematics, 1964).

Mathematical Gems, R. Honsberger (Washington, D.C.: Mathematical Association of America, No. 1, 1973; No. 2, 1976).

Mathematical Problems and Puzzles from the Polish Mathematical Olympiads, S. Straszewicz (New York: Pergamon, 1965).

Mathematical Scholarship Problems, J. C. Burkill & H. M. Cundy (Cambridge: At the University Press, 1962).

1001 Problems in High School Mathematics, E. J. Barbeau, M. Klamkin, & W. Moser (Montreal: Canadian Mathematical Society, 1978).

St. Mary's College Mathematics Contest Problems for Junior and Senior High School, A. Brousseau (Palo Alto, Calif.: Creative, 1972).

The Stanford Mathematics Problem Book With Hints and Solutions, G. Polya & J. Kilpatrick (New York: Teacher's College Press, 1974).

The USSR Olympiad Problem Book, D. O. Shklarsky, N. N. Chentzov, & I. M. Yaglom (San Francisco: Freeman, 1962).

REFERENCES

Aiken, L. R. Ability and creativity in mathematics. *Review of Educational Research*, 1973, *43*, 405–432.

Albert, R. S. Toward a behavioral definition of genius. *American Psychologist*, 1975, *30*, 140–151.

Anastasi, A. Commentary on the precocity project. *Journal of Special Education*, 1975, *9*, 93–103.

Ashley, R. M. Ideas for those who are mathematically bright. In R. M. Ashley (Ed.), *Activities for motivating and teaching bright children*. West Nyack, N.Y.: Parker Publishing, 1973.

Banks, R., Belanger, B., Bettiol, I., Borthwick, B., Donnelly, B., & Smith, A. *Gifted/talented children*. Curriculum Ideas for Teachers series. Toronto: Ministry of Education, Ontario, 1978.

Bell, F. H. *Teaching and learning mathematics (in secondary schools)*. Dubuque, Iowa: William C. Brown, 1978.

Collins, D. Mathematics. In S. A. Bridges (Ed.), *Gifted children and the Brentwood Experiment*. London: Pitman & Sons, 1969.

Collins, W. D. Animal mathematics. *Mathematical Spectrum*, 1977, *10*, 52–58.

Crockenburg, S. B. Creativity tests: A boon or boondoggle for education? *Review of Educational Research*, 1972, *42*, 27–45.

Dellas, M., & Gaier, E. L. Identification of creativity: The individual. *Psychological Bulletin*, 1970, *73*, 55–73.

DuBois, P. H. *A history of psychological testing*. Boston: Allyn & Bacon, 1970.

Engel, A., et al. *Elements of mathematics: Book B problem book*. St. Louis: CEMREL, 1975.

Flener, F. Mathematics contests and mathletes. *Mathematics Teacher*, 1976, *69*, 246–261.

Fox, L. H. Identification and program planning: Models and methods. In D. P. Keating (Ed.), *Intellectual talent, research and development*. Baltimore, Md.: Johns Hopkins University Press, 1976.

Fremont, H. The low achiever and the gifted. In H. Fremont (Ed.), *How to teach mathematics in secondary schools*. Philadelphia: W. B. Saunders, 1969.

Gallagher, J. J. *Analysis of research on the education of gifted children*. Urbana, Ill.: Office of the Superintendent of Public Instruction, 1960.

Gallagher, J. J. Mathematics for the gifted. In J. J. Gallagher (Ed.), *Teaching the gifted child* (2nd ed.). Boston: Allyn & Bacon, 1975.

Gallagher, J. J. The gifted child in elementary school. In W. Dennis & M. W. Dennis (Eds.), *The intellectually gifted: An overview*. New York: Grune & Stratton, 1976.

George, W. C., & Solano, C. H. Identifying mathematical talent on a statewide basis. In D. P. Keating (Ed.), *Intellectual talent: Research and development*. Baltimore, Md.: Johns Hopkins University Press, 1976.

Guilford, J. P. Some new looks at the nature of creative processes. In N. Fredrickson & H. Gilliksen (Eds.), *Contributions to mathematical psychology*. New York: Holt, Rinehart & Winston, 1964.

Havighurst, R. J. Conditions productive of superior children. In W. Dennis & M. W. Dennis (Eds.), *The intellectually gifted: An overview*. New York: Grune & Stratton, 1976.

Hayman, W. K., Dowker, Y. N., Buxton, L. G., & Hayman, M. Mathematics for gifted children. In J. Gibson & P. Chennels (Eds.), *Gifted children, looking to their future*. London: Latimer with the National Association for Gifted Children, 1976.

Holland, J. L., & Astin, A. W. The prediction of the academic, artistic, scientific and social achievement of undergraduates of superior scholastic aptitude. *Journal of Educational Psychology*, 1962, *53*, 132–143.

Hoyt, D. P. *The relationship between college grades and adult achievement: A review of the literature.* Iowa City, Iowa: American College Testing Program Research Report No. 7, 1965.

Jaffar, N. Creativity and brain mechanisms. In J. Gibson & P. Chennels (Eds.), *Gifted children: Looking to their future.* London: Latimer with the National Association for Gifted Children, 1976.

Johnson, D., & Rising, G. A program for the talented. In D. Johnson & G. Rising (Eds.), *Guidelines for teaching mathematics* (2nd ed.). Belmont, Calif.: Wadsworth, 1976.

Krutetskii, V. A. An investigation of mathematical abilities in schoolchildren. In J. Kilpatrick & I. Wirszup (Eds.), *The structure of mathematical abilities.* Soviet Studies in the Psychology of Learning and Teaching Mathematics, Vol. 2. Stanford, Calif.: School Mathematics Study Group, 1969. (Available from the National Council of Teachers of Mathematics.)

Lomon, E., Beck, B., & Arbetter, C. Real problem solving in USMES: Interdisciplinary education and much more. *School Science and Mathematics*, 1975, *75*, 53–64.

MacKinnon, D. W. The creativity of architects. In C. W. Taylor (Ed.), *Widening horizons in creativity.* New York: Wiley, 1964.

MacKinnon, D. W. Personality and the realization of creative potential. *American Psychologist*, 1965, *20*, 273–281.

Marland, S. P. *Education of the gifted and talented: Report to the Congress of the United States by the U.S. Commissioner of Education and background papers submitted to the U.S. Office of Education.* Washington, D.C.: U.S. Government Printing Office, 1972.

Mason, J. *Mathematics: A psychological perspective.* Milton Keynes, England: Open University Press, 1978.

McCurdy, H. G. The childhood pattern of genius. *Horizon*, 1960, *2*, 33–38.

Mednick, M. T. Research creativity in psychology graduate students. *Journal of Consulting Psychology*, 1963, *27*, 265–266.

Michael, W. B. Cognitive and affective components of creativity in mathematics and the physical sciences. In J. C. Stanley, W. C. George, & C. H. Solano (Eds.), *The gifted and the creative: A fifty-year perspective.* Baltimore, Md.: Johns Hopkins University Press, 1977.

Mirman, N. Education of the gifted in the 70's. *Gifted Child Quarterly*, 1971, *15*, 217–224.

Moredock, S. M. Creative mathematics. In L. A. Fliegler (Ed.), *Curriculum planning for the gifted.* Englewood Cliffs, N.J.: Prentice-Hall, 1961.

Mundy, L. A., & Davis, J. C. *Varieties of accomplishment after college: Perspectives on the meaning of academic talent.* Iowa City, Iowa: American College Testing Program Research Report No. 62, 1974.

Nicholls, J. C. Creativity in the person who will never produce anything original and useful: The concept of creativity as a normally distributed trait. *American Psychologist*, 1972, *27*, 717–727.

Nyberg, C. *Square perfect numbers.* Unpublished manuscript, 1976.

Parloff, M. B., Datta, L., Kleman, M., & Handlon, J. H. Personality characteristics which differentiate creative male adolescents and adults. *Journal of Personality*, 1968, *36*, 528–552.

Passow, H. A. Fostering creativity in the gifted child. In J. Gibson & P. Chennels (Eds.), *Gifted children: Looking to their future.* London: Latimer with the National Association for Gifted Children, 1976.

Post, T. R. Making time for the basics: Some thoughts on viable alternatives within a balanced mathematics program. In *Applications in school mathematics*, 1979 Yearbook of the National Council of Teachers of Mathematics. Reston, Va.: The Council, 1979.

Renzulli, J. S. *The enrichment triad model: A guide for developing defensible programs for the gifted and talented.* Wethersfield, Conn.: Creative Learning Press, 1977.

Renzulli, J. S., & Smith, L. H. Two approaches to identification of gifted students. *Exceptional Children*, 1977, *43*, 512–518.

Renzulli, J. S., Smith, L. H., White, A. J., Callahan, C. M., & Hartman, R. K. *Scales for rating the behavioral characteristics of superior students*. Wethersfield, Conn.: Creative Learning Press, 1976.

Ridge, H. L. *Mathematics*. The Student, Subject and Career series. Toronto: Guidance Centre, Faculty of Education, University of Toronto, 1977.

Rising, G. R., & Harkin, J. B. *The third "R," mathematics teaching for grades K–8*. Belmont, Calif.: Wadsworth, 1978.

Roe, A. *The making of a scientist*. New York: Dodd, Mead, 1952.

Shapiro, R. J. Creative research scientists. *Psychologia Africana*, 1968, Supplement No. 4.

Stanley, J. C. Use of tests to discover talent. In D. P. Keating (Ed.), *Intellectual talent, research and development*. Baltimore, Md.: Johns Hopkins University Press, 1976.

Solway, L. School days, school days, *Canadian*, 1979, Sept. 1/2, 12–14.

Syphers, D. F. *Gifted and talented children: Practical programming for teachers and principals*. Arlington, Va.: Council for Exceptional Children, 1972.

Terman, L. M. *The gifted group at mid-life*. Genetic Studies of Genius series. Stanford, Calif.: Stanford University Press, 1959.

Terman, L. M., et al. *Mental and physical traits of a thousand gifted children*. Genetic Studies of Genius, Vol. 1. Stanford, Calif.: Stanford University Press, 1926.

Tilsley, P. Gifted children and their education—a discussion and survey of attitudes and opinions. *Journal of Applied Educational Studies*, 1979, *8*, 13–38.

Torrance, E. P. Prediction of adult creative achievement among high school seniors. *Gifted Child Quarterly*, 1969, *13*, 223–229.

Wallach, M. A. Tests tell us little about talent. *American Scientist*, 1976, *64*, 57–63.

Witty, P. A. Who are the gifted? In N. B. Henry (Ed.), *Education of the gifted*, Fifty-seventh yearbook of the National Society for the Study of Education, Pt. 2. Chicago: University of Chicago Press, 1958.

REFERENCE NOTES

1. Mabee, D. C. Personal communication, May, 1979.
2. Banks, R. G. Personal communication, August, 1979.
3. Fleming, G. A. Personal communication, May, 1979.
4. Conrad, S. R. Personal communication, August, 1979.

Teaching Mathematics to the Visually Impaired

Joseph N. Payne
University of Michigan

Geraldine T. Scholl
University of Michigan

Dr. Joseph N. Payne, professor of mathematics education, University of Michigan, teaches mathematics methods courses and does research on cognitive aspects of mathematics learning. He is the author of school textbooks, articles, and yearbook chapters related to learning and the mathematics curriculum, and was editor of the NCTM yearbook Mathematics Learning in Early Childhood. *He has taught mathematics from elementary school through college and is a past president of the Michigan Council of Teachers of Mathematics.*

Dr. Geraldine T. Scholl is professor of education, School of Education, University of Michigan. She is a former teacher of visually handicapped children and of emotionally disturbed children and was principal of a residential elementary school for the blind. During 1965 she served as chief of the Handicapped Children and Youth Section in the U.S. Office of Education.

IN OUR social contacts, the eye has special significance. Sometimes we judge the motivation of others by their eyes: We are suspicious of persons who do not "look us in the eye." The eyes can be used to control others: A teacher "catches the eye" of a potential troublemaker. In some religions the eye is believed to be the window of the soul, and those who cannot see are treated as outcasts. The eye is used to romantic advantage: The adolescent boy attracts the attention of his favorite girl with a wink of his eye. The eyes tell the doctor a great deal about a person's state of health.

The authors are grateful to Richard Newman and Ronald Schnur for their critical review of the early draft of this chapter; to practicing teacher Eileen Luther for her ideas on what should be included; and to the ten teachers of the visually handicapped who read and reacted to the initial draft while they attended the Optacon Institute at the University of Michigan in August 1979. The photographs in this chapter, taken of children enrolled in the program for the visually handicapped at Mitchell School, Ann Arbor, Michigan, are by Robert J. Lane, Instructional Strategy Services, School of Education, University of Michigan.

THE MEANING OF A VISUAL IMPAIRMENT

Our society holds numerous stereotypical ideas about the blind: They are beggars; they are helpless; their loss of vision is due to venereal disease or to the sins of their parents; they are musical; their life isn't worth living. Most such beliefs arise from a lack of knowledge and experience with persons who are blind.

In reality, those who are blind or have visual impairments possess the same range and variety of physical, mental, emotional, and social characteristics as the general population. They are fat and thin; tall and short; brilliant and retarded; well adjusted and emotionally disturbed; gregarious and reclusive. In all aspects of their lives, the blind appear on a continuum for all other human characteristics just as the sighted do. Even in their degree of vision, they are on a continuum. Relatively few persons, children or adults, are *blind* in the strict meaning that they have no vision. The visually impaired have varying degrees of vision—from total blindness to vision approximating normal. Like all persons, those with visual impairments must be viewed as individuals.

Any impairment hinders to varying degrees the activities of daily life. Such limitations arise from three major sources: the impairment itself, the impaired individual, and society. Three terms used in this regard are *impairment, disability,* and *handicap* (Riviere, n.d.).

An impairment is the medical description of a physically limiting condition. Thus, *visual impairment* refers to a medically defined deviation from the norm that results in defective function, structure, organization, or development of the visual system within the human body. For example, an ophthalmologist examines Tommy and determines that his eye condition is caused by congenital cataracts of unknown origin and that even with the best corrective lenses he has a visual acuity of only 20/200 in the better eye. The parameters of the condition are thus described. The relevance of this information for the teacher is discussed in a later section. Any remediation of an impairment comes through medical or paramedical intervention.

When an impairment limits the performance of normal daily activities, then it is referred to as a disability. Visual disability is not all-pervasive: In school, children with a visual impairment are disabled when they are expected to perform tasks that require normal vision. When vision is not required, such as with oral arithmetic, they are not disabled. Tommy, who has 20/200 best corrected visual acuity, would probably be unable to see a mathematics problem on the chalkboard from a distance of 20 feet. Thus, in this activity, he is disabled. The challenge for teachers is to structure the school environment and activities so that these children are disabled to the least possible degree.

Suggestions for Teaching the Visually Impaired

1. Assess school tasks on the basis of their visual requirements, and plan to include some activities in which the impaired child can compete on an equal basis. (Activities for oral arithmetic are described in a later section.)

2. Use concrete materials for activities that require vision (to be discussed later).

Handicaps are psychosocial in origin and result from limitations imposed by society or the individual. If Tommy's teacher uses the chalkboard without saying aloud what is being written (thereby making him disabled), he may also become handicapped. If the teacher allows him to be a nonparticipating class member, he may feel rejected and unwanted; classmates may follow the teacher's lead and also reject him. Tommy might then withdraw into his own world when the external environment offers no rewards. Students with visual impairments may be more handicapped through social and psychological rejection than through the disabling effects of their impairment.

---

1. Talk while writing on the chalkboard and describe any visual aids you are using. This practice may benefit other learners as well because the oral description is an additional source of sensory input for those who are not visual learners.

2. Mainstreaming children means involving them as participating class members. Involve visually impaired children in both small- and large-group activities.

The Importance of Attitudes

Attitudes of others toward the handicapped and, to a degree, toward anyone who is "different" are important in shaping behavior. Our society in general emphasizes conformity, and those who do not conform, or who are different, are viewed as an "out" group. Frequently this rejection is related to a lack of knowledge about what the difference really means; in the absence of knowledge, old wives' tales take over. Unfavorable attitudes toward blindness and blind persons are deeply rooted in our society partly because of misconceptions (Monbeck, 1973).

Modifying stereotyped beliefs through increased knowledge often helps to change society's behavior and to some extent its attitudes. Teachers who have a child with a visual impairment in their regular classroom for the first

time may feel "funny" about approaching the child. Unfortunately, our society has many prohibitions about touching and even using the sense of touch in gaining information. However, if teachers accept the fact that the visually handicapped child's major contact with the world is through the sense of touch, then they will feel more comfortable in touching the child and will realize that a pat on the head or a touch on the shoulder replaces the glance or the smile.

At first, you might also be uncomfortable in verbal communication. For example, you may be reluctant to use such words as *see* and *look* and search for substitutes such as *feel* or *touch*. There is no need for this. Visually handicapped children learn early to adapt such words as *look* and *see* to their own experience.

It is important to treat the visually handicapped child the same as the other children and to expect the same standards of behavior. For example, a teacher may use some unfortunate pet name, such as "my little one," and through this and also nonverbal communication treat this pupil as a much younger child. The necessity of encouraging mature behavior for the benefit of the child's emotional and social development is discussed in a later section. Assess from time to time whether you are expecting as much from the child as possible. Increased knowledge and understanding will help give you a base from which to examine your own beliefs and correct your misconceptions. Then use this information to examine and attempt to modify your own attitudes in a positive direction. When you know and understand what a visual impairment means for an individual, you will learn more ways to reach out to these pupils.

---

1. Always use the pupil's name to get his or her attention.

2. Reach out with a touch on the shoulder or pat on the head. However, before you touch, make certain that the pupil knows you are there. Otherwise you may startle him or her!

3. Use all the visual words you normally do, such as *look*, *see*, color words, and any descriptive terms. Changing your language is not necessary and, in fact, will make your oral classroom activities artificial.

CHARACTERISTICS OF VISUAL IMPAIRMENTS

Extent of the Problem

Compared with other impairments relevant to school, such as mental and emotional handicaps, children with severe vision problems are few in

number. They account for only about 1% of the total number of handicapped children in our nation's schools (BEH, 1978). In the school-age population, an estimated 1 in 500 has a visual impairment of sufficient severity to require some remediation, usually corrective lenses. Although the number of school-age girls and boys with visual impairments is small, an increasing proportion of the population need corrective lenses as they advance in years; almost all persons 65 years and over require corrective lenses, particularly for reading (Wilder, 1974). Fortunately, most mild to moderate visual impairments can be remedied through a variety of procedures, including medication, surgery, and corrective lenses. School-age children with mild to moderate visual impairments requiring corrective lenses are able to manage with such modifications as sitting near the front of the classroom and being reminded to wear their glasses and keep them clean. Pupils with severe visual impairments, that is, those who are blind, usually require some modifications in the school program. There is particular need for substitute systems in written communication to enable them to participate in the regular class.

Terminology

In the past, pupils with visual impairments were labeled *blind* if their best corrected vision in the better eye was 20/200 or less, that is, if they were able to see at 20 feet what the person with normal vision sees at 200 feet; or if the widest angle of their visual field was no greater than 20 degrees, even though visual acuity in that narrow field might have been better than 20/200. This is often referred to as the legal definition of blindness. Such pupils were automatically placed in classes where tactile methods, including braille, were employed. Pupils with better than 20/200 vision but less than 20/70 best corrected vision in the better eye were labeled *partially seeing* and placed in classes where visual methods, including print materials—most frequently large print—were employed. Some school districts may still use the terms *blind* and *partially seeing* for labeling the pupils in classrooms or programs.

More recently, educators describe pupils with severe visual impairments in more functional terms: *blind* when they must learn through sensory systems other than vision; *low vision* when they can see objects or materials held close to their eyes and do not use tactual materials exclusively in their educational process; and *visually limited* when they have limitations in visual functioning but ordinarily learn through the visual mode (Barraga, 1976). These terms are more meaningful to the teacher.

The visually limited child can ordinarily be instructed in a regular classroom with such modifications as being seated close to the chalkboard or at the front of the room. Their corrective lenses are usually sufficient for them to use regular books and materials effectively. Children who are blind

and those with low vision are the major focus of this chapter, since their school programs usually require more modifications. These two groups will be referred to here as *visually handicapped*.

The Teacher's Role in Identification

Children who have had severe visual problems from birth are usually identified during their preschool years. However, teachers and parents play a vital role in identifying those with mild and moderate vision problems and those who develop a visual impairment while they are in school. Children, especially young children, lack a frame of reference to compare their visual abilities with those of their peers. For example, it is common for young children when first fitted with corrective lenses to discover that a bird's song comes from a tiny creature rather than from a tree.

Although programs for screening visual acuity are increasingly common in most school districts, particularly for children of kindergarten age, many of them test *distance* acuity only. School-related tasks require good *near* vision, and children with defective near vision may be missed by such tests. Some children do not learn to read simply because they are farsighted and cannot see the print in books; often no one, least of all the child, correctly identifies the major source of the difficulty (Brown, 1976).

When a teacher suspects a visual problem, a referral should be made through appropriate school procedures. Usually this process will involve the school principal and the school nurse. In most districts, the parents are notified, and available community resources for referral and diagnosis are recommended.

Specialists skilled in aspects of the diagnosis, treatment, and remediation of visual problems include the following (NSPB, 1964):

Oculists and *ophthalmologists* are physicians who specialize in the diagnosis and treatment of defects and diseases of the eye; they can perform surgery or prescribe treatment, including glasses.

Optometrists are licensed, nonmedical practitioners who measure refractive errors and disturbances of the eye muscles; they prescribe glasses, prisms, and exercises.

Opticians grind lenses, fit them into frames, and adjust frames to the wearer.

Orthoptic technicans are trained in administering scientifically planned exercises for developing or restoring the normal teamwork of the eye muscles.

Be aware of the possibility that poor vision may be contributing to poor academic achievement and refer to the school nurse any child who consistently manifests any of the signs listed below (NSPB, 1978):

Behavior
- Rubs eyes excessively
- Shuts or covers one eye, tilts head, or thrusts head forward
- Has difficulty reading or doing other close work
- Blinks frequently or is irritable when doing close work
- Is unable to see distant objects clearly
- Squints or frowns

Appearance
- Crossed eyes
- Red-rimmed, encrusted, or swollen eyelids
- Inflamed or watery eyes
- Recurring styes

Complaints
- Eyes itch, burn, or feel scratchy
- Cannot see well
- Dizziness, headaches, or nausea following close eye work
- Blurred or double vision

The Eye Report

A teacher receiving a report of an eye examination for the first time may be puzzled. This section briefly explains the elements usually included in an eye report. (For more details see Harley & Lawrence, 1977.) The teacher should not hesitate to seek additional interpretation from the special teacher of the visually handicapped, the school nurse, the child's parents, and the medical specialist.

Visual acuity. Visual acuity, the sharpness or keenness of vision, is usually reported separately for each eye: O.D. (*oculus dexter:* right eye) and O.S. (*oculus sinister:* left eye); O.U. (*oculus uterque*) refers to both eyes. Distance vision is usually measured by a Snellen letter chart and is reported as a fraction in feet (20) or meters (6); the numerator is the distance at which the symbol is clearly seen by the person and the denominator is the distance the symbol would be seen by the normal eye. Thus, an uncorrected visual acuity of 20/100 means that the person sees at 20 feet what the normal person sees at 100 feet. When the visual impairment is so severe that it cannot be measured with the Snellen chart, the examiner's report may include such phrases as "C.F. 4 ft." (the patient can count raised fingers from a distance of 4 feet), "L.P." (the patient can distinguish light from darkness), or "Nil" (the patient has no vision).

Near vision is usually recorded as the smallest type size a person can

read when the card is held at a distance of 14 inches from the eye. The type typically used for this purpose is Jaeger. If the report says "Jaeger 6," this means the patient can read at a distance of 14 inches from the eye the sixth line of Jaeger type, which is the 8-point type used in most newspapers. If the report reads "Jaeger 12" to "Jaeger 20," then the teacher knows the student needs 18-point type or larger.

If the child has a restricted field of vision, the eye report will include a chart showing where in the visual field the restriction occurs. A restricted field in one or both eyes deprives one of the full range (500 degrees) of the normal visual field: up and down and side to side (Vaughan, Cook, & Ashbury, 1965). Children with restricted fields of vision may stumble over objects and be slow readers because the eye takes in only a small amount of information in a single movement.

---

1. Determine through observation the best lighting conditions and distance from the front of the classroom that provide the best visual environment for the pupil with low vision.

2. Pupils with low vision and limited vision should use the vision they have. If vision deteriorates, it is more likely to result from the particular eye condition than from overuse. Holding visual materials close to their eyes will not be harmful.

Age of onset. The report will frequently include a section on history giving the age at which the visual impairment was acquired. *Congenital* means that the patient was born with the condition. Children who lose their sight prior to the age of 5 are often considered congenitally blind because they retain no useful visual imagery (Lowenfeld, 1971).

Among the total population of the visually impaired, those who are born with the condition are in the minority, accounting for approximately 10%; however, in the school-age population, more than 75% are born with impaired vision or acquire it soon after birth (Hatfield, 1975). Congenital impairments are not necessarily hereditary; many result from prenatal factors such as rubella and other infectious illnesses during pregnancy, trauma to the fetus, and poor diet.

---

1. Encourage any pupil with a recent loss of vision to retain such skills as handwriting.

2. If onset occurs during school years, be aware of potential emotional problems and make appropriate referrals for help.

Diagnosis. The cause of the impairment, usually reported for each eye, provides a clue to the teacher about what to expect from the student. Common mild to moderate visual impairments found in the school-age population include amblyopia, astigmatism, hyperopia, myopia, and strabismus (NSPB, 1978).

Amblyopia is a dimness of vision without any apparent disease of the eye; it is usually the result of not using an eye ("lazy eye") in order to avoid the discomfort of double vision caused by a muscle problem, such as strabismus.

Astigmatism is blurred vision caused by irregularities in the shape of the cornea (the transparent covering of the eye) or the lens. Light rays cannot focus on the retina, and so it is difficult to see both far and near objects.

In *hyperopia* (farsightedness), the eyeball is too short from front to back. Therefore, farsighted people see faraway objects well, but things that are close are blurry. Most preschool children are hyperopic and do well on measures of distance vision. This hyperopic condition tends to correct itself as they grow older.

In *myopia* (nearsightedness), the eyeball is too long from front to back. Nearsighted people see nearby objects well but not things that are far away. Children who are myopic usually do well in school-related tasks because they see objects close to them but have trouble seeing those in the distance. Such children are usually not interested in outdoor activities that require good distance vision.

In *strabismus* (squint or crossed eyes), one or more muscles of the eye are out of balance; this causes one or both eyes to turn in toward the nose or outward away from the nose, making it impossible for them to focus on the same object at the same time.

Most of these conditions can be improved with corrective lenses. All are common and not usually disabling in most daily activities.

School diagnostic procedures—especially for children suspected of having learning disabilities, mental retardation, or emotional disturbance—should include an eye examination for near as well as distance vision, fusion (how the eyes work together), and muscle balance to determine whether a visual impairment is contributing to the problem.

Retrolental fibroplasia is still a leading cause of moderate to severe visual impairment among school-age children, although the incidence has decreased dramatically since the administration of oxygen to premature infants has been controlled. This condition is manifested by impairments to the retina, lens, or both. Next to retrolental fibroplasia, the important eye affections causing blindness are cataracts, optic nerve atrophy, and albinism (Hatfield, 1975). *Congenital cataracts* can result from hereditary factors or prenatal conditions. Cataracts, an opacity of the lens, are usually removed surgically, and the child is fitted with corrective lenses. Such

children can often make effective use of visual materials. *Optic nerve atrophy* causes an irreversible loss of vision when optic nerve fibers degenerate. In the congenital or infantile form of the condition, hereditary factors are usually involved. *Albinism* is a hereditary absence of pigment in the irises, skin, and hair. Lowered visual acuity results, but the albino usually retains sufficient usable vision to function as a sighted person.

---

1. Check the eye report for the diagnosis and request clarification from a teacher of the visually handicapped, the school nurse, or the child's parents about what the diagnosis means for the school program.

2. Allow albino children to select a place in the classroom where the light will not be too bright, since they frequently have photophobia, or discomfort from bright light. They should also be cautioned about remaining in direct sunlight, since they tend to sunburn easily.

Other visual dysfunctions. For the information of teachers, two other types of defective visual functioning, *visual perceptual problems* and *color blindness*, are included in this discussion, although neither is considered an impairment.

Success in school tasks depends to a great extent on good *visual perceptual functioning.* Many pupils labeled as learning disabled, for instance, have normal vision but are unable to process accurately what they see. This difficulty may be attributed to faulty reception or to faulty association and interpretation of the visual input. Such pupils require a variety of remedial measures, such as reducing extraneous sensory stimulation to focus more sharply on the task at hand or structuring the learning task so that relationships can be clearly grasped. Pupils with visual-perceptual problems require the assistance of qualified professionals, usually those trained in the area of learning disabilities. It should be noted, however, that any child suspected of having a learning disability should have, as part of the diagnostic procedure, a complete visual acuity examination, especially for near vision. Special techniques for teaching learning disabled children are discussed in chapter 3.

Color blindness is a genetic condition transmitted by the mother primarily to male offspring. Color-blind persons may see the world only in varying shades on the black-white continuum or may simply be unable to perceive certain colors, usually red and green but sometimes blue and yellow. Since this is a congenital defect, the person usually does not know there is a problem until some sensitive individual identifies the real reason for this inability to discern differences in color. Kindergarten and primary school activities depend in large measure on proper identification of colors.

Color-blind children who have difficulty learning their colors are often labeled as slow. Since relatively few women have this condition and since most children's early school experiences are spent under the guidance of female teachers, the child who is color-blind is often not identified. Sensitivity of primary teachers to this potential problem would help the educational functioning of this small group of persons who are handicapped in our color-conscious society.

Children with either of these conditions may be incorrectly identified as having visual impairments and referred to medical personnel. When the report indicates that visual functioning is normal, few educators consider the possibility of faulty perception or color blindness; consequently, valuable school years may be wasted until the true source of the child's poor school performance is discovered.

Prognosis. The report should give information regarding treatment, such as whether corrective lenses will help. Not all eye conditions respond to such remediation, however; sometimes glasses are prescribed for children who derive so little benefit from them that they refuse to wear them. In addition, some glasses restrict the field of vision to such a degree that they are of practical benefit only under certain conditions.

The report will often include what lighting conditions are best, what restrictions should be placed on the use of the eyes, and whether physical activities should be restricted. Finally, examiners often indicate whether vision can be expected to improve, remain the same, or deteriorate.

---

1. If the eye report indicates that the visual impairment will deteriorate, do not assume that instruction in braille should be initiated at once. The pupil may become threatened by this procedure. Wait until the pupil recognizes the need and is motivated to learn tactile reading.

2. Do not hesitate to ask the child and parents about the condition. This is a reality in their lives, and most will talk freely and easily about it.

IMPACT OF THE VISUAL IMPAIRMENT
ON GROWTH AND DEVELOPMENT

Variations in the growth and development of children may be influenced by the age at which they lost their vision, the degree of remaining vision, and the presence of other disabilities. In general, the sequence is the same as that for children in general, with the same variations in rate of growth and development.

Physical Growth

Although research evidence is conflicting, it is generally accepted that physical growth and development is not usually affected by the visual impairment itself (Lowenfeld, 1971). Attitudes of other relevant persons—especially the parents—opportunities to explore the environment, and encouragement to move about independently are all more critical variables. For example, poor hand coordination can usually be attributed to a lack of experience.

Blind children tend to be sedentary because it is safer and easier. Thus, an important aspect of their curriculum is training in orientation and mobility. Every child with a visual impairment should be receiving instruction in this area from a qualified specialist. This training is essential. Regular teachers can assist in facilitating physical growth and development through encouragement and planned activities that can be included in the regular school day.

1. Expect visually impaired children to do as much as possible for themselves, such as getting and putting away books and materials, manipulating equipment, and finding their way around the room. Be patient if they are slow, but do not do for them what they can accomplish independently.

2. Give specific instructions. For example, pointing to a bookcase and saying "Your book is over there" will have little meaning; "Your book is on the second shelf of the bookcase under the windows" gives more information.

3. Use the child's name. Even the child with low vision or limited vision may not be able to see you looking, pointing, or beckoning.

4. Let these children take their turn in going on errands. This provides good experience in mobility and moving about in the environment as well as making them feel part of the class.

5. Teach them, even those who are blind, to write on the chalkboard. This is a good exercise in hand coordination, and many learn their letters and numbers quickly if given the instruction because they are motivated to be like their classmates. Use capital letters at first. Math problems are particularly useful for this experience because the written symbols (numerals and operational signs) are relatively few compared with the 26 letters of the alphabet.

6. Encourage physical activity in teaching concepts. For example, in presenting measurement, have children learn to indicate with their hands how long 10 centimeters is; have them pace off larger measurements, such as 3 meters. These practices accomplish two

objectives simultaneously: They make the pupil physically active, and they help to develop meaningful concepts.

7. On the first day of class orient the pupil to the classroom with a guided tour. Indicate where tables, desks, bookcases, and other furniture and equipment are located. Do not hesitate to rearrange your room from time to time if this is your custom, but be sure to inform the pupil about it, explaining where objects are relocated.

8. It is not necessary to have the pupil sit in the seat nearest the door. Going to another part of the classroom and changing seats from time to time gives good orientation experiences and encourages mobility.

Emotional and Social Growth

As with the physical area, external factors are more significant in retarding emotional and social growth and development than the visual impairment itself. Again, attitudes of parents, teachers, and peers exert a powerful influence (Lowenfeld, 1971).

Blind preschoolers may have difficulty forming a clear self-concept because they lack the opportunity to see and imitate the looks and behavior of peers and grown-ups and to observe themselves in the typical mirror play of toddlers. Later, too, during childhood and adolescence, they are disadvantaged in not being able to observe the behavior and appearance of peers and adults; thus they have difficulty selecting and imitating a role model. To enhance their development in this important area, teachers and parents may need to structure appropriate experiences and to function as their "mirror" (Scholl, 1973).

The desire to be "normal" is strong at all age levels but particularly during adolescence. The lack of the ability to see how peers are dressing and behaving as well as what others are doing may be a distinct deterrent to social development. For example, children who are unable to see what their peers are doing in small groups in the classroom or on the playground are unable to join the group of their choice; this lack of participation may make them appear uninterested. Again, both parents and teachers may need to describe what is going on so blind children can have appropriate social experiences. The adolescent desire for being alike can also work to the disadvantage of the handicapped. Peers might not accept them because they are different. Since the reality of a visual impairment is a "difference," parents and teachers should help such students minimize other differences to as great an extent as possible.

Blind children and, to a degree, those with low vision are disadvantaged in nonverbal communication in two major ways. First, they must depend solely on verbal communication for assessing meaning. In our society,

we frequently do not mean what we say and express our true meaning in nonverbal ways, such as a frown or a smile. These nonverbal cues are unavailable to the blind, and thus they must take the verbal communication at face value. Second, since most nonverbal communciation is learned through imitation—for example, the infant smiles in response to its mother's smile—the blind frequently lack facial and bodily expression because they cannot see to imitate the expressions of others. Common gestures, such as a wave or a wink, must be taught.

---

1. Expect the same behavior you expect of the rest of the class. Peers will be more accepting if pupils with visual impairments act on the appropriate maturity level; they should not be pampered and treated as less mature than they are.

2. Mainstream not only for academics but for all aspects of the school curriculum. Special help is often necessary to encourage pupils with visual impairments to join a group for both formal and informal activities. Describe what the groups are doing and who is in them; let them make a choice and then give them a little assistance in becoming a part of that group.

3. Be the "mirror" for visually handicapped pupils. Praise them when dress and behavior approximate the norm; consult with parents on how you can work together to ensure that they are more like their peers in dress, appearance, and behavior.

4. Stress their strengths and help them know and assess their limitations realistically. You are not doing them a favor by listening approvingly to such unrealistic aspirations as becoming an airline pilot. Help them recognize realistic limitations and capitalize on their capacities.

5. Encourage and praise any facial expression such pupils may have. Help them learn to smile, frown, and so on by talking with them about facial expressions and describing how such forms of nonverbal communication are used. You may need to manipulate their faces to give them an understanding of how the expression feels.

6. Teach the commonly used gestures of peers to the pupil.

Mental Growth

The absence of vision does have a direct impact on cognitive growth and development. The sense of touch is the blind child's major access to the world of objects; even the low vision and the visually limited child have imperfect access because significant details, such as the intricacies of an insect's body, are often not detected. When real objects are too large or too

small to be held in the hands, models are valuable teaching aids. However, teachers must recognize that there are limitations, such as grasping the concept of size or motion. For example, the blind child may learn about the anatomy of a bird through the inspection of a stuffed bird but never grasp the concept of a bird in flight (Lowenfeld, 1971).

For certain concepts that can be taught neither by direct experience nor with models, visually handicapped children must rely on descriptions by those around them. However, a heavy reliance on descriptions rather than direct experience can lead them to parrot words without real comprehension (Harley, 1963). Parents and teachers must provide concrete experiences for concept development and should monitor these, experiences to make certain the child is acquiring an accurate and realistic idea of the object. Of course, some concepts, such as color, may never be grasped, and for these, descriptions are the only alternative.

Two-dimensional representations of two-dimensional shapes in tactile form can be meaningful, but such representations of three-dimensional objects are of no practical value (Lowenfeld, 1971). In a later section, the use of concrete representations of two-dimensional geometric forms is discussed. Teachers of solid geometry, where the concept of three dimensions is critical, should make use of three-dimensional models to give an accurate concept of shape.

Experience plays an important role in the growth and development of visually handicapped children, especially during the preschool years. Research evidence supports the notion that an enriched environment providing many and varied experiences may prevent subsequent retardation in the various aspects of growth and development (cf. Fraiberg, 1977, and Norris, Spaulding, & Brodie, 1957). Visually handicapped children should bring to school with them the knowledge of mathematics found to be typical of more than half of entering kindergartners (Payne & Rathmell, 1975). This includes the following information:

Knowledge Expected of Entering Kindergartners

Oral names for numerals 1–5

Sequence

What comes next? (Count orally: "One, two, three . . .")

What comes next? (Count orally: "Five, six, seven . . .")

What comes after three?

Cardinal number

Give me three disks.

Give me seven disks.

How many pins are here? (Show card with three pins.)

How many stars are here? (Show card with eight stars.)

Ordinal number

Point to the first tree.

Group comparison

Which group has more? (Show four spades and three buckets.)

Is there a disk for each child? (Show four disks and four children.)

Visually handicapped children lacking this type of knowledge should be exposed to a variety of experiences that will help them acquire the necessary concepts on which to base future mathematical instruction.

Even though touch is the most productive sensory system for learning about the world of objects, visually handicapped pupils should be encouraged to make maximum use of all sources of sensory input, including their limited vision. Hearing may be used in teaching about distances; smell and tàste probably have limited application in the teaching of mathematics but are useful in such subjects as biology and chemistry; the kinesthetic sense is also valuable in teaching about distance and measurement. Needless to say, all remaining vision should be used to the maximum. Too often school activities emphasize only vision and hearing, neglecting the contribution of other senses to learning.

1. Do not accept verbal descriptions as the sole assessment of whether the child has acquired a concept. For example, the child may be able to define a triangle as a three-sided figure but may not be able to select the triangle from other figures made from wire or wooden blocks.

2. Make copious use of concrete materials in all aspects of teaching mathematics.

3. Provide experiences that will make mathematical concepts meaningful, particularly those involved in spatial relations and ideas of measurement.

4. Use all sources of sensory input for learning; this helps not only the visually handicapped child but all pupils.

Other Considerations

Throughout this section we have focused on the visually handicapped child with no other impairment. Visually handicapped children present the same broad range of individual differences found in all other categories of

human characteristics and in the various aspects of growth and development. Often the underlying cause of the visual loss, such as rubella, for instance, also produces another impairment. Frequently the other impairment has a greater impact on school learning than the visual impairment. This is particularly evident in the education of visually handicapped pupils who are also mentally or emotionally impaired. Teachers should attempt to assess the potential impact of those other impairments on the growth and development of the visually handicapped pupil.

---

1. Be aware that pupils with visual impairments show the same broad range of individual differences as other pupils; treat each child as an individual, and do not expect that they will all be alike.

2. When a pupil has learning problems that appear unrelated to the visual impairment, make a referral for additional assessment in order to plan a more appropriate individualized education program.

EDUCATIONAL PROGRAMS AND MODIFICATIONS

Types of Programs

Visually handicapped pupils can be educated in a variety of settings, and each one may be the least restrictive environment for a particular child at a particular time in his or her educational career.

The education of visually handicapped children in residential schools began in 1829 in Boston in what is now called the Perkins School for the Blind. There are presently 55 public and private residential schools in this country that serve visually handicapped children.

In the past, residential schools educated the majority of visually handicapped children. The rapid growth of local programs, first in the 1950s and now more recently with the implementation of Public Law 94-142, has resulted in a change of focus within these schools. Some are centers for the education of visually handicapped pupils with additional impairments; some provide a wide variety of specialized services: direct short-term instruction for selected pupils in orientation and mobility, braille, typing, and other skills necessary in the education of blind pupils; consultation for regular teachers on education problems; and a central depository in the state for books and educational materials needed by children enrolled in community schools (Taylor, 1973).

Most community school programs follow one or a combination of three types of services: the special class, the resource room, and the itinerant program. In the *special class model*, the child is enrolled in a classroom with a special teacher for the visually handicapped. The amount of experience

provided with sighted children varies according to the child's individualized education program. Special classes range on a continuum from complete segregation from the school's regular curricular and extracurricular activities to total integration wherein the child uses the special class only as a homeroom.

In the *resource room model*, the student is enrolled in a regular class. The special teacher functions as a consultant to regular teachers on the child's education program, provides any special materials and equipment needed, and, in general, functions as a resource to child, parents, and regular teachers. The primary advantage of the resource room model over the special class is that the visually handicapped student remains the responsibility of the regular educator.

In the *itinerant plan*, pupils attend the school they would attend if they were not handicapped. The special teacher works as a consultant or counselor serving two or more schools. This teacher acts only as a consultant to other teachers and parents when the pupil is independent or gives direct instruction to the pupil in areas of special need. The major disadvantage of the itinerant plan is that the special teacher may not be readily available in an educational emergency. Both the resource room and the itinerant plans provide opportunities for maximum contact with normal children.

Visually handicapped pupils need varying degrees of specialized educational services. Regular teachers should not hesitate to seek consultant help from the special teacher assigned responsibility for serving a specific pupil. Adequate support service is mandated under PL 94-142 and is needed in order for the visually handicapped to receive maximum benefit from their educational experience.

Special Equipment and Materials

One of the major educational disabilities imposed by a visual impairment is the restricted access to the printed word. Various substitutes exist, but none approaches the easy access possessed by a sighted person. The following are the major visual, tactile, and auditory substitutes for regular print.

Visual reading. Children with low vision and limited vision are usually able to read print with some modifications and adaptations. For some, books in large type are used; others can read by magnifying regular print, either with small individually prescribed magnifiers or with one of the larger machines, which is not usually portable; a few can read regular print held close to their eyes. The teacher should recognize that reading speed is greatly reduced for all three methods because the eye cannot take in a normal amount of material in a single movement.

Writing for low vision and visually limited children can be done with

felt-tip or ball-point pens or thick lead pencils. The choice is usually a personal one. Regular lined paper might be used or the wide-lined primary paper; experiment to determine which is most appropriate for the individual child. Teachers should also encourage these pupils to use the chalkboard.

The efficient use of the typewriter is necessary for all visually handicapped pupils, and instruction can begin as early as second grade.

---

1. Anticipate that children with low vision or limited vision may read mathematical problems at a slower rate.

2. Encourage such children to read as much as they can, but be alert to signs of fatigue; reading by any of the methods described above can be physically tiring because of the concentration required.

3. Expect visually handicapped pupils to prepare assignments in a visually written form the same as the rest of the class.

Tactile reading. Blind and some low vision students will need to rely on tactile forms of reading. Braille is probably the most commonly used form of tactile reading and writing. It is a system of embossed dots based on the six-dot cell shown in Figure 7.1. The six dots provide for 63 different characters. Braille numbers and mathematical symbols are included in the illustrations used later in this chapter so teachers can learn the most commonly used signs. Secondary level teachers may wish to consult *The Nemeth Braille Code for Mathematics and Science Notation*, available from the American Printing House for the Blind (see the section on resources).

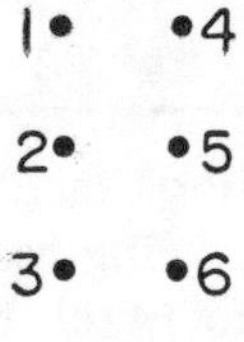

1•   •4

2•   •5

3•   •6

Figure 7.1.

One of the further advantages of braille is that it can be written. Younger children will probably use the *braille writer* for this purpose. This machine has six keys with a space bar between two groups of three keys each. It is about the size of a portable typewriter and thus can be easily carried about.

Older pupils will probably rely on the *slate and stylus*. The slate consists of two pieces of metal hinged at the left side; the upper part has cut-out cells that fit over the lower portion, which contains cells with six-dot depressions. The stylus is a slender rounded metal shaft embedded in a handle.

When paper is inserted, the stylus is used to depress the paper into the lower portion, thus making an embossed dot when the paper is removed and turned over. It is thus necessary to write from right to left.

The *Optacon* (pictured below) is a recent technological development that gives immediate access to print. A miniature camera scans a line of print and translates the optical image into a tactile form that can be read by the finger. It is a useful aid that enables blind students to read mathematical problems in regular texts.

All these forms of tactile reading are slow, and teachers should be aware of this limitation.

> Blind pupils relying exclusively on tactile reading may require some reduction in the amount of reading required or an increase in the amount of time. Be aware that a braille reader can usually read at the speed a sighted person reads print orally. The Optacon reader is even slower.

Aural reading. There are several oral substitutes for print reading. Many visually handicapped persons rely heavily on *readers*. This method would be appropriate for explanatory passages in mathematics, but unless the reader is skilled in describing illustrations and long problems and equations, some necessary information may be lost. Another disadvantage in using readers is that material cannot be reread for full comprehension at the student's convenience. All visually handicapped pupils should learn to

make efficient use of readers, however, and the teacher of mathematics should not hesitate to request some special instruction in listening skills from the special teacher for those who evidence problems in this area.

Recorded materials, cassette or reel-to-reel, have an advantage over readers in that students can read at their own convenience and can go over materials without the embarrassment of requesting a rereading. They should be instructed in using a cassette recorder for taking notes.

The *Kurzweil Reading Machine* and the spoken output accessory for the Optacon are technological aids that translate print material into computerized speech. Their present application is more appropriate for prose than for mathematical problems. Future developments, however, may make both more useful to the pupil in mathematics classes.

---

1. Encourage visually handicapped pupils, especially at the secondary level, to use a cassette recorder for taking notes and recording assignments in class. Ask them to record certain portions of the lesson so they can go over the material at home.

2. Record tests on cassette tape for the student to answer in some written form during the class period.

Mathematical aids. The *abacus* has been used increasingly in the education of visually handicapped pupils (Napier, 1973). Suggestions for using the abacus in the mathematics curriculum are included in a later section.

Calculators are increasing in general use. Calculators with braille or spoken output are available (see the section on resources). In addition, the display of some commercially produced calculators can be read with the Optacon. Teachers who use such aids regularly should explore alternatives for securing one for their visually handicapped pupil.

Various computational aids, such as *cube slates*, are available. The teacher should consult with the special teacher concerning the selection of instructional materials that are most appropriate for a particular pupil.

SUMMARY

Knowing the characteristics of a visual impairment and how society views those who are blind or have severe visual impairments will help the teacher build a sound base of knowledge that might ultimately lead to the development among educators of more positive attitudes toward such students. An appropriate curriculum with well-planned learning experiences can be developed when the teacher knows and understands the impact of the visual impairment on the child's physical, emotional, social, and mental

growth and development. Such information is necessary to assess what can be expected of such pupils in behavior and learning outcomes.

Various ways of managing visually impaired students have been outlined so that teachers will know what to expect of available support personnel when a visually handicapped child is enrolled in their classrooms. Selected special aids and materials have been described so the teacher can request those that will enhance classroom instruction.

From the background information included here, the suggestions for teaching the visually impaired should assist teachers in planning their instructional activities to meet the unique needs of visually handicapped pupils and to improve the education of those who are not handicapped as well.

SUGGESTIONS FOR MATHEMATICS INSTRUCTION

Related Research

A multisensory approach has been used quite successfully in the physical and life science materials for ages 9–12, *Science Activities for the Visually Impaired* (SAVI), produced by the Lawrence Hall of Science, University of California at Berkeley. SAVI emphasizes the development of logical thinking skills and the improvement of manipulative skills, as well as the discovery approach for applying skills to everyday experiences.

In case studies with four children (one educable mentally retarded, one emotionally impaired, and two learning disabled), Goergen, Schnur, Berger, and Vernon (1979) found that with SAVI, special students as a whole showed clear changes in classroom behavior. The changes were noted from data obtained from coding classroom behavior and were analyzed using an intriguing scheme: on-task versus off-task behavior; positive versus neutral versus negative emotional affect; verbal versus nonverbal behavior; social interaction versus nonsocial behavior.

In another article, Schnur and Berger (1979) relate the advantages of SAVI for science teachers in regular classrooms and point to its effectiveness in improving science instruction in general. Especially noteworthy is their statement that science education for the handicapped can carry important benefits for regular education.

The recently published *Sourcebook: Science Education and the Physically Handicapped*, which contains the article by Schnur and Berger, includes many suggestions that can be helpful to mathematics teachers. In a sensitive chapter in the *Sourcebook*, Susanne Johnson (1979) relates her feelings and experiences in having for the first time a low vision child, Tracy, in her junior high school science class. She relates her initial feelings of despair and pity when Tracy appeared without notice the first day of class. Questions about the management of the handicapped child over-

whelmed her. She observed evidence of discomfort and repulsion in her other students. Johnson traces the experiences from this unsettling beginning to a marvelous story of success.

Johnson made an early decision to ask Tracy about her handicap. To her delight, the girl replied freely and easily. With care Johnson chose a dependable student to work with Tracy, selecting one who was consistent, patient, tolerant, and considerate but not overly sympathetic. She describes experiments and the way Tracy participated. She stresses that low vision students should be permitted to participate in classroom activities to their fullest extent. Johnson's concluding two paragraphs should prove helpful to mathematics teachers:

> Probably the most important thing to remember when dealing with any handicapped child is to maintain normalcy. Every child is going to become frustrated at some time. Tracy panics when she has something long to read or must take a test for fear she will run out of time. She has learned to put trust in me, however, and knows I will allow her extra time. Sometimes her classmates become frustrated because she has asked them to repeat something for the fourth time or because they forget momentarily about her handicap. Treating Tracy as though she is normally sighted, and shaping everyday activities to allow for her disability helps to make all involved forget that a problem exists.
>
> Awareness of the problem by the other students and the teacher is the key to helping the handicapped child, not sympathy. A handicapped child will not profit by things being done for her. She, as anyone else, must learn how to do the best she can with what she has. She must learn her capabilities and her own limitations. The best gift we as educators can give is to show her how to use her capabilities and how to deal with her limitations. The rest is up to her. (p. 72)

Utz (1979) describes his experiences with blind students in university mathematics classes. He lists the numerous supportive devices available to them, including textbooks on cassette tape. He cautions about the misconceptions that blind students have superior memories and superior hearing.

Utz describes administering tests by having someone read the test to the blind person. He cautions the blind student to have the test read back when it is completed, since Utz takes exactly what is written. He includes blind students in classroom questions and finds their performance consistent with their homework and tests.

When a blind person recites, Utz writes on the chalkboard what is dictated, and from time to time he gives an oral summary of what has been written.

For drawings and curves he suggests a raised-line drawing board (a board that makes raised figures using thin sheets of acetate), tracing figures on the back of the blind student's hand with the blunt end of a pencil or pen, and making figures on heavy paper with glue. For graphing, he sug-

gests scoring a softwood board for axes, using a flat-headed thumbtack for the origin and round-headed map tacks for points.

The view expressed by Utz is one to be emulated:

> I frequently have blind students in my own classes. I like having them, and the sighted students also appreciate their presence, since the class sessions become especially well organized: I plan what I am going to say, I speak more slowly than usual, and I repeat certain sentences for emphasis. There is no reduction in course content. (p. 492)

Franks (1979) summarizes the small body of research on adapting educational materials in science to tactual materials for blind students. Although the emphasis is on science, much of the data pertain to the teaching of map reading and are relevant to mathematics teaching. Franks states that contrast and simplicity are the two most important characteristics for raised-line diagrams. He suggests that tactile arrays should be simple and the number of symbols minimized. He reports success in using sandpaper with varying degrees of roughness to convey differences in size. For histograms, a difference as small as two millimeters is not detectable to blind students.

Del Regato (1979) describes 6 of 12 case studies with blind students in "Touch-Tone Math: Communicating with the Blind." He taught some blind children to associate the tonal sounds of a telephone touch-tone pad with the speech symbols for numbers. For numbers 10 through 99, two-tone combinations were used. He concluded that learners can develop echoic codes to help them learn arithmetic. (Further information is available from William Loman, Department of Curriculum and Instruction, University of Oregon, Eugene, OR 97403.)

Principles for Mathematics Instruction

Research and experiences in teaching children with visual impairments suggest the following principles for teaching mathematics.

1. *Use concrete materials to introduce new topics.* Some slight modifications in the usual concrete materials may be needed. A teacher must think about the shape, size, and texture of objects used to teach ideas to students with visual impairments.

2. *Make concrete models from readily available materials.* Teachers are more likely to use concrete models if they can be made from readily available materials. Further, research at the primary level has indicated that teacher-made materials are more effective than commercial materials in regular classrooms (Harshman, Wells, & Payne, 1962).

Materials such as the following can be used easily:

- Sandpaper of various textures to illustrate graphs, drawings, and so on

- Gummed dots for number cards and arrays
- Corrugated cardboard to construct models for place value
- Aluminum foil, acetate sheets, or manila folders for drawing or cutting out shapes

3. *Oral work is essential.* All children profit from regular oral work. With visually handicapped pupils, greater emphasis is given to oral arithmetic as a compensation for visual learning. Oral work is essential in learning the basic facts, in doing simple arithmetic in one's head (e.g., adding 47 and 35 without paper and pencil or calculator), and in estimation. With the widespread use of calculators among students, estimation is more important than ever. It is easy to push the wrong button, to omit a decimal point, or to fail to tally a given number; skill in estimation provides the rough check that tells whether a major error has been made.

4. *In arithmetic, complicated paper-and-pencil computation should be reduced from that usually taught.* Here we are talking about work using any writing instrument including slate and stylus, braille writer, typewriter, pen, pencil, crayon, or chalk. Calculators are reducing the need for very complicated computation by paper and pencil for schoolchildren. For visually handicapped pupils, there should be some further reduction. It is sufficient to teach addition and subtraction to four digits, multiplication by a two-digit factor, division by a one-digit factor, fraction computation using only denominators that are small and occur in everyday affairs, and decimals to thousandths. Learning complicated computation is difficult and time-consuming for all students, but it is especially troublesome for students who are visually impaired. Other topics are of greater use. Visually handicapped students need geometry, oral arithmetic, algebraic notation, statistics and probability, graphing, and problem solving. A narrowly defined, highly computational curriculum adds to their handicap.

THE MATHEMATICS CURRICULUM

Mathematics objectives that all students are expected to attain are reflected in curriculum guides and textbooks for Grades K–8. Beyond this, specialized courses of algebra, geometry, advanced algebra, analysis, and calculus are offered in most secondary schools. Students who are visually impaired will probably take the specialized courses in about the same proportion as the general population of students.

Here are special suggestions for teaching some objectives that all students are expected to attain.

Among the most obvious weaknesses in school mathematics are inattention to effective thinking strategies, inadequate development of major concepts, excessive emphasis on standard paper-and-pencil computations,

omission of simple arithmetic without paper and pencil, and inadequate attention to problem solving. Suggestions in this section are directed at improving some of these identified weaknesses for all students, with special suggestions for teaching visually handicapped pupils.

Counting

Children learn to count orally long before they recognize the symbols for numbers. A sighted child handles objects and counts them one by one, but the sighted child also counts by looking at objects and mentally keeping track of the ones counted. Low vision and visually limited children should be encouraged to use their vision for such activities but may need tactile experiences as well. A blind child, of course, cannot count by looking and needs the tactile experience of handling the objects while saying the names orally.

Place beads or buttons on a wire or string for counting. Use beads of two different sizes or shapes and alternate them in fives—five small ones and then five large ones. This will encourage the child to build grouping ideas instead of relying solely on counting by ones to get answers. As a bead is pushed over, it is counted orally. To stress the

idea of cardinal number, have the child hold five beads as you and the child say "five" together. To stress the idea of ordinal number, have the child hold the fifth bead from a predetermined end. "This is number 5, or the fifth one." Relate the counting of objects to the braille symbols for numbers.

Teachers should also learn these braille symbols for checking pupils' work. They are not difficult. In this chapter the corresponding braille symbol will be given for each example. Note that the dots for numbers are in the middle and bottom rows (see Figure 7.2). When a special symbol for "number" is needed, such as on elevators, the braille number symbol ⠼ is used. When it is clear that numbers are intended, the symbol for "number" is usually omitted.

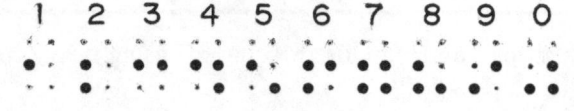

Figure 7.2.

Two-Digit Numbers

For a two-digit number there are five major instructional objectives; these are illustrated below for the number 34.

1. Relate the numeral 34 to objects grouped by tens.

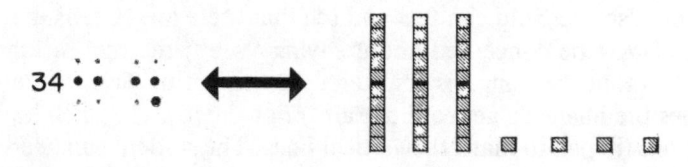

2. Relate the numeral 34 to the oral name.

3. Relate the result of counting by ones to get 34 to the grouping of objects by tens.

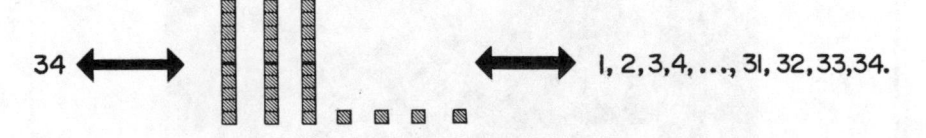

4. Rename 2 tens 14 ones as 3 tens 4 ones. This is needed in the addition algorithm.

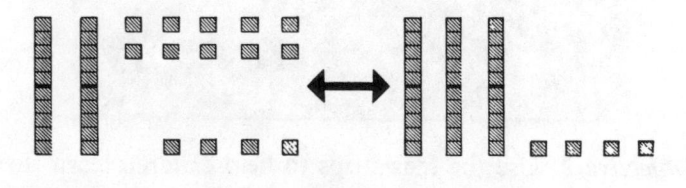

5. Rename 34 as 2 tens 14 ones—that is, $34 = \overset{2}{\cancel{3}}\ \overset{14}{\cancel{4}}$. This is needed for the subtraction algorithm.

Make "tens strips" and "hundreds squares" using heavy corrugated cardboard.

Tens strips: Make a rectangular piece, 1 cm by 10 cm. Draw 1-cm squares. Use a screwdriver or metal instrument to score the marks so that it is easy to feel the squares. Use a knife and score the fifth one gently. The cut suggests the grouping of the squares by fives for ease in counting. A pupil will need at least 20 of the tens strips.

Hundreds square: Make each hundreds square 10 cm by 10 cm. Draw 1-cm squares just as you did for the tens strips. Score the vertical lines so the child can feel and see that there are 10 tens in a hundred. (Don't be concerned about saying "see"; the real meaning of "see" is that an image is registered in the brain. The tactile work enables the image to get to the brain.) For the low vision child, use a thick felt-tip pen to mark the vertical lines. The student can keep these materials in a tray or box.

Objective 2. Use the tens strips to help children learn the oral names. Count the strips two ways, as 1 ten, 2 tens, 3 tens . . . and then use the usual names, ten, twenty, thirty, and so on (Figure 7.3). Twenty, thirty, and fifty are the most difficult to learn because these names

do not correspond well to the root words two, three, and five. The other names come directly from the names four, six, seven, and so on. You can point out that thirty sounds like "third" and fifty sounds like "fifth."

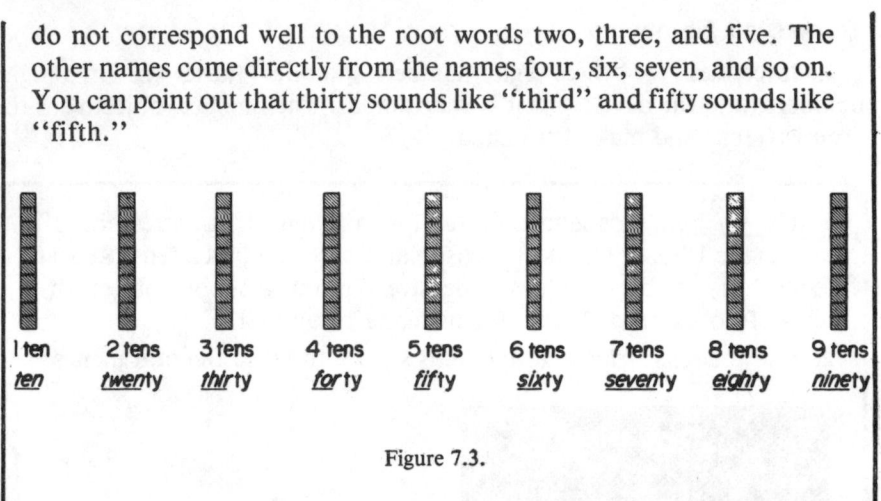

Figure 7.3.

Objective 3. Have the child show 34 by holding 3 tens strips in the left hand and another strip in the right hand with four squares extended. Using both hands this way is preparation for learning place value. Count the number by tens—10, 20, 30, 31, 32, 33, 34. Then count the squares by ones: 1, 2, 3, 4, . . . , 30, 31, 32, 33, 34.

Objective 1. After teaching the oral names for two-digit numbers, teach the place-value notation. Continue to stress the "tens-ones" names for numbers as well as the usual names:

3 tens, 4 ones

thirty-four

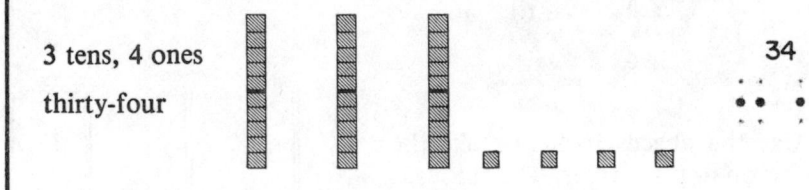

In braille, place value is shown in just the same way.

Objectives 4 and 5. Group 10 single squares to make a tens strip. Alternatively, use only the tens strips. For example, to show that 2 tens 14 ones = 3 tens 4 ones, have the child hold 2 tens strips in the left hand. In the right hand the child holds 1 tens strip and another strip with 4 single squares extended. This shows 2 tens 14 ones. Then the child transfers the tens strip in the right hand to the left hand. Call the number 3 tens 4 ones. For the reverse, 34 = 2 tens 14 ones, the child begins with 3 tens strips in the left hand and 1 strip with 4 squares extended in the right hand, then transfers 1 tens strip to the right hand. Name the number 2 tens 14 ones.

Three-Digit Numbers

Objectives for three-digit numbers parallel those for two-digit numbers, and the development is very similar. The one new objective is to group 10 tens and make 1 hundred.

---

1. Use the hundreds square. Cover it with 10 tens strips. Stress that 10 tens make 1 hundred. Use 12 tens. Name as 1 hundred 2 tens. Repeat for other numbers of tens. The stress is on grouping objects by tens—10 ones make 1 ten; 10 tens make 1 hundred.

2. Use the tens strips and hundreds square to teach the oral names:

2 hundreds　　3 tens　　4 ones
two hundred thirty-four

3. Use the abacus to help make the transition to place value. The abacus is not very helpful in teaching the initial ideas for numbers because it is difficult to sense the grouping by tens. It is best used as a recording device to represent the quantitative ideas built using the tens strips and hundreds squares.

h	*t*	*o*
2	3	4

2 hundreds　　3 tens　　4 ones
two hundred thirty-four

Larger Numbers

For thousands, the key idea is that 10 hundreds make 1 thousand. It is essential that this extension of the grouping concept be illustrated well.

1. Stack 10 hundreds squares. Count by hundreds to 10 hundreds. Then, teach the "new" name, 1 thousand. Review the grouping by 10—10 ones make 1 ten; 10 tens make 1 hundred; extend to 10 hundreds make 1 thousand.

10 hundreds
1 thousand

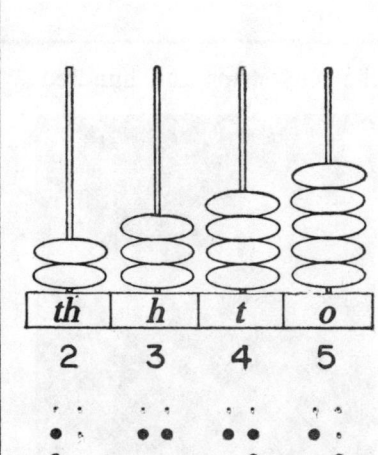

2. Use the abacus to record the number of thousands.

3. Record the number of thousands, hundreds, tens, and ones in place-value notation.

th	h	t	o
2	3	4	5

2 thousands 3 hundreds 4 tens 5 ones
two thousand three hundred forty-five

For larger numbers, stress the major idea that each period is 1000 times the period to its right:

1 million = 1000 thousands
1 billion = 1000 millions
1 trillion = 1000 billions

To teach 1 million, use the stack of 10 hundreds and name it 1 thousand. Have the child begin to think about each of the 1000 small

squares. The child may begin counting them by ones to get the idea, counting perhaps as far as 150. Then have the child count the single squares again, thinking of another stack of 1 thousand each time a square is counted. Say the names: 1 thousand, 2 thousand, 3 thousand . . . 997 thousand, 998 thousand, 999 thousand, 1000 thousand. Another name for 1000 thousand is 1 million.

Such experiences build a sense of the order of magnitude for larger numbers. The sense of size is especially important in estimation and approximation.

Rounding

For all pupils, but especially for the visually handicapped, everyday experiences require that estimation be learned. A major prerequisite for estimation is skill in rounding numbers.

To teach the rounding concept, use the tens strips and hundreds squares.

For 47, hold 4 tens strips and extend 7 unit squares. Use the cut mark at five and feel that the 7 is more than halfway. So 47 is rounded to 50.

To round 130, the child can feel that 3 tens is less than half the 100 square. So 130 rounds to 100. Visually handicapped children will need to learn the same convention as sighted children for "halfway" numbers—halfway numbers usually round *up*:

$$65 \rightarrow 70 \qquad 450 \rightarrow 500$$

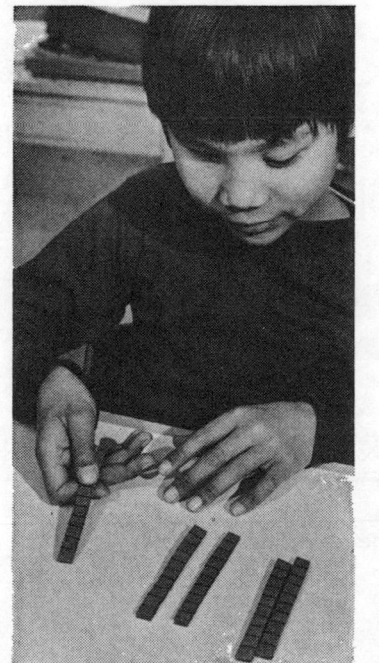

For further suggestions on teaching numbers and place value, see Payne and Rathmell (1975).

Learning Arithmetic Facts

Even for sighted children, learning facts requires much oral work. For the visually handicapped, oral work is even more essential. Learning facts begins with developing thinking models, moves to thinking strategies, and then requires practice to develop speed.

1. *Thinking model.* A child must have a dominant way to think about each of the operations—addition, subtraction, multiplication, and division. Although the thinking is illustrated by the concrete models, the concrete things only suggest the way for the child to think.

The thinking model for addition is easy; it is a combining action. All children have seen addition illustrated in such a way as this: An adult extends three fingers of one hand and two fingers of the other hand and asks, "How many do you see altogether?"

The thinking model for multiplication is not very difficult either. You think of a given number of sets with the same number in each set. For example, the concrete objects shown in Figure 7.4 suggest the kind of thinking we want to develop, namely, 3 fours. The major difficulty with the way we teach the thinking about multiplication is the failure to use such names as "3 fours" long enough for the child to fully understand how to think about multiplication. Too often, we rely solely on the multiplication symbol, ×, expecting the symbol to provide the thinking model for the child.

Figure 7.4. 3 fours.

The thinking models for subtraction and division need much more careful work for all children, sighted and nonsighted. The major idea for a teacher to get in mind for both these "difficult" operations is how to relate them to the "easy" operations of addition and multiplication.

2. *Thinking strategies.* The way children think to find an answer is a *thinking strategy.* For example, after thinking of addition as combining, children must then proceed to find the number in the combined set. A thinking strategy is a process strategy. It is the way a given child processes the initial stimulus of combining to produce the resulting sum.

3. *Practice.* Anything to be learned to automatic recall must be practiced, and practiced a lot. Suggestions are given later for practicing the facts after the thinking models and thinking strategies are developed.

Addition facts

1. *Thinking model.* A child thinks of a combining action and determines the number of the set that results when two sets are joined together.

Two parts are joined to make a whole. Some of the questions that suggest the thinking of addition are these:

- How many are there altogether?
- How many in all?
- What is the total?
- What is the result when the groups are combined?
- What is the cost of the two things?

2. *Thinking strategies*
   a. *Count both sets:* "1, 2, 3, 4, 5, 6, 7, 8, 9."
   b. *Count on,* beginning with the first number: "4 . . . 5, 6, 7, 8, 9."

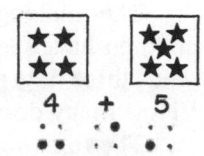

4 + 5

4 ... 5, 6, 7, 8, 9

c. *Count on,* beginning with the greater number: "5 . . . 6, 7, 8, 9."

For the strategies in a, b, and c, touching the beads and counting orally is essential. For the strategies in b and c, hold the first set under one hand and begin counting as you push the next bead over. For example, hold four beads under one hand and say "four." Then say "five" as you push the next one.

d. *Doubles*. It is relatively easy for children to learn the doubles, probably because they need to keep only one number in their working memory while they find the answer. Teach the doubles:

1 + 1   6 + 6

2 + 2   7 + 7

3 + 3   8 + 8

4 + 4   9 + 9

5 + 5

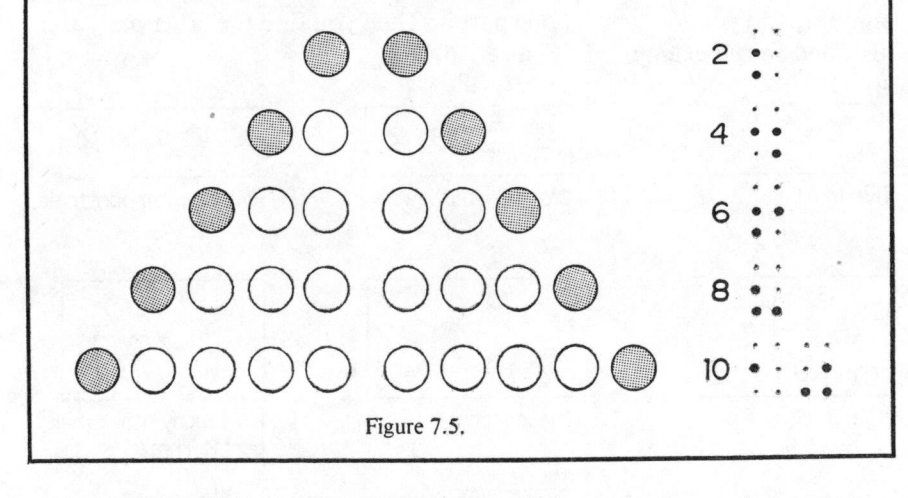

Place gummed dots on a sheet of tagboard with the numerals written in braille at the right. Use sandpaper dots on the ends to suggest that the doubles increase by two. (See Figure 7.5.)

2

4

6

8

10

Figure 7.5.

Practice the doubles orally until children can say each one in three seconds or less, first in order and then randomly.

e. *Near doubles*. Having taught the doubles, use them to teach the sums of numbers that differ by one or by two.

"5 + 5 = 10. So 5 + 6 is 1 more, or 11.
                    5 + 7 is 2 more, or 12."
"7 + 7 = 14. So 7 + 8 is 1 more, or 15.
                    7 + 9 is 2 more, or 16."

(Some children might think: "Put 1 from the 9 with the 7 to make both of them 8; 8 + 8 = 16, so 9 + 7 = 16.")

Give the children practice in recognizing which double can be used to find the sum:

"6 + 7 . . . use 6 + 6, then 1 more.

8 + 6 . . . use 6 + 6, then 2 more."

f. *Relate 9 to 10.* To add 9 to a number, first add 10 and then drop off 1: "5 + 9 . . . 5 + 10 = 15; drop off 1 and that gives 14."

Note that this strategy requires facility in adding single-digit numbers to 10.

With these strategies, there are only a few remaining facts to be learned, such as 5 + 8, 7 + 4, and 6 + 3. For adding 1, 2, or 3, it is not very difficult to count on. This is about the only way to teach the other facts, such as 7 + 4.

Subtraction facts

1. *Thinking model.* The major way to think of subtraction can be called the "part-part-whole" method. You think of the total or whole amount, and you know what one part is. Then you find the other part, as illustrated in the examples in Figure 7.6.

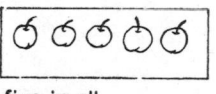

five in all

Cross off a part, two.

Find the other part, three.

eight in all

five in one part

How many in the other part? Three.

Figure 7.6.

Some children find it helpful to think of the "hidden door" model (Figure 7.7). The numeral at the top of a card shows the total number on the card. There are two doors. Open one door to show the part you know. What is hidden behind the other door?

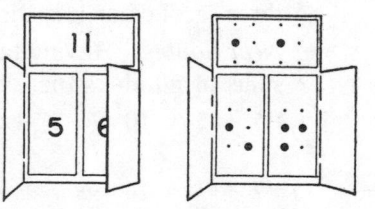

The major goal is to help the child think about addition without stressing the idea of adding. Sentences with missing addends, such as □ + 6 = 11, do *not* usually help because they are highly symbolic.

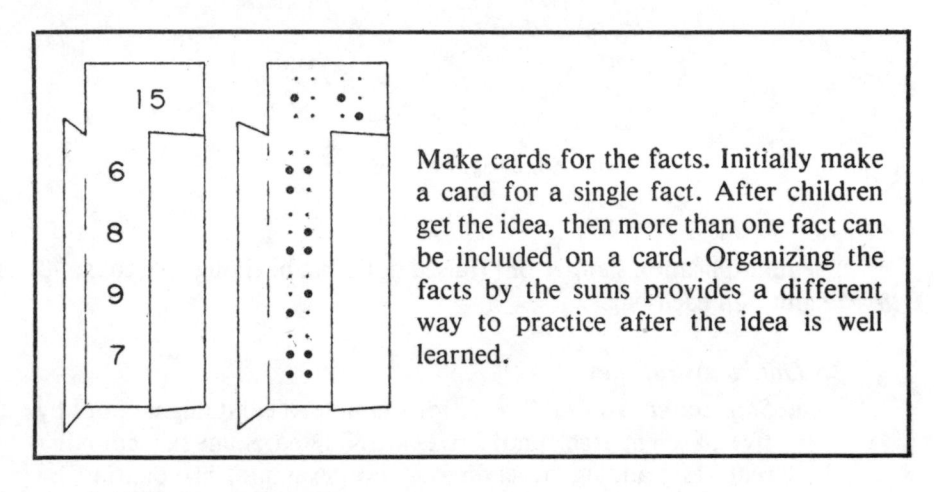

Make cards for the facts. Initially make a card for a single fact. After children get the idea, then more than one fact can be included on a card. Organizing the facts by the sums provides a different way to practice after the idea is well learned.

2. *Thinking strategies*

a. *Count back.* To subtract 1 or 2, it is relatively easy to count back.

For 8 − 2 think "8 . . . 7, 6."

For 9 − 1 think "9 . . . 8."

Counting back is not very effective for subtracting larger numbers because children get mixed up on where they start and where they stop.

b. *Count on.* When children know that the total is 8 and also that 5 must be subtracted (8 − 5 = ?), they count on from the 5 . . . "6, 7, 8," keeping a record of how many are counted.

c. *Add on.* This is a direct outgrowth of counting on.

For 8 − 5 think "5 and *3* make 8. So 3."

For 12 − 6 think "6 and *6* make 12. So 6."

d. *Doubles and near doubles.* Essentially, this is the "add on" strategy, but the use of doubles and near doubles is emphasized.

For 13 − 6 think "6 + 6 = 12. So 6 + *7* = 13. Answer: 7."

For 14 − 6 think "6 + 6 = 12. So 6 + *8* = 14. Answer: 8."

Multiplication facts

1. *Thinking model.* The major multiplication model is illustrated by thinking of three bags with five objects in each bag (see Figure 7.8). The thinking is summarized with the words, "3 fives." You know that the sets

have the same numbers of members, you know the number of sets; you know also the number of members in each set. You are to find how many in all.

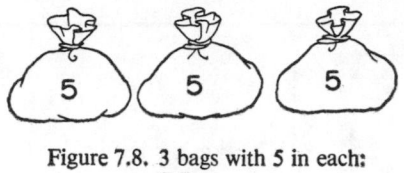

Figure 7.8. 3 bags with 5 in each:
3 fives
3 × 5

The multiplication sign, × or · (raised dot), can be thought of thus: "3 *times* I put 5 in each bag.

2. *Thinking strategies*

   a. *Skip count.* To find 7 × 5, for example, a child might count by fives, keeping track until 7 fives are counted. Some skip counting requires "adding by endings." For example, in counting by eights, one begins "8, 16." To count another 8, 8 is added to 16. A child may think, "8 + 6 *ends* in 4. So the answer is __?__ 4. Since 8 + 6 is more than 10, the number of tens is 2. So, 16 + 8 = 2_4." Practice in adding by endings will improve a child's ability to do skip counting.

   b. *Count on from known product.* To find 7 × 6, for example, a child might start with a known product, such as 5 × 6 = 30, and count on from 30: "7 × 6 . . . 5 sixes = 30 . . . 36, 42. So 7 × 6 = 42." Children should be especially encouraged to count on using the facts with five because these facts are learned easily.

   c. *Doubles.* For facts with one even factor, doubles can be used: "8 × 7 . . . 4 sevens = 28; 8 sevens = 28 + 28, or 56."

   d. *Turn-around factors.* This strategy is an application of the commutative property of multiplication. "5 × 8 . . . 8 fives = 40; so 5 eights = 40, 5 × 8 = 40."

   e. *Relate factors of 9 to 10.* For facts with one factor of 9, first think of 10 times the number. Then subtract the number. "9 × 7 . . . 10 sevens = 70; 70 − 7 = 63; so
   9 sevens = 63; 9 × 7 = 63."

   Beyond these strategies, children should be encouraged to use generalizations about 0 and 1 as factors:

   0 times a number = 0.

   1 times a number = the number.

Division facts

1. *Thinking model.* By far the most productive way to think for division is to use multiplication. In division you know that sets have the same number, the number in all (the dividend), and either the number of sets or the number in each set (the divisor).

To prepare for the initial instruction on division, children need to spend at least a week working through questions and problems finding missing factors. Examples such as these would be included:

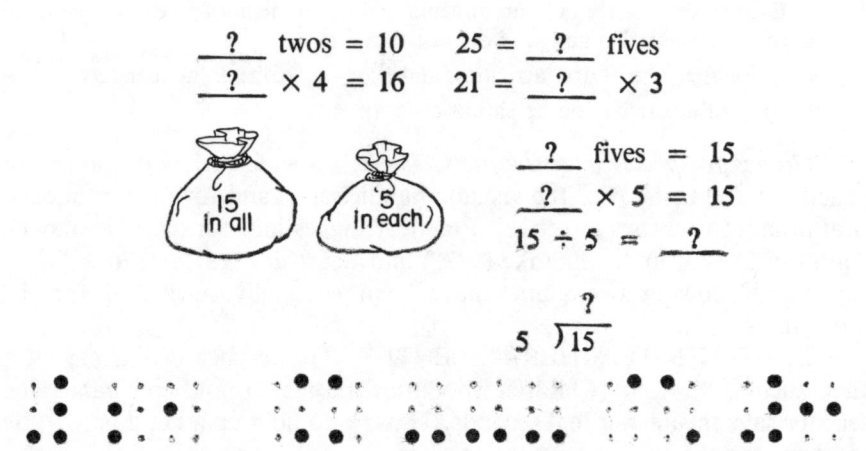

$$\underline{\quad?\quad} \text{ twos} = 10 \qquad 25 = \underline{\quad?\quad} \text{ fives}$$

$$\underline{\quad?\quad} \times 4 = 16 \qquad 21 = \underline{\quad?\quad} \times 3$$

$$\underline{\quad?\quad} \text{ fives} = 15$$

$$\underline{\quad?\quad} \times 5 = 15$$

$$15 \div 5 = \underline{\quad?\quad}$$

15 In all   5 In each

$$5\overline{)15}\ ^{?}$$

When the thinking model of the missing factor is well established, then the division signs $\div$ and $\overline{)}$ are introduced. The signs mean to think of the corresponding multiplication fact.

2. *Thinking strategies.* The most basic strategy is, of course, to think of a multiplication fact.

$$6\overline{)42}\ \ldots\ \text{“}6 \times \underline{\ ?\ } = 42;\ 6 \times 7 = 42;\ \text{so } 6\overline{)42}\ ^{7}\ \text{”}$$

Children who do not know the fact can count on, keeping track of the number of counts: "6, 12, 18, 24, 30, 36, 42 . . . , 7 counts of 6; so the quotient is 7."

For further suggestions on teaching thinking strategies in addition and multiplication facts, see Rathmell (1978, pp. 13–38). For research that supports the use of thinking strategies, see Thornton (1978, pp. 214–227).

Practice on the facts. Any content to be learned to automatic recall must be practiced, and practiced a lot. Davis (1978) gives helpful suggestions for memorizing the facts. He has examples and explanations for these nine principles:

1. Children should attempt to memorize [only] material they reasonably understand.
2. Have children begin to memorize basic arithmetic facts soon after they demonstrate an understanding of symbolic statements.
3. Children should participate in drill with the intent to memorize.
4. During drill sessions, emphasize remembering—don't explain.
5. Keep drill sessions short, and have some drill almost every day.
6. Try to [have them] memorize only a few facts in a given lesson, and constantly review previously memorized facts.
7. Express confidence in your students' ability to memorize—encourage them to try memorizing and see how fast they can be.
8. Emphasize verbal drill activities, and provide feedback immediately.
9. Vary drill activity and be enthusiastic. (p. 52)

Games for practice on the facts. There is a wide variety of games for practicing the facts. (For the visually handicapped and for other students, oral practice is always effective.) Practical suggestions for teachers may be found in Dumas and Schminke (1977) and Beardsley (1973, 1976).

The following two games have been especially successful for the authors:

BEAT THE TEACHER—SILENTLY. The teacher begins saying a fact, such as "5 + 5." Children who know the answer hold up a hand. The teacher says the answer in 4 seconds. Those who hold up a hand before the teacher says the answer beat the teacher.

GIVE ME THE HARD FACT. The teacher chooses five facts (four easy ones and one hard) for practice during a short oral drill. Two teams are formed. The teacher chooses a fact, and one member of a team responds. Then another fact is chosen for the other team. An "easy" fact scores one point; a "hard" fact scores five points. This provides incentive to learn even the hard facts, and children will begin to ask for the hard fact.

Oral Arithmetic

All children need to learn to do simple arithmetic in their heads. They will use it in their everyday transactions to calculate the cost of purchases or an amount of change. Estimation and approximation, furthermore, demand that one be able to do simple arithmetic in one's head. A teacher should plan 10 minutes of oral arithmetic each day, following a systematic plan leading to mastery.

The major objectives for oral arithmetic with whole numbers are these:

- To add and subtract any two-digit numbers
- To add and subtract any three-digit numbers ending with zero
- To multiply a two-digit number by a one-digit number

- To divide multiples of 10 and multiples of 100 by one-digit numbers without determining the remainder
- to count change

The examples below illustrate a planned sequence that can be followed to attain these objectives. All arithmetic done in one's head depends on quick recall of the facts. So oral arithmetic begins by mastering the facts.

1. *Addition*

   a. Adding ones to tens:

   $$30 + 7 \qquad 50 + 4 \qquad 70 + 6$$

   b. Adding ones to two-digit numbers with no bridging of the next decade:

   $$31 + 4 \qquad 73 + 4 \qquad 82 + 7$$

   c. Adding ones to two-digit numbers with bridging required:

   $$42 + 9 \qquad 65 + 7 \qquad 88 + 9$$

   For 42 + 9, think: "2 + 9 ends in 1. So 42 + 9 ends in 1. The sum is in the 50s. So 51." This is called "adding by endings."

   d. Adding two two-digit numbers with no bridging:

   43 + 35—"43 and 30 more is 73. 5 more is 78."

   27 + 81—"81 and 20 more is 101. 7 more is 108."

   e. Adding two two-digit numbers *with* bridging:

   36 + 57—"57 and 30 more is 87. 6 more is 93."

   45 + 76—"76 and 40 more is 116. 5 more is 121."

   86 + 94—"94 and 80 more is 174 (9 + 8 = 17). 6 more is 180."

   f. Adding hundreds:

   200 + 400—"2 + 4 = 6. So 600."

   g. Adding two three-digit numbers that end in zero, where the tens do not bridge to hundreds:

   670 + 310—"67 and 30 is 97; 1 more is 98. So 980."

   h. Adding two three-digit numbers that end in zero, where the tens *do* bridge to hundreds.

   370 + 480—"48 + 30 = 78. 7 more is 85. So 850."

The oral arithmetic for g and h will be difficult for some children. Stressing addition of the two-digit number makes it a bit easier. Teachers may wish to reserve these steps for their more advanced pupils.

2. *Subtraction.* Again, the development ranges from easy to difficult. The mastery of each is prerequisite for learning the next.

   a. Subtracting tens:

   $$70 - 30 \qquad 80 - 20 \qquad 90 - 50$$

b. Subtracting tens from two-digit numbers:

78 − 50—two ways to think: (1) "50 to 70 is 20. 8 more is 28" (a count-on strategy). (2) "7 − 5 = 2. So 28."

87 − 40—(1) "40 to 80 is 40. 7 more is 47." (2) "8 − 4 = 4. So 47."

c. Subtracting two-digit numbers with no renaming required:

78 − 24—(1) "24 to 74 is 50. 4 more is 54." (2) "78 − 20 = 58. 4 less is 54."

96 − 45—(1) "45 to 95 is 50. 1 more is 51." (2) "96 − 40 = 56. 5 less is 51."

d. Subtracting two-digit numbers *with* renaming required:

78 − 29—(1) "29 to 69 is 40. 9 more is 49" (a count-on strategy). (2) "78 − 20 = 58. 9 less is 49."

63 − 28—(1) "28 to 58 is 30. 2 more is 32. 3 more is 35." (2) "63 − 20 = 43. 8 less is 35."

3. *Counting change.* Use real money. Make sure the child can identify each coin tactually and knows its value.

The thinking strategies for counting change are essentially the same as for subtraction. The "counting on" strategy is used more often in practical affairs, as illustrated in this example.

Buy a pen for 69¢. Give the clerk a dollar.

Think: "1¢ makes 70¢; 5¢ makes 75¢; 25¢ makes a dollar. So 31¢ is the change."

4. *Multiplication*

a. Multiplying ones times tens:

3 × 20—"3 × 2 = 6. 3 × 2 tens = 6 tens. So 3 × 20 = 60."

5 × 70—"5 × 7 = 35. 5 × 7 tens = 35 tens. So 5 × 70 = 350."

b. Multiplying ones times hundreds:

3 × 400—"3 × 4 = 12. 3 × 4 hundreds = 12 hundreds. So 3 × 400 = 1200."

5 × 700—"5 × 7 = 35. 5 × 7 hundreds = 35 hundreds. So 5 × 700 = 3500."

c. Multiplying ones times two-digit numbers with no renaming:

3 × 23 (no renaming)—"3 × 20 = 60. 3 × 3 = 9. So 69."

4 × 71—"4 × 70 = 280. 4 × 1 = 4. So 284."

d. Multiplying ones times two-digit numbers *with* renaming:

4 × 35—"4 × 30 = 120. 4 × 5 = 20. 120 + 20 = 140."

7 × 56—"7 × 50 = 350. 7 × 6 = 42. 350 + 42 = 392."

e. Multiplying tens times tens:

40 × 50—"Ten × ten = 100. So the answer will be hundreds. 4 × 5 = 20. So 20 hundreds or 2000."

   80 × 90—"8 × 9 = 72. So 7200."

f. Multiplying hundreds times tens:

   600 × 50—"Ten × hundred = 1000. So the answer will be thousands. 6 × 5 = 30. 30 thousands. So 30 000."

   800 × 40—"8 × 4 = 32. The answer will be thousands. So 32 000."

The oral arithmetic in a, b, e, and f is critical to estimate results on a calculator.

Written Algorithms

Long, tedious calculations will almost always be done on the calculator by all students, including the visually handicapped. In using a calculator, the visually handicapped can be expected to produce in the same way as other pupils.

In teaching computation, stress the process or understanding of all four algorithms. Understanding is built by oral work and by using concrete materials. Slow, careful development is required, especially when a new algorithm, or a new step in an algorithm, is introduced.

Use tens strips to illustrate algorithms. Use the names "ones," "tens," and "hundreds" orally as you work problems through with children.

```
  73        7 tens 3 ones   =   6 tens 13 ones
 −28       −2 tens 8 ones   =   2 tens  8 ones
 ───       ─────────────        ──────────────
  45                            4 tens  5 ones
```

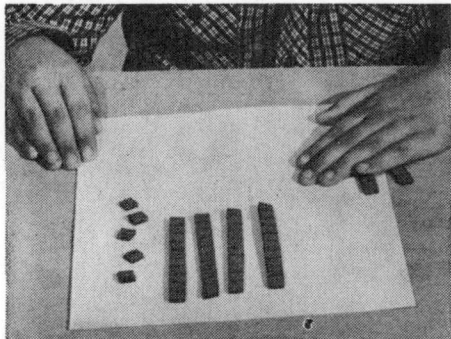

$$\begin{array}{r} 23 \\ \times\ 4 \\ \hline 92 \end{array}$$

2 tens   3 ones
×   4
─────────────
8 tens 12 ones, or
9 tens   2 ones

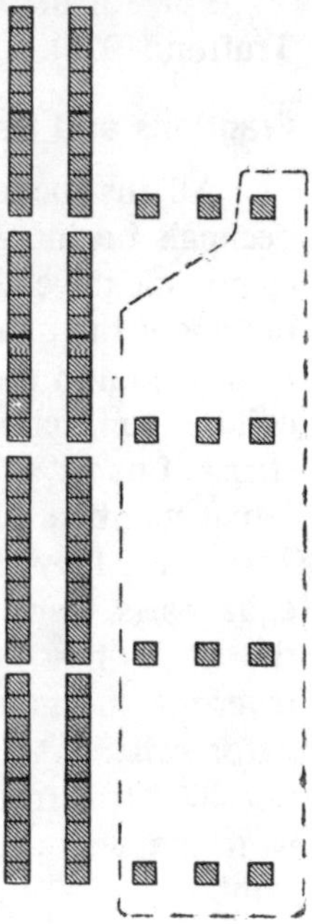

$$3\ \overline{)\ 69}\quad ^{23}$$

2 tens 3 ones
3) 6 tens 9 ones

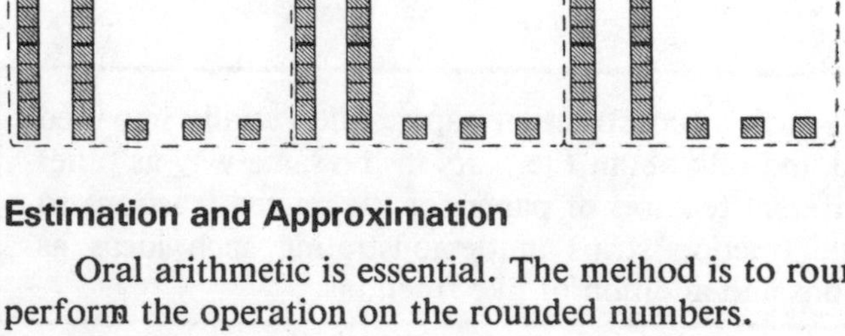

Estimation and Approximation

Oral arithmetic is essential. The method is to round the numbers and perform the operation on the rounded numbers.

Estimate

$$367 \rightarrow 400$$
$$+285 \rightarrow \underline{300}$$
$$700$$

Estimate

$$695 \rightarrow 700$$
$$-136 \rightarrow \underline{100}$$
$$600$$

Estimate

$$78 \rightarrow 80$$
$$\times 6 \quad \underline{6}$$
$$480$$

Estimate

$$7\,\overline{)\,865\,} \rightarrow 7\,\overline{)\,900\,}^{\,100}$$

For further suggestions on estimation and mental arithmetic, see Trafton (1978).

Fractions and Decimals

All instruction on fractions and decimals begins with concrete objects to provide the children a way of thinking about the quantities involved. The most common method of introducing children to fractions is having them use strips of paper and fold them into different numbers of equal parts (Figure 7.9). Then they should talk about the equal parts, learning the oral names for the parts first. (This helps prevent reversing the numerator and denominator when the symbols are introduced.) Then from concrete ideas and word names, they learn the written symbols.

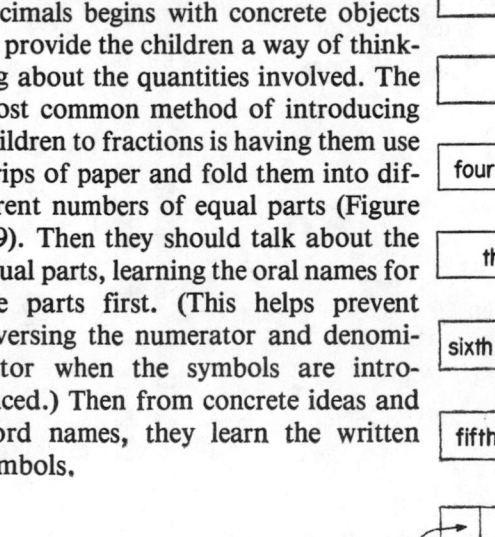

Figure 7.9.

Use heavy paper, such as construction paper. The visually impaired can learn to fold and talk about the parts in the same way as other children. Use different textures of paper for the related fractions so they can use the fraction strips in demonstrating such ideas as equivalent fractions and addition of like fractions.

The teacher will want to include tenths because of the increased use of the metric system.

Geometry and Measurement

The work with geometry in most classes requires visualization. Even with sighted children, a teacher begins with concrete objects, talks about the shapes of the objects, and helps the children focus on the essential features. For example, a block is noted to have six faces, each one flat. The features can be confirmed by the child's running his or her hands over the object. The edges are noted as being straight; the corners, sharp. The entire block is named a cube. Such an effective teaching procedure is just as good with visually handicapped pupils.

When you teach figures on a plane to your visually handicapped pupils, it is also necessary to provide something they can feel.

1. Make plane figures from wire. Pipe cleaners are effective.

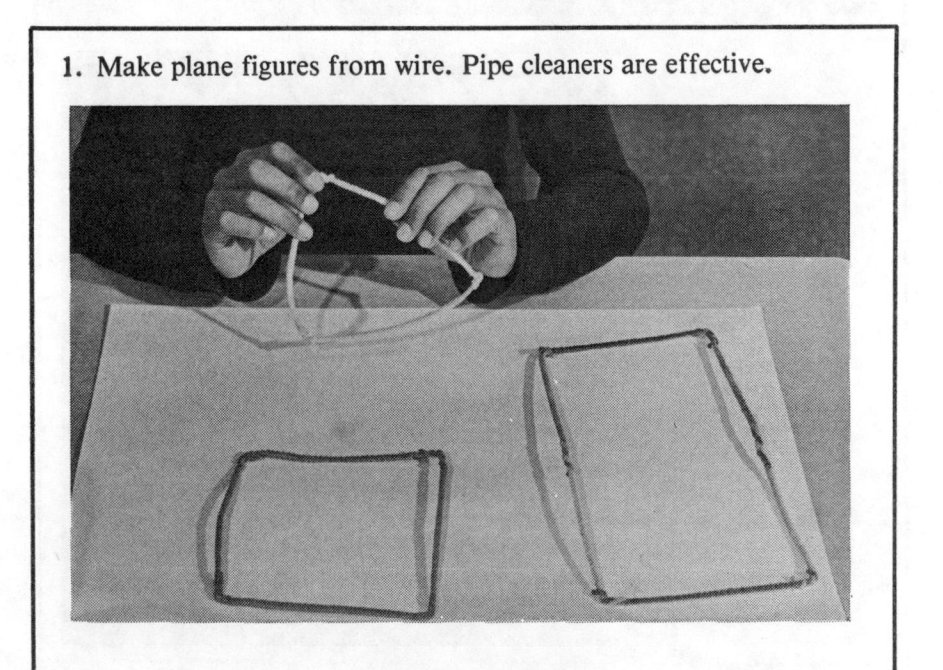

2. Trace the figures onto aluminum foil with the blunt end of a pen. Do this before beginning instruction. The child with a visual impairment can then follow your presentation to the class just by feeling the figures in the foil.

3. Braille rulers are readily available.

RESOURCES

PL 94-142 requires that needed supplementary services be provided when handicapped children are placed in a regular class. Thus, teachers of mathematics should have a qualified teacher of visually handicapped pupils available to them for consultation and assistance with any instructional problems that may arise in the regular classroom. The regular teacher should contact the local or intermediate director of special education to ascertain who that person is. If there is no one, the teachers should contact the state department of education to seek help.

Funds for professional development are allocated to each state under PL 94-142. Teachers should write to their state department of education regarding the possibility of participation in the development of the state plans to ensure that the in-service needs of mathematics teachers with handicapped pupils enrolled in their classes are included in the plans.

In addition to local and state resources, the following national agencies may be of service:

The American Foundation for the Blind
15 W. 16 St.
New York, NY 10011

The American Printing House for the Blind
1839 Frankfort Ave.
Louisville, KY 70206

Recordings for the Blind, Inc.
215 E. 58 St.
New York, NY 10022

The American Foundation for the Blind sells by mail order a wide variety of aids and appliances. Such items as clocks and measuring instruments are of special interest to teachers of mathematics. You may wish to write for their free catalogs of publications, *Aids and Appliances* and the *International Guide to Aids and Appliances for Blind and Visually Impaired Persons*.

The American Printing House for the Blind sells textbooks, both braille and large print, and other instructional materials. Teachers of mathematics should consult with the teacher of the visually handicapped or the director of special education concerning the purchase of such materials on the quota account allotted to all states for the education of blind children. Materials of special interest include measuring instruments, the Speech-Plus Talking Calculator, geometric figures, graphic aids, and the abacus. Teachers should write for a free catalog.

Recordings for the Blind has available for loan a wide variety of textbooks on open reel and cassette tapes. Teachers should write for a catalog.

SUMMARY

The foregoing suggestions for the mathematics curriculum are intended to broaden the teacher's view of learning opportunities for visually impaired students. All too often these students have been limited to a curriculum consisting only of a work book type of drill and practice on computation. Such a narrow curriculum will only accentuate their handicap.

We have suggested a curriculum that includes much oral work in arithmetic, substantial work on estimation, and the calculator for more complicated computations. We have stressed the need for concrete materials, especially to introduce new content. We are confident that an improved mathematics program for visually impaired pupils will mean an improved mathematics program for all pupils.

APPENDIX A

Nemeth Braille Code for Math and Science Notation

The authors are grateful to Eileen Luther, teacher of the visually handi-capped, for compiling this listing of braille mathematical symbols especially for teachers.

Numeral sign:

Numbers: In mathematics, numbers are more frequently shown in the lower cells (i.e., 1 , 2).

Note: 4 is the reverse of 6, 5 is the reverse of 9, and 8 is the reverse of 0.

1

2

3

4

5

6

7

8

9

0

Letters of importance:

m a

n b

x c

y z

a – same as 1 in upper cells

b – same as 2 in upper cells

c – same as 3 in upper cells

Comparison signs:

equals =

greater than >

less than <

not equal ≠

Operational signs:

addition +

subtraction −

multiplication ×

multiplication ·

division ÷

slash (per, over, divided by) /

Decimal sign:

Comma in math:

Parentheses:

opening

closing

Money:

¢ (cents) (after #, i.e., 1¢)

$ (i.e., $2.00)

Other symbols:

% (i.e., 2%)

° (degrees, i.e., 10°)

$\overset{=}{?}$

π

subscript

ellipses

square root $\sqrt{\ }$ number

exponent (i.e., x^2) superscript

REFERENCES

Barraga, N. C. *Visual handicaps and learning: A developmental approach.* Belmont, Calif.: Wadsworth, 1976.

Beardsley, L. *1,001 uses of the hundred square: Activities and ideas for teaching mathematics.* West Nyack, N.Y.: Parker (Prentice-Hall), 1973.

Beardsley, L. *Elementary math activities with model behavioral objectives.* West Nyack, N.Y.: Parker (Prentice-Hall), 1976.

Brown, D. A. What are the issues? *Sight-Saving Review,* Summer 1976.

Bureau of Education for the Handicapped. *BEH Data Notes.* Washington, D.C.: BEH, September 1978.

Davis, E. J. Suggestions for teaching the basic facts of arithmetic. In M. N. Suydam (Ed.), *Developing computational skills,* 1978 Yearbook of the National Council of Teachers of Mathematics, Reston, Va.: The Council, 1978.

del Regato, J. Touch-tone math: Communicating with the blind. *Trying out some ideas: Final report of the Oregon system in mathematics education* (NSF Grant No. SER 72-05821), March 1979.

Dumas, E., & Schminke, C. W. *Math activities for child involvement.* Boston: Allyn & Bacon, 1977.

Fraiberg, S. *Insights from the blind.* New York: Basic Books, 1977.

Franks, F. The tactile modality in adapting and developing science materials. In H. Hoffman & K. Ricker (Eds.), *Sourcebook, science education and the physically handicapped.* Washington, D.C.: National Science Teachers Association, 1979.

Goergen, A. C., Schnur, R., Berger, C., & Vernon, D. *The use of activity-centered science education to facilitate the mainstreaming of elementary school children with special needs.* Unpublished report, School of Education, University of Michigan, 1979.

Harley, R. K. *Verbalism among blind children.* New York: American Foundation for the Blind, 1963.

Harley, R. K., & Lawrence, G. A. *Visual impairment in the schools.* Springfield, Ill.: Thomas, 1977.

Harshman, H. W., Wells, D. W., & Payne, J. Manipulative materials and arithmetic achievement in grade 1. *Arithmetic Teacher,* 1962, *9,* 188–192.

Hatfield, E. M. Why are they blind? *Sight-Saving Review,* 1975, *45,* 3–22.

Hoffman, H., & Ricker, K. (Eds.). *Sourcebook, science education and the physically handicapped.* Washington, D.C.: National Science Teachers Association, 1979.

Johnson, S. Science for a partially sighted junior high child. In H. Hoffman & K. Ricker (Eds.), *Sourcebook, science education and the physically handicapped.* Washington, D.C.: National Science Teachers Association, 1979.

Lowenfeld, B. Psychological problems of children with impaired vision. In W. M. Cruickshank (Ed.), *Psychology of exceptional children and youth.* Englewood Cliffs, N.J.: Prentice-Hall, 1971.

Monbeck, M. *The meaning of blindness.* Bloomington: Indiana University Press, 1973.

Napier, G. D. Special subject adjustments and skills. In B. Lowenfeld (Ed.), *The visually handicapped child in school.* New York: John Day, 1973.

National Society for the Prevention of Blindness. *Signs of possible eye trouble in children* (Pub. No. G-102). New York: NSPB, 1978.

National Society for the Prevention of Blindness. *Vocabulary terms relating to the eye* (Pub. No. P-607). New York: NSPB, 1964.

The Nemeth Braille Code for Mathematics and Science Notation (1972 ed.). Louisville, Ky.: American Printing House for the Blind, 1973.

Norris, M., Spaulding, P. J., & Brodie, F. H. *Blindness in children.* Chicago: University of Chicago Press, 1957.

Payne, J., & Rathmell, E. Number and numeration. In J. N. Payne (Ed.), *Mathematics learning in early childhood*, Thirty-seventh Yearbook of the National Council of Teachers of Mathematics. Reston, Va.: The Council, 1975.

Rathmell, E. Using thinking strategies to teach the basic facts. In M. N. Suydam (Ed.), *Developing computational skills*, 1978 Yearbook of the National Council of Teachers of Mathematics. Reston, Va.: The Council, 1978.

Riviere, M. *Rehabilitation codes: Five year progress report*. New York: Rehabilitation Codes (1790 Broadway, New York), n.d.

Schnur, R., & Berger, C. Benefits from science education for the handicapped. In H. Hoffman & K. Ricker (Eds.), *Sourcebook, science education and the physically handicapped*. Washington, D.C.: National Science Teachers Association, 1979.

Scholl, G. T. Understanding and meeting developmental needs. In B. Lowenfeld (Ed.), *The visually handicapped child in school*. New York: John Day, 1973.

Taylor, J. L. Educational programs. In B. Lowenfeld (Ed.), *The visually handicapped child in school*. New York: John Day, 1973.

Thornton, C. A. Emphasizing thinking strategies in basic fact instruction. *Journal for Research in Mathematics Education*, 1978, *9*(3), 214–227.

Trafton, P. R. Estimation and mental arithmetic: Important components of computation. In M. N. Suydam (Ed.), *Developing computational skills*, 1978 Yearbook of the National Council of Teachers of Mathematics. Reston, Va.: The Council, 1978.

Utz, W. R. The blind student in the mathematics class. *American Mathematical Monthly*, 1979, *86*(6), 491–494.

Vaughan, D., Cook, R., & Ashbury, T. *General opthalmology*. Los Altos, Calif.: Lange Medical Publications, 1965.

Wilder, M. H. *Characteristics of persons with corrective lenses, United States—1971* (DHEW Pub. No. 75-1520). Washington, D.C.: Superintendent of Documents, 1974.

8

Teaching Mathematics to the Hearing Impaired

Charles H. Dietz

Model Secondary School for the Deaf

Clarence M. Williams

Gallaudet College

Dr. Charles H. Dietz is a mathematics instructor of deaf students at the Model Secondary School for the Deaf, Gallaudet College, Washington, D.C. Previously he taught mathematics and mathematics education at various universities, directed a secondary student teaching program, and taught both science and mathematics in high schools for hearing students. His current research interests are in the area of mathematics learning, especially as it relates to concept formation, visualization, and deaf students.

Dr. Clarence M. Williams is coordinator of faculty and graduate student research, Gallaudet College, Washington, D.C. He is a fellow in the American Association for the Advancement of Science; a member of Psi Chi, Phi Delta Kappa, and the American Education Research Association; founder of the Society for Study of Technology in Education; cofounder of the National Conference on Visual Literacy; and director of the Center for Visual Literacy. He has published a number of professional books and articles.

W HEN Helen Keller (1933) was asked which condition she considered more handicapping, deafness or blindness, her answer was deafness. The response surprised many; deafness is a more all-encompassing handicap than it at first appears. Deaf persons are closed out of social interactions and lack a major source of nonconcrete information on which to base their perceptions and understandings of the world. Deafness affects not only what a person hears but also what that person sees. A deaf person is more than a person who cannot hear; hearing impaired individuals can be different culturally, socially, and cognitively. According to Mulholland and Fellendorff (1968),

Today our nation faces a crisis in the education of its hearing impaired children. . . . The proliferation of scattered day classes, frequently supervised by educators who are not knowledgeable in the field of deafness, staffed by poorly qualified teachers, and limited in their educational opportunities has aroused educators and parents alike. Few states have recognized the problem of educating hearing impaired children beyond narrow limits and still fewer have developed comprehensive state plans. (p. 3)

Although the existence of PL 94-142 has now encouraged the development of such comprehensive plans, little specific help is available yet today for the classroom teacher in working with deaf students in particular content areas, such as mathematics.

The purpose of this chapter is to provide such help by—

1. describing some characteristics of hearing impaired students and how these characteristics can affect mathematics learning;
2. discussing specific problems hearing impaired students may experience in the classroom setting that might prevent them from effectively learning mathematics;
3. suggesting general and specific principles the classroom teacher can use to assist hearing impaired students learn mathematics.

A brief description of deafness, its causes and effects, is given for the purpose of orientation; detailed analyses of physiological, psychological, and sociological factors are not included. References are listed throughout as important sources of additional information on these matters.

HEARING IMPAIRMENT

Deafness erects unseen walls between deaf individuals and all the other people with thom they should interact. These walls have their most telling consequences on the individual's attempts to communicate and the development of that most important aspect of human capabilities— language in the common tongue. The successes of hearing handicapped persons in education, social interactions, work achievements, and in personal development hinge on their ability to surmount these communication barriers. All aspects of development are related in significant ways to different and specific kinds of communication problems encountered by deaf persons and to their achievement of some measure of success in this area of life behavior. Most importantly, their experiences and performance in learning environments are likely to be seriously affected unless prodigious effort is exerted both by and with them (Meadow & Trybus, 1979).

Hearing impairment is a generic term referring to any loss of hearing regardless of type, severity, or age of onset. It conveys little meaning with

regard to educational placement, communication skills, or the social and emotional abilities necessary for growth-producing interactions with the hearing world. The term *hard of hearing* is not synonymous with hearing impairment or deafness. There has always been some controversy in distinguishing between the definitions of *hard of hearing* and *deaf*. It has been said that the hard of hearing child fits neither into the world of the hearing nor into the world of the deaf. For this reason it is imperative that the hard of hearing be recognized as a specifically defined population with unique characteristics and needs (Ross & Calvert, 1977).

The most common method of classifying persons as hard of hearing is based on their remaining amount of usable residual hearing. Unlike deaf persons, hard of hearing individuals use their residual hearing to learn speech and language, although both of these acquisitions may be deviant to some degree (DiCarlo, 1964). It is said that a hard of hearing child (a) learns vocabulary and sentence structure more slowly or to a lesser extent than the normal hearing child (Berg, 1976, p. 312) and (b) understands most of what is said only under optimal conditions with or without the use of a hearing aid (Vernon & Mindel, 1971).

Furthermore, it seems that most hard of hearing classifications are made on the basis of audiometry alone (Davis & Silverman, 1970). Other considerations, such as social and emotional needs, communication ability, age of onset, previous training, intelligence, and environment, should also be taken into account when placement, planning, and implementation are being considered (Birch, 1975).

Incidence

The incidence of hearing impairment in the U.S. population has been difficult to measure because of the invisible nature of the handicap. Some recent estimations are available. Using 1980 U.S. Census Bureau results, and applying prevalence rates of Schein and Delk (1974), the Office of Demographic Studies (1980) offers these estimates:

14 640 000 hearing impaired individuals

7 175 000 individuals with significant bilateral loss

1 936 000 deaf persons

450 000 prevocationally deaf persons

222 000 prelingually deaf persons

An estimated 370 000 children (Moores & Maestas y Moores, in press) may need careful consideration or additional services because of a hearing impairment. It has been reported that approximately 5% of the school-age population have undetected mild losses that would require medical intervention and that 3% have significant hearing losses that may interfere with academic achievement.

Although it is difficult to determine precisely how hearing loss affects academic achievement, it is clear that students with differing degrees of hearing loss will, in all probability, function quite differently from each other. They will evidence differences in speech intelligibility, channels used in gathering information, social interactions, communication patterns, and behavioral mannerisms.

Two factors affecting the perceived variability of estimates of hearing loss among studies are that those children with fluctuating losses due to ear infections and allergies are not counted among the handicapped population, and that some very mild losses and unilateral losses are not detected by the schools. In addition, variability among survey designs, identification procedures, test environment, calibration of audiometric equipment, student interest, and the qualifications of personnel administering the tests must be taken into consideration when attempting to determine the incidence rates of hard of hearing and deaf children (Alpiner, 1971).

Causes of Hearing Impairment

Five major causes of childhood deafness have been identified in the literature: heredity, maternal rubella, prematurity, meningitis, and mother-child blood incompatibility (Ries, 1979; Vernon, 1968; Hudgins, 1973). It is possible to estimate from various sources that approximately 33% to 50% of hearing impaired children have deafness caused by heredity, 5% to 7% by meningitis, and for approximately 30%, the cause is unknown. Percentages associated with maternal rubella, mother-child blood incompatibility, and prematurity are unknown, according to Moores (1978). A more recent study reports that 22% is due to maternal rubella, 11% to heredity, 12% to other childhood diseases and infections, 19% to other birth and pregnancy complications, and 34% to unknown causes (Karchmer et al., 1979).

Most studies show that 20% to 40% of hearing impaired children and youth, as a group, have additional disabilities. The distribution of these problems depends to some extent on the cause of the loss. In rubella children, almost half have cardiac defects and about one-third have visual problems; about 20% are of below average intelligence. Meningitis as a cause of deafness is associated with a high rate of mental retardation (Gentile & McCarthy, 1973). One school survey showed that one-third of all deaf children had significant visual problems (Pollard & Neumaur, 1974).

Communication and Cultural Patterns

The means a hearing impaired individual uses in communication with others is determined by a number of conditions. Among these are preference of the family, friends, and those in the school setting and the degree of the individual's hearing loss. Oral methods, manual methods, or a

combination of these can be used. Although many programs emphasize oral training and methods exclusively, an increasing majority of programs and individuals working with deaf students in the United States prefer some form of manual methods. The philosophy increasingly being accepted is that in an educational setting the most effective combination of methods should be used.

Various methods of manual communication include (a) Signed English, in its varying degrees of purity, where the signs have a more or less one-to-one correspondence with English; (b) the Rochester Method, which uses the manual alphabet to fingerspell all words; and (c) American Sign Language (ASL or Ameslan), a language in its own right that is substantially different in character and structure from spoken language but that shares many signs with Signed English.

Among many deaf persons, ASL, or a mix of ASL and Signed English, is the preferred means of communication, and many deaf children of deaf parents grow up with ASL as their native language. Although ASL is a very efficient means of communication, it is not a written language and thus native "speakers" of ASL are placed at a disadvantage in learning written English. Since many deaf native ASL users do not share a common native language with the hearing society in which they live, the development of a separate deaf culture having different mores, attitudes, and perceptions from the predominant hearing culture is encouraged. Detailed descriptions of these differences are not possible here, but the teacher of the deaf student needs to be aware that *some* deaf students will tend to interact with the hearing society in much the same way as a member of a cultural minority.

Differences of Perspective

The idea of schemata, as used by researchers in reading, information processing, and cognitive psychology, can be useful in understanding how the thinking patterns of the hearing impaired person can differ from those of the hearing person. All information gathered by an individual through the senses is organized and stored in the brain. The connections, or associations, between elements of this information constitutes a structure called a schema, used here in the broad sense. The way an individual organizes these networks of associations, or schemata, may depend on the kind of information available, the context in which it is obtained, and previous schemata established by the individual.

The well-known story of the blind men and the elephant is illustrative of this viewpoint. In learning about an elephant, one man felt its tail and decided an elephant was much like rope. Another felt its leg and decided the animal was similar to a tree. Still another felt the side and thought an elephant to be like a wall. The schema associated with the concept of an

elephant for each of these men was different, a function of their different experiences.

In the same way, all of us have had different experiences and, to some extent, have built different kinds of schemata. The deaf person's experience and information are vastly different from those of a hearing person in both type and character, especially if the deaf person was born deaf. Ways in which a deaf person organizes that information may differ greatly. From this perspective, it should not be surprising that the attitudes, views, and knowledge of deaf persons can be substantially different from those of hearing persons. The hearing person who wishes to interact with deaf people needs to be open and accepting of any such major differences, just as the deaf person needs to be aware and accepting of the differences in the hearing person.

Emotional/Behavioral Problems in Deaf Children

Although a number of different attempts have been made to assess the prevalence of hearing impaired children and youth who have "an educationally significant emotional/behavioral problem," no clear-cut answer is presently available. This is thought to be true because of different methods, different definitions, and surveys focused on a variety of large and small groups. However, it has been estimated that emotional/ behavioral problems are from three to six times as common among deaf children as among hearing children (Meadow & Trybus, 1979). Teachers at a state residential school for the deaf described their disturbed students' behavior as (a) hyperactive lack of control (behavior that was impulsive, unreflective, and uninhibited), (b) anxious inhibition, and (c) preoccupation, descriptors related to immaturity (Reivich & Rothrock, 1972). In another study, it was concluded that deaf children described in school records as emotionally or behaviorally disturbed had a lower need for achievement and higher aggressiveness, anxiety, and hostile isolation. Additional handicapping conditions were related to significantly higher anxiety, academic disability, and hostile isolation. The presence of handicaps in addition to emotional disturbance appeared to be independent and additive so that those children in the second group were thought to have the most pathology (Goulder, 1976). It is believed that the shock most parents suffer on learning that their child is deaf leads to actions or inactions which make up an important factor in the development of emotional disorders in deaf children. Those around deaf children tend to react by not communicating with them. All our early feelings, understandings, appreciations, hopes, fears, anticipations, goals, values, and more are derived from our communication contexts. Deaf children can participate in communicating human emotions and transactions to the

degree that effective messages can be received and expressed in interacting with all of those who are important in their lives.

In summary, it is evident that a sizable number of schoolchildren have hearing problems. These problems may range from a mild loss to a profound one, and it behooves the teacher to be ever sensitive to communication problems in the classroom, school, and other related educational activities. This sensitivity needs to begin as early in the child's life as possible because the preschool years from birth to age 4 are considered extremely critical for language acquisition.

The causes of hearing impairment are important to know but perhaps not as important to know as *when* the deafness occurred. For those who are born with a hearing impairment, some or all of the opportunities to acquire a language base may be lost or, in the most favorable of circumstances, simply attenuated. For those whose loss occurs after language acquisition, the communication problem is much less severe. For the typical elementary and secondary school teacher, the vigilance necessary to detect and try to deal in appropriate ways with communication and behavioral problems as early as possible cannot be relaxed as more and more hearing impaired students are being placed among the other students. The amount and kinds of available support services will vary considerably, and those classroom teachers will need to exert their utmost in seeking creative ways to help these worthy children.

TEACHING THE HEARING IMPAIRED STUDENT

The goal of any educational program is to help students grow toward more efficient and effective functioning as individuals in society. When we consider the societal roles of handicapped individuals, the ideas of adequate functioning or minimum functioning frequently arise. Recent attempts to ensure adequate functioning of individuals in our society have been made by many state and local education authorities through the mandating of programs of minimum competencies or basic skills. These activities have had their effects on programs for handicapped children. Florida recently adopted a program of minimum education competencies and developed lists of them by age level for hearing impaired students. Although such lists can be quite useful in defining school programs, they carry with them several dangers. These include losing the overall perspective of the curriculum, teaching to specific limited objectives, and the overall lowering, not raising, of the levels of expectation for the majority of students. Programs for such handicapped groups as the hearing impaired are especially susceptible to these dangers, and they need to be carefully avoided.

Developing Literacy

Helping the student toward literacy is another way of expressing the

goal of educational programs, that is, helping the student become a well-rounded, educated individual able to establish and achieve realistic life goals. A balanced program needs to work toward verbal, visual, social, and mathematical literacy.

Verbal literacy. Verbal literacy is the ability to understand and use written and nonwritten language effectively. Hearing impaired students often have great difficulty with written language, since it is based on a spoken language that they cannot hear and have not learned from experience as hearing children have. The ability to use and understand written English is often determined in large part by the age at which a child becomes deaf. Those who are born deaf or become deaf before they begin to talk find learning a written language much more difficult. Those who become deaf later, say at about 10 or 12 when written language skills have been well developed, find their reading and writing skills little affected. Because the development of written language skills is a difficult task, the school program needs to emphasize English and language skills at every opportunity. All teachers of the hearing impaired must be teachers of language, whether they are English teachers or mathematics teachers. Consistent emphasis on effective verbal expression throughout the school experience by all professionals involved can greatly aid these students in overcoming their language difficulty and lead them toward verbal literacy.

Another dilemma now arises. Where is the appropriate balance between language instruction and, for example, mathematics instruction to be struck? An emphasis on language will not necessarily reduce the amount of time devoted to mathematics. However, it is possible to emphasize language instruction to such an extent that the amount of time devoted to mathematics is significantly reduced and student achievement suffers. This may be the situation in many programs for hearing impaired students at the primary level (cf. Johnson, 1976). It is desirable that a balance be set where instruction in language and other areas is complementary and the student achieves at an optimum level in all areas.

Visual literacy. Visual literacy is an often overlooked aspect of school programs. *Visual literacy* refers to a group of vision competencies a human being can develop by seeing and at the same time having and integrating other sensory experiences. The development of these competencies is fundamental to normal human learning; they enable visually literate persons to discriminate and interpret the visual actions, objects, or symbols that they encounter in their environment. Through the creative use of these competencies, they are able to communicate with others (Williams & Debes, 1970). Since, for the hearing impaired person, the majority of sensory input for communication purposes is through the visual channels, the development of effective visual means to communicate is especially

important. This includes the receiving and interpreting of visual information as well as the visual expression of ideas (Williams & Debes, 1970). It is entirely possible that in this area certain deaf students may be even more literate than their teacher, and the teacher should be open for opportunities to learn from the student. The development of an effective visual communication of ideas is an important and necessary skill for the teacher of any hearing impaired student. The use of manipulative materials that embody concepts to be taught and the use of diagrams illustrating the important relationships encountered can increase the effectiveness of classroom instruction for all students, not only the hearing impaired. These materials can, at the same time, help hearing impaired students develop their own ability to express themselves effectively in visual modalities (Skemp, 1971).

Social literacy. Social literacy can be defined as a person's ability to understand the social behavior of others and to control one's behavior to the extent that it is acceptable to others and will achieve the person's social goals. Deaf children may exhibit negative social behavior that could be considered immature, hyperkinetic, autistic, egocentric, and so on. This behavior "may be attributed to unsatisfactory environmental conditions that developed because a child's parents were not helped to adjust to the fact of deafness and therefore did not provide the child sufficient environmental support to develop to his or her potential" (Moores, 1978, p. 142). Because the majority of parents of deaf children are hearing and know little about deafness, they are often afraid and not able to deal with the situation very well. Communication between the parent and the hearing impaired child is greatly reduced from normal. Normal two-way communication between parent and child may not exist (Moores, 1978). Since the child is deprived of normal social interactions with other children and adults, the social sense is affected.

Neither the school program nor the teacher must overlook this aspect of the child's development. Opportunities need to be afforded for interaction with other children—both hearing and hearing impaired children. Teachers need to give students continuous positive and supportive feedback regarding their social behaviors. Deaf adults are invaluable as models in this respect. The difficulty of communication between hearing and hearing impaired individuals will continually give rise to social misunderstandings. The hearing impaired student must learn to appreciate this problem and learn to deal with the resulting frustration. The hearing teacher of hearing impaired students must learn not to overreact to negative behaviors but patiently guide the student toward more socially acceptable ones. The hearing teacher also must learn to accept communication difficulties with deaf students patiently and not avoid meaningful

conversation with them. This frequently requires hard work and a great deal of time. The teacher could do nothing as important as opening and maintaining communication channels with the hearing impaired student.

Mathematical literacy. The inclusion of mathematics as one of the foundation subjects of any education program is based on the fact that mathematics, including its tools and the development of the cognitive skills necessary to be successful in it, contributes significantly to the effective functioning of any individual in society. Mathematics helps one to understand the world by helping a person build appropriate schemata with which to understand his or her perceptions. Mathematics provides the computational skills without which no one can independently perform many daily tasks or function in a wide variety of occupations. The study of mathematics provides the student with valuable problem-solving skills that can be brought to bear on many situations requiring careful analysis.

Specifically, a typical set of goals for school mathematics is given by Johnson and Rising (1967):

- The student knows and understands concepts such as mathematical processes, facts, or principles;
- The student understands the logical structure of mathematics and the nature of proof;
- The student performs computations with understanding, accuracy, and efficiency;
- The student has the ability to solve problems;
- The student develops attitudes and appreciations which lead to curiosity, initiative, confidence, and interests; and
- The student learns how to develop proper methods of learning mathematics and communicating mathematics, and also develops study habits essential for independent progress. (pp. 12–14)

The goals of school mathematics involve much more than computation.

When considering these goals for students with physical or other handicapping conditions that tend to slow progress through formal school experiences, priorities must be set to determine the directions and emphasis of the program for the time available. For the deaf, as for other handicapped groups, decisions have generally been made toward the social curriculum, as indicated by Glennon in an earlier chapter. Along with this decision go all the listed disadvantages. For some hearing impaired students this can lead to the tragedy of unfulfilled potential. Unlike students who are mentally retarded or those with serious learning disabilities, the intellectual abilities for superior achievement can be present in the student with a hearing impairment. These abilities may be relatively untapped, partly because of the low expectations of educators. The teacher of deaf students needs to guard constantly against unjustifiably lowering the goals for the

students and yet balance that with realistic expectations that will not frustrate students with continual failure. The teacher's expectations for students are very important. On the one hand it is easy to underestimate the levels of achievement that hearing impaired students can attain. On the other hand, unrealistically high expectations can lead to frustration and discouragement for both the student and the teacher. A realistic setting of goals and priorities is a critical need when teaching the hearing impaired. Too often when the educational programs for deaf students are outlined, the only goal of the mathematics program that receives emphasis is computation. To limit these students' progress to computation without appropriate attention to the other five areas is, in most cases, to expect too little of them.

Understanding and Learning

Earlier in this chapter the idea of a schema was introduced to help characterize how the thinking of hearing and hearing impaired individuals can differ. Although these networks of associations differ as well from individual to individual, they can be similar enough to allow for communication, the sharing of common experiences, and an understanding of another person's logical analyses. The development of similar schemata to allow these interactions and understandings to occur must be a prime concern of education.

Learning can be thought of as the development and modification of schemata. Understanding could be defined as the incorporation of a limited abstract concept into a larger, more general schema. When this happens we say that we understand the concept because we can relate it to other remembered experiences and associations. In using the idea of schemata as a model for the way humans organize and use sensory data, we have a valuable means of characterizing what happens in classroom learning and how the classroom learning experience of the hearing impaired student differs from that of the hearing student.

Schemata and Learning Mathematics

Any stimulus coming to the brain must either be ignored or processed. If the information is processed, then it must be attached to an existing schema, incorporated into a modified schema, used with other information to build a new schema, or stored as an unrelated piece of information (a one-point schema).

The process of attaching information to an existing schema is sometimes called *assimilation* (Skemp, 1971). A child who is first learning subtraction as a missing addend problem is attempting to relate the concept of subtraction to addition; the subtraction schema is being tied to the addition schema. If Amanda has a well-developed schema ("understands"

addition), this process should improve her understanding (broaden her schema) of subtraction. She is *assimilating* the concept of subtraction as a missing addend situation.

The modification of an existing schema is called *accommodation*. If Mark has been exposed to the concept of number only in the discrete sense, then the thinking of number in the continuous sense will require an accommodation of the original schema. Points in the curriculum at which a schema needs to be modified will be trouble spots, since accommodation is a much more difficult process than assimilation. The individual will try any means possible to assimilate information before accommodation will occur. Examples of transitions often required are—

1. the discrete use of number to the continuous use of number as in measurement;
2. whole numbers to fractions and mixed numbers;
3. extension of the whole numbers to the integers;
4. arithmetic to algebra, algebra to geometry, and the beginning of calculus.

The goal of instruction should be to encourage the development of schemata that will require a minimum of accommodation for future learning to take place. The child who is taught that a larger number can never be subtracted from a smaller number is being encouraged to limit subtraction only to whole number instances. At that stage the child is not applying subtraction to other situations, and so it would appear that no harm is being done. This is not true; when the child is asked later to apply subtraction to the subtraction of real numbers, where it is proper to subtract a larger number from a smaller, the child will need to accommodate the subtraction schema already built up. Attempts to assimilate the new schema and not accommodate the original schema will lead to a variety of errors in applying subtraction to these situations and lead to a difficulty in understanding the meaning of the positive and negative signs describing the numbers. Teachers seldom see the results of their oversimplification because the problems often occur long after they are no longer teaching the student or because the cause of a difficulty is not readily apparent.

Possibly the development of the faulty subtraction schema could be obviated if we would carefully avoid structuring teaching experiences that might lead students to the impression that subtraction, as a mathematical operation, can only be applied to whole number situations. Certainly, we should never state directly that subtraction is so limited. It should be obvious that such considerations in designing instruction require that the teacher possess an understanding of mathematics far beyond what is being taught to the students. Students can develop inappropriate schemata even without misinformation and misguidance. Also the accommodation of an

existing schema can be the key to great strides in learning and insight. But the overcoming of some previously developed inappropriate schema is a difficult task often requiring a great deal of instructional time and student experience. When it is possible to ensure the development of an appropriate schema, the learning process is greatly facilitated.

The development of such appropriate schemata by the student needs to be the major concern of the teacher in teaching mathematics. If a schema is appropriate, it must (a) allow assimilation of concepts to be learned later, (b) be connected to applicable situations, (c) incorporate previously developed related schemata, and (d) be tied to appropriate stimuli so as to allow for retrieval at appropriate times.

Consider several approaches to the teaching of some early concepts of fractions:

1. Use paper strips, all of the same length, divided into equal divisions with certain numbers of these divisions shaded.

2. Use circular regions divided into equal sectors with certain numbers of the sectors shaded.

3. Use sets of objects divided into equivalent subsets and consider a group of these subsets.

4. Use a number line, with endpoints labeled 0 and 1, divided into equal segments and naming specific points on the line.

5. Use a combination of approaches (1–4 above).

Which of these approaches is "best"? To make a decision, each approach should be evaluated on each of the four criteria. Which do you consider "best"?

The use of the four criteria to evaluate a variety of approaches to the teaching of a mathematical concept can become quite complex. Often the result of such evaluations will not result in a clear-cut "best" approach. The teacher will be required to make a judgment in terms of the background and need of the students. Although it may not be either possible or practical for a classroom teacher to evaluate completely all approaches to the teaching of each concept, considering the four criteria will help make instruction more effective. These four criteria can be summarized by the following questions:

1. Does the selected approach conflict with what the student will need to learn later?

2. How will the student use this concept later? Does the approach assist the student to apply it?

3. How does the approach relate to what the student already knows? How is the approach consistent with approaches used before?

4. How easy will the concept be to remember using the approach? If

the student forgets the concept, can it be reconstructed from related concepts?

Consulting these questions when designing instruction should help raise red flags for inappropriate methods. For example, the approach of teaching multiplication by drilling the facts and teaching the algorithms would be questioned under these criteria. Teaching transposition initially as a way of simplifying equations is another technique that would appear to be of doubtful value under the criteria. If the teacher considers these issues in instructional design, the student's development of appropriate schemata could be facilitated.

A student can learn an unrelated concept or an idea in total isolation. The process of changing quarts to gallons by dividing the number of quarts by 4 is one example. This can be taught easily and quickly. However, the student will forget it just as quickly, since there is no schema to which to relate the process; it is difficult to recall one or a myriad of isolated processes. A better approach is always to have the student relate the process to other familiar processes. The conversion of quarts to gallons can be related to the general regrouping process where units are changed to groups and groups to units by a specific conversion factor. Into this larger schema of regrouping, numeration and all measurement conversions, both customary and metric, fall as specific cases. The student needs to remember only the one process of changing from units to groups or groups to units and the specific conversion factor to recall how to do any specific conversion. Teaching unrelated concepts is neither efficient nor effective.

One question might cross the reader's mind at this point. Some students who are taught with methods that have been questioned in this section may still learn mathematics very well. If the consideration of the issues related to schemata is so important in designing instruction, why have students learned in the past? One explanation is that some students have a wide variety of relevant, real-world experiences on which to base mathematics learning. They also are very good at constructing their own schemata, testing them for appropriateness, and accommodating them if they do not stand up against the test. These are the students who are "good in mathematics." They learn in spite of the instruction. Students without these experiences and without these abilities are those that "do not have a mathematical mind." They "can't do mathematics." These are the students who are hurt most by inappropriate, incorrect instruction. These are the students who will benefit most from carefully designed instruction.

Learning, Understanding, and the Hearing Impaired

One can now look at the classroom learning of deaf students and begin to understand what kind of learning problems they might experience and

why they experience them. Consider 13-year-old Jon, who has been deaf from birth. His parents, like many hearing parents of deaf children, were at a loss on how to deal with their son's handicap. Jon's hearing loss was not discovered until he was about 2 1/2, and at that time professional help was sought. He lived at home and attended special classes in the public school until he was 10; then his parents sent him to a special school for the deaf. His home life was very sheltered and dull. Much of the time he sat watching television, observing things he had never experienced; without the audio portion of the programming, he could not relate these things to his life. His parents did not allow him to play outside without continuous supervision by an adult or hearing children because they were afraid that since he could not hear the horns of approaching cars or other danger signals, he might be injured. In school, much of Jon's instruction was aimed at teaching him to speak and read a language he had never heard—words that were hardly more than bewildering symbols on a page.

Much of Jon's mathematics instruction involved the use of a workbook or textbook exercises. These exercises required a specific answer that seemed to be derived by following specific procedures illustrated by examples given by the teacher and included at the beginning of each section in the book. His hearing impairment deprived him of much of the incidental learning of abstract and vicarious information that constitutes a major portion of the real learning of students who can hear the radio and television, the stories and experiences of their parents and friends, and the comments of strangers on the street.

Of course he saw the world differently from his hearing peers, since all information received by any individual is perceived and interpreted using the schemata already acquired. So the kinds and degrees of information that Jon received were very different from his hearing peers. This does not mean that all of the schemata built up in school or life experiences by a deaf student are wrong or inappropriate, only different. Indeed some schemata built up by such students may enable them to perceive the world more realistically than other persons coming to a situation with a variety of preconceived notions acquired by hearsay and from inaccurate information.

In school, then, deaf students can be much more affected by what a teacher does than by what that teacher says. Deaf students build up conceptions of the purpose of a given educational exercise and the importance of various school activities by observing what the teacher does and observing the context of the experience. It is easier to build up misconceptions of what learning is and how one is supposed to learn when those learning experiences are not moderated by more abstract, verbal guidance. When students are subjected to learning primarily by having them imitate examples and fill in blanks or do short-answer exercises, it is natural

for some to feel that completing the pages in a workbook and following examples is learning. If the pages are completed, learning has happened and there may be no reason to repeat forgotten concepts because the important thing was covering the pages. Students may also take this position to mask their frustration at not understanding the concepts in the first place. A student who has all the prerequisite understandings necessary to do a problem but has not been given an example may say he or she cannot attempt the problem.

It should become obvious that such problems as (a) a lack of persistence in working through difficult problems or attempting to discover new relationships, (b) an inability to apply what has been learned to life situations, (c) an inability to transfer old learning to new, (d) poor study habits, (e) an inability to remember what has been learned for more than a few days, hours, or minutes, and (f) a tendency to have the learning of one skill interfere with what has previously been learned should not be unusual with deaf students. We should note that many of these problems are not unusual among hearing students. The spouting of verbal platitudes by a teacher does not always overcome inappropriate learning experiences. Hearing students pick up the same behavioral signals as deaf students, but, perhaps because of the possibility of their having more opportunities with which schemata about school and learning can be developed and used, their further learning is not as much affected.

How can a reasonable number of these problems for hearing impaired students be decreased in their negative effects? (a) By good, well-conceived, and well-designed school experiences not much different from those appropriate for all students; (b) by taking into consideration the kinds of previous experiences in and out of school that students have had and thus building on the schemata they have set up; (c) by providing them with life experiences or substitutes for those they have probably missed that are important bases of school concepts; and (d) by providing them with opportunities to apply what was learned to new situations accompanied by rich opportunities for discussion playing with the "big" ideas of human thought.

Language Structure

The teacher needs to be aware that certain linguistic structures appear to cause hearing impaired students some difficulty. Rudner (1978) lists the following:

- Conditionals (if, when)
- Comparatives (greater than, most)
- Negatives (not, without, answer not given)
- Inferentials (should, could, because, since)

- Low-information pronouns (it, something)
- Lengthy passages

During instruction, when using text material, or in testing, the teacher needs to realize that these kinds of structures may pose problems and either try to avoid them or assist the student in dealing with them.

Evaluation

An essential part of any educational program is the evaluation of learning. This evaluation can be used for placement, diagnosis, or assessment. The evaluation of the knowledge and achievement of deaf and hearing impaired students involves serious problems that can affect both the validity and reliability of the instruments and procedures used.

The language structure and vocabulary difficulties outlined earlier contribute to the difficulty and possible misinterpretation of any verbal form of evaluation, whether written, spoken, or signed. Frequently it appears that hearing impaired students do not understand some concept or are not able to apply a concept because they have performed poorly on test items. Had the item been adequately designed and communicated to the students, they might have been able to demonstrate successful acquisition of the concept.

Care must be taken here not to fall into a form of language discrimination. At times a student is not able to perform the school tasks requested by the teacher within the context of the teacher's language. There is often the temptation to decide that the student has not understood the instruction or is unable to perform the task under any socially *important* situations, even if the teacher sees the student adequately perform in a more familiar context, such as through the use of ASL. Indeed, if the student cannot perform a task in the context of the prevailing language, there is cause for concern. The problem, however, is not a conceptual or a cognitive problem as much as it is a language/cultural problem. The difficulty may have nothing to do with the student's ability to learn mathematical concepts or to reason logically.

Diagnostic Testing

The past misdiagnosis and institutionalization of deaf individuals as mentally ill or retarded because they did not develop adequate language has led to a hesitancy to diagnose a deaf student as having any kind of learning disorder, from retardation to learning disability. Since some of the causes of deafness and some of the causes of various forms of retardation and learning disabilities are thought to be the same—for example, rubella, disease with high fever, or birth defects—it should be suspected that the proportion of individuals with learning problems in addition to their

deafness is higher than it is in the general population (cf. Karchmer et al., 1979).

Although it is known that a hearing impaired child's chances of having additional handicaps that affect learning are greater than those of a hearing child, the ability to diagnose such problems in a hearing impaired child is limited. It is difficult to determine whether faulty responses are due to such a problem or due to poor communication, lack of relevant experience, and inadequate previous instruction. Only through long-term experience with a child—experience involving a knowledge of the child's learning environment and the child's reactions to that environment—can the existence of definite learning disabilities or retardation be suspected. Fortunately, the general kinds of remediation suggested for children with learning problems, such as small-group instruction or tutoring and the use of manipulative materials, are also the approaches that can be effective in helping the hearing impaired child. Only when the treatment becomes very specific for a learning disability should caution be especially indicated lest time and money be wasted and the expectation of the student's achievement be lowered.

With these general comments, let us look at some considerations specific to the different uses of evaluation as related to mathematics. As hearing impaired students move from one program to another and as they are considered for placement in regular school programs, some form of testing occurs. Extreme care must be exercised to avoid misinterpreting placement tests. Usually with hearing students it is possible to sample items from across the mathematics curriculum and get a pretty good idea where to place a student. With the hearing impaired student, however, these patterns do not necessarily match. Because of experiential gaps and nontraditional previous school experiences, it is possible, for example, to find students who are excellent at computing with whole numbers using all four operations but who cannot tell time or, more frequently, do not seem to have a sense of time duration. Frequently a student can multiply both single and multidigit numbers well but cannot subtract.

When using testing and other evaluation procedures, care must be taken to consider the possibilities outlined earlier. A student's failure on first trial might be caused by misunderstanding or a lack of experiences, not a lack of understanding of the mathematical knowledge involved. For diagnostic purposes, a one-on-one testing situation is usually preferable to group testing so that the test administrator can observe the student's responses. Also, the student can be asked questions at the appropriate times to evaluate the tester's conclusions. When a student has already been tested extensively by a diagnostic specialist, the teacher doing additional diagnostic work in mathematics needs to be aware of these earlier tests and try to make sensible use of the diagnostic information already available.

Achievement Testing

Most often students are placed in testing situations for the purpose of measuring their progress. The instrument can be either a standardized or a teacher-made test. The standardized achievement test most frequently used with hearing impaired students is the Stanford Achievement Test. This is the only one of its type to have a special edition for the hearing impaired (Office of Demographic Studies, 1974). The version for the hearing impaired was developed from the original by revising the norms, the instructions, and the conditions under which the testing occurs. In addition, a screening test was developed that uses language level instead of age to determine what level of test is to be given.

Unfortunately, the items on the Stanford Achievement Test have not been revised on the hearing impaired versions. This may result in the same kinds of language structure and vocabulary problems and, to some extent, a form of cultural bias as would be a problem with any test standardized on hearing children. The revised norms do allow for some comparisons among hearing impaired students and with hearing students. There is a question, however, whether hearing and hearing impaired scores can be compared, since there could be questions on the construct validity of some items on the mathematics tests for the hearing impaired.

Considering all this, scores for hearing impaired students on standardized achievement tests do need to be interpreted with a great deal of caution and understanding. Even more caution needs to be exercised when using such scores to compare individual students. The Stanford Achievement Test—H.I. (for the hearing impaired), while an improvement, does not alleviate all these problems, and any decisions about students or evaluations or programs based solely on such scores should be discouraged.

All these problems and issues are compounded when it comes to teacher-constructed classroom tests. Of special concern should be the writing of one test for use with both hearing and hearing impaired students—such as in classrooms where hearing impaired students are mainstreamed. When writing a test, teachers make assumptions about students' schemata. These schemata involve the students' knowledge of test taking, which is often called test-taking ability, the concept schemata built up during classroom instruction, and the schemata relating to their general experience base.

Some hearing impaired students may have quite limited knowledge of test taking. They tend to determine the kind of response wanted on a test item by looking at the entire set of items. Changing item type within a section, such as multiple choice, short answer, essay, drawing responses, and the solving of problems, can cause difficulty. Many students ignore the directions for each section of the test and guess what the response type

should be. For example, an algebra student who is given a set of equations and asked which ones have a solution might instead attempt to solve each equation in the set. If the test items are not exactly like the homework problems, difficulties are more likely. This is not to say that various kinds of test items should not be presented or that they should not deviate from the homework format. Indeed, this problem may have been created by teachers attempting to avoid the need to read directions on tests in the first place. But the teacher does need to be aware of potential problems of test administration and phrase directions simply and carefully, use a language structure that the students can understand, and then check on the students frequently during the test to be sure they understand what they should be doing.

Students, especially hearing impaired children, need to experience testing situations in the classroom and be taught how to handle them. Also the valid and reliable evaluation of hearing impaired students requires that more than one form of evaluation be used. The teacher constantly needs to question the assessment processes to avoid, as much as possible, the misinterpretation of evaluation results. The complete process should involve consistent observation of the student at work, clinical interviews with the students about what is being learned, and continuous evaluation of homework errors, not only the number correct or the number wrong. If the classroom teacher has this broad view of the assessment of students' progress and is sensitive to the specific kinds of language and experience-based problems that hearing impaired students are likely to have, the chances of misevaluation can be greatly reduced.

Many questions of how to construct tests and evaluate the performance of hearing impaired students have not been answered, and many problems of the validity and reliability of evaluation measures remain unresolved. The watchword in the use of any kind of evaluation tool must be caution. Decisions must be made and programs evaluated. If many sources for evaluative information are considered, the chance of serious mistakes can be minimized.

Deaf Students in a Hearing Classroom

With the implementation of PL 94-142, more and more hearing impaired students are being placed in classrooms with hearing peers. Although under certain circumstances mainstreaming can be beneficial for both handicapped and nonhandicapped students, the mainstreaming of the hearing impaired can be more difficult than the mainstreaming of students with other handicaps.

Often the classroom teacher will be able to look for help to a resource teacher assigned to the hearing impaired students. This resource teacher may be responsible for monitoring the achievement of the deaf student and

providing supplementary instructional assistance and diagnostic services. It is necessary that the classroom teacher carefully observe the student and provide as much information as possible to the resource teacher. In many programs the resource teacher will be able to see the student only once a week. This is hardly sufficient time to give substantial assistance, and in these situations, the brunt of the diagnosis, remediation, and instructional planning and implementation is the responsibility of the classroom teacher no matter how ill prepared he or she is for the task.

The typical classroom teacher within a departmental setting may be responsible for more than 100 students daily. This does not allow time for much individual planning for students with special needs. Even in this kind of situation, however, there are procedures teachers can follow that will greatly assist the hearing impaired student and often improve the overall effectiveness of the instruction for all students in the class.

1. *Provide opportunities for individualization.* When data have been gathered about students' special needs, it should become clear that they will have specific weaknesses or gaps in their understanding of mathematics that need to be accommodated. Providing them the opportunity to study the topics they need to ensure that prerequisites for learning are met is critical. Also, learning techniques and materials that prove effective for them are extremely important. Practically, this cannot mean an entirely unique approach for each student in a class, but it does suggest the provision of a significant and sufficient variety and choice within the instruction program. Sources such as the NCTM Yearbook *Organizing for Mathematics Instruction* (1977) can be quite helpful in this regard.

2. *Use diagnostic-prescriptive teaching approaches.* It is necessary to have some basis on which to individualize instruction. Formal and specialized diagnosis of learning problems and special needs may be beyond the time available as well as beyond the training of the typical classroom teacher. If so, it is possible that services can be provided through the other professionals in the school organization. The classroom teacher can, however, do a good deal of informal evaluation, primarily in terms of instructional and conceptual prerequisites. The teacher can collect assessment information through the use of written tests, conversations with the student, and observation of the student in class and then ask questions such as the following, based on the information collected:

- Does the student have the prerequisite concepts necessary to understand the approach the teacher plans to use? (It should be remembered from previous discussions that hearing impaired students are likely to have a number of conceptual and procedural gaps in their background.)

- Does the student have the necessary relevant experiences in the real world from which to understand the applications and examples of the instruction? (Remember the restricted environment of the hearing impaired child.)
- Can the student tolerate an indirect instructional approach? (The hearing impaired student tends to need more structure in the instructional situation and also needs to know the context of instruction.)
- How well does the student understand various forms of communication in instruction? (The teacher needs continually to seek feedback from the student to discover if meaningful and accurate communication is occurring.)

The teacher must teach with a diagnostic frame of mind, continually adjusting the instruction on the basis of feedback from the students. With hearing impaired students, where communication is probably difficult, a special effort needs to be made so that such communication attempts are not avoided but instead facilitated.

3. *Provide real-world experiences and examples.* Students need to see how the mathematical concepts they are learning relate to life situations with which *they are familiar.* Unfamiliar examples serve to enhance an abstract concept little more than drill and practice without any application. If hearing impaired students are expected to apply what they have learned to real life, this direct or indirect application must be explicitly taught to them in the classroom. They cannot be expected always to see the life connections with school learning by themselves.

4. *Teach all instances of a concept.* Frequently a teacher gives instruction in a concept, such as subtraction, by demonstrating one way in which that concept is used—for instance, demonstrating subtraction with the "take away" use. Later the students are expected to know how to apply the operation of subtraction in a comparison situation. Usually, they won't understand that subtraction is the appropriate operation, since the situation is completely different. They have a limited schema for subtraction that includes only "take away." Specific instruction is needed to extend their subtraction schema to situations involving *comparison, missing addend,* and *how many more.* For an excellent description of the various situations in which mathematical concepts are used, see Kennedy (1975).

Discrete and continuous uses for the operations should not be overlooked. In a geometry class, relatively high-level and successful hearing impaired students were presented with a line segment of a given length and were also given the length of one part of it. Not one student in the class could determine the length of the other part. All these students were

competent in the use of subtraction with whole numbers, fractions, and decimals, and they appeared to understand the problem. It was presented with a clear diagram. They evidently had not had sufficient practice with subtraction using continuous quantities like those found in measurement problems.

5. *Include all three levels of abstraction.* It has been suggested that all new learning must proceed through three stages: *concrete, iconic* (pictorial), and *symbolic* (Bruner, 1960). Concrete representations of concepts using manipulative materials—the necessary first stage of any learning, according to Bruner—may be necessary for the formation of appropriate and useful schemata. The gradual movement from using concrete devices, such as colored rods, multibase blocks, counters, chips, and so forth, to the symbolic stages of computation needs great care. It is very possible for students to use concrete materials when first learning to multiply, then diagrams, and finally numerals alone and from these experiences to develop in their minds three different and, therefore, unrelated schemata. What they did with the counters they do not see as related to the numerals. This occurs most frequently when concrete materials are introduced after unsuccessful attempts have already been made to teach the student to compute. Early instruction moving through all three stages, with careful attention to the transition points, is very important.

With hearing impaired students these considerations are of utmost importance. It is possible that concrete materials can be of help in reducing some of the differences between the teacher's and the students' schemata. Of course many students do learn mathematics without going through all the likely formal classroom instruction stages, but a case can be made that those students have had experiences in real life that have allowed them to understand and develop useful learning schemata. To assume that this will be true for most hearing impaired students is an open gate to an underprepared, inadequately planted, and unfertilized learning garden.

6. *Set the stage well.* Up to this point, the procedures suggested for use in classrooms for hearing impaired students are those that would enhance the learning of all students. A case can be made that the kind of mathematics instruction needed for the handicapped is little more than exemplary instruction in mathematics for any student. The hearing impaired student has additional special needs about which the classroom teacher needs to be aware. Most of these are obvious, but it is surprising how often they are overlooked.

Hearing impaired students need especially to be shown in some way the reasons for a lesson and its objectives. They benefit also if they can be shown how the particular lesson fits with the whole course. This is necessary in order to orient them to the instruction that is to take place. Additionally

it becomes more likely that any information lost in the communication during the lesson itself might be more easily filled in by them. A knowledge of the context of the lesson is important to enable them to recall or develop the appropriate schema for the lesson, which then can guide their perceptions. This may be the reason that for many hearing impaired students, discovery lessons can be more difficult and frustrating than for hearing students. Successful visual communication requires a knowledge of context. In American Sign Language, the order of concepts is designed to establish the context first, before the critical information is presented. Students look for that same organization in the classroom, and if they do not find it they may become frustrated and give up.

7. *Emphasize the language elements of instruction*. Language must be continually emphasized with the hearing impaired. "Every teacher is a teacher of language" is one of the guidelines of teachers of the hearing impaired, and for good reason. Since deaf and many hard of hearing students do not have the continuous input of spoken language, the amount of incidental learning time devoted to mathematics is minimal when compared to that of hearing children.

Facility with language helps pupils learn mathematical meanings, and conversely (Bruner, 1960). So, emphasis on language will aid not only the students' language skills but also their learning of mathematics. A point often overlooked is that when students are learning mathematics well, they will be improving their language skills also.

Several suggestions can be made that will assist hearing impaired students with language problems and not unduly affect the nature of instruction for other students.

Be aware of difficult language structures and use them with care. It is not necessarily helpful to avoid completely such structures as compound sentences, if-then forms, and so on. One needs to know, however, where difficulties could lie and be sure the student understands. If it is needed, provide a short explanation. What should be avoided is the continual use of such structures without testing the students' understanding and without providing the necessary assistance. Do not introduce too many difficult structures on the same day. A little practice is good. A flood of unfamiliar language can breed frustration. It is surprising how much teachers can adjust their use of language in the classroom to make it more appropriate for hearing impaired students without diminishing its effectiveness for the hearing students. In fact, it might be found that hearing students will also benefit.

Do not introduce new terms and words casually. When a new term is introduced to the class, be sure to write it clearly on the chalkboard, then write it phonetically, pronounce it carefully, and use it in a sentence. Give the students practice with the new terms as if they were words from a new

vocabulary list. Finally, in that same class period if possible, test for correct spelling and understanding of the word. Many mathematics teachers do not place this kind of emphasis on new vocabulary, but this emphasis would probably be helpful to both hearing and hearing impaired students.

8. *Emphasize visual communication.* Emphasizing visual communication means two things for the teacher in a mixed classroom. First it means trying to increase the amount of information that is communicated visually through an increased use of the chalkboard, overhead projector, bulletin boards, and gestures. Second, it means making communication easier for those who are taking in information primarily through sight. Several suggestions, which seem obvious, are often forgotten by teachers in the press of the classroom activity:

- Face the students whenever you are talking to them. (This is especially necessary when the student is not using an interpreter.)
- Time your speaking not to conflict with writing on the board or on the overhead projector, or at other times when the students' gaze needs to be directed to another place (as when the student is writing). This will require slowing the pace of instruction quite a bit at times. You should also direct the attention of the students.
- Seat the hearing impaired students where they can see the entire class at once, such as in the front corners of the usual seating arrangement. If the class is small enough, seating them in a semicircle is best. That way the special students can benefit from classroom discussion and questions.
- When a new person begins talking, direct the attention of the hearing impaired students toward that person. This can be done subtly and naturally through the movement of the eyes or head or another gesture toward the speaker. Other students in the class can also be of help in this way. This should make it much easier for the hearing impaired student to follow the discussion.

9. *Work with the notetaker or interpreter.* Some older hearing impaired students who are mainstreamed have the services of a notetaker or an interpreter supplied either by the school or another public agency. Much can be added to the effectiveness of these assistants if they have some direction from the teacher before the lesson. Preparing a list of technical terms that will be used during the class, providing an outline of the lesson, or scanning the notes after class can ensure that the hearing impaired student will be getting accurate information for study. In all cases, however, remember it is the hearing impaired student and not the interpreter or the notetaker who is being served.

DEVELOPING AND USING MATHEMATICAL CONCEPTS

The Stanford Achievement Test indicates that deaf students lag significantly behind in the acquisition of mathematical concepts. Why is the learning of mathematical concepts so difficult for them? Pendergrass and Hodges (1976) have suggested that this difficulty could be caused by their lack of relevant experiences and that these experiences need to be tied to the concepts to be learned in school. Others have suggested that deaf students have a rigidity of thought, which makes the generalization and abstraction process very difficult for them. Pendergrass and Hodges also suggest that deaf students need special training in asking information and seeking suggestions and opinions from others. However, Furth (1966) found that if concepts are directly taught to deaf students, then they can usually learn, use, and apply them.

Another consideration is that because of the different experiences deaf persons have, the concepts they develop will be connected in different ways, that is, the deaf will have different schemata. How do these schemata differ from those of the hearing person? One suggestion, which experience tends to bear out, is that deaf students tend to build narrower schemata, which incorporate fewer experiences and fewer concepts in a single structure. Recall from the previous section that to develop an appropriate schema, four things must happen. A schema must—

1. allow assimilation of later concepts;
2. be connected to applicable situations;
3. incorporate previously developed related schemata;
4. tie to appropriate stimuli for retrieval.

The question then becomes, How can the teacher of mathematics assist students in developing appropriate schemata? Another way of saying this is, How can the teacher of mathematics provide meaning in instruction?

Providing Focused Experiences

Among the ways a teacher of mathematics can provide experiences that will help the hearing impaired student develop these appropriate schemata would be to provide *focused* learning experiences. Active experiences in the classroom are necessary to fill experience gaps. Unfortunately, classroom experiences can only partially fill the gaps created by a lack of natural experiences—those occurring outside the school environment.

Care has been taken not to suggest that just any kind of classroom experiences or well-designed classroom experiences on a particular topic are sufficient to provide for the development of an appropriate schema. It is necessary that these classroom experiences be appropriately focused. For

example, consider a geoboard experience to develop the formula for the area of a parallelogram as it relates to the area of a rectangle (see Figure 8.1). Students work through a series of examples. It is easy for them to do this without focusing on the relevant variables—that is, that the height and the base are all the same, as is the area of the appropriate figure. As another

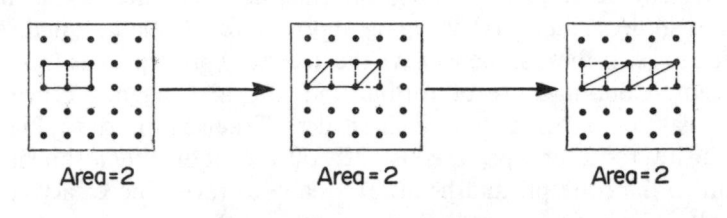

Figure 8.1. Geoboard presentation of the area of a rectangle and related parallelograms.

example, students can make all the necessary exchanges with base-10 arithmetic blocks for renaming without associating these exchanges with borrowing in subtraction. It is necessary for the teacher to focus the attention of the student on the important variables in any experience and to help the student tie to the concepts. For many hearing students it is possible to discover relationships and concepts. Discovery, however, may be quite difficult for most. Furth (1966) found this in his extensive studies of the deaf. In his experiment with transfer after attainment, he found that most subjects could not transfer concepts learned, perhaps because most attained these concepts by rote whereas hearing subjects sought some meaning in the original concept that aided them in transfer. Furth says that deaf students, "once taught concepts directly, can apply as well as hearing subjects" (p. 152). Furth and others have suggested that these patterns may result from past school and intellectual experiences of the deaf child caused by lower levels of communication with teachers, parents, and others.

What can be done? As early as possible, discovery and play experiences should be designed to stimulate the intellectual curiosity. Pendergrass and Hodges (1976) suggest that deaf students need special training in such questioning, information, and acquisition skills as how to ask for information, suggestions, and the opinions of others. The teacher, especially of older deaf students, faces the dilemma of either using discovery progress or using more directed approaches and not helping the students develop the intellectual skills and curiosity that can increase their learning effectiveness later. Here the teacher must strike a balance in approaches for the classroom that enables students to progress in the learning of mathematical ideas with minimal frustration but also does not overlook opportunities to help them become more intellectually alive and independent learners. The teacher needs to provide the necessary experiences for building concepts and to focus the students' attention on the

relevant attributes of those experiences, yet encourage them to seek relations and patterns of their own.

Checking for Prerequisites

Skemp (1971) emphasizes that mathematical concepts are usually built on previously developed concepts. Considering the difficulty that hearing impaired students have in developing appropriate schemata, it makes sense to check to see if these students have the necessary prerequisites for learning a concept. Continual use of formal and informal diagnostic evaluation within classroom instruction is in order. Teachers need to know the prerequisites for a concept, be constantly observant of students' behavior in relation to the concept, and be always ready to review necessary concepts and skills. Take, for example, in the teaching of long division, a student who does not understand regrouping for subtraction. This can easily happen because the student originally learned regrouping in subtraction by rote and thus cannot use subtraction in the new situation, even though he or she may be able to work the subtraction problem very appropriately and correctly when it is presented in the usual format. Gagné's (1963) use of task analysis and diagrams is a worthwhile exercise to help the teacher become sensitive to prerequisites even if it is not possible to do this all the time.

Not only *contact* prerequisites but also *developmental* prerequisites need to be considered. Implications of the work of Piaget and other developmental psychologists are that the child may not be ready to learn abstract concepts or even be ready to use concrete materials to learn. Although the particular stages of developmental readiness proposed by Piaget have been the basis of controversy, it would be well worthwhile, especially for the primary and lower elementary teacher, to be aware of these stages and their possible implications for instruction. (Much is written elsewhere on this topic; a good source for mathematics learning is Copeland, 1971.)

The sequencing of instruction is more critical with deaf students. If instructional sequences are not complete, hearing students can fill the gaps better than deaf students either from experience or through a discovery strategy. Often they are not even aware that there is a gap or that they are not understanding something.

This is illustrated by one deaf high school student who was completing the first year of algebra. The boy had done inconsistent work and was barely getting by. While working in a one-on-one situation with him, an instructor found that the student was not aware of the connection between fractional notation and division. Never having made this link, the student created two separate schemata—one for division and the other for working with rational expressions—never realizing they were the same. As a result, his schema for rational expressions was not efficient. He continually made

errors and did not understand the explanation of teachers when division was used to "clear up" his error with rational expressions. A short digression by the instructor resulted in substantial improvement and achievement. The boy saw that 1/2 is indeed the answer to 1 divided by 2, and that 2/4 is the answer to 2 divided by 4, which is, in both cases, 1/2, and finally that A divided by B is A over B. Practice to fix this task make it possible for him to incorporate the two schemata into one larger and more complete schema.

Any teacher can point to such situations, where identifying a previously unidentified gap in a student's knowledge and then providing instruction to remedy the situation have resulted in substantial gains. Mathematics teachers of the hearing impaired need to be alert for such problems, since they seem to occur frequently with these students.

Earlier it was mentioned that deaf people tend to create schemata different from those of hearing people. Since learning occurs when information (such as from a teacher, a book, or experience) is interpreted and incorporated through the use of a schema already constructed by the student, it is important for the teacher to be as familiar as possible with the student's schema. Failure to do this can result in the gaps or misunderstandings mentioned earlier.

One teacher of the deaf related how the topic of instruction for several days had been finding the volume of solids. One student did not seem to understand any explanation about volume but attempted all problems by rote. If any situation was even slightly different from an example given, the girl had no success. Finally, in desperation, the teacher asked her to give an example of volume. She promptly went to a nearby bookshelf and showed the teacher a volume of an encyclopedia.

This is an extreme example of where the schema of the teacher and that of the student did not match; no communication was possible until this problem was remedied. Similar problems can arise from such sources as specialized mathematical meanings of common words, misunderstood sentences, and differences in experiences. Teachers need to structure lessons so they receive frequent feedback from their students, not only on whether an answer is correct, but also on how the student is thinking about a problem situation. For hearing impaired students working with hearing teachers, this is a special problem because the level and quality of communication between teacher and student may not be high. It is easier to ask only for answers or check papers than to discuss situations or ask for explanations. Yielding to this temptation can have dire consequences for the student. Aids for structuring feedback can be derived through the observation of students as they use manipulatives—counters, rods, shapes, measuring instruments, balances, and so forth, where the teacher can in some indirect way perceive the student's thinking processes. They can also

be derived through the use of group work and interaction where other students can detect and correct incorrect approaches to a concept.

Using Manipulative Materials

The use of manipulative materials can be of great help in designing reasonable sequences for instruction, especially for students at the elementary level. Instruction that begins with manipulative concrete materials and gradually becomes more and more abstract through the use of more abstract materials can lead students successfully to abstract concepts in a meaningful way.

For example, when working with the concept of place value, materials can be found or devised at many different levels of abstraction. Consider the representation of the number 127. Initially the idea of 127 can be represented by individual counters, such as coffee stirrers or sticks (see Figure 8.2). Ten sticks can be bundled into a group, and groups of 10 can be bundled into a group of 10 tens, or 100. Then 127 is represented by one group of 10 tens (100), two groups of 10, and 7 individual sticks. Renaming in addition or sbutraction is done by making or breaking bundles.

In order to achieve a higher level of abstraction, a different manipulative (such as multibase arithmetic blocks) can be used that still incorporates countable objects. This added step helps enforce the correct grouping. The arithmetic blocks, base ten, consist of small cubes (units), longs (10 units fixed together), squares (10 longs joined side to side to form a square of 100 units), and cubes (10 squares joined face to face, resulting in a group of 1000). With the blocks, 127 is represented by one square, two longs, and seven units. The renaming process here is one of exchanging, for example, 10 units for 1 long. The student can still see the individual units.

The next stage might be to use longs, squares, and cubes without the markings showing the individual units. The student must remember that 10 units make up 1 long, and so forth. If the student forgets, it is possible to place 10 units side by side to show that they are the same length as a long.

Now the student is ready for materials that abstractly represent place value, such as colored chips. Here the colors of the chips represent the values 1, 10, 100, and so forth; so the number 127 is now represented, for instance, by one green, two blue, and seven yellow chips. The renaming process is still changing chips, but here it comes very close to what occurs in the written algorithm. The last stage before a written algorithm could be the use of an abacus, which substitutes position for color.

These examples show that the degree of abstraction of manipulative materials can be quite different. One material may be very close to the meaning of the symbol (127 actual counters for the number 127) and the other, the abacus, almost as abstract as the written numeral itself. Many institutional materials are designed to use some kind of manipulatives. Few

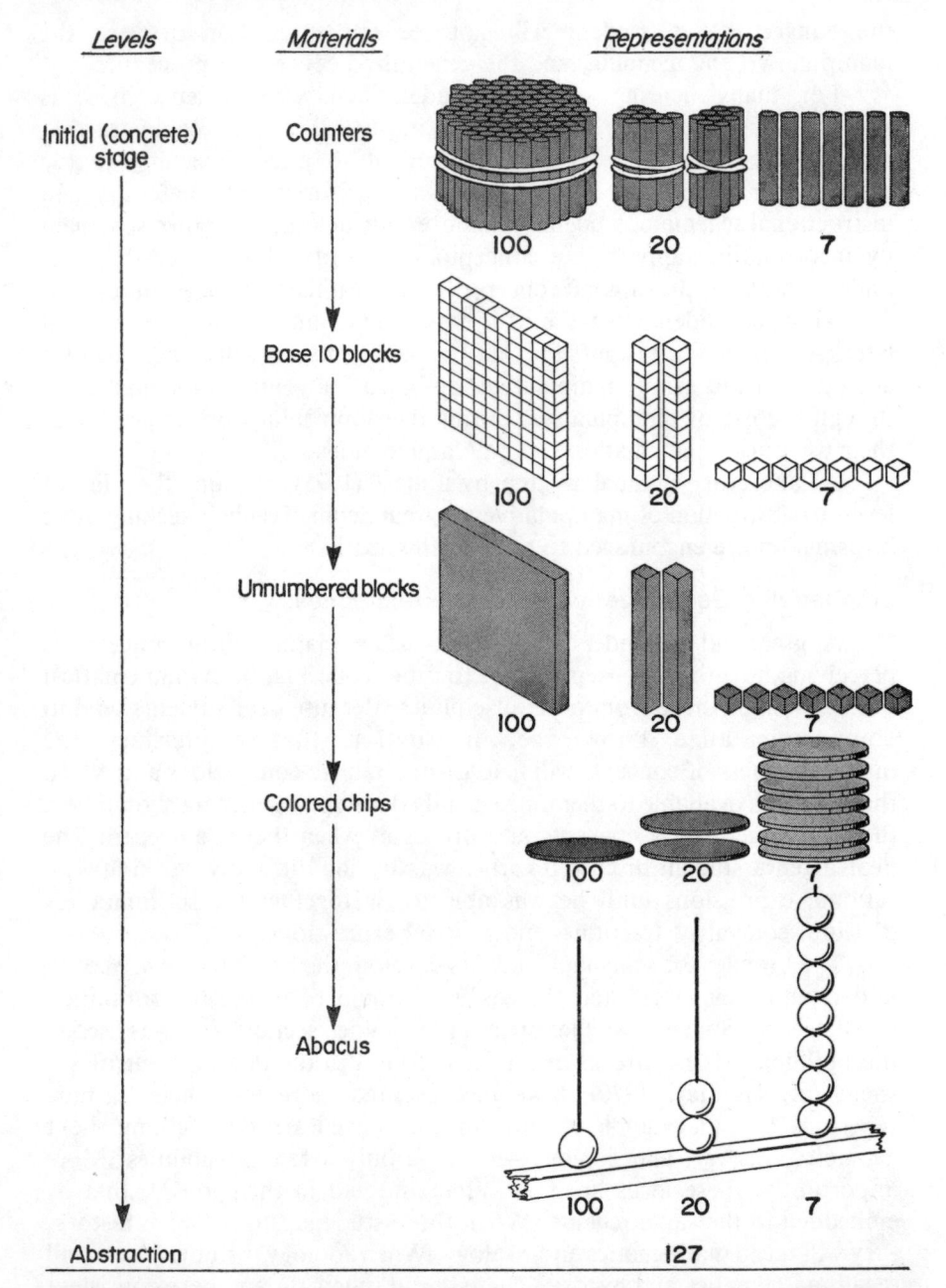

Figure 8.2. Levels of abstraction in developing the place value concept using manipulatives.

teachers or curricula use as structured a variety of experiences as suggested here. The leaps to abstraction can be great. The longer the leap, the greater

the danger that a student will not see the connection between the manipulative, the meaning, and the generalized concept or procedure.

For many hearing impaired students whose experience base is somewhat restricted, the use of more or most of these steps to abstraction may be necessary in order for the student to attach meaning to the mathematical concepts. By working with a variety of materials and instructional schemata, students can more fully develop their own schemata by incorporating appropriate conceptual elements, thus increasing their understanding of the original concept. It is critical that this be accomplished with younger students because of the inordinate amount of time required later. Additionally, it is possible that the older students will evince negative attitudes toward using manipulatives designed for younger students. Even though the use of manipulatives during developmental work is preferred, their use during remediation can pay large dividends.

A laboratory manual written by Jungst (1975) develops the idea of levels of abstraction of manipulatives in great detail. Teachers seeking more information are encouraged to refer to this work.

Emphasizing Generalizations and Interrelatedness

A great aid to understanding and using mathematical concepts is perceiving how these concepts relate to other concepts, both mathematical ones as well as those from other disciplines. Because deaf students tend to compartmentalize knowledge, instruction that emphasizes the interrelatedness of concepts will help them establish connections and widen the schemata available to them. More fully developed schemata should help them recall necessary concepts and processes when they are needed. The deaf algebra student discussed earlier was having difficulty working with rational expressions until he was able to tie together the schemata for division, equivalent fractions, and rational expressions.

The broader the schemata students develop, the fewer they will need to understand their world and the easier it should be to recall information when needed. Students who learn about the golden section, as it was used in the buildings of the Greeks and as it is found in the development of sea shells (cf. Huntley, 1970), have incorporated more into their learning repertoire than an example of ratio, for they have learned something about geometry, history, and zoology—to name only a few possibilities. More importantly, these ideas are now interconnected in their minds, that is, embedded in the same schema. When those students study Greek history, they will recall mathematics and zoology. When zoology is studied, they will recall mathematics and history. These broad schemata are more consistent with the needs of daily life when one is confronted with a problem and are the essence of understanding one's world. Instruction for deaf students, then, should emphasize the connectedness of concepts both within

mathematics and as connected with other disciplines. When multiplication can be thought of as repeated addition, subtraction as a missing addend problem, and division as repeated subtraction, then all these operations will be tied together in the mind of the student. Emphasizing that decimals are fractions and percents are fractions can be an aid to a student who is working with fractions, decimals, and percents. Indeed, mathematics itself is a way of making these kinds of links or broad schemata. The system of fractional numbers (positive rationals) is a link for the concept of ratio, describing parts of a whole, and for the division of whole numbers. Mathematics is the very essence of the abstraction and generalization process.

Instruction in mathematics does not automatically assist students in developing broad schemata. Instruction characterized by explaining examples, followed by the drill and practice of specific skills, followed by more examples and more drill, does not foster generalization. Instruction characterized by puzzles and problem solving, group discussion and interaction, exploring the "big ideas," and emphasizing meaningfulness or understanding of concepts should provide a basis for the development of broad schemata and the eventual greater achievement and usefulness for deaf students.

Emphasizing Real-World Experiences

The use of mathematical ideas in the real world is a type of generalization. It is primarily because of the need to use computational mathematics in our society that most people admit to the importance of mathematics in the school program. This emphasis on computation has, however, made the true goals of mathematics in life less frequently realized.

Overemphasis on computation has occurred in the mathematics education of deaf students to an even greater extent than with hearing students. In part this has happened because of the wish to provide deaf students with the basic skills of addition, subtraction, multiplication, and division needed to function in our society. What may result is a student with good computational skills who has no idea where or how to apply these skills. The relatively sheltered childhood of many deaf students does little to alleviate this problem.

Mathematics instruction needs continually to incorporate real-world experiences that deaf students may not have had. These experiences can be incorporated either as motivation before instruction or as application after instruction on a concept. Field trips to stores, banks, museums, and camps, and school activities, such as recording measurements, record keeping, selling, and planning, can, if carefully constructed, contribute to students' realization of the importance of mathematics in life and to their ability to apply mathematics to real situations.

Using real materials, such as order pads from local fast-food chains or invoice statements from business firms can also be of great assistance in both motivation and application, but materials of this type are a poor substitute for actually going to the restaurant or business first to see the materials in the real setting. Designing lessons around such activities as sporting events, buying a car, keeping an apartment, or riding the bus can make mathematics very real to these students.

Another advantage of using real-world experiences in instruction is that the student can see that the same mathematical concept can be used in a number of contexts. For example, multiplication of whole numbers can be used in repeated addition, areas and arrays, and multiple combinations (Cartesian product). The teacher of the deaf especially needs to be certain that the student has opportunities for experiences in all applications contexts for a given mathematical idea, since it is not likely that the deaf student has had related focused experience outside the school environment in which the necessary mathematics was used.

Using Visual Teaching Approaches

The obvious approach to instruction for the deaf is visual. Some educators hypothesize that because deaf students must learn primarily through visual channels, their visual sense must be superior. Unfortunately, there has been little research in this area, and thus there is little evidence to support this hypothesis. Although many deaf people are expert in observations regarding nonverbal communication—such as body language—arguments could be made that deaf students may not be as efficient as most hearing students at school learning through visual means, especially when the material to be learned is as abstract as mathematics. Whether or not deaf students can learn better visually, most educators of the deaf agree that visual approaches are more effective than verbal approaches for nonlanguage learning and are therefore important tools to consider when designing instruction for the deaf.

Again, it is useful to think in terms of schemata. Earlier it was suggested that the deaf must construct schemata that are different from those of hearing individuals because of their different kinds of experiences. It has been hypothesized that the nature of the schemata of some hearing impaired people could be different from those of hearing people. If hearing impaired persons' schemata do tend to be more visual, attempting to provide experiences that lead them to develop visual schemata may be useful. For example, using a double pan balance to illustrate the solution of linear equations in algebra or using the simple harmonic motion of the shadow of an object on a rotating disk to describe the trigonometric functions may provide students with visual images to incorporate into their schema for the corresponding concepts. Using the transformational

approach to teaching geometry at both the secondary and elementary levels appears to be very helpful in teaching a subject considered the most difficult for the hearing impaired mathematics student (O'Neill, 1968). In this approach, geometric figures are analyzed and compared through the use of slides (translations), flips (reflections), and turns (rotations). Materials that use this approach are becoming increasingly available at all levels.

CONCLUSIONS AND SUGGESTIONS

This chapter can be summarized by the following five guidelines:

1. Watch out for the narrow curriculum. Be sure that on the elementary and the junior high school levels the mathematics program is more than just computation. Basing a program on the ten basic skills suggested by the National Council of Supervisors of Mathematics (1977) would be one way to do this. The mathematics department at the Model Secondary School for the Deaf has attempted to implement these basic skills in objectives that could be used as bases for an individualized educational plan available to anyone as a reference. At the secondary level the emphases on algebra or geometry should be not on simple memorization of facts or skills but on problem solving, reasoning, and application.

2. Watch out for the narrow methods. The continued use of the example/practice method does not provide the student with an opportunity to explore and understand mathematical concepts. Teachers using the textbook as the only guide for instruction frequently fall into this trap. Although the use of a textbook in mathematics is necessary for almost all teachers, teaching exclusively from a text leads students to equate "covering" pages in a book with learning. Further, textbooks cannot stand alone as a substitute for a teacher, especially with deaf students. Books do not usually stimulate the curiosity or the understanding of a concept in naive students. Setting a hearing impaired student aside with a textbook and an occasional tutor is not doing that student a favor.

3. Watch out for points of accommodation. Points in the mathematical curriculum where students need to change the way they have been thinking about something are areas of potential difficulty. The introduction of fractions, changes in the context of an operation, and beginning other new areas of study are examples of such points. The amount of accommodation students need to accomplish as they move through the mathematics curriculum is directly related to the quality of instruction and the knowledge of mathematics on the part of the teacher. When students are at a point of accommodation, carefully designed experiences to encourage correct development of the new schemata are needed, not the usual drill and practice activities.

4. Do not assume a student thinks the way you think. Everyone's experiences are different. The kind and type of experiences and the kinds of information understood by a hearing impaired student can be vastly different from those of teachers. For teachers to assume that an approach that appears logical and effective to them will appear so to their students is a mistake. Teachers of the hearing impaired need to be sensitive to this fact and also try their best to gain a better understanding of the life and environment of their students.

5. Do not assume a hearing impaired student is retarded. Hearing impaired students may not appear to function as well intellectually as hearing students do. This may be for a number of reasons: (a) The deaf may think differently. Their schemata are different from those of the hearing, and our society is a hearing society with which the deaf person may not even share a native language. To judge the way a hearing impaired person functions in a hearing society is as fair as judging the survival skills of an industrial society urbanite in the midst of the Amazon jungle. (b) The home and school environment of the deaf child is not likely to be as varied and rich as that of the hearing child. This deprivation may well affect the thinking habits of some hearing impaired people. Furth says that "there seems to be an inability [in deaf persons] to look for reasons, not inability to reason" (Furth, 1966, p. 152). Language bias may make a deaf person appear less intelligent in the same way that a foreign-born individual speaking only broken English may appear less intelligent to a native speaker of English. Learn to communicate with the students on their terms first whenever possible.

Teaching mathematics is a challenging task. Teaching mathematics to students with impaired hearing is even more demanding. Little research exists to guide the teacher in designing instructional programs for these students. Well-designed research into instructional problems of, and strategies for, hearing impaired students is critically needed in all disciplines, including mathematics. Until the time that more information is available, decisions on curriculum and methodology lie to a great extent within teachers' professional judgments. It appears that with a few obvious adjustments, what constitutes good mathematics instruction for hearing children is also good mathematics instruction for many hearing impaired children. There will never be good substitutes for well-prepared teachers who know their subjects, know their methods, and know their students very well.

REFERENCES

Alpiner, J. G. Public school hearing conservation. In D. E. Rose (Ed.), *Audiological assessment*, pp. 133–166. Englewood Cliffs, N.J.: Prentice-Hall, 1971.

Berg, F. S. *Educational audiology: Hearing and speech management.* New York: Grune & Stratton, 1976.

Birch, J. W. *Hearing impaired pupils in the mainstream.* Minneapolis: University of Minnesota, 1975.

Bruner, J. H. *The Process of education.* Cambridge, Mass.: Harvard University Press, 1960.

Copeland, R. W. *How children learn.* New York: Macmillan, 1971.

Davis, H., & Silverman, R. *Hearing and deafness.* New York: Holt, Rinehart & Winston, 1970.

DiCarlo, L. *The deaf.* Englewood Cliffs, N.J.: Prentice-Hall, 1964.

Furth, H. G. Thinking without language: Psychological implications of deafness. New York: Free Press, 1966.

Gagne, R. M. Learning and proficiency in mathematics. *Mathematics Teacher*, 1963, *56*, 620–626.

Gentile, A., & McCarthy, B. *Additional handicapping conditions among hearing impaired students, United States: 1971–72.* Series D, Number 14. Washington, D.C.: Gallaudet College, Office of Demographic Studies, 1973.

Goulder, T. J. *The effects of the presence or absence of being labeled emotionally/behaviorally disturbed on the classroom behaviors of hearing impaired children, ages 7–13.* Unpublished doctoral dissertation, American University, Washington, D.C., 1976.

Hudgins, R. Causes of deafness among students of the Clark School for the Deaf. In *Clark School for the Deaf: 106th annual report*, pp. 59–60. Northampton, Mass.: Clark School, 1973.

Huntley, H. E. *The divine proportion, a study in mathematical beauty.* New York: Dover, 1970.

Johnson, D. A., & Rising, G. R. *Guidelines for teaching mathematics.* Minneapolis: University of Minnesota, 1967.

Johnson, K. *A survey of mathematics programs, materials, and methods in schools for the deaf.* Unpublished doctoral dissertation, Syracuse University, 1976.

Jungst, D. C. *Elementary mathematics methods: Laboratory manual.* Boston: Allyn & Bacon, 1975.

Karchmer, M. S., Rawlings, B. W., Trybus, R., Wolk, S., & Milone, M. N. *Educationally significant characteristics of hearing impaired students in Texas, 1977–78.* Series C, No. 4. Washington, D.C.: Gallaudet College, Office of Demographic Studies, 1979.

Keller, H. *Helen Keller in Scotland: A personal record written by herself* (with introduction by J. Love). London: Methuen, 1933.

Kennedy, L. M. *Guiding children in mathematical discovery.* Belmont, Calif.: Wadsworth, 1975.

Meadow, K. P., & Trybus, R. J. Behavioral and emotional problems of deaf children: An overview. In L. J. Bradford (Ed.), *Hearing and hearing impairment.* New York: Grune & Stratton, 1979.

Moores, D. F. *Educating the deaf: Psychology, principles, and practices.* Boston: Houghton Mifflin, 1978.

Moores, D., & Maestas y Moores, J. Special adaptations necessitated by hearing impairment. In J. Kauffman & D. Hallahan (Eds.), *Handbook of special education.* New York: Prentice-Hall, in press.

Mulholland, A., & Fellendorf, G. *Report of the National Research Conference on day programs for hearing impaired children.* Washington, D.C.: A. G. Bell Association, 1968.

National Council of Supervisors of Mathematics. *Position paper on basic skills.* Minneapolis: Author, 1977. Also available in *Arithmetic Teacher*, 1977, *25*, 19–22.

National Council of Teachers of Mathematics. *Organizing for mathematics instruction.* Reston, Va.: Author, 1977.

Office of Demographic Studies. *The Stanford Achievement Test—Hearing Impaired Version.* Washington, D.C.: Gallaudet College, Office of Demographic Studies, 1974.

Office of Demographic Studies. Personal communication, September 1980.

O'Neill, V. Developing deaf children's thinking through mathematics. *Volta Review*, 1968, 426–430.

Pendergrass, R., & Hodges, M. Deaf students in group problem solving situations: A study of the interaction process. *American Annals of the Deaf*, 1976, *121*, 327–330.

Pollard, G., & Neumaur, R. Vision characteristics of deaf students. *American Annals of the Deaf*, 1974, *119*, 740–745.

Reivich, R. S., & Rothrock, I. A. Behavior problems of deaf children and adolescents: A factor-analytic study. *Journal of Speech and Hearing Research*, 1972, *15*, 84–92.

Ries, P. Reported causes of hearing loss for hearing impaired students: 1970–1971. In *Annual Survey of Hearing Impaired Children and Youth*, Series D, Number 11. Washington, D.C.: Gallaudet College, Office of Demographic Studies, 1979.

Ross, M., & Calvert, D. R. Guidelines for audiology programs in educational settings for hearing impaired children. *Volta Review*, 1977, *79*, 153–161.

Rudner, L. M. Using standardized tests with the hearing impaired: The problem of item bias. *Volta Review*, 1978, *80*, 31–40.

Schein, J., & Delk, M. *The deaf population of the United States.* Silver Spring, Md.: National Association of the Deaf, 1974.

Skemp, R. *The psychology of learning mathematics.* Baltimore: Penguin Books, 1971.

Vernon, M. Current etiological factors in deafness. *American Annals of the Deaf*, 1968, *113*, 106–115.

Vernon, M., & Mindel, E. *They grow in silence.* Silver Spring, Md.: National Association of the Deaf, 1971.

Williams, C. M., & Debes, J. L. *First national conference on visual literacy.* New York: Pitman, 1970.

Teaching Mathematics to Children and Youth with Physical and Health Impairments

Stephen S. Willoughby
New York University

Jerome Siller
New York University

Dr. Stephen S. Willoughby is a professor and the director of the Mathematics Education Program at New York University. He holds degrees from Harvard and Columbia, and has taught all levels from first grade through graduate courses in education and mathematics. Willoughby has served on the Board of Directors of NCTM and has been active in other professional organizations. He has written many articles and books. Most recently, he is the senior author of the elementary series Real Math.

Dr. Jerome Siller is professor and chairman, Department of Educational Psychology, New York University. He is past president of the Division of Rehabilitation Psychology of the American Psychological Association; Clinical Division, New York State Psychological Association; New York Society of Clinical Psychologists; and Psychoanalytic Psychologists of Long Island. He is a former consultant, Social Rehabilitation Service of HEW; a consulting editor, Rehabilitation Psychology; *and contributor to the literature on psychosocial aspects of physical disability.*

A T THE outset of this discussion of the consequences for children who have a physical disability or health impairment, a vital point must be made. Perhaps the most disabling aspect of the situation for such children is the attitude of parents, peers, and professionals toward them. These children may be viewed as objects to be taught, treated, or handled rather than as unique persons whose behavior will be highly structured by our own attitudes and behavior toward them. We shall discuss later, however, the attitudes of teachers, family, and peers toward exceptional children. For now,

let us emphasize that aside from certain sensory, motoric, or cognitive limitations imposed by a child's condition, any view that places "the problem" within the child rather than on the total interactive system within which the child must exist is not only unfair but incorrect. Thus, there is no psychology, sociology, education, and so on, of "the disabled." The true state of affairs is best understood as involving the complex network of interactions of those having certain impairments with the immediate and larger communities. A special focus of this understanding must be the subjective state and viewpoint of those involved. Behavior is governed by what we believe to be true rather than by an "objective" reality.

The term *somatopsychology* has been introduced to describe the social and psychological consequences of disablement. Somatopsychology is concerned with those variations in physique that affect the psychological situation of a person by influencing the effectiveness of one's body as a tool for actions or by serving as a stimulus to oneself or others (Barker, Wright, Meyerson, & Gonick, 1953). Somatopsychological analysis stresses dynamic interactions and fluid, evolving situations amenable to change and modification that reflect a potent rehabilitation orientation.

Educators who work with children that have specific conditions should, of course, have specialized knowledge. Common problems for children and the adults dealing with them, such as incontinence, sensory loss, or motor loss, have already been dealt with, and special materials, curriculum, tools, and so on are often available for these types of problems. But trepidation on the part of teachers can be reduced and educational and personal effectiveness can be enhanced when one's knowledge of the *psychological* situation is increased and supportive materials are provided.

Aspects of Impairment Salient to the Psychoeducational Situation

Some of the factors that enter into the formation of the self-image of children with an impairment and that can exert decisive influence on their psychosocial situation (see Freeman, 1967; Nagi, 1971; Siller, 1976a) will be reviewed. Obviously, these factors do not operate automatically or have an inevitable impact, but they can orient one to the determining forces in a child's condition and life. We shall consider the etiology of the condition, the child's age at onset, the degree and quality of the limitations, the onset and duration, the course of the condition, and the cosmetic appearance.

1. *Etiology.* The orgin of a condition can present a salient stimulus to oneself and to others. Thus, conditions that are fortuitously arrived at differ from those induced by carelessness, just as both differ from "heroic" causative circumstances such as war injuries. Familial stress may be imposed if assumptions regarding neglect or genetics are made. Guilt feelings by the parents can thus be part of the family dynamics. How the child and

the family conceive of the etiology of the condition, therefore, becomes an important factor in how one thinks about the situation. Fantasies regarding this matter further confound the picture.

The actual causes of physical disabilities include such factors as genetic contribution, fetal insult, the birth process, anoxia, infections and disease, dietary deficiencies, accidents and injuries, and effects of radiation and drugs.

2. *Age at onset*. Differing effects may be assumed depending on the time in the life cycle that a condition arises. Socially, the occurrence of a condition at one age may be more intrusive than at other ages, for example, puberty or at the time of entrance to school. If the child already has a fairly well-formed self-concept and a circle of friends, the effects of the disability will likely be less disruptive than they would otherwise. If one's sense of self has been shaky and one's peer relationships insecure, sickness or trauma can have much more profound consequences. School under such conditions becomes rather irrelevant. When sensory impairments are involved, disturbances in early life can make for developmental paths qualitatively different from those formed when such disabilities occur after skills and conditions have been developed. Distinctions between congenital and adventitious origins are often stressed by clinicians. Congenital defects are more likely to produce diffuse personality alterations, and acquired disabilities are more likely to produce acute disturbances. Individual reactions, of course, are highly variable.

3. *Degree and quality of limitations*. The effectiveness with which one may deal with the physical demands of the environment or the processing of information is significantly determined by this element. Disabilities vary greatly in the degree to which loss of function is involved; even within a particular disability, persons with identical physical conditions show grossly different degrees of personal effectiveness. A not inconsiderable number of children have multiple handicaps. There is much conflicting data regarding the relationship between the amount of physical limitation or severity of a condition and its effects on personality, sociability, and other psychological dimensions. In general, one may assume that no simple relationship exists. It is important to emphasize that no direct relationship exists between the physical fact of illness or disability and one's psychological reaction to that condition.

For children, the consequences of severe disability may be profound, since contact with the environment may be reduced, with adverse results for cognitive and social development. The isolation of many of the disabled, of all ages, is frequently noted. Socialization skills may be retarded, and one's access to the usual social correctives (consensual validation) of one's behavior and thinking may be limited. An implication of this is that the

school situation may be called on to supplement qualities that ordinarily are taken for granted.

4. *Onset and duration of the condition.* Disabilities vary greatly in suddenness of onset, antecedent conditions, and expected direction. Opportunities to deal effectively with the stress of the situation differ greatly and are reflected in the manner in which persons manage. Profound disruptions to the self-image can and do result. However, the self-image is slow to change, and the period from one psychological position to another can be replete with problems. With a permanent disability, the ability to assume a self-image that is realistic to one's actual situation can make the difference between a successful or an unsuccessful adjustment.

5. *Course.* Disabilities may remain stationary, be progressive, improve, or be episodic with periods of normality. When stationary (e.g., amputation), there is a stable base on which to predicate the future and, to that extent, make coping easier. Progressive conditions, such as muscular dystrophy and other degenerative diseases, pose the problem of uncertainty and continued demoralization. Improving conditions leave residual feelings (real or feared) of a sense of vulnerability. Episodic conditions, such as seizures or diabetes, create uncertainty and can be particularly bothersome if they intrude into a relationship where it was not known that the situation existed. Not unexpectedly, persons with such ailments may find it expedient to develop pervasive protective systems, such as withdrawal, designed to avoid such experiences.

6. *Cosmesis.* The appearance and visibility of a condition may be a prime determining factor in the social consequences of a disability. That disfigurement, particularly if it's facial, has tremendous social relevance has been amply documented. Its impact on the self-image of the disabled person and on familial interactions and adaptations is equally profound.

In addition to the factors mentioned above, which are general to most disabilities or health impairments, condition-specific restrictions also operate. Thus, in each instance, conditions where motor functioning is limited, where incontinence is involved, or where sensory disability results will present a common problem for those sharing that experience. Individual resolutions of these general and condition-specific elements must be made.

Body-Image and Self-Image

The concepts of body-image and self-image are useful in helping to understand approaches to helping children with physical or health impairments. It is assumed that the self emerges developmentally from a body ego. One's first impressions are physical—pain, discomfort, satisfaction. These impressions then coalesce into some memory formation that

ultimately leads to a differentiated feeling of "selfness."

Self-image and body-image exist together throughout life after each has emerged. Both are capable of change throughout life, but these are mostly stable processes, and once formed, they act conservatively to maintain an essential identity. Most personality and developmental theories, therefore, place considerable emphasis on the early formative years as having special significance for subsequent outcomes and assume a restricted receptivity to change afterwards. Virtually all systems do see change as possible. In later years, however, the extent and difficulty of envisioned change varies from theoretical system to system. Whereas at times the relationship of self-image to body-image is minimal, at other times there are intense narcissistic involvements that make them very close.

The presence of physical or health impairments (e.g., the effects of aging in older persons) may bring feelings of body and self closer. This would be most true when social forces in the child's environment promote the identification of oneself in terms of one's physical state. Physical self-preoccupation is *not* an inevitable consequence of disability but almost always reflects the environmental climate. (The one notable exception would be when constant pain exists, but this is a limited case.) Placement of children in special classes, of course, could promote the salience of the physical state to a child.

One can differentiate between the situation for a child whose condition is of congenital origin, or develops even a year or so after birth, from that of a child whose condition is adventitious in origin and who is already in the school situation. In the former instance, the very sense of integrativeness, balance, and symmetry that enters into the acquisition of numerical and reading concepts may be involved. Essentially, a coordinated sense of self and of body facilitates the ability of young children to abstract and to conceptualize. This does not mean that children with impairments are necessarily going to be disadvantaged in their school work, but the timing of attainment and the manner and procedure of learning may be affected. (See below for specific examples.)

An illness or accident to a child already in school is an intrusion on an already structured body-image. An early issue is whether the condition is seen by the child as real or permanent. If correctly perceived, changes in body-image and self-image are more likely to occur without pathological defense formations. Once again, the supporting (or nonsupporting) environment will be highly influential in producing outcomes.

So far, we have considered the body-image as having import for education in terms of its affective importance for all involved, its importance as a prerequisite for concept learning, and its role in the development of the self-image. The rest of this section will stress aspects of the self-image.

The self-image of the child with a physical disability or health impair-

ment has been the subject of numerous research and clinical studies. Because of measurement problems and difficulties in conceptualizing the real issues, much of the research is inconclusive. Whereas there may be some value in such composite statements as "The self-image of the disabled group, as measured by X, was lower than that of the nondisabled group" to characterize populations, it would seem to be more valuable to formulate the question differently. If we accept that any consequential aspect of a person, such as color, religion, intelligence level, or one's body as a physical stimulus to others or to oneself, must enter into one's self-image, a more appropriate question is, "How does this fact enter into one's picture of oneself?"

The self-image is important because it assumes a directive function for the person. To the extent that one feels pleased with what one perceives oneself to be, life is colored much more differently than when the opposite is true. How one develops a positive or negative self-image depends on the quality of one's environment and certain intangible qualities of the person. When disability or health conditions intrude, the child must contend not only with developmental vicissitudes common to all children but also with the special circumstances imposed by the condition or conditions.

One might characterize the adjustment process as successful or unsuccessful to the extent that the child's self-image is predicated on worth rather than on deficiency and self-contempt. In practice, this means that the protective and adaptive mechanisms typifying that child are essentially based on reality and are nonpathological. Such adaptive children (and adaptive does *not* mean conventionally conforming) are directed toward positive gratifications, are goal directed in socially useful ways, and are usually socially adept. In contrast, children with less fortunate adaptive resolutions seem to avoid the implications of their conditions rather than seek positive gratifications; their primary motivation is to ward off anxiety, shame, and other noxious effects. This latter resolution is the basis for residual self-hate.

The role of the teacher and other professionals for the disabled and the health-impaired child is to extend every aid possible to help him or her have the self-regard that is necessary for a constructive and happy life. A specific contribution that can be made here is to help the child enlarge his or her scope of values. Dembo, Leviton, and Wright (1956), in a brilliant analysis of what it means to "accept one's loss," introduce the idea that by loss is meant the absence of something valuable felt as a personal misfortune. They analyze the changes, within the value system of the person, that are instrumental in overcoming the feeling of shame and inferiority resulting from disability as a value loss.

These changes are elaborated on by Wright (1960) as (a) enlarging the scope of values—that is, the emotional realization of the existence of other

values, the nondisabled aspects of oneself; (b) containing the effects of the disability—where the effects of the physical condition are seen improperly as spreading to other aspects of the person, such as intelligence, personality, or character; (c) subordinating physique—where one's physique becomes less important in terms of appearance and physical ability; and (d) transforming comparative values into asset values—whereas the former is to evaluate oneself in terms of generalized and stereotyped standards, the latter arises from qualities inherent in oneself.

Although the importance of a positive self-image is obvious insofar as adjustment processes are concerned, its importance for cognitive functioning and educational purposes may be overlooked. Without entering into questions of definition, there clearly is an intimate relationship between self-image and ego functioning. Ego functions, which would include such qualities as memory, attention span, and capacity for delay, readily become intruded on when one's self-image is poor. One is not just being "nice" to the child to consider his or her feelings of self—the child's very ability to deal with the school material is involved.

Certain elements in the development of the child with physical or health impairments may impinge directly on the child's learning of mathematics. Foremost among these is the frequent interruption of academic work by medical visits or even hospitalization. Whereas this factor encroaches on all school learning situations, in subjects such as mathematics, where sequencing and a systematic laying down of foundations is particularly vital, there may be profound disruption, resulting in demoralization and actual deficiencies of knowledge.

Learning mathematics, except in its most rote and trivial sense, requires concentration, attention, and some comfort with abstractions. The child, already harrassed by interruptions as just described, might also have to contend with physical pain, medication routines, prosthetic devices or other appliances, and social issues, among other distractions. All these factors interfere directly with conditions that are necessary for promoting attention and the ability to concentrate. Abstract ideas and processes ordinarily require a certain amount of attention and concentration for conceptualization to be effective. One may also note that self-absorption, a by-product of pain, discomfort, and social factors such as isolation, tends to promote a concreteness of thought and an intolerance of generalization.

On a more direct and obvious level, motoric difficulties in actually forming letters and numbers can present problems. Research on the effect of using electronic calculators in learning mathematics will have to be assessed in relation to the motor, sensory, and cognitive properties of those with physical impairments. Children with paralytic, athetotic, and other crippling conditions particularly will require electronic aids that do not presume fine motor control.

The problems introduced by medical visits, hospitalization, impairment of concentration and attention, interference with abstract processes, and motor deficiencies are far from insurmountable. Means of rectification already should be a part of every teacher's repertoire. Minor modifications involving scheduling, using supplementary tools, and providing reasonable individualized attention should suffice for almost all children.

Personal Impact of Disability

In subsequent sections, social factors that have an impact on the life of children with impairments will be discussed. Here the more private aspects of the person with such impairments will be considered. It is our contention that unless the private nature of such children is understood and some appreciation of their phenomenology is gained, a gulf will exist between educators and other professionals and the children that will sharply limit our effectiveness.

An immediate issue for the educator in this context is whether the fact of impairment is even relevant for a particular child either in the educational situation or in that child's general life. We must avoid the basic error of attributing that certain things are so *because of* the condition. It frequently has been observed that persons will make assumptions that the child's behavior (e.g., nervousness, irritability, inattentiveness) results from the physical condition when this may be totally unrelated to it.

Individual ways of coping with one's total situation—including that of disablement or health conditions—vary from person to person, and for a person from time to time. Nonetheless, certain consistencies in the situation of the recently traumatized have been observed (Siller, 1976a). Whereas children at this stage of a disability are not likely to be seen by the educator (unless in the hospital), some feeling for this period might help educators to understand later developments. In the earliest phases of a traumatic condition, a fairly consistent sequence for adults has been described: shock, grief or depression involving defensive retreat, healthy or pathologic resolutions of the mourning state, and finally success or failure in rehabilitation. Clinically, anxiety and depression are universally identified as the primary effects associated with disability. Whereas the picture may not be as clear for young children owing to their inability, at least on some level, to appreciate the full extent of the situation, the sequence described above probably also prevails.

Unlike adults, whose denial mostly refers to the nonacknowledgment of the full implication of the condition, young children are more likely to deny that the condition actually exists. In any event, denial can have a positive function when it serves to help the child over a bad time. One should become concerned when denial becomes too prominent an aspect of the child's defensive structure—persisting beyond the original upsetting

period and leading to a distortion of reality that interferes with rehabilitation. Direct confrontation of the child's use of denial by teachers or others should be avoided, since supportive groundwork that would enable the child to relinquish this manner of defense needs to be done first.

Hospitalization, pain, physical dependency, immobilization, and even institutional rules promote regressive behavior. The avoidance, or at least minimization, of regressive behavior can be facilitated when the institutional structure is geared to promote appropriate strivings for independence while offering necessary support in ways that do not "infantilize." For example, a frequent complaint of those in wheelchairs is that they are placed facing a blank wall or that their caretakers act as if they do not exist.

At times, well-intentioned persons try to deal with the reactions of grief or mourning that follow impaired health or disablement by trying to help the person "tough it out." In effect, denial is being reinforced, and respect for the need for the child or adult to work through the feelings of loss through mourning is absent. This can be a most dangerous maneuver, since clinicians generally agree that without an opportunity to deal with the strong feelings associated with the loss of a valued function or part, emotional disturbance can result. Thus, for some, the inability to mourn at the "right" time leads to those feelings being displaced to other inappropriate objects at later times. For others, there are feelings of vague uneasiness or emptiness that can be traced to the missed opportunity to experience grief at the time of the experience. In these and other reactions, what results is a dissociation of the feelings appropriate to the trauma and a sense of inner deadness or an inappropriate affective state.

For children, the state regarding mourning described above is particularly significant, since the very pattern of emotional development may be structured around lines of avoidance. One may stress the functional and immediately pragmatic as a way of blunting the affective reaction, with the ultimate consequence being the missed opportunity to become a feeling and emotionally complex adult.

The immediate reactions to disablement just described—depression, grief, anxiety, denial, and regression—are almost normative, although wide variations in their extent and manner of expression exist. Greater individualization is observed in long-range adjustments because of variations in personality, ego strength, coping styles, and environmental forces. Depending on the particular disability, different need systems may be intruded upon, and specific unresolved, unconscious conflicts may be activated.

Despite the diversity of patterns of long-term adjustment, six partial modes can be noted: passivity, dependency, aggression, compensation, withdrawal, and coping. The term *partial modes* is used to describe important rather than totally definitive characterological behavioral patterns.

With adults, these modes of adaptation are fairly fixed. Children, however, are more influenced by the situation in which they find themselves. The educational environment can play a significant role in helping to fix favorable or unfavorable patterns. We shall briefly consider each of the six patterns of adjustment.

Passivity as a mode of adaptation involves backing away from one's environment. It has, as do all the patterns, its adaptive use. In this instance passivity protects one against embarrassing situations by limiting initiatives. In effect, one does not try, and so one does not confront the possibility of failure. Professional personnel can mistakenly construe this adaptive stance as indifference or an acceptance of the status quo. The inability to accept responsibility for initiating one's rehabilitation should not be mistaken for unwillingness to be rehabilitated.

Dependency is a natural aspect of the prolonged need of the infant and child for adult care. However, emotional dependency should not be seen as synonymous with physical dependency. Although serious health impairment or disablement may require helping actions from others, emotional dependency on the helper is most often promoted by infantilization by the latter. Some children deal with the need for others by becoming overdependent, whereas others try to deny their need and manifest what might be called pseudoindependence. An overdependent child looks for frequent approval, needs to be close to others, is fearful, indecisive, and clinging. One gets a feeling of a child that is overwhelmed by his or her circumstances. Temporary relief from responsibility may be useful in helping such persons ultimately relinquish the dependency. Our own values of self-reliance and achievement may make it difficult to react nonnegatively to such children.

Pseudoindependent behavior is expressed in obstinacy, inappropriate confidence, unwillingness to accept appropriate offers of help, and the setting of unrealistic goals. Because so much of reality must be denied and interpersonal situations are made awkward, this mode of adaptation generally fails to be successful in the long run.

The meaning of help for the disabled is an extemely important issue, since this is one of the most sensitive issues for such persons. A classic analysis of the meaning of help for the disabled can be found in Ladieu, Hanfmann, and Dembo (1947).

Aggression as a major mode of adaptation to impairment has two particular aspects. In one, active, and sometimes even obnoxious, aggressive behavior and attitudes can arouse retaliatory attitudes on the part of educators or others. The fact that the hostility might be based on a struggle against passivity or against a sense of devaluation might be unnoticed.

A second aspect of aggression is that it might be expressed passively. Passive aggressive behavior is manifested by those who unconsciously

realize that direct expression of one's angry feelings is dangerous—frequently true with children. Passive aggressive behavior is expressed in such ways as not taking medicine, not doing homework, losing assignments, "forgetting," and many other spiteful or devious means.

Compensatory behavior as used in a broad sense signifies a generalized orientation toward maintaining feelings of significance and effectiveness. In a positive sense it leads to real accomplishment and is one of the most frequent and effective of the restitutive mechanisms. Such behavior becomes problematic mostly when it is overdone and leads to impoverishment in other aspects of functioning. Concern has been raised by theorists in disability that the positive aspects of compensation should not be taken simply to mean that disablement in itself is necessarily a "bad" value. That is to say, just because one has a certain condition does not mean that one is inferior.

Withdrawal as an adjustive mode is most obviously seen as the retraction of the person from active interaction with the environment, decreased sociability, and a psychological orientation of noninvolvement. Unlike the passive form of adaptation in which such persons need external initiators of action, the withdrawal reaction leads one to resist opportunities for interchange. Whereas for adults some outlets might be found in affiliating with other persons with disabilities, for children the consequence more likely would be isolation. As with some of the other modes of adaptation described, withdrawal as a temporary expedient acting to give a person a "breathing space" should be interpreted differently from a long-term orientation.

The patterns of adaptation described so far can be better understood if the importance of shame and guilt are recognized. Shame about one's appearance or diminished ability to function may, in our opinion, be the single most noxious emotional consequence of impairment and undercuts one's ability to deal constructively with one's condition. Much of a child's or adult's functioning can be understood as an attempt to avoid the experience of shame. Educational experiences that subject children to the possibility of shame—and for the child with an impairment, this may be a daily experience—inevitably lead to motivational and behavioral problems. For example, one child refused to acknowledge that he had an obvious speech problem (tongue thrusting) and would not go to a remedial speech class. The resistance became easily intelligible when the circumstances were described. The boy, who was of superior intelligence and quite arrogant about it, had poor general relations with his classmates and teachers. He was in a regular class for all his courses; however, remediation sessions were initiated by the speech teacher coming to the door of the classroom and calling out his name and that of two others who were to have speech remediation. The boy experienced this singling out as a great humiliation and

fought it by denying the whole issue of the tongue thrusting. The situation was easily rectified when the humiliation aspect was directly considered. His other problems were dealt with by psychotherapy.

Guilt, as shown in self-recriminations, depression, and masochistic patterns, is also easily observed. Disability as punishment for sins is an ancient notion. Cultural and religious factors may promote such notions either in the child or in the persons dealing with him or her. Guilt may serve as a double-edged motive. On the one hand, it may lead to paralysis, self-doubt, and anxiety. On the other hand, it may be expressed by overstriving as a penitent act. In either event the personal consequences are unhappiness and subjective strain. Accomplishments from this frame of reference cannot be really satisfying. A major source of guilt and shame for the impaired child is the feeling of not coming up to standard and falling short in the eyes of parents, teachers, and other significant persons.

Secondary gains afforded the child by others may serve to fix unnecessary dependencies. Thus, if a teacher does not require of a child what is appropriate because of a mistaken notion of sympathy or an incorrect assessment of the child's capabilities, the child may be seduced into a pattern of invalidism. Generally, it is best for the teacher to assume that even the most seriously impaired child is capable of most everything; this can be checked out with parents, previous teachers, and other personnel. Advantages gained by being "disabled" may keep children from a more functional level of operation. This discussion, of course, assumes that one will be reasonable and knowledgeable about the specific child involved.

The final partial mode of adaptation to be described has been called *coping* (Wright, 1960). Disabililty generally has been discussed from a one-sided, deficient point of view. Wright, in her many writings and public appearances, has been a major champion of the importance in viewing the coping aspects of disability. She properly takes to task the almost invariable manner in which the capabilities of persons with disabilities are ignored. It would seem from discussions and the literature that only loss, incapability, and deficit predominate in the world of the disabled. She penetratingly points out that often the disability is background to a field of competence.

Two basic orientations have been discussed by Wright (1960; 1979), one called *coping* and the other *succumbing*.

> The coping framework presents the person with a disability as an active participant in valued activities. What the person can do is viewed as being highly differentiated, the disability being only one aspect of life. In the succumbing framework, in contrast, the negative consequences of disability are emphasized and made equivalent to the whole person who is portrayed as passively defeated. (Wright, 1979, p. 1)

It is our strong recommendation that educators and others who deal

with children with various impairments be made aware of the coping and succumbing orientations and become positive factors in promoting the former.

So far, the focus of our discussion has been mostly on the child with a disability. We shall now give specific attention to the social forces that impinge on the child, such as social and cultural norms, and more extensively, the attitudes of those without disabilities toward those with disabilities. First, however, let us consider a question that is essential to attitudes toward the disabled. Namely, are those with physical disabilities really different from nondisabled persons?

Are the Physically Disabled Really Different?

Some of the reactions toward out-groups, be they racial, religious, or otherwise, are claimed to rest on actual qualities of the objects being appraised ("kernel of truth" hypothesis). This belief provides an easy "out" for those holding prejudiced attitudes and is an attempt to shift the responsibility of change from them to the stigmatized person. This issue of differentness will be considered before examining the structure of attitudes toward the disabled and specific findings in this regard.

Do those with impairments actually present themselves so as to promote differential treatment by others? Writers in the area of blindness, for example, have found such points of difference as "unevenness in level of functioning from one cognitive area to another" (Witkin, Birnbaum, Lomonaco, Lehr, & Herman, 1968, p. 767), developmental delays (Fraiberg, 1968), differential ego delays (Sandler, 1963), and lost interplay with the mother due to the inability to look and smile at each other (Burlingham, 1964). Other writers indicate that delays or deviations in the development of the blind occur that are specific for blindness and do not have the same significance that such delays would have for a sighted child (Fraiberg, 1968; Gillman, 1973; Jastrzembska, 1976). In effect, despite differences of timing the standards for the blind should be based on the growth and development of the nonhandicapped child.

Regardless of whether profound developmental consequences do result for the blind, there can be no question that such things as the "blindisms" and stare of many blind persons do present stimuli with decided social effects.

The possibility of actual systematic differences in social perception of the disabled has been examined by Schiff and Thayer (1974) in regard to deafness. They conclude that deaf persons lose key nonverbal information from the face—especially the eye region—because they concentrate their peripheral and central visual attention on decoding linguistic information. Deaf and hearing persons also weigh kinetic social information differently,

and differences in the perceived degree of several interactive characteristics result. As part of the different informational currents and emphases, impaired communication and resulting communication discomfort on the part of both the disabled and the nondisabled result. Although the studies reviewed by Schiff and Thayer and most of the other work on this problem used adults, the findings likely are generalizable to children.

Blau (1964) conducted research to determine whether the loss of one primary communicating channel would lead to compensatory sensitivity in the remaining channel. He concluded that whereas blind people were more attentive to the technical aspects of auditory communications, they were less accurate at judging the emotional characteristics of the communication itself. Schiff and Thayer (1974) couple the Blau study with their own study on deafness and conclude that for neither condition does the compensatory process largely work. As they point out, "This substitution leads to an overloaded visual system, and deaf-hearing differences appear which increase problems of social misunderstanding" (p. 66).

Other studies also have directly concerned themselves with the question of the social perception of the disabled. Richardson, Hastorf, and Dornbusch (1964), working with 9- to 11-year-olds, conclude that restricted access to direct experience in social interaction leads to the impoverishment of perceptual categorization. Richardson (1963) earlier had concluded that the evidence is consistent in suggesting that *blunting* rather than *sensitizing* is the more likely consequence of handicapping. This finding is consistent with Ingwell, Thoreson, and Smits (1967), who found orthopedically disabled women less socially sensitive than their nondisabled matched controls.

Kleck has demonstrated experimentally how the behavior of a nonhandicapped person is modified in the presence of a handicapped person, for example, giving shorter responses to questions and distorting opinion more (Kleck, 1969; Kleck, Ono, & Hastorf, 1966). Comer and Piliavin (1972) demonstrated that disabled persons experienced considerable discomfort in encounters with physically normal persons. That there is mutual difficulty in disabled-nondisabled interactions, therefore, has been both clinically and experimentally documented. However, as Schoggen (1963) and others point out, behavioral settings in addition to the physical characteristics of the child may be determining outcomes, a position at variance with the usual tendency to identify problematic interaction within the individuals involved. Such behaviors on the part of nondisabled persons as staring, rude questions or actions, and devaluative and subordinating actions precipitate resentment and anger in reaction to the unthinking and unempathic person. The disabled person's justified anger might then be misperceived by the other person as an inevitable distortion of character resulting from the disablement. (See the attitudinal dimension described below as "Inferred Emotional Consequences.")

Disturbances in nondisabled-disabled interactions have been attributed to an assumed "impairment in empathic ability" due to the supposedly different developmental tracks imposed by disability. Although an early study by Black (1964) involving the disabled in helping roles reported that physically normal people found it difficult to think of a disabled person as a helper, two more recent studies found quite opposite results in that nondisabled undergraduates responding to hypothetical counseling situations preferred disabled over nondisabled counselors (Brabham & Thoreson, 1973; Mitchell & Fredrickson, 1975).

From the review above (which is fairly representative), one can infer that as soon as one departs from the direct fact of disability, evidence can be provided to demonstrate either the presence or the absence of psychological differences resulting from disability. The obvious physical differences cannot define resulting reactions. Much of the data suggests that if the disabled do present themselves as "different," this often enough is a secondary consequence of the social climate rather than an inherent disability-specific phenomenon. As Moriarty (1974) points out, "Only when minority group members are stigmatized do they feel and act like social deviants" (p. 849). However, as Schiff and Thayer (1974) and others demonstrate, there are real psychological consequences to disablement, particularly when the senses are affected, that also create interpersonal stresses.

To respond to the question posed at the beginning of this section on whether there are "real" differences in the disabled, one might conclude that such contributions by the disabled, if they exist, still would not preclude untoward reactions rooted in the character and experience of the nondisabled or deny the definitiveness of the interactive aspect of such relationships (somatopsychological considerations). There can be no static "right" answer to the question of the degree to which an undefined person with an ambiguously perceived disability is "different." Different to whom and for what purpose?

The Social Context of Disablement

There is no meaning to the concept of disability independent of the contexts in which it occurs. In fact, whether or not a condition is even considered a disability can be determined by cultural factors. Thus, historical, cultural, religious, and socioeconomic factors all enter into the matrix of meanings from which reactions to a specific child by specific persons emerge. Nonetheless, particular subcultures do seem to have fairly common attitudes, as demonstrated by the ease with which stereotypes about the disabled can be elicited (Siller, 1976b).

After a brief characterization of some of the background factors in-

volved, we shall consider some of the parental, sibling, peer, school, and communal attitudes obtained from research and clinical studies, ending with a description of a set of basic attitudinal dimensions that seem to encompass the primary salient dimensions of attitudes toward the disabled.

Historically, disability or the impairment of the health of a child has been viewed as a negative feature. Although certain conditions may have received special exemption for one reason or another at a particular period in time, disability as a stigmatized condition has been the rule. No fully satisfactory reasons have been advanced to account for the consistent negativity expressed (Siller, Chipman, Ferguson, & Vann, 1967a; Wright, 1960). Certain religions have attached negative moral meanings to disability—sin on the part of parents—or positive ones—having been specially chosen by the Creator. For example, if a teacher or administrator holds a religious belief that disability involves sinfulness (as certain fundamentalist and orthodox believers do), it is possible that this will have an influence on actual behavior. Social class has also been found to enter into the way in which someone with a disability is perceived.

In addition to social class and cultural and historical background, a wide variety of factors have been identified as having import in the interaction of the disabled with the nondisabled. Some of these include the age, sex, and other demographic characteristics of the nondisabled, the personalities of the disabled and the nondisabled, the physical status of the person (i.e., disabled or not), specific experiences, amount and quality of contact, type of teaching situation, whether the child remains in a single classroom, the achievement level of the disabled, the coping style, the acknowledgment or nonacknowledgment of the disability by the disabled, and the context of the interaction. Almost any variable identified for the disabled or the nondisabled has its counterpart in the other. We shall briefly characterize our impression of the general status of these factors.

Age, sex, and other demographic variables are important mostly in the manner in which attitudes toward the disabled are expressed rather than in their formation. Thus, females may have attitudes similar to males but will be more likely to express them in ways influenced by their sex role. Negative response to disabled children is seen in preschoolers. Adolescents of both sexes tend to be more rejecting than younger or older persons. Hard generalizations regarding the influence of these various demographic factors cannot be made, since their operations are complex and unlikely to be described in a direct and simple way.

The personality of the nondisabled person has been studied in relation to attitudes toward the disabled. In general, significant but weak relationships have been found for a variety of personality dimensions having "positive" variables, such as ego strength, body-image boundaries, upbringing, and good adjustment and social-interaction measures, which cor-

relate with acceptance; more "negative" variables, such as anxiety, hostility, alienation, and authoritarianism correlate with rejection (Noonan, Barry, & Davis, 1970; Siller et al., 1967a; Yuker, Block, & Young, 1966). Particular ego-defensive structures of the nondisabled have been shown to be particularly related to negativity (Gladstone, 1977). The pattern of results from numerous studies suggests that "ego strength" and the ability to attain stable relationships with others underlie positive reactions toward the disabled. Ethnocentrism is clearly related to negative attitudes and is highly general in nature. Those who express ethnocentrism toward other out-groups tend to express negative attitudes toward the physically disabled.

The particular context in which a disabled-nondisabled interaction takes place can be most important, for instance, physical activities in schools or camps or competitive situations where the disability may be seen as limiting achievement. In fact, in one study on the effects of the presence of a blind person on verbal learning and associative clustering, a belief was found that one's performance was impaired when interacting with the blind individual rather than when interacting with a sighted one, even though the objective evidence was to the contrary (Jones, 1970). Fear of negative social implications from others for the nondisabled also has been shown to be an element in their attitude orientation (Siller et al., 1967a; Siller, Ferguson, Vann, & Holland, 1967b).

Recent research studies are beginning to specify concrete ways that can enhance or retard disabled-nondisabled interactions. Thus, presenting oneself as coping and simply acknowledging one's condition received favorable responses (Bazakas, 1977). Interestingly, either coping or acknowledgment alone was insufficient to promote positive response in the experimental interaction situation. Achievement level and type of school service received has also been shown to influence acceptance.

Contact with those who have impairments is clearly related to attitudes. However, the relationship between contact and its consequences can be either favorable or unfavorable depending on other contingencies. Conditions favoring positive or negative interactions have been explored in previous research in the area of ethnic attitudes (e.g., Allport, 1954; Amir, 1969) and need not be repeated here. In general, we have found that it is the quality rather than the quantity of the contact between the disabled and the nondisabled that is important (Siller et al., 1967a). Structuring the environment in the school and other settings will substantially affect interaction outcomes and should be an important aspect of educational planning for the health impaired and disabled child.

Families with health impaired or disabled children face such obvious problems as financial costs, time for care, restrictions on movements, emotional stress, and so on. The extent of any of these as real problems varies,

but their general relevance cannot be doubted. As a consequence, the child can carry into the school situation the effects of overprotectiveness, infantilization, rejection, and other interfering feelings. However, not all or even necessarily most parents of children with impairments have such emotionally distorting attitudes and behaviors. Many parents have been able to deal very successfully with the complexities introduced by the condition. What most likely holds true is that the normal ambivalence present in *all* parent-child relationships is the rule and that individual children will bring into their emotional life both constructive and destructive identifications and behavioral patterns. The educator, by avoiding oversimplistic reasoning and stereotyping, can build on the strengths of the child to try to avoid reinforcing secondary gains (advantages derived by being "sick") and other by-products of disturbed family environments. Needless to say, a clear relationship between parental acceptance and the child's self-esteem exists. The educator, as a parental surrogate and in his or her own right, can play an important role in supporting the child's positive feelings of self. In turn, children with positive self-esteems have better capability to deal with the opportunities and demands of the school situation.

Attitudes of educators toward the disabled child have received considerable attention. Unfortunately, the results of these studies are far from unequivocable owing to such factors as sample size and representativeness, measurement weaknesses, experimental design, statistical problems, and the very conceptualization of the problem. Another element clouding the interpretation of results is that the milieu of the schools is changing due to Public Law 94-142. Data from the past will become increasingly obsolete because of the influx and mixture of children with disabilities into the regular school system and classroom.

Without attempting a methodological critique of the literature, we shall summarize some of the outstanding findings as reported in the general research literature. Not surprisingly, familiarity with a condition generally lessens negativity, and teachers who have had specific experience with one kind of disability tend to prefer to continue to work with that kind. Our own experience with special education teachers and students suggests that although many would willingly work with children of most any type of impairment, many others have distinct preferences for a particular type. One might expect that greater familiarity and knowledge would help make teachers more comfortable in working with new populations. Elementary school teachers were found to express attitudes similar to the general population, which would suggest the need for special training. Although some have found that attitudes of teachers toward the handicapped are mildly favorable, it is also possible that experience with the handicapped (at least for a retarded population) may increase rejection by the teacher. At this point the question cannot be whether training for teachers should be

undertaken, but rather what would be the most effective training for helping *all* teachers, regardless of special education status.

At least one study (Harasymiw & Horne, 1975) found an absence of a relationship between the number of special education courses and favorable attitudes. The nature of what constitutes special education courses might be in question. Can one infer that course work geared to the cognitive dimension without dealing with the more affective aspects of disabled-nondisabled interactions is insufficient to effect favorable attitudinal growth?

Teachers, as do other populations, can view the disabled both in terms of the specificity of their conditions and in a more generalized way. For example, Wechsler, Suarez, and McFadden (1975) surveyed 547 teachers and found that children with asthma or heart conditions and children requiring crutches and braces were viewed as more easily integrated into the regular classroom than children with visual or hearing problems or histories of convulsions and seizures. Those teachers with previous experience teaching physically handicapped children were most optimistic about integrating these children into the regular classroom. Other studies also document how the sensorially impaired are least preferred to be taught by educators of various levels of training and responsibility.

Studies on teachers' attitudes are becoming supplemented by an appreciation of the role of educational administrators. The literature here, however, is rather sparse and should be supplemented by future intensive work.

We have only briefly characterized what by now has become an extensive literature. Scores of other studies have examined the social position of the physically disabled by means of various preference and ranking studies. It is clear from all this work that physical disability is in most instances a stigmatized condition with distinct social implications. One early study found that physically disabled children were not accepted by normal children in integrated classes and that few of these children had enough positive assets to offset completely the negative effect of being labeled handicapped by their classmates (Force, 1956). A general pattern of the early studies (which mostly used sociometric approaches) seems to indicate that despite the practice of placing exceptional children in regular classes on the basis that this enables them to maintain normal relations with their peers, this does not prevent segregation from their peers (Gronlund, 1959).

Later studies in the 1960s continued to support the findings of the earlier reports. A general orientation of status devaluation repeatedly emerges. As the pressure for mainstreaming increases in the 1980s, one would expect that the greater influx of disabled children into the regular school system would have an impact greater than in the past. Although definitive studies are yet to be done, future work can build on the following

suggestive results of past work: There is a need to create a milieu that will maximize successful interactions, since children have pronounced early attitudes toward disability. These attitudes tend to be negative and maintained and built on with development, tend to isolate or at least lead to differential treatment of children with impairments, and are highly influenced by parental and teacher attitudes. The actual performance of the child may or may not influence interaction outcomes for the good, but it rather easily affects such interactions for the bad. Careful attention to setting the stage for constructive interactions is necessary, since contact alone may have negative rather than positive consequences.

Some clarification of the manner in which those with disabilities are perceived by the nondisabled has been offered in a series of studies, which are thus suggestive of strategies for changing attitude (Siller, 1976b; Siller et al., 1967a, 1967b). Essentially, the position was taken that attitudes toward the disabled are multidimensional rather than just reflective of a unidimensional acceptance-rejection position. Accordingly, a series of empirically based studies was undertaken to identify and measure salient dimensions of attitudes toward the disabled. Factor analytic procedures were used on sets of attitude questionnaires dealing with a variety of disability conditions; seven major attitude dimensions were identified, and scales to measure these attitudes were developed. These seven components are as follows:

- *Interaction strain*—uneasiness in the presence of disabled persons and uncertainty about how to deal with them.

- *Rejection of intimacy*—rejection of close, particularly familial, relationships with the disabled.

- *Generalized rejection*—a pervasive negative and derogatory approach to disabled persons with a consequent advocacy of segregation.

- *Authoritarian virtuousness*—ostensibly a "prodisabled" orientation, this factor is really rooted in an authoritarian context that manifests itself in a call for special treatment that is less benevolent and more harmful than it seems.

- *Inferred emotional consequences*—intense hostile references to the character and emotions of the disabled person.

- *Distressed identification*—personalized hypersensitivity to disabled persons, who activate anxiety about one's own vulnerability to disability.

- *Imputed functional limitations*—devaluation of the capacities of a disabled person in coping with his or her environment.

These seven dimensions are fairly comprehensive in describing attitudes toward disability and can be taken to provide a discriminative separation of important components of attitudes toward a wide variety of stigmatized conditions.

Disabilities in the Mathematics Classroom

Disabilities come in many forms and degrees. By some standards virtually all of us are disabled to some extent. By law, no more than 12% of us are disabled. For the purposes of the teacher of mathematics, a physical disability is of importance in the mathematics classroom precisely to the extent that it affects the learning of mathematics.

Disabilities can affect the learning of mathematics in many ways. A child who has fewer than 10 fingers will be unable to use fingers in the usual way as a model for the base ten numeration system. A child with visual difficulties will be unable to see pictures and writing produced by the teacher at the front of the classroom. A child who is in constant pain may be unable to concentrate on long abstract mathematical derivations. As we mentioned earlier, a pupil who is often absent (physically or mentally) will be at a disadvantage in learning a sequential subject like mathematics in which the understanding of one concept often depends on a knowledge of previously taught concepts.

Teaching mathematics is difficult under the best of circumstances. The teacher of mathematics deals with the human mind (the most complex and remarkable entity known) and with a subject that has historically been as difficult to learn as any other school subject. Since the beginning of recorded history, only a small minority have become proficient in mathematics. Surely, teaching mathematics to "normal" children would seem to be sufficiently difficult without making matters worse by mainstreaming children who have disabilities and who will further complicate the teacher's life. Yet, there is some reason to suppose that the teacher who modifies his or her teaching to accommodate students with certain obvious disabilities may learn through that process to be a better teacher for other students with less obvious individual variations. In discussing the role of blind students in his university mathematics classes, Utz (1979) notes that by being a more effective teacher for special students, he became a more effective teacher for all.

One or more disabled students in a classroom may help the teacher remember to deal with individual differences of all sorts. Many of the techniques that teachers have used successfully with the disabled are also helpful with the nondisabled, and vice versa. Thus, the following suggestions for teaching mathematics to disabled students may be helpful in teaching those who are not disabled, even though the emphasis here is on the physically disabled.

Recognizing the Problem

Physical disabilities range from those that are easily identified, such as serious orthopedic abnormalities, to those that are unlikely to attract any special attention in the classroom, such as epilepsy or leukemia. In general, the teacher should be alert in watching for unusual behavior that may signal

underlying physical problems. Children often manage to hide the symptoms of such disabilities for surprisingly long periods of time. Some years ago a teacher noticed a bright high school senior who always sat in the front row and squinted at the chalkboard. Questioning established that he could hardly make out anything written on the board (though it was less than 3 meters from him). He had had the problem for at least 3 years, but his family adhered to a religion that disapproves of medical intervention in physical problems. By moving the boy's seat still closer to the board and writing larger, the teacher was able to solve the problem temporarily. A discussion with the family convinced them that he really needed glasses to succeed in school as well as to lead a normal life, and he soon appeared in class with a pair of glasses that greatly improved his ability to do mathematics. Often young children have almost completely lost the ability to hear before anybody notices. They read lips, watch what others do, and generally avoid talking when possible.

Other physical problems, including paralysis, emotional problems, heart and lung diseases, speech defects, allergies, and many brain dysfunctions, may be noticed first by an alert teacher who has a good measure for assessing normal behavior and sees children in situations that make such recognition particularly easy. The identification and referral of children with untreated and possibly unidentified physical problems is an important part of the teacher's job, and there is much material elsewhere in this book that will help teachers do this task efficiently. Here we concentrate primarily on certain negative effects physical disabilities are likely to have on the learning of mathematics and what the teacher can do to alleviate those negative effects.

Physical disabilities often have serious, unexpected negative consequences for learning mathematics. For example, the ability to perform certain Piagetian conservation tasks is apparently delayed in deaf children by one or more years (e.g., Springer, 1978). Interestingly, a small sample of deaf children from Springer's study who were raised by deaf families conserved about as soon as and as well as the hearing group. Presumably the reason for this is that the acquisition of conservation concepts comes through social contact with people (usually adults) who conserve. Any interference in such social contacts slows the acquisition of conservation. This interpretation is further supported by the observation that blind institutionalized children conserve later than those who live at home. Thus, any physical disability that interferes with the usual social activities of children can be expected to produce late development of important concepts that teachers usually take for granted in children of a given age. The lack of such concepts should not suggest intellectual inability so much as a probable lack of appropriate experience.

For children whose development seems to be delayed for lack of certain

kinds of experience, the usual teaching can be delayed while appropriate experiences are made available. For example, for conservation of number, have children work with bunches of things (Popsicle sticks, pieces of candy, etc.) and with one or more persons who do conserve. However, there is considerable evidence that conservation is supported by the ability to measure as well as vice versa; so teaching a child to count and measure while supplying appropriate conservation experiences may be helpful, contrary to some of the early Piagetian pronouncements.

A related problem that often results from physical disabilities involves absences from school. If the absence occurs while the child is registered for your course, you should keep track of what is being missed and either arrange for remedial work when the child returns or, if the absence is likely to be a long one and the child is able to study at home or in the hospital, make arrangements for the child to continue with the work the class is doing. Parents, siblings, friends, visiting teachers, and others may be available to help in this endeavor. Some ways to work with such helpers are discussed further in another section of this chapter.

Sometimes the work you plan to introduce in class will be so complex and unusual that you do not believe others will be able to do the subject justice. If you are unable to do it yourself, you may wish to suggest various kinds of practice that the student can do to prepare for an efficient introduction on returning to school. For example, if you plan to introduce a two-digit addition algorithm, you might propose that the child practice addition and subtraction facts to be more proficient in these and thus be able to learn the two-digit algorithms for these operations more readily.

Absences from school that have occurred in previous grades are usually much harder to track down. For example, a child may have been absent for many months while his or her classmates were learning to operate with fractions. The resulting deficiencies may not become obvious or crucial until the student is studying rational expressions in algebra or possibly during the study of trigonometric functions. Improved methods of tracking students through the educational system can greatly reduce the seriousness of this sort of problem. First, teachers should make records of difficulties children have for whatever reason, and these records should be passed on to the student's subsequent teachers. Presumably, such records would have included information about physical or other disabilities a student may have. Second, cumulative diagnostic tests should be administered early enough in the school year so that remedial action can be taken. Third, teachers should get into the habit of pretesting and preteaching topics that are prerequisite for material that is about to be introduced. Before attempting to teach children to add fractions with unlike denominators, for example, you should check to see that children can add and multiply whole numbers and that they have a good intuitive understanding of the meaning of fractions. Of course, a

well-organized textbook should provide opportunities to teach and test such prerequisite material before the new topic is introduced.

Speaking of tests, there are many reasons to view the results of formal tests with some skepticism. The literature is full of critiques of standardized and nonstandardized tests, but a further caution should be noted when dealing with the physically handicapped. The form and specific content of a test may prevent children with certain specific physical deficiencies from showing their true intellectual abilities. This has been shown to be true for certain standard tests and some physical disabilities (Heil, 1978) and is certainly true for others. Thus, appropriate testing may require one-to-one oral communication between teacher and pupil, special kinds of written assignments, or other creative evaluation procedures on the part of the teacher (see the section below regarding communication).

Perhaps the most common kind of absence from mathematics class is one that is sometimes difficult to recognize and hard to deal with: mental absence. This problem exists under the best of conditions, and students who have other problems, such as serious physical disabilities, learning disabilities, and possibly the taking of medication for such disabilities, may have greater cause to "turn off" from time to time. Methods for reducing the duration and frequency of such mental absences are discussed in other sections of this chapter ("Communication" and "Making Mathematics Meaningful"), but beyond this, the teacher ought to come back to different topics from time to time, preferably in a new context so as not to bore those who remember. Usually this will reduce the overall cumulative effects of mental absences.

Teachers should remember that differences among children identified as physically handicapped (and among "normal" children as well) will be greater than the average difference between the physically handicapped as a group and the "normal" children as a group. Thus, all the comments made here are likely to be more pertinent for some "normal" children than for some disabled children. Further, it is important to remember that having recognized one physical disability does not free the teacher from watching for others. Disabilities often come in bunches, and contrary to popular myth a person who is disabled in one faculty is not necessarily stronger in others—often the opposite is true. So teachers must look for, and respond to, differences among all students, disabled or not.

Coping with Prejudices

Most people have a tendency to be prejudiced against things and people that are different. Such prejudices are magnified when the differences are of such a nature that they may cause us extra work or in some way reduce the benefits or pleasures we are accustomed to having. A physically disabled student in the classroom is likely to elicit prejudices from both fellow

students and teachers. One of the teacher's first responsibilities is to recognize and deal with these prejudices in a rational and constructive manner.

Salvia, Algozzine, and Sheare (1977) demonstrated that young children who have attractive faces get better grades from teachers than those who are less attractive when effects of achievement are controlled. Apparently, teachers expect attractive children to do better than unattractive children, and these expectations are known to be self-fulfilling to at least some extent. Thus if a disability has characteristics that make the victim seem less attractive to teachers and others, the problems inherent in the disability will be greatly magnified.

Even if the child does not seem physically less attractive than others, the child's teacher or peers might resent the extra time, effort, and facilities needed to accommodate the child's disabilities. The psychological, emotional, and physical demands on a teacher are generally greater for a handicapped child than for a nonhandicapped child.

There are ways to reduce the negative effects of teacher and peer prejudice if the teacher is prepared to take an active leadership role in doing so. The first step is to recognize both your own and your pupils' concerns (legitimate and otherwise). Then try to take actions that will remove or reduce the legitimate objections. Try not to spend so much of your time looking after the needs of the disabled that you ignore the needs of the others. Try not to accept social behavior from one child that would be totally unacceptable in another. Try not to neglect the legitimate needs of one child for the less legitimate needs of another.

Second, try to identify the strong points of each of your students (disabled or not) and build from those strong points (this suggestion is pursued further in the next section of this chapter).

Third, plan group activities in which mathematical and other intellectual activities are the center of attention and in which the disabled child will be able to work closely and positively with others. Careful planning may be necessary to improve the opportunities for success in such activities. Try to arrange for the disabled child to work first with other students who are reasonably sensitive and accepting of differences in others—preferably leaders if possible—and gradually expand the contacts to include other class members. But the essential point is to try to include situations in which each person can make positive contributions and in which everybody has the opportunity to learn about others' weaknesses and strengths, similarities and differences.

Improving Students' Self-Image

Everybody thinks of himself or herself as special. Some of us think of ourselves as being especially good, some of us think of ourselves as being

especially bad, and most of us realize that we have both strong and weak attributes and that in fact our strengths and weaknesses change from time to
time and situation to situation. Somebody who has a particular disability or
weakness may tend to overemphasize it and begin to believe that there is no
hope for real success. This can become a self-fulfilling belief and, unless
broken, destructive of attempts to help the individual succeed.

For various reasons, mathematics has a special place in the development of students' self-images. Many people think of mathematics as a particularly difficult subject to learn, and some people still think of it as a subject designed only for certain people (usually male, "brainy," middle class,
etc.). Young women, people from lower socioeconomic groups, and others
who do not fit the stereotype of a mathematics learner may come to believe
that mathematics is not important for them and that even if it is important,
they cannot learn it. Lately there has been much written on "math
anxiety," especially as it affects females. The teacher who faces this problem in students, disabled or not, should refer to some of that material.

Because of its special place as a difficult or esoteric subject in the minds
of many people, success in mathematics can be especially important to a
person who otherwise has a poor self-image. "If mathematics is a very hard
subject and I can succeed at that, then I should be able to succeed at
anything." The teacher of mathematics, then, has a special opportunity to
help erase low self-images as well as a special challenge.

In order to foster success you should first strive for success at *anything,*
then build on that. For example, some years ago a young boy in a California
high school approached the advisor of the student paper and asked to join
its staff. The advisor knew the boy and his family had a reputation for being
limited intellectually as well as in the social graces. The teacher refused. As
the boy was about to leave, the advisor remembered that the advisor of the
photography club seemed to enjoy working with troublemakers and suggested that the boy join the photography club. Within a year the boy had
won a prize in a national photographic contest and decided that he would
like to go to college. Although his academic record was bad, it was
theoretically possible for him to complete all the necessary work to get into
college except the mathematics. He agreed to take mathematics through a
correspondence course with the help of the photography club advisor's
wife, who happened to be a physicist. He completed 9th-grade algebra and
10th-grade geometry in short order and then decided he liked them so much
that he would continue. Today the young man is not only the first person in
his family to have graduated from college but also the first person in his
family to be a Ph.D. mathematician and a professor at a major university.
Had he not been given the opportunity to succeed at photography, he would
probably never have even graduated from high school.

Success breeds success, and the teacher should try to create situations

in which each student has an opportunity to succeed. The success, however, *must be real.* To compliment a normally intelligent 8-year-old for knowing that $2 + 2 = 4$, for example, is patronizing and insulting. You should make realistic demands on children and then do everything in your power to see to it that they succeed. When they do succeed, they should be told explicitly that they have succeeded and encouraged to continue succeeding.

The fine line between being too demanding and not sufficiently demanding is often hard to tread, but some suggestions may help:

1. Arrange the task so that essentially nonpertinent disabilities do not interfere with it.

2. Make assignments short, specific, and clear and be sure the student understands what is expected.

3. Until considerable confidence is developed, have the students do some or all of the assignment under supervision. This allows you to recognize and help with unexpected difficulties whether or not they are related to disabilities and also increases the chance that the student will make a real effort to do the assignment. Help children get started if they seem not to be proceeding efficiently. Such help may be very specific or quite general, depending on circumstances.

4. Assignments should be checked, so that the student knows how successful he or she has been. (Checking can be done by the teacher, by a helper, by another student, or by the student who did the assignment.)

5. Frustration is good in small quantities but can be very bad in large doses. Make the task sufficiently frustrating so that the student feels a sense of accomplishment when it is completed but not so frustrating that it is unlikely to be completed.

6. Remember that the most precious resource you have at your disposal is the children's time. Do not waste it by giving inane busywork. If there is no appropriate homework assignment, do not give one. If there is appropriate work that can be done independently, decide what you want to achieve with it and assign work that will achieve your aims as efficiently as possible without wasting time. Teacher time is also limited, and you ought not to spend time checking papers that could be spent working with individual children or planning creative lessons. There are many ways you can get help checking mathematics papers. Paid or volunteer assistants can often do this work, or good students can help: The first person with a perfect paper checks the rest of the papers (this is usually considered a reward for success), or students can sometimes exchange papers or even check their own. Of course, some work ought to be checked by the teacher, but you should consider carefully which work really needs your personal attention and which can be read by somebody else.

All this activity should be designed to lead to real, solid achievement

for each child and an accompanying sense of satisfaction and feeling of self-worth.

Deciding Who Should Learn Mathematics

No more than 40 years ago it was widely believed that mathematics should be studied by people who were going to be engineers, physical scientists, accountants, or mathematics teachers. Virtually everybody else could get along nicely with no more than the rudiments of arithmetic. Today, professions such as biology, the social sciences, designing, medicine, and so on that once required little or no mathematics now require at least calculus and statistics and often mathematics that is considerably more advanced and esoteric. This trend shows no signs of abating, and we shall certainly see a time within 40 years when most desirable professions will require some mathematics that is well beyond that usually taught in the secondary school. A person who does not have a strong mathematical background is at a distinct disadvantage in today's world and will be even more disadvantaged in the future. People who have physical disabilities are already at a disadvantage. To increase that disadvantage by also not knowing mathematics would be inexcusably shortsighted. Thus, there is little doubt that disabilities, rather than being used as an excuse for not learning a lot of mathematics, should generally be a sign that as much mathematics as possible should be studied.

As for what mathematics should be studied, disabled people will need essentially the same mathematical skills and understandings as other people. Many good statements of such needs are available (e.g., Association of Mathematics Teachers of New York State, 1977; National Council of Supervisors of Mathematics, 1977). Recent statements on appropriate mathematics differ from much previous practice in that they emphasize such things as understanding at the student's level, estimation and approximation, the use of calculators and computers, probability, statistics, and most important, the ability and desire to think and solve real problems using mathematics. Leaders in mathematics education generally seem worried about the "back to basics" movement and so continually emphasize the fact that thinking is the most basic skill and the other skills should be taught in such a way as to foster thinking. This point of view is at least as appropriate for the disabled as for the nondisabled.

Communication

The word *communicate* can mean either "to give or impart knowledge" or "to have an interchange of thoughts and information." Most teaching is more effective if the second meaning is emphasized more heavily than the first. This is likely to be particularly true when there are substantial differences in experiences and outlook between teacher and

pupil. When the pupil is handicapped and the teacher is not, the need for two-way communication is especially important. The teacher should try to find out as much as possible about the pupil's interests, abilities, fears, and problems. Then the teacher should use this information to help improve communication.

For example, a Connecticut teacher who was trying to teach the standard division algorithm to an emotionally disturbed girl had no success until she discovered that the girl loved to dance and was an excellent dancer. The teacher choreographed the steps of the division algorithm so the girl could dance through the whole thing on the floor. The procedure was gradually adapted to pencil and paper, and the girl became adept at dividing.

In emphasizing two-way communication and building on children's strengths and interests, the teacher must not relinquish the professional obligations inherent in the teacher's job. The teacher is responsible for deciding what mathematics is to be learned and how it is to be learned. Communications from the student should supply information with which to discharge these obligations more effectively but should not be used to avoid the responsibility of making the decisions. If the students are as qualified as the teacher to decide what is to be learned and how it is to be learned, there would appear to be some injustice in paying the teacher to teach or insisting that the students learn.

Two-way communication should continue during virtually all the time there is interaction between the teacher and the class. Especially with younger children and children with problems that may negatively affect learning, there should be no long lectures and there should be ways for the teacher to get immediate responses from all members of the class. There are many ways to get these responses, several of which are listed here:

1. Encourage children to join in the discussion voluntarily.

2. Call on specific children to answer certain questions or discuss certain points.

3. Have the class respond in unison to questions that have unambiguous and short answers.

4. Have each student respond with a predetermined signal to multiple choice questions (yes or no, etc.). For example, holding the hands out with the thumbs up would mean yes, thumbs down would mean no, and holding the hand flat so the thumb and fingers point sideways might mean that there is not enough information to decide.

5. Have each pupil respond to numerical questions by using response cubes. For answers from 0 through 10, two cubes are used. One cube has the digits 0, 1, 2, 3, 4, 5 on it; the other has 5, 6, 7, 8, 9, and 10 on it. If the teacher asks, "What is 3 plus 5?" each student finds the 8 on the face of the second cube and wraps a hand around the cube so only the 8 is showing.

Then the hand and cube are held against the student's chest so nobody else can see until the teacher says "Show me" or some similar command, and all the students show the answer. The teacher says, "That's right. 3 + 5 = 8." Using this technique, the teacher can quickly see whether everybody is participating and also identify anybody who is making mistakes. Children have the advantage of knowing immediately whether they are right or wrong (and what the correct answer is if they were wrong) and also are not embarrassed by having the rest of the class know when they have made a mistake. For two-digit numbers, two more cubes designating 0–5 tens and 5–10 tens can be used. Having the tens cube slightly larger than the units cube (a 2-cm cube for units and a 2.5-cm cube for the tens is a good size for most 6-year-old's hands) and a different color is beneficial to help both the teacher and the students distinguish them from each other. Obviously, if a child is orthopedically disabled in such a way as to make this difficult or impossible, other alternatives are available. The disabled child might whisper the answer directly to the teacher, write it, or show it in some other way. Often this will require the teacher to go to that child (or have the child sit near the teacher) for such response exercises.

6. Use response cards with four number wheels on them to show more than two digits. The card can be made with eyelets holding the number wheels to the card and allowing them to turn, with notches cut to show only one digit at a time for each wheel. Such a card can show four-digit numbers, digital time (when the little hand is between 3 and 4 and the big hand points to the 7, the time is shown as 0335), fractions (the first two digits show the numerator and the last two show the denominator; so 2/5 is shown as 0205), and even decimals (have the student hold the card from behind and point one finger over the top to the place where the decimal point would be).

Of course, if some disability interferes with any of the procedures above for a specific child, make the necessary modifications. Usually this is not as difficult or traumatic as you might expect if you have a good healthy relationship with the child and with the class. For example, in one class that was field testing material using finger sets, the teacher consulted the program director about a child who was missing all the fingers on one hand. In the procedure, children show the numbers from 0 to 10 on their fingers, but each number is always shown the same way so that finger counting can be reduced as children memorize the finger sets. Ultimately, it makes it much easier to wean children away from counting on their fingers. The director could not suggest a good way to solve the teacher's difficulty and so consulted the authors of the material. The authors suggested two or three rather cumbersome solutions, which the teacher planned on suggesting to the girl after the first class on finger sets. This turned out to be unnecessary, since

the girl approached the teacher after the lesson and explained, "You'll have to watch me carefully for numbers greater than 5 because I'll show them by holding up all five fingers first and then the extras." Children often come up with the best solutions to problems of this sort if given a chance, and solving their own problems is good for them when they are able to do it.

There are many people, other than the children themselves, who can help you do a better job of teaching. Certainly the most important such people are parents or parent surrogates. Members of the family provide most of the early experiences of children and a major share of the experiences children have even after they start school. As mentioned earlier, those experiences are important in the development of the various Piagetian concepts and other concepts that we take for granted in teaching mathematics. We build on experiences children have elsewhere when teaching mathematics, and if those experiences have not occurred, or for some reason were not productive, we may fail to communicate with the child. Thus, the family situation is important in the mathematical development of the child.

If a child has been institutionalized or is in an abnormal family situation, special attention must be paid to the kinds of understandings children usually develop outside of school. Conservation, some numeral recognition and understanding of numbers, simple geometric concepts and words, and so forth are commonly assumed for a 5- or 6-year-old child. If these have not developed, some specific experiences can be planned that will help the child develop the concepts. The teacher may supply some of these experiences in school but should also try to enlist the help of parents or parent surrogates to provide more experiences.

Getting the cooperation of parents or parent surrogates is the first step in upgrading out-of-school experiences. Generally this is easier than some teachers expect. Parents and others responsible for the welfare of children almost always are interested in the child's education and will do what they can to improve it. Just as parents are willing to see that children take medicine or do the exercises that are prescribed by a physician, they are also generally willing to see that a child does the specific things prescribed by a teacher. The problem is to communicate clearly what is needed and why. For example, if a 7-year-old child has not yet learned the addition facts and most of the other children in the class have, you might send a letter of the following sort home:

Dear Mr. and Mrs. Jones:

In about two weeks I plan to start teaching the class a procedure for adding two numbers greater than 10. This is easier if everybody in the class knows well the addition facts up to 10. John is one of the children in the class this year

who does not yet know all of these facts as well as I would like, so I would appreciate your help in this matter.

I suggest that you spend four or five minutes at a time with John in a quiet place asking him addition questions such as "What is 7 + 8?" When he gets the correct answer, reward him with a compliment, such as "That's good" or "Right" and give him another problem. If he gets a wrong answer, simply say "No" or some other noncritical statement. Do not become irritated during these sessions, and if you believe either you or John is getting tired, stop even before the four or five minutes is up.

You should not worry about John, since he is working hard and learning much in school, but he will do even better if you or some member of the family can spend a few minutes working with him in this way two or three times each day.

If you have any questions about John's progress or what we are doing in school this year, please write, call, or come in and talk with me.

Sincerely,

Such a letter will usually elicit the desired response, and you should see a noticeable improvement in the skill. Beyond that, it offers an opportunity for parents or other responsible adults to become actively involved in the child's education and thus to show their support for that education. Another good result that sometimes comes from such letters is an improved relationship between parent and child. In some cases where this has been tried, either the parent or the chld has later admitted that this produced the only regular time the two were together without the parent being critical of the child or too busy to pay attention to the child's needs.

Of course, such letters should not be the only communication from school to home. You may wish to telephone the parents. Parent-teacher conferences in school are often effective, and meetings of the teacher with large numbers of parents may also be used to help communicate. Each of these methods has the advantage that communication from the parent to you is more likely but the disadvantages that the parent usually does not have anything specific in writing and some parents will be unable or unwilling to come to school. These disadvantages can be reduced by using more than one technique (give letters to parents at a conference or follow up a telephone call with a letter, for example).

In addition to the preceding communications, there are other specific ways of making use of the child's family to help teach mathematics. So-called homework is a standard technique. Less common but known effective procedures include establishing a lending library of mathematical games (see the next section for more suggestions about these), flash cards, or electronic equivalents to flash cards. Check each item in and out as you

would a library book and allow them to stay out for only a specific length of time.

All of these are effective methods of developing skills and can be used with some pleasure and positive effects in the home.

Perhaps the most important thing to remember in communicating with parents or parent surrogates is that they have information you do not have that may be useful in helping their child learn mathematics. Give the parents an opportunity to talk about their physically disabled child—ask about the child's interests, strengths, and weaknesses, and then use this information to teach more effectively.

In addition to parents, some of the people with whom you must communicate to help you do a better job of teaching mathematics include special resource teachers, guidance counselors, the child's other teachers if your school is departmentalized, volunteers or paid teacher's aides, other school personnel such as the school secretary, the school nurse, the custodian, and so on. Each of these people may have information about a child that will help you do a better job of teaching. For physically disabled children, the school nurse, a resource teacher, and the guidance counselor are likely to have especially helpful information about the child as well as general information about the particular disability. An alert, intelligent school secretary is also likely to be the source of much useful information. There is no one set pattern for communicating with these various people, but it is generally well to remember that helpful suggestions and information are often available in apparently unlikely places, and the teacher should try to keep two-way lines of communication open with everybody who might be able to help either with information or by their direct actions. For example, under social services or some similar title in the yellow pages of your local telephone directory you will find a long list of organizations that may be able to provide or tell you about materials and information that are available to help people who have the particular physical disabilities with which you are dealing. Try to use these communications in creative, effective ways that will improve the child's education.

Making Mathematics Meaningful

Unfortunately, mathematics seems to be perceived by many adults and children as a sort of dreary branch of theology, designed principally for the purpose of keeping young children busy when they might otherwise be idle and perhaps, therefore, doing something of which their elders would disapprove. In this view, mathematics has replaced the 19th-century custom of having children make samplers, except that whereas samplers were beautiful and cherished when finished, mathematics, when completed, is seen as a product that is immediately disposable. Teachers and children alike must understand and remember that mathematics should be used to develop the

mind, not the soul. Mathematics is useful. Mathematics should save work or make possible the achievement of some goal that would otherwise be unattainable. Mathematics should be taught so that students see it as useful, enjoyable, and a way of avoiding unnecessary work or of solving otherwise unsolvable problems that they wish to solve.

There are many things a teacher can do to foster this positive attitude toward mathematics. All are appropriate for any student, but some are especially useful in teaching disabled children.

1. *Socialize mathematics.* Mathematics is a social activity and should be taught that way. Normal adults who use mathematics in their everyday lives usually try to involve others. Whether the activity involves doubling a recipe, paying taxes, or creating new mathematics, most people try to talk to somebody else about what they are doing in order to get the benefit of the other person's judgment and creativity. In fact, university mathematics departments tend to be very social, and it is nearly impossible to hire a mathematician to teach at a university unless the school has or will hire another mathematician with a sufficiently similar specialty for them to talk to each other about their research.

Both because it is more realistic and because it is more enjoyable, mathematics ought to be taught in a social context whenever possible. Many times a concept or skill can be taught or practiced through some form of group project. For example, measurement activities lend themselves naturally to projects; groups of pupils can collect information for analyses of good and poor buys in the grocery store, thus learning some statistics, the use of decimals (money and measures), ratios, and geometry (size and shape of containers). Games can be used to practice skills and develop concepts. Students can help each other practice specific skills in pairs or in small groups. Virtually all mathematics can be discussed in small or large groups. Of course, there are times when you will have to insist that children work in isolation, but these times ought to be kept to a minimum. Under no circumstances should individualization be equated with isolation or solitary confinement.

In planning projects, be sure you arrange the groups so every member can contribute, and try to make it clear that if one member does not contribute, the others will suffer. Children are more inclined to do the expected work if they realize others will be hurt if they fail. Use the same principle when having children learn the addition facts, for example. Have an addition table in front of the class that everybody can see. Mark off those facts that everybody knows well. Then tell children to help each other learn the remaining facts. They can use flash cards, practice orally, try to explain relations to known facts, or use other techniques, but make the children responsible for and to each other. For children who have disabilities, you should make a special attempt to make them responsible for other students

who need their help to emphasize the fact that we are all interdependent and we can each help others in some ways while being helped by others in different ways.

2. *Use games.* Games can be used for skill practice but should also have mathematical thinking problems inherent in them to encourage students to identify and solve their own problems rather than just solve so-called word problems, which are often of little interest to the student. Games should also generally require both luck and skill to win, since a game that is all skill will quickly become boring because it will usually be won by the better player and a game that is all luck may become boring because there is little challenge.

A game that has these desirable characteristics can be played with the response cubes mentioned in the "Communication" section. Start with two cubes that have numbers from 0 to 5 on the faces and two cubes that have numbers from 5 to 10 on the faces. The goal is to get a total of 15 or as close to 15 as possible (so 14 and 16 are equally good, 13 and 17 are equally good, etc.). Roll the cubes one at a time, adding the numbers on top. For example, you might roll a 2 and then another 2, then an 8. Your score so far is 12. You may stop after two or three rolls or you may roll all four cubes. Notice that as well as practicing addition, this game requires the player to solve a problem. Should the player roll the last cube? What numbers are on the last cube (a person playing the game could look to see that the numbers are 5, 6, 7, 8, 9, 10)? Would there have been a better order in which to have thrown the cubes? These questions are asked, not by the teacher, but rather by the player in the midst of the game. If you watch 7- and 8-year-old children play this game, you will see that they gradually develop better strategies as they ask themselves questions about which cube to roll when and whether they should roll one of the remaining cubes if they have a certain score. Thus the child sees a clear advantage to thinking mathematically in order to solve a problem that is the child's problem and from which the child benefits by solving. Incidentally, games should be introduced to children by playing several demonstration rounds rather than by having them read or listen to the rules. Learning a game from the rules is very difficult for most people. There are, of course, hundreds of games of this sort that allow practice in virtually all mathematical skills while encouraging thinking and the development of intuitive probability concepts. (See, for example, Willoughby, Bereiter, Hilton, & Rubinstein, 1981.)

3. *Use the strengths of individuals.* Most students have some special area in which they know more than others or in which they are more interested than others. If you know what these are, you can often modify a particular lesson or series of lessons to use such special interests. For example, a teacher in Wisconsin had several students who seemed very bright but

not at all interested in mathematics. One of the brightest and least interested was Jewish and had studied Hebrew when she was younger. The teacher decided to teach a short unit on infinite sets and called attention to the fact that the man who created this material in the 19th century (Cantor) was Jewish and had named the smallest infinite set $\aleph_0$—the first letter of the Hebrew alphabet with a subscript 0. The teacher called this "aleph sub-zero" or "aleph null" and then asked if anybody could improve on the pronunciation. The girl corrected the pronunciation. The teacher's pronunciation gradually improved, but the very fact that she could correct the teacher on this point made the student the most alert and best student in the class for that entire unit, and the benefits carried over into several later units.

4. *Emphasize the usefulness of mathematics.* Children should learn that mathematics is useful—not only in adult life and scientific activities but in their own present activities. Help them to see that they can plan their financial lives better, play games more intelligently, make useful recommendations to adults, and do many other things that are useful with mathematics. For example, the class could make a project out of deciding what modifications could be made in the school building to make it more accessible to somebody in a wheelchair. Many measurements and estimates would be necessary (the width of a wheelchair, how much leeway is needed, approximating the height of the head of a person in a wheelchair for using water fountains, appropriate incline for somebody rolling a wheelchair up or down a grade, etc.), and the results might easily be put into a final report to the authorities with some estimate of the cost and the inconvenience to individuals if the modifications were not made.

5. *Provide opportunities for visible success.* Most people are pleased when they have succeeded at something that is impressive to others. Even if they have done or learned something that seems useless, if they have done it well and others are impressed, it seems worthwhile. Therefore, if you set a task for students, you should encourage them to do the task well so they will have something to be proud of when they are finished. If the task is learning the multiplication table, for example, show children how to use all their ability to learn it successfully. Explain how to relate unknown facts to known facts (for example, you know $10 \times 7 = 70$; so 9×7 must be $70 - 7$, or 63). Show how to learn facts by simple practice using flash cards or electronic equivalents. Provide games and practice sessions for children to work together to learn the needed facts. Have practice sessions with the whole class in which everybody has an opportunity to shine occasionally. Use all your skills to encourage everybody to achieve success. Success breeds success and failure breeds failure; so try not to rush on quickly to the next topic before gaining real success with the one at hand. One of the most meaningful results a child can achieve is to be able to do something well and

to know that it is being done well and that other people recognize the achievement.

Evaluating Mathematical Learning

The main purpose of evaluation ought to be for diagnostic and remedial purposes. It is also commonly used in an extrinsic motivational process that is quite effective for many students. Unfortunately, since this last purpose often becomes the principal purpose, many teachers begin to believe that only objective evaluations that can be preserved and shown to parents, administrators, and others are of any value. This is unfortunate under any circumstances and particularly serious for children who have disabilities that are likely to make conventional forms of evaluation invalid.

There are many other forms of evaluation, some of which have been mentioned in passing earlier in this chapter:

1. *Response mechanisms,* such as the number cubes or number-wheel cards that allow each child to respond independently but at the same time as other class members.

2. *Direct observation* by the teacher of the students in natural situations such as mathematical projects or games. Here you can notice whether a child responds quickly and accurately when called on for an arithmetic fact or calculation, who seems to be creative in identifying and solving problems, and so on. Quietly watching a group for 2 or 3 minutes can be a very effective evaluative procedure.

3. *Class or small-group discussions* can often be used to pinpoint specific strengths or weaknesses, although this tends to be less efficient than other procedures because usually only one child speaks at a time and often these are the ones who are least in need of help.

4. *Daily written work* should be helpful in evaluating progress. In addition to examining the final product, you should try to observe the activities that produce the product. Watch for children who are particularly slow starting or who seem to rely unduly on others, and who show other signs that a modification of work habits might provide a more reliable estimate of the pupil's knowledge and perhaps a better chance of improving that knowledge.

For all these forms of evaluation as well as others you may use, you should keep records of achievement for those skills and attributes you feel are important. You might, for example, write children's names down the left-hand margin of a sheet of squared paper and the skills along the top. Then when a student has achieved as well as you expect on a particular attribute, put a check in the appropriate box. For children who do not satisfy your criteria by the time the class is moving on to another topic, you might use pencil notations such as "t," meaning the child does not understand the

concept and needs further teaching, and "p," meaning the child does understand but is not proficient and so could use more practice. But whatever form of evaluation you use and keep, you should certainly use it to help plan your activities so as to strengthen each pupil's overall understanding and skill in mathematics.

Summary

Surprisingly little is known and publicly available about teaching mathematics to physically handicapped people. Johnson (1977) collected data on mathematics programs for the deaf and concluded that "little systematic and broad effort is being made to design math programs to meet the needs of deaf children." Essentially the same conclusion can be drawn for children with other physical disabilities.

In light of this lack of real knowledge, the teacher must rely on what is known about the teaching of mathematics to all people but must modify that with a generous dose of common sense, humaneness, and good judgment. The teacher should expect and get help from many other people, both professional educators and other people who are able to provide help. Some specific suggestions about how to provide the best mathematical education for each child include these:

1. Be aware of the strengths and weaknesses of each child. Build on the strengths and try to strengthen the weak areas where possible or otherwise try to avoid allowing the weaknesses to cause other problems.

2. Recognize your own probable prejudices as well as the prejudices of others and try to cope with them as best you can. This involves modifying opinions where possible, usually by increasing one's knowledge of the individual against whom the prejudice is directed, and at the very least trying to avoid allowing the prejudices to influence professional decisions and the opportunity for individuals to learn and succeed.

3. Try to provide opportunities for success and to build on past successes and previously identified strengths. Encourage self-reliance and responsibility toward others. We often can get over feeling sorry for ourselves (whatever the justification) if we feel a responsibility to do something for others.

4. Teach children that thinking is the most important mathematical skill, but help them learn the many subsidiary skills that make thinking more efficient and more useful. Solving complex problems will be easier if the problem solver does not have to think and be creative about each of the normal skills that is used to solve the general problem.

5. Two-way communication with students and all others involved in the educational process should always be used to improve everybody's ability to work together to improve learning.

6. Strive always to make mathematics meaningful in the world of the student.

7. Evaluate progress using many different techniques so as not to allow the limitations of one procedure to influence the evaluation unduly. Keep records of your evaluations and take specific steps to alleviate weaknesses.

8. Continually try to learn new and better ways to achieve your goals. There is much to be learned about helping the physically disabled master mathematics, and each individual will respond differently. The best resource to achieve better mathematics education for the physically handicapped is the dedicated, educated, creative professional teacher.

REFERENCES

Allport, G. W. *The nature of prejudice*. Reading, Mass.: Addison-Wesley, 1954.

Amir, Y. Contact hypothesis in ethnic relations. *Psychological Bulletin*, 1969, *71*, 319–342.

Association of Mathematics Teachers of New York State. A quality education in mathematics. *New York State Mathematics Teachers' Journal*, 1977, *27*, 112–115.

Barker, R. G., Wright, B. A., Meyerson, L., & Gonick, M. R. *Adjustment to physical handicap and illness: A survey of the social psychology of physique and disability* (2nd ed.). New York: Social Science Research Council, 1953.

Bazakas, R. *The interpersonal impact of coping, dependency, and denial self-presentations by the disabled*. Unpublished doctoral dissertation, New York University, 1977.

Black, K. V. *Attitudes toward the disabled acting in the helper role*. Unpublished master's thesis, University of Colorado, 1964.

Blau, S. An ear for an eye: Sensory compensation and judgments of affect by the blind. In J. R. Davits (Ed.), *The communication of emotional meaning*. New York: McGraw-Hill, 1964.

Brabham, R. E., & Thoreson, R. W. Relationship of client preferences and counselor's physical disability. *Journal of Counseling Psychology*, 1973, *20*, 10–15.

Burlingham, D. T. Hearing and its role in the development of the blind. *Psychoanalytic Study of the Child*, 1964, *19*, 95–112.

Comer, R. C., & Piliavin, J. A. The effects of physical deviance upon face-to-face interactions: The other side. *Journal of Personality and Social Psychology*, 1972, *23*, 33–39.

Dembo, T., Leviton, G. L., & Wright, B. A. Adjustment to misfortune—A problem of social-psychological rehabilitation. *Rehabilitation Psychology*, 1975, *22*, 1–100. (Originally completed in 1948; published in 1956 in *Artificial Limbs* and most available in reference above)

Force, D. G. Social status of physically handicapped children. *Journal of Exceptional Children*, 1956, *23*, 104–107.

Fraiberg, S. Parallel and divergent patterns in blind and sighted infants. *Psychoanalytic Study of the Child*, 1968, *23*, 264–300.

Freeman, R. D. Emotional reactions of handicapped children. *Rehabilitation Literature*, 1967, *28*, 274–282.

Gillman, A. E. Handicap and cognition: Visual deprivation and the rate of motor development in infants. *New Outlook for the Blind*, 1973, *67*, 309–314.

Gladstone, L. R. A study of the relationship between ego defense style preference and ex-

perimental pain tolerance and attitudes toward physical disability (Doctoral dissertation, New York University, 1977). *Dissertation Abstracts International*, 1977, *37*. (University Microfilms No. 77-5306)

Gronlund, N. E. *Sociometry in the classroom*. New York: Harper & Brothers, 1959.

Harasymiw, S. J., & Horne, M. D. Integration of handicapped children: Its effect on teacher attitudes. *Education*, 1975, *96*, 153–158.

Heil, E. Correlational study of the Wide Range Achievement Test, Peabody Individual Achievement Test, and the Key Math Diagnostic Arithmetic Test with learning disabled children with a modality deficit. *Dissertation Abstracts International*, 1978, *38A*, 5394. (University Microfilms No. 7801760)

Ingwell, R. H., Thoreson, R. W., & Smits, S. J. Accuracy of social perception of physically handicapped and non-handicapped persons. *Journal of Social Psychology*, 1967, *72*, 107–116.

Jastrazembska, Z. S. (Ed.). *The effects of blindness and other impairments on early development*. New York: American Foundation for the Blind, 1976.

Johnson, K. A. A survey of mathematics programs, materials & methods in schools for the deaf. *Dissertation Abstracts International*, 1977, *38A*, 2704. (University Microfilms No. 77-24546)

Jones, R. L. Learning and association in the presence of the blind. *New Outlook for the Blind*, 1970, *64*, 317–329.

Kleck, R. E. Physical stigma and task oriented interaction. *Human Relations*, 1969, *22*, 53–60.

Kleck, R. E., Ono, H., & Hastorf, A. H. The effects of physical deviance upon face-to-face interaction. *Human Relations*, 1966, *19*, 425–436.

Ladieu, G., Hanfmann, E., & Dembo, T. Studies in adjustment to visible injuries: Evaluation of help by the injured. *Journal of Abnormal and Social Psychology*, 1947, *42*, 169–192.

Mitchell, D. C., & Fredrickson, W. A. Preferences for physically disabled counselors in hypothetical counseling situations. *Journal of Counseling Psychology*, 1975, *22*, 477–482.

Moriarty, T. Role of stigma in the experience of deviance. *Journal of Personality and Social Psychology*, 1974, *29*, 849–855.

Nagi, S. Z. Rehabilitation and visual impairments. Some issues in research and practice. In *Blindness and services to the blind*. Cambridge, Mass.: OSTI Press, 1971.

National Council of Supervisors of Mathematics. *Position paper on basic mathematical skills*. Minneapolis: NCSM, 1977. (Available from Ross Taylor, Minneapolis Public Schools, 807 Broadway N.E., Minneapolis, MN 55413.)

Noonan, J. R., Barry, J. R., & Davis, H. C. Personality determinants in attitudes toward visible disability. *Journal of Personality*, 1970, *38*, 1–15.

Richardson, S. A. Some social psychological consequences of handicapping. *Pediatrics*, 1963, 291–297.

Richardson, S. A., Hastorf, A. H., & Dornbusch, S. M. Effects of physical disability on a child's description of himself. *Child Development*, 1964, *35*, 893–907.

Salvia, J., Algozzine, R., & Sheare, J. B. Attractiveness and school achievement. *Journal of School Psychology*, 1977, *15*, 60–67.

Sandler, A. M. Aspects of passivity and ego development in the blind infant. *Psychoanalytic Study of the Child*, 1963, *18*, 343–360.

Schiff, W., & Thayer, S. An eye for an ear? Social perception, nonverbal communication and deafness. *Rehabilitation Psychology*, 1974, *21*, 50–70.

Schoggen, P. *Environmental forces in the lives of children with and without physical disability*. Paper presented at the American Psychological Association Convention, New York, September 1963.

Siller, J. Psychosocial aspects of disability. In J. Meislin (Ed.), *Rehabilitation medicine and psychiatry*. Springfield, Ill.: C. C. Thomas, 1976. (a)

Siller, J. Attitudes toward disability. In H. Rusalem & D. Malikin (Eds.), *Contemporary vocational rehabilitation*. New York: New York University Press, 1976. (b)

Siller, J., Chipman, A., Ferguson, L. T., & Vann, D. H. *Attitudes of the nondisabled toward the physically disabled*. New York: New York University, School of Education, 1967. (a)

Siller, J., Ferguson, L. T., Vann, D. H., & Holland, B. *Structure of attitudes toward the physically disabled: Disability factor scales—Amputation, blindness, cosmetic conditions*. New York: New York University, School of Education, 1967. (b)

Springer, S. A. A study of the performance of deaf and hearing subjects on Piagetian and new-Piagetian tasks. *Dissertation Abstracts International*, 1978, *38B*, 5618.

Utz, W. R. The blind student in the mathematics classroom. *American Mathematical Monthly*, 1979, *86*, 491–494.

Wechsler, H., Suarez, A. C., & McFadden, M. Teachers' attitudes toward the education of physically handicapped children: Implications for the implementation of Massachusetts Chapter 766. *Journal of Education*, 1975, *157*, 17–24.

Willoughby, S. S., Bereiter, C., Hilton, P., & Rubinstein, J. H. *Real math, K–6*. LaSalle, Ill.: Open Court, 1981.

Witkin, A., Birnbaum, J., Lomonaco, S., Lehr, S., & Herman, J. L. Cognitive patterning in congenitally totally blind children. *Child Development*, 1968, *39*, 767–786.

Wright, B. A. *Physical disability—A psychological approach*. New York: Harper & Row, 1960.

Wright, B. A. *The coping framework and attitude change: A guide to constructive role-playing*. Paper presented at the American Psychological Association Annual Convention, New York, September 1979.

Yuker, H. E., Block, J. R., & Young, J. H. *The measurement of attitudes toward disabled persons*. Albertson, N.Y.: Human Resources Center, 1966.

10

Improving Preservice and In-Service Programs for Teaching Mathematics to the Exceptional

Jasper Harvey

United States Department of Education

Dr. Jasper Harvey was director, Division of Personnel Preparation, Office of Special Education and Rehabilitative Services, U.S. Department of Education. He chaired and developed the Department of Special Education, University of Alabama, and chaired the Department of Special Education, University of Texas at Austin. He was a past president of the Council for Exceptional Children; member, American Psychological Association; American Speech, Language and Hearing Association; and American Academy for Cerebral Palsy and Developmental Disorders.

O VER the years the federal government has often become involved where specific needs were not being met by state and local governments or by private sources. The training of teachers and leadership personnel for the education of the handicapped was recognized as one of these great needs in the late 1950s. In 1958 Public Law 85-926 was passed to provide support for the training of leadership personnel in the area of mental retardation, and Public Law 85-905 provided for media services for the deaf. Three years later, Public Law 87-276 provided for training teachers of the deaf, and the United States had the beginnings of what has become a comprehensive package of federal legislation supporting education programs to train specialists and support personnel for handicapped children (Harvey & Siantz, 1979).

In 1966 Congress added Title VI to the Elementary and Secondary Education Act to provide funds to assist state and local governments in serving handicapped children in regular elementary and secondary schools. Title VI also established the Bureau of Education for the Handicapped (BEH) within the U.S. Office of Education. With a bureau to administer them, Congress rapidly expanded programs for the handicapped: It enacted

legislation to provide for the training of physical educators and recreation personnel for the handicapped (1967); the Captioned Films for the Deaf Program was expanded to include all types of handicaps (1967); 15% of the Grants to the States under Title III of the Elementary and Secondary Education Act was earmarked for the handicapped (1967) as well as 10% of the Grants to the States for Vocational Education (1967); and the Handicapped Children's Early Education Assistance Act (1968) was enacted. Harvey and Siantz (1979) noted that this rapid expansion of educational programs for the handicapped by Congress indicated the beginning of a change in national priorities. Administrators of programs not specific to the handicapped were encouraged to contribute to the advancement of their education. The prime example of such a contribution was the informal earmarking of 15% of the funds under the Education Professions Development Act for the support of training programs for regular teachers and other related personnel to work more effectively with handicapped children and youth.

All existing legislation for the handicapped was incorporated into one authority in 1970 with the passage of Public Law 91-230, the Education of the Handicapped Act, which expanded and changed Title VI of the Elementary and Secondary Education Act. Part D of Title VI was designated "Training Personnel for the Education of the Handicapped." Title VI-D has subsequently been extended by Public Laws 93-380 and 95-49 through fiscal year 1982. The safeguards contained in Public Law 93-380 were given new emphasis and impetus with the passage of Public Law 94-142, the Education for All Handicapped Children Act of 1975, which renewed and expanded Title VI-B of Public Law 93-380. An unusual aspect of Public Law 94-142 is that it has no expiration date and funding to the states is tied to assurances of, and provision for, a free appropriate public education for all handicapped children and to providing individual protections for them and for their parents. These protections consist of procedural safeguards, nondiscriminatory testing, the assurance of an individual education plan (IEP), and the provision of services for each child in the least restrictive environment appropriate for delivery of those services as outlined in the child's IEP.

Major enabling legislation has not solved but, instead, has raised a wide variety of complex issues involved in the education of children and youth who are handicapped and who are entitled to the protections of Public Law 94-142. Halperin (Andringa, Finn, Halperin, Timpane, & Wolanin, 1976), in a discussion of federal education policy, noted:

> P.L. 94-142, the new Equal Opportunity for All Handicapped Children Act [sic], isn't primarily an innovative program as much as it is a regulatory or civil rights advance with a relatively small financial inducement to the states to get moving—and a great deal more enforcement clout. (p. 4)

The civil rights aspect of Public Law 94-142 grew, in part, out of the fact that although most states *already* had legislation *requiring* that all handicapped children receive an education, most states had not been stringent in enforcing such requirements.

In the annual program plans submitted to the Bureau of Education for the Handicapped for funding approval under Public Law 94-142, the states continue to indicate the need for additional certified specialists and for the in-service training of both regular education and special education teachers, administrators, and support personnel. The states include teacher needs data in the section of the plan entitled "Comprehensive System of Personnel Development" and indicate the ways they will meet specific requirements in personnel preparation as required in the act and in the regulations for Public Law 94-142. In response to these needs, the BEH and its Division of Personnel Preparation (DPP) began shifting funding priorities toward in-service training and the training of regular educators as early as 1974, prior to the passage of Public Law 94-142. In fiscal year 1974, 27 projects were funded for a total allocation of $1.459 million. During fiscal year 1975, $3.874 million was allocated to 90 projects to train regular educators. This constituted 10.2% of all funds allocated by the DPP for that fiscal year. Beginning with the budgeting for fiscal year 1976, allocations were made on both a preservice and in-service basis for each of the division's funding areas. This preservice and in-service allocation pattern allowed applicants to target specific populations and their training needs.

Funding levels for in-service training in regular education have increased from $4.098 million in 1976 to $11.875 million in 1979. Over that period, the regular educators trained have increased from 11 543 to 46 929. During that same period, special educators and regular and special education support personnel have also received training, increasing in number from 12 668 for fiscal year 1976 to 32 085 for fiscal year 1979. In-service expenditures for that group have increased from $7.605 million in 1976 to $12.568 million for 1979.

In-Service Delivery System

The Bureau of Education for the Handicapped has committed significant financial resources to develop in-service training programs for both regular and special education personnel and for support personnel for both groups. Beginning with funding for fiscal year 1978 (academic school year 1978–79), the Division of Personnel Preparation selected nine in-service projects to begin the development of a network. The purpose of the network was to provide assistance to in-service projects funded by the DPP and to maximize the efficient and effective use of these collective resources. Indiana University manages this effort through the National Inservice Network Project (NIN). This evolving and developing network provides a

forum for sharing successful training approaches or techniques with other interested trainers.

Siantz (1978) pointed out a number of implications for in-service training required to fulfill the mandates of Public Law 94-142:

- Both regular and special education personnel will be needed to serve handicapped children who are not fully served in present programs.

- Serving the most severely handicapped within each disability will, in most instances, require the development of new preservice and in-service programs and curricula.

- Providing these services in the least restrictive environment requires that the handicapped child be integrated into the school's regular programs wherever and as much as possible.

- Developing the required Comprehensive System of Personnel Development in each state will require the identification of personnel needs and a focusing of resources on those needs.

Each of these will require that the DPP focus its resources on those needs in its funding decisions for each state's applications for funding assistance.

During the 1979–80 academic year, more than 200 projects were funded by the DPP to focus on the in-service training of personnel needed to implement the law. The actual delivery of training depends on those funded projects and the training needs they have identified.

In addition to the Title VI-D personnel preparation funds, largely untapped resources for funding in-service training are the funds from Public Law 94-142 VI-B that flow to the states and their local education agencies (LEA). In some instances—for example, Illinois—the state board of education has mandated that 10% of these funds be used for the in-service training of the LEA's personnel.

Preservice Delivery System

With the passage of Public Law 85-926 in 1958, the number of colleges and universities offering programs in one or more areas of special education has increased from 15 to more than 400. The Division of Personnel Preparation funds program components in more than 300 of these. This pattern has changed drastically since 1976 when the DPP, as part of its forward planning to assist in the implementation of Public Law 94-142, published in the *Federal Register* (1976) 11 priority areas of training. "Volunteers (including parents)" was added as a 12th in 1977. These priority areas are divided into four broad training areas:

1. *Preparation of special educators*
   a) early childhood
   b) severely handicapped

    c) general special education

2. *Preparation of support personnel for regular and special education*
   a) vocational/career education
   b) paraprofessional
   c) physical education
   d) recreation
   e) interdisciplinary
   f) volunteers (including parents)

3. *Instructional models*
   a) developmental assistance
   b) model implementation (special projects)

4. *Special education training for regular education teachers*
   a) preservice training (Deans' Grants) and regular education in-service training

Saettler (1976) and Harvey (1978b) have both written explanations of the ways in which these priorities for the DPP have been developed. Essentially, they have come from the following:

- Congressional hearings
- Congressional intent as expressed in the conference reports accompanying a legislative packet
- The *Congressional Record* (both Senate and House)
- Joint conference reports on legislation and appropriations
- State plans submitted for various BEH funds
- State legislation
- General Accounting Office studies and audits
- National Center of Educational Statistics studies
- U.S. Office of Education general counsel interpretations of the law and the intent of the Congress
- Budget review testimony given by the Office of Education, its assistant secretary, and the Office of Management and Budget concerning BEH programs
- National Education Association studies
- Application data from institutions of higher education
- Professional organizations
- Professional judgment of staff within the BEH

Senate and House reports emphasize the need for the targeting of training of personnel. The U.S. Senate Report (1977) states:

The enactment of Public Law 94-142 raises additional challenges to projects authorized under this program. Individualized planning for handicapped children and the requirement that educational services be provided with supportive services in the least restrictive environment appropriate to the handicapped child's needs necessitates thorough and adequate training of both special and regular education personnel. (p. 7)

With the need for regular educators to have a basic knowledge and understanding of handicapped children, the BEH asked deans of schools, colleges, and departments of education to submit applications directed toward a reconceptualization of teacher education. It was recommended that the deans, who had the authority, responsibility, and decision-making latitude to bring about change, serve as project directors; that the project be directed toward the inclusion ("infusion") of basic special education knowledge, skills, and understandings into the undergraduate (and graduate) elementary and secondary teaching curricula; and that the entire faculty of the college of education be involved on an equal basis. The BEH also urged including other areas of the university or college that were involved in teacher preparation. Since 1975, these projects have proved to be catalytic. The success of individual projects has relied specifically on the genuine forces for change that were generated from within the college and institution and the impact of those forces on the existing system (Harvey & Siantz, 1979).

Data for Consideration

The improvement of preservice and in-service programs for teaching mathematics to the exceptional has been treated from the federal funding agency framework; that is, "What can a federal discretionary program do to facilitate the development of appropriate training programs and mechanisms that will improve the teaching of subject matter to exceptional children?" and "What has the Division of Personnel Preparation done since the passage of Public Law 94-142 to facilitate funded programs to provide appropriate preservice and in-service training that is targeted toward fulfilling the mandates of the act?" These questions have already been addressed here.

The following suggestions and comments may be of assistance to the subject matter specialist:

1. Experience has indicated over time that handicapped children generally differ more from each other than from their normal or nonhandicapped peers. Teachers have always had "unidentified" handicapped children in their classes and probably will continue to do so. As the delivery system for the least restrictive environment concept is fine tuned, they will be appropriately placed, but they and their teachers will need support services.

2. Neither the act nor the regulations for Public Law 94-142 use the term *mainstream*. They use, instead, the term *least restrictive environment*. Paragraphs 121a.550, 551, and 552 address the least restrictive environment in the regulations (p. 42497). A continuum of alternative placements is required, and *placement* is based on a child's individualized education program. In the *Comment* to Section 121a.552, it is stated that the analysis of regulations for Section 504 of the Rehabilitation Act of 1973 includes several points regarding the educational placement of handicapped children. A pertinent point is this:

> Where a handicapped child is so disruptive in a regular classroom that the education of other students is significantly impaired, the needs of the handicapped child cannot be met in that environment. Therefore regular placement would not be appropriate to his or her needs. (p. 42497)

3. In a discussion of "Legislative Intent and Progress," Harvey (1978a) wrote:

> One of the more critical issues facing the broad area of special education is to change the ways educators and others view the needs of handicapped children. . . . As achievement and development are considered, comparison is between the present and potential achievement status, that is, discrepancy analysis. Learning or nonlearning takes place in all environments, not just in a formal school setting. Both the human and physical aspects are influential in forming one's cognitive, affective, and psychomotor behaviors. (p. 234)

When regular classroom placement is indicated by a child's individualized education program, it is critical that the school system realize its implementation is not a workbook or curriculum match with the child. Such an approach nullifies the professional role of the teacher. Available software is not this precise, nor are the techniques for matching the child and the materials. The intent is not that the IEP be a full and sufficient guide to the instructional strategies for a child, nor is the IEP a series of lesson plans. The less certain one is of the data on which the IEP was based, the more critical it becomes to review the plan and modify it on a periodic basis. Many IEPs require specialized materials and equipment, and access to these continues to be problematic in many geographic areas. In addition, there are time limitations for individual teachers in relation to the teacher-pupil ratios being imposed by various local education agencies. The fine tuning of the individual child's or youth's curriculum is the teacher's role and responsibility. The critical factors are that the child's least restrictive environment is the direct outgrowth of her or his IEP and that the fine tuning of the curriculum is done by the teacher, not the IEP participants.

4. A study by the Stanford Research Institute's Policy Center (1977) indicated that the factor that most affects parents' satisfaction with the IEP

process was a concerned, competent, and resourceful teacher or administrator.

5. Since the mid-1960s the Bureau of Education for the Handicapped has funded activities to develop materials and other supportive strategies for the use of teachers. A series of Regional Resource Centers currently are funded through the Division of Media Services. Adapted curricula materials are available in most states through the systems developed under the Associate Learning Resource Center Program, which was a precursor of the Regional Resource Centers. Also funded by the same division is the National Information Center for Special Education Materials (NICSEM) at the University of Southern California. Extensive data on subject matter, including mathematics, are available from NICSEM. However, it should be stressed that the fine tuning for a child has to be done by her or his teacher.

6. In chapter 2, Glennon makes the point that all mathematics is not of equal worth to exceptional children and youth. Lazarus (1978) used this analogy to explain the use and need for mathematical skills and ideas:

> If mathematics were music, professional mathematicians would be composers—the creators of new works in the medium. The composer's place is unique and special, for without the composer, there is no music at all—and without the mathematician, no mathematics. But not everyone need compose music. For most, it is enough to play an instrument a little, or perhaps to understand enough music to enjoy it. Likewise, not everyone has the talent, interest, drive, or need to create new mathematics. Those who do are a most important body of students, needing the close guidance of working mathematicians at every step in their education. But for most people, it is enough to know how to use mathematics, and for some, enough to understand how others use it. (p. 8)

Glennon's paradigm, "Major Sources of the Curriculum," shown in chapter 2, can serve as a meaningful guide to curriculum development for the mathematics teacher who has a handicapped child or youth in class.

7. In a discussion of assumptions about change in educational institutions, Hall (1978) notes that (a) change is a process, not an event, (b) change is made by individuals first and then by institutions, (c) change is a highly personal experience, (d) change entails developmental growth in feelings and skills in relation to the innovation, and (e) the change facilitator must function in highly adaptive, systemic, and personalized ways if change is to be facilitated most efficiently and effectively for the individuals and for the institution as a whole (pp. 50–51).

8. It is appropriate to be concerned about what the introduction of exceptional children does to one, personally, and to one's classroom structure; however, it is necessary to move forward in the process through inservice training. To be effective, such training must be based on the

teacher's needs and the needs of the peer group and carried out over a period of time in a planned and systematic manner, evaluated, and then recycled.

9. In-service trainers are learning that when regular teachers are first assigned handicapped children, they frequently respond to a needs questionnaire in a negative way. It appears that many teachers feel they have so little knowledge and information concerning the exceptional that they frequently feel powerless to deal with the situation. Teachers given the opportunity to state their in-service training needs should begin with the basics if they feel insecure with a handicapped child in the classroom. They should ask for information about who handicapped children are and some strategies for working with them in a group of children, then progress to the specifics of subject matter over a period of time.

10. When dealing with in-service training situations, teachers should ask questions even though they feel they will be too simple. The question they want to ask is probably one that most of their peers in the group will want answered.

REFERENCES

Andringa, R., Finn, C., Halperin, S., Timpane, M., & Wolanin, T. *Perspectives on federal education policy: An informal colloquium.* Washington, D.C.: George Washington University, Institute for Education Leadership, 1976.

Federal Register, 41, September 1, 1976. Washington, D.C.: Superintendent of Documents, U.S. Government Printing Office.

Federal Register, 42, (163), August 23, 1977. Washington, D.C.: Superintendent of Documents, U.S. Government Printing Office.

Hall, G. Facilitating institutional change using the individual as the frame of reference. In J. Grosenick & M. Reynolds (Eds.), *Teacher education: Renegotiating roles for mainstreaming.* Reston, Va.: Council for Exceptional Children, 1978.

Harvey, J. Legislative intent and progress. *Exceptional Children*, 1978, *44*, 234–237. (a)

Harvey, J. Focus on national priorities. *Focus on quality*, Program of Fifth Annual Conference, American Association of the Education of the Severely/Profoundly Handicapped, October 1978. (b)

Harvey, J., & Siantz, J. Public education and the handicapped. *Research and Development in Education*, 1979, *12* (4).

Lazarus, M. The mathematical arts. In *edc news*. Newton, Mass.: Education Development Center, Fall 1978.

Saettler, H. Setting priorities for the preparation of personnel. In Roy Littlejohn Associates (Ed.), *Conference summary of Public Law 94-142.* Washington, D.C.: Division of Personnel Preparation, BEH, USOE, 1976.

Siantz, J. *Special education manpower development: Program coverage, priorities, and examples of successful innovations.* Washington, D.C.: Division of Personnel Preparation, BEH, USOE, February 1978.

Stanford Research Institute. *Three states' experience with IEP requirements similar to P.L. 94-142.* Palo Alto, Calif.: SRI Policy Center, 1977.

U.S. Senate, 95th Cong., 1st sess., Report No. 95-124, 6 March 1977.

Date Due